MW01027371

HOLMAN
Old Testament
Commentary

HOLMAN *Old* *Testament* Commentary

Proverbs

GENERAL EDITOR AND AUTHOR

Max Anders

HOLMAN
REFERENCE

NASHVILLE, TENNESSEE

Holman Old Testament Commentary
© 2005 B&H Publishing Group
Nashville, Tennessee
All rights reserved

ISBN 978-0-8054-9472-3

Bible versions used in this book:

Unless otherwise stated all Scripture citation is from the HOLY BIBLE, NEW INTERNATIONAL
VERSION®. Copyright © 1973, 1978, 1984 by International Bible Society. Used by permission
of Zondervan Publishing House. All Rights Reserved. The "NIV" and "New International Version"
trademarks are registered in the United States Patent and Trademark Office by International Bible
Society. Use of either trademark requires the permission of International Bible Society.

Scripture citations marked NASB are from the New American Standard Bible. ©The Lockman
Foundation, 1960, 1962, 1968, 1971, 1973, 1975, 1977, 1995. Used by permission.

The King James Version

Dewey Decimal Classification: 223.7
Subject Heading: BIBLE. PROVERBS

Proverbs / Anders, Max
        p. cm. — (Holman Old Testament commentary)
        Includes bibliographical references. (p.).
        1. Bible. Proverbs—Commentaries.   I. Title.   II. Series.
        —dc21

Printed in China

8 9 10 11 12 13 • 19 18 17 16 15

To our children, Tanya and Chris, who have brought life and joy to our world, and who make me want to be the best possible father.

⤳ Max Anders ⤳

2005

Contents

Contents

Contents

Contents

Editorial Preface

Today's church hungers for Bible teaching, and Bible teachers hunger for resources to guide them in teaching God's Word. The Holman Old Testament Commentary provides the church with the food to feed the spiritually hungry in an easily digestible format. The result: new spiritual vitality that the church can readily use.

Bible teaching should result in new interest in the Scriptures, expanded Bible knowledge, discovery of specific scriptural principles, relevant applications, and exciting living. The unique format of the Holman Old Testament Commentary includes sections to achieve these results for every Old Testament book.

Opening quotations stimulate thinking and lead to an introductory illustration and discussion that draw individuals and study groups into the Word of God. Verse-by-verse commentary interprets the passage with the aim of equipping them to understand and live God's Word in a contemporary setting. A conclusion draws together the themes identified in the passage under discussion and suggests application for it. A "Life Application" section provides additional illustrative material. "Deeper Discoveries" gives the reader a closer look at some of the words, phrases, and background material that illuminate the passage. "Issues for Discussion" is a tool to enhance learning within the group. Finally, a closing prayer is suggested. Bible teachers and pastors will find the teaching outline helpful as they develop lessons and sermons.

It is the editors' prayer that this new resource for local church Bible teaching will enrich the ministry of group, as well as individual, Bible study and that it will lead God's people truly to be people of the Book, living out what God calls us to be.

Acknowledgments

*My thanks to
Dr. John Bechtle
for his scholarly
contribution to
this volume.*

Holman Old Testament Commentary Contributors

Vol. 1 Genesis
ISBN 978-0-8054-9461-7
Kenneth O. Gangel and Stephen Bramer

Vol. 2 Exodus, Leviticus, Numbers
ISBN 978-0-8054-9462-4
Glen Martin

Vol. 3 Deuteronomy
ISBN 978-0-8054-9463-1
Doug McIntosh

Vol. 4 Joshua
ISBN 978-0-8054-9464-8
Kenneth O. Gangel

Vol. 5 Judges, Ruth
ISBN 978-0-8054-9465-5
W. Gary Phillips

Vol. 6 1 & 2 Samuel
ISBN 978-0-8054-9466-2
Stephen Andrews

Vol. 7 1 & 2 Kings
ISBN 978-0-8054-9467-9
Gary Inrig

Vol. 8 1 & 2 Chronicles
ISBN 978-0-8054-9468-6
Winfried Corduan

Vol. 9 Ezra, Nehemiah, Esther
ISBN 978-0-8054-9469-3
Knute Larson and Kathy Dahlen

Vol. 10 Job
ISBN 978-0-8054-9470-9
Stephen J. Lawson

Vol. 11 Psalms 1-72
ISBN 978-0-8054-9471-6
Steve J. Lawson

Vol. 12 Psalms 73-150
ISBN 978-0-8054-9481-5
Steve J. Lawson

Vol. 13 Proverbs
ISBN 978-0-8054-9472-3
Max Anders

Vol. 14 Ecclesiastes, Song of Songs
ISBN 978-0-8054-9482-2
David George Moore and Daniel L. Akin

Vol. 15 Isaiah
ISBN 978-0-8054-9473-0
Trent C. Butler

Vol. 16 Jeremiah, Lamentations
ISBN 978-0-8054-9474-7
Fred C. Wood and Ross McLaren

Vol. 17 Ezekiel
ISBN 978-0-8054-9475-4
Mark F. Rooker

Vol. 18 Daniel
ISBN 978-0-8054-9476-1
Kenneth O. Gangel

Vol. 19 Hosea, Joel, Amos, Obadiah, Jonah, Micah
ISBN 978-0-8054-9477-8
Trent C. Butler

Vol. 20 Nahum, Habakkuk, Zephaniah, Haggai, Zechariah, Malachi
ISBN 978-0-8054-9478-5
Stephen R. Miller

Holman New Testament
Commentary Contributors

Holman Old Testament Commentary

Twenty volumes designed for Bible study and teaching to enrich the local church and God's people.

Series Editor	Max Anders
Managing Editor	Steve Bond
Project Editor	Dean Richardson
Product Development Manager	Ricky D. King
Marketing Manager	Stephanie Huffman
Executive Editor	David Shepherd
Page Composition	TF Designs, Greenbrier, TN

Introduction to

Proverbs

AUTHOR AND DATE

Solomon is generally thought to have authored the entire Book of Proverbs except for three sections: the Sayings of the Wise in Proverbs
22:17–24:34, Proverbs 30, and Proverbs 31. He may have collected and compiled the Sayings of the Wise, but it is generally agreed that he did not write
them. We do not know who wrote them, nor do we know anything about the
authors of Proverbs 30–31. They are attributed to Agur and Lemuel, but we
do not know who they are. Some scholars think that Lemuel was just another
name for Solomon, but others do not. Since there is language in Proverbs 31
that some believe has Arabian influence, there is some support for Lemuel
being from Arabia.

Solomon ruled Israel from 971 to 931 B.C. He seems to have written his
proverbs early in his reign, before his heart was turned from the Lord (1 Kgs.
11:1–11), since the book reveals a heart given completely to God. The Sayings of the Wise appear to have been written at some undetermined time
before that. The Book of Proverbs was not compiled in its final form until
Hezekiah's day or after since Proverbs 25:1 says, "These are more proverbs of
Solomon, copied by the men of Hezekiah king of Judah." Hezekiah ruled
about 715–686 B.C.

THE PURPOSE OF PROVERBS

First Kings 4:30 says that Solomon was wiser than any other man. The
Book of Proverbs is a compilation of short sayings or maxims designed to
present important truth in memorable form. The Hebrew word for *wisdom*
means "skill in living." The purpose of Proverbs is to give the reader skill for
living life from God's perspective and, in doing so, give the wise person
greater happiness. Wisdom begins with a fear of the Lord (reverence and
respect, not terror) and includes knowledge, understanding, discretion, discernment, and obedience. Proverbs is to be used to help succeeding generations be successful in life, primarily by contrasting the difference between the
wise person and the fool.

INTERPRETING PROVERBS

As Wisdom Literature, Proverbs must be interpreted with special care. Proverbs presents general truth that is often not intended to be taken literally in every situation. For example, Proverbs 22:29 says, "Do you see a man skilled in his work? He will serve before kings." Yet many men skilled in their work do not literally stand before kings. We don't even have many kings in the world today. But there is a greater general truth to which this proverb points—that if a person does skilled work, he will tend to be recognized and rewarded for it. This is just one example of the kind of mind-set that must be used in interpreting Proverbs. Otherwise, the book will appear to be a hodge-podge of hopeless promises.

The proverbs are intended to present brief, catchy statements of truth, designed to hit home with maximum impact. One American proverb says, "An apple a day keeps the doctor away." It is not literally true that an apple a day will keep the doctor away. It is a pithy and memorable way of saying that if you eat well, you will experience a health benefit. Also, brief statements of truth, while generally true, are too brief to explain potential exceptions to that truth. If a proverb were written to explain all the potential exceptions to it, it would no longer be catchy or memorable.

It would be preposterous to say, "An apple a day, as well as other fresh fruit, will not always keep the doctor away but will in general give you improved health so long as you do not eat green apples or eat them unwashed with too much pesticide residue. And keep in mind that during the winter you may not be able to find apples or other fresh fruit to eat, but there will still be residual health benefits from eating fresh fruit in moderation whenever you can." The proverb loses some of its punch that way.

The same is true of Hebrew proverbs. They are often not intended to be technically true in all situations, and they do not state everything about a given truth. They point to a general truth that may not be absolutely true if applied to all situations and interpreted technically.

Proverbs are not promises but general statements of truth. Rather than being thought of as exacting promises from God, they must be understood as general guidelines for living a successful life. For example, Proverbs 22:6 says, "Train a child in the way he should go, and when he is old he will not turn from it." Yet many brokenhearted parents have trained up their children in the way they should go, and when their children grew up, they abandoned Christianity.

I know of a well-known pastor who had four daughters. He and his wife gave every appearance of being model Christians. Three of the daughters grew up to be exemplary Christians, but the fourth defected from the faith. There is no apparent reason the fourth daughter gave up her faith. It certainly had nothing to do with any significant failure on the part of the parents to bring her up "in the nurture and admonition of the Lord" (Eph. 6:4 KJV). In addition, children in other families, raised in less consistent Christian homes, have grown up to embrace the faith. Does this mean Proverbs 22:6 is unreliable?

No, it means that it should not be seen as a blanket promise but a general truth. All of church history points to the fact that, when parents live out authentic faith, their children tend to become Christians as well. The vast majority of Christians in America come from Christian homes and accept Christ before their eighteenth birthday. That is the general truth to which Proverbs 22:6 points. If Solomon were here, he would likely explain that he did not intend this proverb to be understood as having no exceptions.

Proverbs are not intended to be technically exact. Take Proverbs 6:27–29, for example: "Can a man scoop fire into his lap without his clothes being burned? Can a man walk on hot coals without his feet being scorched? So is he who sleeps with another man's wife; no one who touches her will go unpunished."

In their book *How to Read the Bible for All Its Worth* (Grand Rapids: Zondervan, 1993), Fee and Stuart make this comment about that proverb:

> Someone might think, "Now that last line is unclear. What if the mailman accidentally touches another man's wife while delivering the mail? Will he be punished? And are there not some people who commit adultery and get away with it?" But such interpretations miss the point. Proverbs tend to use *figurative* language and express things *suggestively* rather than in detail. The point you should get from the proverb is that committing adultery is like playing with fire. God will see to it that sooner or later, in this life or in the next, the adulterer will be hurt by his actions. The word 'touch' in the last line *must* be understood euphemistically (cp. 1 Cor. 7:1), if the Holy Spirit's inspired message is not to be distorted. Thus a proverb should not be taken too literally or too universally if its message is to be helpful (Fee and Stuart, 218–19).

Proverbs must be culturally translated into today's meaning. There are some proverbs that cannot be understood unless we understand the culturally obsolete thing they are talking about. When the proverbs talk about kings, we don't have kings in the United States, but the proverb will still be true if we understand a king to be representative of leaders in our lives. So when we read, "He who loves a pure heart and whose speech is gracious will have the king for his friend" (Prov. 22:11), we can substitute the idea of important leaders in our lives. When we do that, it is understood in this way: when we have a pure heart and speak graciously, we will make a positive impression on leaders and responsible persons who are generally impressed with honesty and gracious speech.

Proverbs rely heavily on imagery in order to be memorable. Often the intent of a proverb is to create a mental picture so that you remember its basic truth. We must understand the image and take its symbolic truth. In Proverbs 20:26, we read, "A wise king winnows out the wicked; he drives the threshing wheel over them." Of course, a wise king would never drive a threshing wheel over the wicked. If capital punishment were warranted, he would use some other means, and if capital punishment were not warranted, the threshing wheel would be too severe. The point is that a wise king will not look the other way when he sees evil. He will do what is necessary to weed out evil from his kingdom.

Of course, the principle applyies to any position of leadership. The president of a company, the principle of a school, and the coach of a team have the opportunity to do what they can to cleanse their "kingdom" of evil, and they will do so if they are wise.

CONCLUSION

Many additional examples could be given, but these are sufficient to establish the basic principle. Proverbs are often not intended to be taken literally. They use many figures of speech and suggest general principles that point to basic truth. Through Proverbs's use of stark contrasts, bold relief, and overstatement to communicate truth, we will find powerful and timely guidance for wise living.

INDEX TO ALL PROVERBS BY CHAPTER AND VERSE
(AND WHERE TO FIND THEM IN THIS COMMENTARY)

While there is some general overall organization to the Book of Proverbs, the individual proverbs within the book are often arranged randomly. This can present a challenge when studying the book because it is often helpful to study similar proverbs at the same time. Therefore, this commentary has rearranged all the proverbs into thirty-one topical studies rather than going through the proverbs in the order they are found in the Bible. The organizational structure is seen in the contents page at the front of this book. Following is a list of the proverbs in order and the chapter in this commentary where they are found.

Proverbs Passage	HOTC Chapter	Proverbs Passage	HOTC Chapter
Proverbs 3:9–10	Chapter 23	Proverbs 10:31–32	Chapter 18
Proverbs 3:11–12	Chapter 11	Proverbs 11:1	Chapter 21
Proverbs 3:13–24	Chapter 2	Proverbs 11:2	Chapter 16
Proverbs 3:25–26	Chapter 29	Proverbs 11:3	Chapter 14
Proverbs 3:27–28	Chapter 24	Proverbs 11:4	Chapter 23
Proverbs 3:29–32	Chapter 20	Proverbs 11:5–10	Chapter 12
Proverbs 3:33–35	Chapter 13	Proverbs 11:11	Chapter 18
Proverbs 4:1–27	Chapter 3	Proverbs 11:12-13	Chapter 19
Proverbs 5:1–23	Chapter 4	Proverbs 11:14	Chapter 10
Proverbs 6:1–5	Chapter 26	Proverbs 11:15	Chapter 26
Proverbs 6:6–8	Chapter 26	Proverbs 11:16–17	Chapter 15
Proverbs 6:9–11	Chapter 25	Proverbs 11:18–20	Chapter 12
Proverbs 6:12–15	Chapter 14	Proverbs 11:21	Chapter 13
Proverbs 6:16–19	Chapter 20	Proverbs 11:22	Chapter 27
Proverbs 6:20–35	Chapter 4	Proverbs 11:23	Chapter 12
Proverbs 7:1–27	Chapter 5	Proverbs 11:24–26	Chapter 24
Proverbs 8:1–36	Chapter 6	Proverbs 11:27	Chapter 13
Proverbs 9:1–6	Chapter 7	Proverbs 11:28	Chapter 23
Proverbs 9:7–9	Chapter 10	Proverbs 11:29	Chapter 27
Proverbs 9:10–18	Chapter 7	Proverbs 11:30–31	Chapter 13
Proverbs 10:1	Chapter 27	Proverbs 12:1	Chapter 11
Proverbs 10:2	Chapter 21	Proverbs 12:2–3	Chapter 12
Proverbs 10:3	Chapter 13	Proverbs 12:4	Chapter 27
Proverbs 10:4	Chapter 25	Proverbs 12:5–8	Chapter 12
Proverbs 10:5	Chapter 26	Proverbs 12:9	Chapter 16
Proverbs 10:6–7	Chapter 12	Proverbs 12:10	Chapter 15
Proverbs 10:8	Chapter 10	Proverbs 12:11	Chapter 26
Proverbs 10:9	Chapter 13	Proverbs 12:12	Chapter 12
Proverbs 10:10	Chapter 14	Proverbs 12:13–14	Chapter 18
Proverbs 10:12	Chapter 15	Proverbs 12:15	Chapter 10
Proverbs 10:13-14	Chapter 9	Proverbs 12:16	Chapter 17
Proverbs 10:15	Chapter 23	Proverbs 12:17	Chapter 22
Proverbs 10:16	Chapter 12	Proverbs 12:18-19	Chapter 19
Proverbs 10:17	Chapter 11	Proverbs 12:20	Chapter 21
Proverbs 10:18	Chapter 19	Proverbs 12:21	Chapter 12
Proverbs 10:19-21	Chapter 18	Proverbs 12:22	Chapter 19
Proverbs 10:22	Chapter 13	Proverbs 12:23	Chapter 18
Proverbs 10:23	Chapter 9	Proverbs 12:24	Chapter 25
Proverbs 10:24–25	Chapter 13	Proverbs 12:25-26	Chapter 15
Proverbs 10:26	Chapter 25	Proverbs 12:27	Chapter 25
Proverbs 10:27	Chapter 8	Proverbs 12:28	Chapter 12
Proverbs 10:28–30	Chapter 12	Proverbs 13:1	Chapter 10

Proverbs Passage	HOTC Chapter	Proverbs Passage	HOTC Chapter
Proverbs 13:2-3	Chapter 18	Proverbs 14:24	Chapter 9
Proverbs 13:4	Chapter 25	Proverbs 14:25	Chapter 22
Proverbs 13:5	Chapter 21	Proverbs 14:26–27	Chapter 8
Proverbs 13:6	Chapter 13	Proverbs 14:28	Chapter 28
Proverbs 13:7	Chapter 16	Proverbs 14:29	Chapter 17
Proverbs 13:8	Chapter 23	Proverbs 14:30	Chapter 16
Proverbs 13:9	Chapter 12	Proverbs 14:31	Chapter 24
Proverbs 13:10	Chapter 16	Proverbs 14:32	Chapter 29
Proverbs 13:11	Chapter 21	Proverbs 14:33	Chapter 9
Proverbs 13:12	Chapter 29	Proverbs 14:34	Chapter 12
Proverbs 13:13	Chapter 10	Proverbs 14:35	Chapter 28
Proverbs 13:14-16	Chapter 9	Proverbs 15:1-2	Chapter 18
Proverbs 13:17	Chapter 28	Proverbs 15:3	Chapter 8
Proverbs 13:18	Chapter 11	Proverbs 15:4	Chapter 19
Proverbs 13:19	Chapter 29	Proverbs 15:5	Chapter 11
Proverbs 13:20	Chapter 15	Proverbs 15:6	Chapter 12
Proverbs 13:21	Chapter 12	Proverbs 15:7	Chapter 18
Proverbs 13:22-23	Chapter 24	Proverbs 15:8	Chapter 14
Proverbs 13:24	Chapter 11	Proverbs 15:9	Chapter 12
Proverbs 13:25	Chapter 12	Proverbs 15:10	Chapter 11
Proverbs 14:1	Chapter 27	Proverbs 15:11	Chapter 14
Proverbs 14:2	Chapter 8	Proverbs 15:12	Chapter 11
Proverbs 14:3	Chapter 18	Proverbs 15:13	Chapter 29
Proverbs 14:4	Chapter 26	Proverbs 15:14	Chapter 9
Proverbs 14:5	Chapter 22	Proverbs 15:15	Chapter 24
Proverbs 14:6	Chapter 9	Proverbs 15:16	Chapter 23
Proverbs 14:7	Chapter 15	Proverbs 15:17	Chapter 15
Proverbs 14:8	Chapter 9	Proverbs 15:18	Chapter 17
Proverbs 14:9	Chapter 11	Proverbs 15:19	Chapter 25
Proverbs 14:10	Chapter 29	Proverbs 15:20	Chapter 27
Proverbs 14:11	Chapter 12	Proverbs 15:21	Chapter 9
Proverbs 14:12	Chapter 8	Proverbs 15:22	Chapter 10
Proverbs 14:13	Chapter 29	Proverbs 15:23	Chapter 18
Proverbs 14:14	Chapter 13	Proverbs 15:24	Chapter 9
Proverbs 14:15	Chapter 9	Proverbs 15:25	Chapter 16
Proverbs 14:16–17	Chapter 17	Proverbs 15:26	Chapter 13
Proverbs 14:18	Chapter 9	Proverbs 15:27	Chapter 21
Proverbs 14:19	Chapter 12	Proverbs 15:28	Chapter 18
Proverbs 14:20	Chapter 23	Proverbs 15:29	Chapter 14
Proverbs 14:21	Chapter 24	Proverbs 15:30	Chapter 29
Proverbs 14:22	Chapter 13	Proverbs 15:31	Chapter 10
Proverbs 14:23	Chapter 25	Proverbs 15:32	Chapter 11

Proverbs Passage	HOTC Chapter	Proverbs Passage	HOTC Chapter
Proverbs 15:33	Chapter 8	Proverbs 17:16	Chapter 23
Proverbs 16:1	Chapter 8	Proverbs 17:17	Chapter 15
Proverbs 16:2	Chapter 14	Proverbs 17:18	Chapter 26
Proverbs 16:3-4	Chapter 8	Proverbs 17:19-20	Chapter 19
Proverbs 16:5	Chapter 16	Proverbs 17:21	Chapter 27
Proverbs 16:6	Chapter 15	Proverbs 17:22	Chapter 29
Proverbs 16:7	Chapter 13	Proverbs 17:23	Chapter 21
Proverbs 16:8	Chapter 24	Proverbs 17:24	Chapter 9
Proverbs 16:9	Chapter 8	Proverbs 17:25	Chapter 27
Proverbs 16:10	Chapter 28	Proverbs 17:26	Chapter 22
Proverbs 16:11	Chapter 21	Proverbs 17:27-28	Chapter 18
Proverbs 16:12-15	Chapter 28	Proverbs 18:1	Chapter 16
Proverbs 16:16	Chapter 9	Proverbs 18:2	Chapter 8
Proverbs 16:17	Chapter 29	Proverbs 18:3	Chapter 13
Proverbs 16:18–19	Chapter 16	Proverbs 18:4	Chapter 8
Proverbs 16:20	Chapter 8	Proverbs 18:5	Chapter 22
Proverbs 16:21	Chapter 18	Proverbs 18:6–7	Chapter 18
Proverbs 16:22	Chapter 9	Proverbs 18:8	Chapter 19
Proverbs 16:23-24	Chapter 18	Proverbs 18:9	Chapter 25
Proverbs 16:25	Chapter 8	Proverbs 18:10	Chapter 8
Proverbs 16:26	Chapter 25	Proverbs 18:11	Chapter 23
Proverbs 16:27-28	Chapter 19	Proverbs 18:12	Chapter 16
Proverbs 16:29	Chapter 20	Proverbs 18:13	Chapter 18
Proverbs 16:30	Chapter 14	Proverbs 18:14	Chapter 29
Proverbs 16:31	Chapter 27	Proverbs 18:15	Chapter 9
Proverbs 16:32	Chapter 17	Proverbs 18:16	Chapter 24
Proverbs 16:33	Chapter 8	Proverbs 18:17	Chapter 22
Proverbs 17:1	Chapter 20	Proverbs 18:18–19	Chapter 20
Proverbs 17:2	Chapter 27	Proverbs 18:20-21	Chapter 19
Proverbs 17:3	Chapter 14	Proverbs 18:22	Chapter 27
Proverbs 17:4	Chapter 18	Proverbs 18:23	Chapter 23
Proverbs 17:5	Chapter 15	Proverbs 18:24	Chapter 15
Proverbs 17:6	Chapter 27	Proverbs 19:1	Chapter 18
Proverbs 17:7	Chapter 28	Proverbs 19:2	Chapter 9
Proverbs 17:8	Chapter 21	Proverbs 19:3	Chapter 8
Proverbs 17:9	Chapter 19	Proverbs 19:4	Chapter 23
Proverbs 17:10	Chapter 10	Proverbs 19:5	Chapter 19
Proverbs 17:11	Chapter 28	Proverbs 19:6–7	Chapter 23
Proverbs 17:12	Chapter 9	Proverbs 19:8	Chapter 9
Proverbs 17:13	Chapter 13	Proverbs 19:9	Chapter 22
Proverbs 17:14	Chapter 19	Proverbs 19:10	Chapter 16
Proverbs 17:15	Chapter 22	Proverbs 19:11	Chapter 17

Proverbs

Proverbs Passage	HOTC Chapter	Proverbs Passage	HOTC Chapter
Proverbs 19:12	Chapter 28	Proverbs 20:26	Chapter 28
Proverbs 19:13–14	Chapter 27	Proverbs 20:27	Chapter 14
Proverbs 19:15	Chapter 25	Proverbs 20:28	Chapter 28
Proverbs 19:16	Chapter 10	Proverbs 20:29	Chapter 27
Proverbs 19:17	Chapter 24	Proverbs 20:30	Chapter 11
Proverbs 19:18	Chapter 11	Proverbs 21:1	Chapter 28
Proverbs 19:19	Chapter 17	Proverbs 21:2-3	Chapter 14
Proverbs 19:20	Chapter 10	Proverbs 21:4	Chapter 16
Proverbs 19:21	Chapter 8	Proverbs 21:5	Chapter 17
Proverbs 19:22	Chapter 19	Proverbs 21:6	Chapter 19
Proverbs 19:23	Chapter 8	Proverbs 21:7	Chapter 20
Proverbs 19:24	Chapter 25	Proverbs 21:8	Chapter 13
Proverbs 19:25	Chapter 10	Proverbs 21:9	Chapter 27
Proverbs 19:26	Chapter 27	Proverbs 21:10	Chapter 15
Proverbs 19:27	Chapter 10	Proverbs 21:11	Chapter 9
Proverbs 19:28	Chapter 22	Proverbs 21:12	Chapter 13
Proverbs 19:29	Chapter 13	Proverbs 21:13	Chapter 24
Proverbs 20:1	Chapter 17	Proverbs 21:14	Chapter 21
Proverbs 20:2	Chapter 28	Proverbs 21:15	Chapter 22
Proverbs 20:3	Chapter 19	Proverbs 21:16	Chapter 13
Proverbs 20:4	Chapter 25	Proverbs 21:17	Chapter 25
Proverbs 20:5	Chapter 9	Proverbs 21:18	Chapter 12
Proverbs 20:6	Chapter 15	Proverbs 21:19	Chapter 27
Proverbs 20:7	Chapter 12	Proverbs 21:20	Chapter 26
Proverbs 20:8	Chapter 28	Proverbs 21:21	Chapter 13
Proverbs 20:9	Chapter 16	Proverbs 21:22	Chapter 8
Proverbs 20:10	Chapter 21	Proverbs 21:23	Chapter 18
Proverbs 20:11	Chapter 14	Proverbs 21:24	Chapter 16
Proverbs 20:12	Chapter 9	Proverbs 21:25–26	Chapter 25
Proverbs 20:13	Chapter 25	Proverbs 21:27	Chapter 14
Proverbs 20:14	Chapter 14	Proverbs 21:28	Chapter 22
Proverbs 20:15	Chapter 9	Proverbs 21:29	Chapter 20
Proverbs 20:16	Chapter 26	Proverbs 21:30–31	Chapter 8
Proverbs 20:17	Chapter 21	Proverbs 22:1	Chapter 29
Proverbs 20:18	Chapter 10	Proverbs 22:2	Chapter 23
Proverbs 20:19	Chapter 19	Proverbs 22:3	Chapter 29
Proverbs 20:20	Chapter 27	Proverbs 22:4	Chapter 16
Proverbs 20:21	Chapter 21	Proverbs 22:5	Chapter 29
Proverbs 20:22	Chapter 20	Proverbs 22:6	Chapter 11
Proverbs 20:23	Chapter 21	Proverbs 22:7	Chapter 23
Proverbs 20:24	Chapter 8	Proverbs 22:8	Chapter 13
Proverbs 20:25	Chapter 17	Proverbs 22:9	Chapter 24

Proverbs Passage	HOTC Chapter	Proverbs Passage	HOTC Chapter
Proverbs 22:10	Chapter 19	Proverbs 24:30–34	Chapter 25
Proverbs 22:11	Chapter 28	Proverbs 25:1–7	Chapter 28
Proverbs 22:12	Chapter 8	Proverbs 25:8	Chapter 17
Proverbs 22:13	Chapter 29	Proverbs 25:9–10	Chapter 29
Proverbs 22:14	Chapter 5	Proverbs 25:11	Chapter 18
Proverbs 22:15	Chapter 11	Proverbs 25:12	Chapter 10
Proverbs 22:16	Chapter 24	Proverbs 25:13	Chapter 28
Proverbs 22:17–21	Chapter 1	Proverbs 25:14	Chapter 24
Proverbs 22:22–23	Chapter 24	Proverbs 25:15	Chapter 18
Proverbs 22:24–25	Chapter 17	Proverbs 25:16–17	Chapter 15
Proverbs 22:26–27	Chapter 26	Proverbs 25:18	Chapter 22
Proverbs 22:28	Chapter 21	Proverbs 25:19	Chapter 15
Proverbs 22:29	Chapter 26	Proverbs 25:20	Chapter 29
Proverbs 23:1–3	Chapter 28	Proverbs 25:21–22	Chapter 15
Proverbs 23:4–5	Chapter 23	Proverbs 25:23	Chapter 19
Proverbs 23:6–8	Chapter 14	Proverbs 25:24	Chapter 27
Proverbs 23:9	Chapter 10	Proverbs 25:25	Chapter 29
Proverbs 23:10–11	Chapter 21	Proverbs 25:26	Chapter 20
Proverbs 23:12	Chapter 9	Proverbs 25:27	Chapter 16
Proverbs 23:13–14	Chapter 11	Proverbs 25:28	Chapter 17
Proverbs 23:15–16	Chapter 18	Proverbs 26:1	Chapter 13
Proverbs 23:17–18	Chapter 29	Proverbs 26:2	Chapter 19
Proverbs 23:19–21	Chapter 17	Proverbs 26:3	Chapter 13
Proverbs 23:22–25	Chapter 27	Proverbs 26:4–11	Chapter 9
Proverbs 23:26–28	Chapter 5	Proverbs 26:12	Chapter 8
Proverbs 23:29–35	Chapter 17	Proverbs 26:13	Chapter 29
Proverbs 24:1–2	Chapter 15	Proverbs 26:14-15	Chapter 25
Proverbs 24:3–4	Chapter 9	Proverbs 26:16	Chapter 16
Proverbs 24:5–6	Chapter 10	Proverbs 26:17	Chapter 20
Proverbs 24:7	Chapter 9	Proverbs 26:18–19	Chapter 21
Proverbs 24:8–9	Chapter 13	Proverbs 26:20-22	Chapter 19
Proverbs 24:10	Chapter 29	Proverbs 26:23–26	Chapter 14
Proverbs 24:11–12	Chapter 22	Proverbs 26:27	Chapter 13
Proverbs 24:13–14	Chapter 9	Proverbs 26:28	Chapter 19
Proverbs 24:15–16	Chapter 12	Proverbs 27:1	Chapter 8
Proverbs 24:17–18	Chapter 15	Proverbs 27:2	Chapter 16
Proverbs 24:19–20	Chapter 16	Proverbs 27:3	Chapter 20
Proverbs 24:21–22	Chapter 28	Proverbs 27:4	Chapter 16
Proverbs 24:23–25	Chapter 22	Proverbs 27:5–6	Chapter 10
Proverbs 24:26	Chapter 21	Proverbs 27:7	Chapter 23
Proverbs 24:27	Chapter 26	Proverbs 27:8–10	Chapter 15
Proverbs 24:28–29	Chapter 20	Proverbs 27:11-12	Chapter 29

Proverbs Passage	HOTC Chapter	Proverbs Passage	HOTC Chapter
Proverbs 27:13	Chapter 26	Proverbs 28:26	Chapter 8
Proverbs 27:14	Chapter 18	Proverbs 28:27	Chapter 24
Proverbs 27:15–16	Chapter 27	Proverbs 28:28	Chapter 12
Proverbs 27:17	Chapter 10	Proverbs 29:1	Chapter 10
Proverbs 27:18	Chapter 26	Proverbs 29:2	Chapter 12
Proverbs 27:19	Chapter 14	Proverbs 29:3	Chapter 5
Proverbs 27:20	Chapter 29	Proverbs 29:4	Chapter 28
Proverbs 27:21	Chapter 16	Proverbs 29:5	Chapter 19
Proverbs 27:22	Chapter 9	Proverbs 29:6	Chapter 29
Proverbs 27:23–27	Chapter 26	Proverbs 29:7	Chapter 24
Proverbs 28:1	Chapter 29	Proverbs 29:8	Chapter 17
Proverbs 28:2–3	Chapter 28	Proverbs 29:9	Chapter 9
Proverbs 28:4	Chapter 11	Proverbs 29:10	Chapter 13
Proverbs 28:5	Chapter 22	Proverbs 29:11	Chapter 17
Proverbs 28:6	Chapter 23	Proverbs 29:12	Chapter 28
Proverbs 28:7	Chapter 11	Proverbs 29:13	Chapter 24
Proverbs 28:8	Chapter 23	Proverbs 29:14	Chapter 28
Proverbs 28:9	Chapter 11	Proverbs 29:15	Chapter 11
Proverbs 28:10	Chapter 20	Proverbs 29:16	Chapter 12
Proverbs 28:11	Chapter 23	Proverbs 29:17-19	Chapter 11
Proverbs 28:12	Chapter 12	Proverbs 29:20	Chapter 17
Proverbs 28:13	Chapter 11	Proverbs 29:21	Chapter 11
Proverbs 28:14	Chapter 8	Proverbs 29:22	Chapter 17
Proverbs 28:15–16	Chapter 28	Proverbs 29:23	Chapter 16
Proverbs 28:17	Chapter 20	Proverbs 29:24	Chapter 15
Proverbs 28:18	Chapter 13	Proverbs 29:25	Chapter 8
Proverbs 28:19	Chapter 25	Proverbs 29:26	Chapter 22
Proverbs 28:20–22	Chapter 23	Proverbs 29:27	Chapter 12
Proverbs 28:23	Chapter 19	Proverbs 30:1–33	Chapter 30
Proverbs 28:24	Chapter 27	Proverbs 31:1–31	Chapter 31
Proverbs 28:25	Chapter 16		

Chapter 1

The Source of Wisdom

Proverbs 1:1–7; 22:17–21

I. **INTRODUCTION**
The Wisest Man Who Ever Lived

II. **COMMENTARY**
A verse-by-verse explanation of these verses.

III. **CONCLUSION**
Follow the Yellow Brick Road

An overview of the principles and applications from these verses.

IV. **LIFE APPLICATION**
Lessons from Robin Hood

Melding these verses to life.

V. **PRAYER**
Tying these verses to life with God.

VI. **DEEPER DISCOVERIES**
Historical, geographical, and grammatical enrichment of the commentary.

VII. **TEACHING OUTLINE**
Suggested step-by-step group study of these verses.

VIII. **ISSUES FOR DISCUSSION**
Zeroing these verses in on daily life.

| Q u o t e |

"*K*nowledge is horizontal. Wisdom is vertical—

it comes down from above."

B i l l y   G r a h a m

Proverbs

1:1–7; 22:17–21

I N   A   N U T S H E L L

*P*roverbs 1:1–7 introduces the entire Book of Proverbs, identifies its primary author, calls for the reader to gain wisdom, knowledge,
understanding, and prudence, and declares that the beginning point of
this kind of wisdom is to fear the Lord. Then, Proverbs 22:17–21 tells us
that if we commit ourselves to a study of the proverbs, it will be pleasing
to us, our trust will be in the Lord, and we will have sound answers to the
questions of life.

The Source of Wisdom

I. INTRODUCTION

The Wisest Man Who Ever Lived

*Y*ou are already familiar with one of the most amazing stories of wisdom ever told. Two women brought an infant son to the king, each claiming to be the true mother. They both claimed that the other woman had suffocated her own son in the middle of the night by rolling over on top of him without realizing it. And, having suffocated her own son, she was trying to steal the other woman's son, claiming it to be her own.

The king called for a swordsman to cut the baby in half and give half to each woman. The first women said, "Fine with me! If I can't have him, I don't want her to have him either." The second woman screamed in horror and begged the king to give the son to the first woman.

The king, revealing his wisdom, said, "Give the baby to the second woman. She is his mother."

When the people heard about the judgment the king had handed down, they were stunned! The implications of this kind of wisdom were actually frightening. It was as though the king could peer into their souls. There was no pulling the wool over this man's eyes! It was time for honesty and integrity!

The king who handed down this judgment was Solomon, regarded as the wisest man who ever lived. His wisdom was a gift from God. When he was crowned king, he asked God not for riches or success over his enemies but for wisdom. God was pleased with the request and granted it in greater measure than any other human being except Christ.

It is this man—renowned as the wisest man who ever lived—who wrote the Book of Proverbs. He knew what he was talking about. When he spoke, it was time to listen. Now we begin our study of Proverbs. Solomon will speak. We should listen.

II. COMMENTARY

The Source of Wisdom

MAIN IDEA: *Wisdom is the most important thing a person can acquire in life. It comes from God. Pay attention to these proverbs and apply your heart to them so that you can profit from them.*

A The Purpose of Proverbs (1:1–7)

SUPPORTING IDEA: *These proverbs were written to impart wisdom. The fear of the Lord is the beginning of wisdom.*

1:1. The Hebrew word for "proverb" can have a broader meaning than the typical American usage. It means a "comparison," or a "brief, pithy saying," or an "ethical saying." In this context the word refers to several different kinds of insightful sayings and observations.

Though **Solomon** is declared to be the author of Proverbs in 1:1, it is clear that someone other than Solomon wrote some of the content of this book. The entire contents of the book were collected over a period of time. Solomon's name appears three times in this book, each time apparently introducing a section in the book that was written by him. His name appears in 1:1, probably announcing authorship for Proverbs 1:1–9:18; in 10:1, probably announcing his authorship of 10:1–22:16; and in 25:1 for chapters 25 through 29.

1:2. Verse 2 begins a summary statement about why the Book of Proverbs was written: first, **for attaining wisdom, discipline,** and **understanding,** Lofty goals for sure! The Hebrew word for "wisdom" is transliterated *hokmah* and means "skill or expertise in living." Just as a person might be a skilled craftsman, musician, or mediator, so a person might be skilled in the living of life. The purpose of Proverbs is that a person might gain such skill.

The Hebrew word for "discipline" is *musar,* meaning "moral discipline, instruction, or correction." Even after a person knows how to live skillfully, he must have the personal discipline to do so. Finally, the Hebrew word for "understanding" is *binah* and carries the idea of "discernment."

In summary, then, the purpose of Proverbs is that the reader might gain skill for living life, the discipline to carry through with it, and the discernment to know whether one is "on course."

1:3. Verse 3 expands the summary statement, repeating the need for discipline, adding prudence, which includes having good judgment with high moral standards, along with a high sense of justice and fairness.

1:4. Solomon targets a **simple** person and a **young** person, hoping to give both persons **prudence, knowledge,** and **discretion.** A simple person refers to someone who is untaught and naïve. It does not mean that he is intellectually limited or that he is a fool. Instead, he is one who is inexperienced, who simply hasn't lived life long enough, or who has not been instructed in wisdom. It is similar with the young person, though this person's need is perhaps clearer. A young person is one who is beginning to enter into the adult world; he has not had the range of life experiences or the physical and mental maturity to develop wisdom.

1:5. The target group is now expanded to include not just simple or young people but also **wise** and **discerning** people. Even they can learn from the Proverbs. We should all continue to grow in our knowledge, understanding, and wisdom as long as we live. No one should get complacent or feel that he has arrived.

1:6. The learning and guidance that the wise and discerning gain is for the purpose of **understanding proverbs, parables**, and **sayings and riddles of the wise**. This list of subjects helps us understand more of what is meant by the term *proverbs*. It is more than just a pithy saying. Part of Solomon's strategy to impart wisdom was to sharpen the mind by challenging wise and discerning people to increase their wisdom and discernment by pondering and interpreting proverbs, parables, and riddles.

1:7. Having stated his purpose in writing the proverbs, Solomon now gives his first and perhaps most important piece of instruction. The beginning point for becoming a wise person is **the fear of the LORD**. To fear the Lord does not mean to be frightened of him. Rather, it means to revere him, to honor him, to give him the proper place in one's life. If a person does not start out at the right place, he cannot expect to end up at the right place. Fearing the Lord is the place to begin in gaining wisdom to live life skillfully.

In contrast to the person who is wise and discerning because he fears the Lord, Solomon spotlights the fool. **Fools despise wisdom and discipline**. To *despise* means "to hold in contempt, to belittle, to ridicule" (Num. 15:31; Neh. 2:19). If anyone holds God in contempt, he will never be a wise person, and he will tend to live his life in violation of God's will. This will bring trouble into his life. As a man sows, that shall he also reap. A person cannot break the laws of God. He can only break himself against them when he violates them. Solomon is giving us an implicit choice: fear God or be a fool. There seems to be no middle ground.

B The Result of Proverbs (22:17–21)

SUPPORTING IDEA: *If you commit yourself to a study of the proverbs, it will be pleasing to you, your trust will be in the Lord, and you will have sound answers to the questions of life.*

22:17. Solomon now exhorts the reader to commit himself to a life of study and a pursuit of wisdom. Solomon's spirit is similar to Jesus' when he said, "He who has ears to hear, let him hear" (Mark 4:9). In other words, don't let this information go in one ear and out the other. Take it in. Think about it. Ponder it. Let it change you.

22:18. The goal of paying attention, listening, and applying (v. 17) is so that it will be **pleasing** for you. The idea here seems to be to memorize the sayings of the wise (**keep them in your heart**) so that you will be able to quote them and talk knowledgeably about them (**ready on your lips**). What we say about wisdom will have little value unless it has changed us from the inside out.

22:19. Solomon teaches his student so that his **trust may be in the LORD**. This is reminiscent of Paul's statement, "The goal of this command is love, which comes from a pure heart and a good conscience and a sincere faith" (1 Tim. 1:5). Neither Paul nor Solomon was teaching to satisfy curiosity but to change lives.

22:20–21. Solomon now refers to thirty sayings of counsel and knowledge that he has written. These sayings are **true and reliable words** and, when learned by the student, can help him **give sound answers to him who sent you** (possibly meaning his teacher or employer).

> **MAIN IDEA REVIEW:** *Wisdom is the most important thing a person can acquire in life. It comes from God. Pay attention to these proverbs; apply your heart to them so that you can profit from them.*

III. CONCLUSION

Follow the Yellow Brick Road

When Dorothy's house landed in Munchkin Land, killing the Wicked Witch of the North and throwing all the Munchkins into gala celebration, all Dorothy wanted to know was, "How do I get home?" The Munchkins didn't know. They told her she needed to go to Oz and ask the wizard. The Munchkins told her to "follow the Yellow Brick Road." The Yellow Brick Road began at the very point where Dorothy's house had landed, spiraled out like a bull's-eye, and eventually headed toward Oz. Stay on it, they said, and she would eventually get to Oz.

There was one road to Oz. It began right there. To stay on it would take her to Oz. To depart from it would take her anyplace except to Oz. If you want to get to Oz, you have to follow the Yellow Brick Road to the final destination.

The principle is true, too, of having a rewarding life. The beginning point—the origin of the Yellow Brick Road leading to a rewarding life—is reverence for God (1:7). The fear of the Lord is the beginning of knowledge, and knowledge leads to wisdom, prudence, and discretion (1:2–6), which in turn lead to a pleasing life (22:18). Start with reverence for God; stay on the road of knowledge, wisdom, prudence, and discretion, following them to their ultimate destination; and you will arrive in the land of a pleasing life. That is the message of the Book of Proverbs.

PRINCIPLES

- A life of wisdom cannot be gained apart from reverence for God.
- A person who turns his back on God is a fool. A wise person will pursue learning and listen to counsel.
- Wise sayings are not always easy to understand at first. Sometimes it takes effort, time, and maturity to comprehend a deeper insight.

APPLICATIONS

- Revere God. Honor him in your life. Give him first place. Everything you want in life is based on this decision.
- Commit yourself to the pursuit of wisdom. Wisdom is hard to gain even after you have given yourself to it. It is impossible without commitment to it.
- Be willing to struggle to understand things that are difficult to comprehend. The struggle sharpens your understanding and increases your wisdom.

IV. LIFE APPLICATION

Lessons from Robin Hood

In *The Adventures of Robin Hood,* a 1938 movie starring Errol Flynn as the legendary English hero, Robin Hood and his merry men were conducting guerilla warfare from Sherwood Forest against Prince John, younger brother of King Richard the Lionhearted. Richard had led a crusade to the Holy Land, leaving England in the hands of his younger brother, who taxed the people of England beyond reason and pocketed the money himself. Robin stole from the rich (Prince John and his cohorts) and gave to the poor (the common people from whom the money was taken in the first place), as Prince John and the Sheriff of Nottingham tried to eliminate him.

After years of absence, King Richard returned to England, disguised as a common traveler. The men of Sherwood Forest captured King Richard and took him to Robin Hood. King Richard asked Robin if he supported the king's crusade to the Holy Land. Robin replied that he did not support the king, since he had left England in the hands of the wicked Prince John. "So are you loyal to King Richard?" the traveler wanted to know. "I'd lay down my life for him," replied Robin. Assured that he was safe among loyalists, King Richard removed his outer robe to reveal his royal armor beneath. Robin and his men were astonished to realize they were in the presence of their king. Immediately they dropped to one knee and bowed in silence before their monarch.

Respect. Reverence. Awe. These were the responses of people who knew who they were and knew who their king was.

Today the American people are hardly capable of that kind of respect. We have so flattened our world, bringing leaders down to our level, that we would be more apt to high-five a king than to kneel before him.

Unfortunately, the same is true of our capacity to revere God. Our capacity for reverence is so stunted that we are almost incapable of revering God on an appropriate level. Americans are unable to offer God the reverence that marks the beginning point of wisdom. As a result, we are not a wise people.

One reason for the lack of respect in America is that no one person has any great authority over us. Litigation, politically correct tolerance, labor strikes, and mass demonstrations have removed any sense in America that anyone is "over" us as individuals. Respect in ancient England was heightened by the realization that the king had the unquestioned power of life and death in his hands. The king was respected because he deserved respect. The welfare of the common man depended on his respect for the king.

The same is true with God. His sovereignty is unquestioned and carries with it the power of life and death, heaven and hell, blessing and cursing. If we are in touch with reality, we understand the logic of revering God. In his hands lies our eternal destiny. Jeremiah said it is "because of the LORD's great love we are not consumed" (Lam. 3:22). The person who is doctrinally sound—the person who is in touch with reality—is a person who reveres God and cultivates his capacity for reverence. Not only is reverence for God a good thing in and of itself; it also places us at the beginning of the Yellow Brick Road that leads to wisdom.

V. PRAYER

Father, help us realize that wisdom is a by-product of our relationship with you, and that it is a heart issue, not a head issue. Your wisdom often takes us 180 degrees in the opposite direction of our natural inclinations. Help us to keep our hearts close to you so our minds might be rooted in wisdom and our actions might bring honor to you. Amen.

VI. DEEPER DISCOVERIES

A. Fear of the LORD

The expression "fear of the LORD" occurs fourteen times in the Book of Proverbs. Solomon said it was the "beginning of knowledge" (Prov. 1:7), "the beginning of wisdom" (9:10), "a fountain of life" (14:27), and "the instruction for wisdom" (15:33 NASB). The fear of the Lord "is to hate evil" (8:13), it prolongs life (10:27), it imparts "strong confidence" (14:26 NASB), it keeps one from sin (16:6), it is the pathway to life (19:23), and its rewards include "wealth and honor and life" (22:4).

A number of words are translated as "fear" in the Old Testament. But in this context (fear of the Lord), it does not mean being afraid of God. Rather, it means having an attitude of honor and trust that cause a person to esteem and obey God. It means that we give God "weight," and consider him to be worthy of respect and deference. If a person fears the Lord, he recognizes who God is and responds correctly to his greatness.

B. Wisdom

Hokmah, the Hebrew word for wisdom, often refers to the mental and physical skills of craftsmen, singers and musicians, sailors, counselors, and others. But at other times, as in Proverbs, it focuses on the application of moral and ethical principles to the living of life, so that one might be said to "live skillfully," as compared to a sailor who might sail skillfully or a metal worker who might craft metal skillfully. A person with wisdom has expertise in living in a way that makes life go as well as possible for him.

The ability to live this way depends on a person's "fearing the Lord." When a person tries to be wise in his own abilities, the best wisdom he can produce is "earthly, unspiritual, of the devil" (Jas. 3:15). When Christians draw on their own wisdom, rather than wisdom that comes from "fearing the Lord," the best wisdom they are able to produce is the same as the world is capable of producing (earthly). This form of "wisdom" often does not take into account spiritual principles such as turning the other cheek and doing unto others as we would have others do unto us.

There is an example of this in 2 Timothy 2:25–26. In this passage, we see Christians who have been trapped by the devil to do his will because they do not have a knowledge of the truth because they have not repented. Unrepentance makes a Christian vulnerable to mental distortion at the hands of the enemy.

Much conflict in the church might be a result of Christians using wisdom that is earthly, unspiritual, and of the devil, rather than the wisdom that comes from fearing the Lord.

C. Fool

Many proverbs in this book contrast the wise man with the fool. The wise person has knowledge and wisdom, while fools "despise wisdom and discipline" (Prov. 1:7). Three Hebrew words are translated "fool" in Proverbs. The first one, *kesil*, refers to one who is stubborn and bullheaded, with a closed mind. This fool rejects information or counsel from others, thinking he knows it all, or doesn't need to know it. It is the most common word for "fool" used in Proverbs.

A second word for "fool" is *nabal*, which means "a person who lacks spiritual perception." This word is used only three times in Proverbs. It is the same word used for Abigail's husband (1 Sam. 25), who rejected David's request for food and drink for his men. David was offended by his attitude and prepared to avenge the insult. Abigail prepared food and drink for David's men and went out to appease him. She begged David to "pay no attention to that wicked man Nabal. He is just like his name—his name is Fool, and folly goes with him" (1 Sam. 25:25).

The third word for "fool" is *ewil*. This fool is arrogant, coarse, and hardened in his ways. This word is used nineteen times in Proverbs and only seven times in other places in Scripture. This is the word used in 1:7. The arrogant, coarse fool, hardened in his ways, rejects God and the wisdom he gives. The contrast in chapter 1 is between the wise person who fears God, and as a result gains true wisdom, and the arrogant fool who rejects God and holds true wisdom and discipline in contempt.

VII. TEACHING OUTLINE

A. INTRODUCTION

1. Lead Story: The Wisest Man Who Ever Lived
2. Context: Solomon describes the purpose of his writing proverbs and the consequences of fearing the Lord.
3. Transition: If a person wants to learn how to live life skillfully, he must begin by fearing the Lord.

B. COMMENTARY

1. The Purpose of Proverbs (1:1–7)
2. The Result of Proverbs (22:17–21)

C. CONCLUSION: FOLLOW THE YELLOW BRICK ROAD

VIII. ISSUES FOR DISCUSSION

1. Do you believe that fearing the Lord produces instantaneous wisdom? If not, how long do you think it takes to gain true wisdom?
2. What are some specific instances of foolish words or behavior that you have witnessed? What are some examples of wise words or behavior that you have witnessed?
3. Where are you on the wise/fool spectrum? Closer to the wise, or closer to the fool? What do you think you need to do to become a wiser person?

Chapter 2

The Benefits of Wisdom

Proverbs 2:1–22; 3:13–24

I. **INTRODUCTION**
The Cremation of Sam Magee

II. **COMMENTARY**
A verse-by-verse explanation of these verses.

III. **CONCLUSION**
Seeing Life Through Solomon's Eyes

An overview of the principles and applications from these verses.

IV. **LIFE APPLICATION**
Breaking the Laws of God

Melding these verses to life.

V. **PRAYER**
Tying these verses to life with God.

VI. **DEEPER DISCOVERIES**
Historical, geographical, and grammatical enrichment of the commentary.

VII. **TEACHING OUTLINE**
Suggested step-by-step group study of these verses.

VIII. **ISSUES FOR DISCUSSION**
Zeroing these verses in on daily life.

"*Wisdom is the power to see and the inclination to choose the best and highest goal, together with the surest means of attaining it.*"

J . I . P a c k e r

Proverbs
2:1–22; 3:13–24

IN A NUTSHELL

Wisdom must be sought, like any rare treasure. When found, it will save one from violent men and seductive women. It is more valuable than gold, and it brings true happiness.

The Benefits of Wisdom

I. INTRODUCTION

The Cremation of Sam Magee

*T*here is no end to the lengths to which people will go to find gold. In Robert W. Service's poem "The Cremation of Sam Magee," he tells the story of hardship, cold, deprivation, and loneliness experienced by Sam Magee and his partner Cap as they prospected for gold in Alaska. Sam was from Tennessee, and he hated the cold with a passion. Gold fever was the only thing that would make him endure such ongoing misery as prospecting in Alaska. Bad circumstances caught up with him, and his darkest fear was realized. He was going to freeze to death. As his partner, Cap, recounted the story:

> Well, he seemed so low that I couldn't say no;
>> then he says with a sort of moan:
> "It's the cursed cold, and it's got right hold
>> till I'm chilled clean through to the bone.
>
> Yet 'tain't being dead—it's my awful dread
>> of the icy grave that pains;
> So I want you to swear that, foul or fair,
>> you'll cremate my last remains."

So, faithful partner, Cap, suffered untold hardship getting Sam's frozen corpse by dogsled to some place where he could fulfill his promise to cremate him. He finally found an old steamship half submerged in a lake. Cap pulled up some boards, built a roaring fire in the ship's boiler, and stuffed in Sam. Then he walked around for a while before coming back to make sure the cremation had gone all right. He finally worked up the courage to open the door of the boiler to inspect Sam's remains.

> And there sat Sam, looking cool and calm,
>> in the heart of the furnace roar;
> And he wore a smile you could see a mile,
>> and he said: "Please close that door.
> It's fine in here, but I greatly fear
>> you'll let in the cold and storm—
> Since I left Plumtree, down in Tennessee,
>> it's the first time I've been warm."

Of course, Service's poem is pure folly, but even in this elaborate spoof, we understand that the life of a prospector in Alaska's cold, gold country was a harsh life. But people thronged to the area in the hope of getting rich. They paid any reasonable price, and many times an unreasonable price, to look for gold, and more often than not, never got rich.

Solomon says that if you look for wisdom with the same commitment, dedication, and intensity, you will find it. And having found it, it will be well worth the price and worth much more than gold.

II. COMMENTARY

The Benefits of Wisdom

MAIN IDEA: *Wisdom can be found, if a person searches for it diligently enough, and once found, it will save a person from disaster and lead to satisfaction.*

 ### Wisdom's Conditions and Consequences (2:1–22)

SUPPORTING IDEA: *If you dedicate yourself to an intense search for wisdom, you will find it. And with the wisdom, you will find God. You will be protected from violent men or seductive women who would otherwise entice you to disaster. You will be able to choose the right paths because you know where each path ends.*

2:1–2. Solomon used chapter 1 to describe the disaster in store for anyone who ignores the warnings of wisdom. Now in chapter 2, he extols the wonderful blessings that **wisdom** brings. In 2:1–4, Solomon lists three conditions, each beginning with the word *if* (vv. 1,3,4). First, one must choose attentiveness (2:1–2). Passive listening is not enough. The father uses verb after verb urging his son to focus on wisdom—welcoming it, accepting it, and storing away its truths in memory. A wise learner leans closer to hear, choosing to listen with his heart, not just his ears.

2:3. The second condition for gaining wisdom is to ask for it. The writer uses verbs that refer to loud, insistent pleas for help, like the desperate cry of a man begging for deliverance from trouble (cp. Ps. 4:1; Mark 10:46–48). We will gain wisdom when we yearn for it strongly enough to **call out** for it.

2:4. A third step in gaining wisdom is to commit oneself to a determined **search** for it. People go to incredible lengths to find gold or silver or to dig in search of **hidden treasure**; the search for wisdom demands the same dedication.

2:5. If you fulfill these three conditions and throw yourself into a disciplined search for wisdom, God promises that you will find what you are looking for. The passage gives two promises: You will gain God (2:5–8), and you will gain God's wisdom (2:9–11).

The person who searches for wisdom will find more than he looked for because God is the source of all wisdom. When you set out to find wisdom, God waits for you at the end of the search. **The fear of the LORD** and **the knowledge of God**, two classic Old Testament descriptions of true devotion, are linked in Proverbs 1:7. When we recognize God's majesty, we will be ready to listen to him, and thus we will know him better by experience.

2:6–8. You will find God when you search for wisdom because he is the one who **gives wisdom** (see Jas. 1:5). In one sense, we find wisdom at the end of a diligent search; in another sense, God gives it freely. The Lord also "stores up sound wisdom" (Prov. 2:7 NASB) for his people. The Hebrew *tushiyyah* (victory, NIV) refers to sound wisdom and common sense and the success such wisdom brings. Verses 7–8 mention the **upright** and **blameless**, the **just** and **faithful**, showing that God's wisdom is more than cleverness; it is linked to holiness. Those who give themselves to this godly wisdom will experience God's protection. He is a protective shield, and he guards the paths where his people go.

The word for **blameless** refers to total submission that chooses God with the whole heart. And **his faithful ones** comes from the Hebrew word *chesedh*, which describes the loyal love that God displays to people as he keeps his covenants with them. When used of people, it means those who are loyal to God with a heart of love.

2:9. A second result of the search for wisdom is that God's wisdom will give you a sense of right and wrong. This concern for moral ethics is described by three words with closely related meanings. **Right** refers to actions that conform to God's standard of right and wrong. **Just** comes from the verb "to govern," calling us to render decisions that reflect God's character of justice. **Fair** stems from a word meaning "straight, upright," so that we do nothing underhanded or morally questionable.

2:10. At first, **wisdom** may seem to go against your natural instincts. But the person who searches for wisdom will soon acquire a taste for it. It becomes part of his **heart**, his inmost being. The truths that once seemed distasteful are now delightful.

2:11. The second half of the chapter explains how wisdom rescues its possessors from those who are out to trap them. It begins with a general statement that God's wisdom provides protection, just as God himself protects us (2:7–8).

2:12. A young man faces two perils: the perverted or **wicked** man (2:12–15) and the sensual woman (2:16–19). Wisdom helps you see these villains as they really are, penetrating their contrived image. This passage, like 1:10–19, gives a vivid description of these criminals, using the image of a path to describe their way of life. They have turned away from what is right, their values have become distorted, and they have twisted the truth with **perverse** words in order to persuade others to join them.

2:13. They have forsaken **the straight path**s (literally, the paths of uprightness, using the same word as 2:7). They have chosen to adopt a lifestyle of darkness, cloaking their sin in obscurity (see John 3:19).

2:14. The wicked get their greatest **delight in doing wrong**, particularly enjoying the twisted lifestyle they have adopted. Paul describes a similar depravity in Romans 1:32.

2:15. Anyone who follows these deceivers will soon lose his sense of direction. The **paths are crooked**, and the men themselves **are devious**, constantly turning to the left or the right and leading others off the right path.

2:16. The sensual woman is the second danger from which wisdom will rescue a young man. She is called an **adulteress**, literally "a strange or foreign woman." Though the term might refer to a non-Israelite like Ruth (Ruth 2:10), women from Gentile cultures were much more likely to be involved in immorality. She is also called a **wayward wife**, either a foreigner or a Jew acting as shamelessly as a foreigner.

The sensual woman seduces by her words, not just her physical appearance. Her words are, literally, "smooth" and flattering, deceiving an unsuspecting young man by appealing to his ego.

2:17. Like the wicked man who left the path of uprightness (2:13), the sensual woman has forsaken her original commitments. She has deserted her husband, **the partner** (intimate friend) **of her youth**. And in the process, she has chosen to ignore **the covenant** of her God. This phrase refers to marriage vows in Malachi 2:14, but it may also allude to the fact that God's covenant with the nation Israel outlawed adultery.

2:18–19. Those who become involved with a sensual woman soon find that they have made a ghastly mistake. **Her house** is literally a place of "sinking down" **to death**. This does not mean that anyone who gets involved with a sensual women will die but that her lifestyle is a lifestyle of death—perhaps alluding to spiritual, emotional, and financial death, and if pursued to the ultimate extreme, physical death.

2:20–22. A person who pursues wisdom can escape this fate by staying on the right path. Like the conclusion of Christ's Sermon on the Mount (Matt. 7:13–27), the final verses depict the fate that waits at the end of each path. **The upright** or **blameless will remain in the land**, **but the wicked** will **be cut off** or removed from the land, like a tree that is cut down, dug out by the roots, and hauled off. "Land" (Heb. *eretz*; also translated "earth" in Gen. 1:1) looks back to the covenant of Deuteronomy 28 where the Lord warned that Israel would be expelled from the promised land if they failed to remain faithful to him.

ⓑ The Value of Wisdom (3:13–24)

SUPPORTING IDEA: *Wisdom is more valuable than money because it bestows the gift of true happiness in addition to riches and honor. Just as God used wisdom to create the universe, he provides wisdom that preserves us from sin and fear.*

3:13. This is the first of eight "beatitudes" in the Book of Proverbs (8:32,34; 14:21; 16:20; 20:7; 28:14; 29:18). The word **blessed** is plural (as in Pss. 1:1; 119:1) and might be rendered, "Oh the blessednesses!" The word appears again at the conclusion of the section in Proverbs 3:18.

3:14–15. Like a merchant, the writer evaluates the treasures available to him. What acquisition will produce the greatest gain or profit? Though **gold** and **silver** are undeniable measures of wealth, they can provide only the things that money can buy, and wisdom provides what money cannot buy. The verses that follow outline some of those benefits. Verse 15 may refer either to **rubies** or coral, certainly something reddish (Lam. 4:7), extremely valuable, rare, and beautiful. Wisdom, however, surpasses all of these treasures.

3:16. Wisdom is pictured as a woman bearing gifts in each hand. Her left hand offers **riches and honor.** In her right hand, the position of preference, she bears the gift of **long life.** But wisdom is even better than these.

3:17. Unlike the confused darkness of the path to destruction in chapter 2, the paths of wisdom are **pleasant** and peaceful. Wisdom puts us on the path of highest pleasure, not boredom. **Peace** (Heb. *shalom*) stands for the joy and prosperity that accompany the full blessing of God, not merely the absence of conflict.

3:18. Wisdom is portrayed as **a tree of life** (Prov. 11:30; 13:12; 15:4), giving refreshment and nourishment. In Genesis 2:9, the tree of life gives life, and the replanted tree of life in Revelation 22:1–2 gives healing. Wisdom gives life to those who cling to her.

3:19–20. God used **wisdom** to create the world in Genesis 1, a picture expanded in Proverbs 8:22–31. Although Genesis 1:7 mentions the separating of waters, the Hebrew words for **the deeps were divided** in Proverbs 3:20 are the same as those used in the description of the flood in Genesis 7:11. God's wisdom produces both great destruction and gentle **dew.**

3:21. A new section begins with the father's appeal not to lose sight of **sound judgment and discernment.** The NIV reverses the Hebrew order of the two phrases for smoother English, but the idea is clear: do not let wisdom **out of your sight.** To **preserve** means "to watch or guard," as Adam was instructed to keep the garden (Gen. 2:15).

3:22. The core idea of Proverbs 3:21–26 is that wisdom will preserve your life. It will **grace your neck**, suggesting the addition of **ornament.** Grace can sometimes be translated "fair, beautiful," making this verse a promise of both life and beauty.

3:23. The path of sound judgment and discernment is the place of greatest **safety**. Though godly people sometimes suffer, they avoid the ultimate consequences of sin.

3:24. As a result, the wise person does not need to be plagued by anxiety. Night will be a time of refreshing, not fear (cp. the judgment of sleeplessness in Deut. 28:65–67). Proverbs 3:25–26 continues the discussion of the peace that comes to those who trust in God's wisdom.

> **MAIN IDEA REVIEW:** Wisdom can be found if a person searches for it diligently enough, and once found, it will save a person from disaster and lead to satisfaction.

III. CONCLUSION

Seeing Life Through Solomon's Eyes

Solomon asked the Lord for wisdom at the beginning of his reign as king of Israel, and God gave it to him. According to 1 Kings 4:31, he was the wisest man who ever lived. His wisdom was sharpened through the life he lived and the things he observed. He had seen his father's life complicated through sin. He had seen his brother seduce his sister and then another brother kill the one who seduced her. He had seen the destructive influence of greed, lust, and violence. When Solomon spoke, he knew what he was talking about.

This father longed for his children to live a happy, peaceful life, and he knew there were certain things they had to do and other things they had not to do if their lives were to be rewarding on earth. He didn't want them to ruin their lives as he had seen so many young people do, including his own brothers. In this chapter he practically falls to his knees and begs his son to acquire wisdom. He pleads, begs, wheedles, and cajoles his son to have the right attitude toward wisdom and then gives him the best advice he can.

Listen to the verbs in Proverbs 2:1–4: *accept, store up, turning your ear, applying your heart, call out, cry aloud, look, search.* It is as though he is on his knees saying, "Please, please, please—don't ruin your life. Listen to me. I've experienced, I've observed, I know. 'This' will help you, and 'that' will hurt you. Choose wisely. Become a person of character." Then he begins to lay out the principles of a life of wisdom and character.

PRINCIPLES

- God is the source of all wisdom.
- God wants to impart wisdom to human beings.
- Wisdom must be sought.

- Strive for wisdom with the same drive and intensity as people seeking wealth.
- Let wisdom guide you in choosing your friends.
- Enjoy wisdom's protection against taking harmful and destructive paths.
- Ask God for wisdom and pay attention to his Word.

IV. LIFE APPLICATION

Breaking the Laws of God

Someone has said that you cannot break the laws of God. You can only break yourself against them when you violate them. It is true. Every action builds an attitude, every attitude forges a character, and every character yields a destiny. Galatians 6:7 says, "Do not be deceived: God cannot be mocked. A man reaps what he sows."

God knows this, of course, and because he loves us, he has told us how to live and what to do so we can sow good and reap good, rather than sowing harm and reaping harm.

We read in Deuteronomy 8:1–2:

> Be careful to follow every command I am giving you today, so that you may live and increase and may enter and possess the land that the LORD promised on oath to your forefathers. Remember how the LORD your God led you all the way in the desert these forty years, to humble you and test you in order to know what was in your heart, whether or not you would keep his commands.

Then, we read further in Deuteronomy 8:15–16:

> He led you through the vast and dreadful desert, that thirsty and waterless land, with its venomous snakes and scorpions. He brought you water out of hard rock. He gave you manna to eat in the desert, something your fathers had never known, to humble and to test you so that in the end it might go well with you.

In this principle, we see that everything God asks of us, he does because he wants to give something good to us and to keep us from harm. If you believe this, you are obedient to God's laws. If you don't, you aren't. If you want to measure your faith, you measure your obedience. If you are not obedient, it is because you don't believe that your life goes better when following God's laws. The life we long for is found in total obedience to Christ. These conclusions are the fruit of wisdom.

V. PRAYER

Father in heaven, we read in the life of Solomon that you are pleased with the prayer for wisdom and that it is a prayer you are happy to answer. So we ask you, Father, please give us wisdom that we might follow you closely. Bless us and give us your joy as we follow you. Amen

VI. DEEPER DISCOVERIES

A. Attentiveness: The Springboard to Wisdom

It is very easy to overlook the most common command in the first nine chapters of Proverbs: the call to attention. Almost every major section begins with the father urging his son to pay attention (1:8; 2:1–2; 3:1,21; 4:1,10; 5:1,7; 6:20; 7:1–3,24). Any parent can understand the importance of this point because every parent has watched a child blunder into trouble right after our warnings. Even the inspired wisdom found in Proverbs will do little good if we pay no attention to it.

There is much repetition in these exhortations, but several practical steps to attentiveness are clear.

First, *"make your ear attentive"* (Prov. 2:2 NASB). Jesus frequently finished his statement by saying, "He who has ears, let him hear" (Matt. 13:9). He complained of those who had ears but did not hear (Matt. 13:13–15). We will benefit from Proverbs when we choose to listen actively and receptively.

Second, *"incline your ear"* (Prov. 4:20; 5:1 NASB). When we want to be sure we hear someone, we turn toward them and lean forward, in order to give them our full attention. This is a picture of the attitude that enables us to gain wisdom.

Third, *"incline your heart"* (Prov. 2:2 NASB). Lean forward mentally as well as physically. When we give full attention to a speaker, we show how much value we place on his words.

Fourth, *"treasure"* what you hear (Prov. 2:1; 7:1 NASB). Place a high value on it and make it a point to retain what you learn. The one who treasures wisdom will devise practical ways to ensure that the insights are not lost. This might involve journaling or keeping some other written record, or it might lead to conversations with others. In any case, a person who treasures wisdom will act on it, rather than lose the benefit of its help.

Fifth, *"do not forget"* (Prov. 3:1; 4:5; cp. 3:21; 4:21). Wisdom is so valuable that the sensible person wants it to be a permanent part of life. This involves lodging it in your memory, as well as building it into your habits of life. Proverbs 7:3 asks us to "write them on the tablet of your heart." Writing on a tablet often meant to engrave permanently on a clay or stone tablet.

B. The Father-Son Connection

The opening chapters of Proverbs are largely presented as counsel from a father to his son. Though the principles apply to mothers and daughters as well, the specific advice is addressed directly to a young man, preparing him for adult life.

Some Bible students have suggested that the references to fathers and sons in the first nine chapters are actually talking about wise men or sages giving advice to their disciples. It was not unusual for Jewish teachers to be called fathers and to speak of their younger followers as "sons." There seems to be no reason, however, why the chapters cannot be taken as father-son conversations.

Since we know the identity of the primary author of Proverbs, we can make some observations about the family situations behind these fatherly conversations.

Proverbs 1:1 announces that Solomon was the source of these discussions. With his hundreds of wives and concubines, he had the opportunity to instruct many offspring. But it seems clear that he would have attempted to pass on these teachings to Rehoboam, the son who would follow him on the throne. History shows that Rehoboam failed to profit from all this wise advice. He even disregarded the wise counsel of Solomon's advisors (1 Kgs. 12:8) and lost most of his kingdom. We can speculate that Solomon's failure to take his own advice (1 Kgs. 11:1–14) might have soured his son.

Proverbs 4 opens the door to another aspect of the family background. Solomon recounts a bit of his own childhood when he was the focus of loving instruction from his father and mother. This would be a reference to his father David and his mother Bathsheba. Though David failed to provide adequate training for his older sons like Absalom and Amnon (2 Sam. 13–18), it seems likely that he devoted considerable energy to grooming Solomon for his future responsibilities as king of Israel (1 Kgs. 2:1–4).

VII. TEACHING OUTLINE

A. INTRODUCTION

1. Lead Story: The Cremation of Sam Magee

2. Context: Solomon describes the elusiveness and worth of wisdom, as well as the benefits.

3. Transition: If you want wisdom, you must realize how valuable it is and be willing to pay the price to get it.

B. COMMENTARY
1. Wisdom's Conditions and Consequences (2:1–22)
2. The Value of Wisdom (3:13–24)

C. CONCLUSION: SEEING LIFE THROUGH SOLOMON'S EYES

VIII. ISSUES FOR DISCUSSION

1. What life lessons about wisdom can you glean from your childhood and family life?
2. How vulnerable are you to the influence of violent men? Seductive women? If violent men or seductive women are not your greatest threats, what are?
3. Who is the wisest person you know? Why did you pick that person?

Chapter 3

The Safety of Wisdom

Proverbs 4:1–27

I. **INTRODUCTION**
The Urgency of Wisdom

II. **COMMENTARY**
A verse-by-verse explanation of these verses.

III. **CONCLUSION**
It Won't Be Different with You!

An overview of the principles and applications from these verses.

IV. **LIFE APPLICATION**
When You Come to a Fork in the Road,
Take It!

Melding these verses to life.

V. **PRAYER**
Tying these verses to life with God.

VI. **DEEPER DISCOVERIES**
Historical, geographical, and grammatical enrichment of the commentary.

VII. **TEACHING OUTLINE**
Suggested step-by-step group study of these verses.

VIII. **ISSUES FOR DISCUSSION**
Zeroing these verses in on daily life.

Quote

"A wise man learns by the experience of others. An

ordinary man learns by his own experience.

A fool learns by nobody's experience."

Anonymous

 IN A NUTSHELL

It is the duty of a father, and the privilege of a child, for the father to pass wisdom down to his son. The choice is between a path that leads to life and one that leads to destruction. The father must teach wisdom. The son (child) must heed it.

The Safety of Wisdom

I. INTRODUCTION

The Urgency of Wisdom

*I*t is only natural for youth to think that adults are out of it, don't know what's really important, and that for the first time in history, their generation sees things clearly. Every generation thinks that, and every generation is wrong. Mark Twain once said that when he was eighteen, his father was so ignorant that Twain could hardly stand to be in his presence. Yet Twain remarked that by the time he was twenty-one, he felt that his father had smartened up considerably in only three short years. The difference, of course, was in Twain, not his father.

Young people are in desperate need of wisdom. Yet, typically, they are resistant to it. Nevertheless, parents must try to pass wisdom down to the next generation. They may not appreciate it at the moment, but in time they will respect the counsel and advice given by their parents. Solomon sounds almost desperate to get his sons to listen to reason. Perhaps that desperation is because Solomon saw so little wisdom in his own family. His brother raped his sister, and another brother killed the one who raped her. Then the murderous brother also tried to depose, and if necessary kill, his own father, the king. Solomon knew firsthand the need for wisdom, and he also knew the calamity that can occur without it.

We need to catch Solomon's sense of urgency. Whether it is our own children or the spiritual children we are ministering to, we need to work hard at passing down wisdom to the next generation.

II. COMMENTARY

The Safety of Wisdom

MAIN IDEA: *A father can give no greater gift than to pass on a thirst for wisdom so that his children can stay on the right path in life.*

🅰 Passing Wisdom Down Generations (4:1–9)

SUPPORTING IDEA: *Solomon learned from his father David how crucial it is to make wisdom the goal of life.*

4:1–2. This chapter begins with a father exhorting his son to pay close attention to the instructions he is about to give. Though such calls to attentiveness occur often in the first eight chapters of Proverbs, this one gives the clearest portrait of a father's heart for his son. The mention of **sons** in the plural shows that Solomon intended his teaching for more than just the son who would take his throne, but he switches back to the singular in verse 10. This father bestows the gift of **sound** or good **learning**, so the son should be careful not to **forsake** his **teaching**. Teaching here is *torah* in Hebrew, usually translated "law," often referring to the law given by God to Moses (Prov. 28:9; 29:18). But in a phrase like "my *torah*," it may be rendered "teaching."

The word "taught" in verse 4 is the root from which "torah" is derived.

4:3. Solomon paints a picture of the loving atmosphere he experienced as a child. He was David's son, living in the king's home, in constant contact with him. Though his mother Bathsheba eventually had more children (1 Chr. 3:5), he was **an only child** for some years. Obviously his parents devoted much energy to his training.

4:4. Beginning in verse 4, Solomon presents a quotation from his father David, which probably runs through verse 9. Solomon builds on his boyhood experience to show why he is so insistent on passing on this heritage to his own son. The next verses are peppered with commands. First, he must hold on to his father's **words** wholeheartedly. Next, choose life by keeping these **commands** (see Deut. 30:19).

4:5. A son must choose his goal. Aim to obtain **wisdom** and **understanding**. One might wonder if David's charge to get wisdom motivated Solomon to ask God for wisdom later in life (1 Kgs. 3:5–14). The son must also keep up the pursuit; he cannot afford to forget his instructions **or swerve** to one side.

4:6. Wisdom is pictured as a gracious, desirable woman in verses 6–9, just as in other portions of the first nine chapters. How beneficial it is to devote one's energies to wooing this lady rather than the neighborhood girls! Verse 6 contains only four words in Hebrew, promising that wisdom will **protect** the person who remains loyal in loving her.

4:7. This verse has been translated in various ways. The opening phrase is literally, "beginning of wisdom," using the same word that opens Genesis 1:1. We might render the idea as, "The beginning of wisdom is, **get wisdom!**" The first step in gaining wisdom is to determine that we will pursue it. The second line contains a play on words, "with all your getting, **get understanding.**" The overall thrust of the passage is clear: Wisdom is the greatest possession a person can have, so we should make it our highest goal in life.

4:8. Pursuing wisdom is worth the effort. **Esteem** means to raise higher and higher in value, as a purchaser would raise his bid. When you esteem wisdom, she will **exalt** you by rewarding you with a high position. **Embrace** wisdom with tender love, and she will **honor you** so that others will treat you with respect.

4:9. Falling in love with Lady Wisdom will benefit you. She will bestow the honor mentioned in verse 8 by placing a crown on your head. You will win the prize of a **garland of grace**, a beautiful wreath. And she will present you with a **crown of splendor**. These are unnamed blessings in life, and we must be on the lookout to spot them in our own lives. We may think that they involve being invited to the White House or something else on a grand scale, but the verses may be fulfilled by much smaller things in everyday life.

B Picking the Right Pathway (4:10–19)

> **SUPPORTING IDEA:** *We must choose between the path that leads to life and the paths that lead to destruction. Choose the path of life.*

4:10–11. The father renews his plea for careful attentiveness, marking the beginning of a new section. If the son will **accept** or appropriate what he hears, he will enjoy **many** years of **life**.

This promise does not guarantee immunity from trouble, as Job discovered. But a son who heeds these warnings will avoid the paths that lead to disaster and early death. Verse 11 introduces the picture of life as a journey, one where it is vital to choose the right **way** or **paths**. The father has explained how to choose the way marked out by wisdom and has led his son in **straight** paths, paths characterized by uprightness. These are the routes that are right both morally (2:13) and practically (3:6). And the son must now choose which paths he will follow. Verses 10–13 describe the path of life.

4:12. When you walk in straight paths, **your steps will not be hampered**. That is, you will not be tripped up by the obstacles of sin, but you will have ample room to walk. Even if you run, the path will be clear of obstacles, and **you will not stumble**.

4:13. The proper response is obvious: **hold on** tightly to the instruction you have received. **Do not let it go; guard it well**! The command actually uses a feminine form, "Guard her well," to point back to the picture of wisdom as a desirable woman. Picking up the emphasis of verses 4 and 10, Solomon reminds his son that this instruction holds the key to **life** itself.

4:14–15. In verses 14–17, the discussion turns from the path of life to the ways of death. Solomon warns against **the path of the wicked**, a reminder that the issue goes beyond practical issues. The root of the danger is evil, not ignorance. These two verses consist primarily of six urgent commands. It is so dangerous to take even the first step down the path to sin that the father shouts a series of warnings. Do not enter that trail or **set foot** on it. Do not start walking down it. Stay clear of it. Don't keep traveling in that direction. **Turn from it**, not toward it. Keep going in your original direction, rather than even pausing to consider it.

4:16–17. What makes the path so dangerous? The evil people whom you are following. They live in a morally upside-down world where sin has become duty. They can't **sleep** soundly unless they have been active in practicing **evil**

themselves and causing others to **fall**. Their restless wickedness is second nature to them; it is like **bread** and **wine**, their standard diet.

4:18–19. The father summarizes his comparison of the two paths: one is a path of **light**, the other is a trail of **darkness**. For the righteous, the road is like **the first gleam of dawn**, which may start in darkness, but grows gradually **brighter** until the sun has risen and they walk in broad daylight.

For **the wicked**, however, the path winds deeper into unending **darkness** where they cannot even see the things over which they **stumble**. The picture of walking in the light (1 John 1:7) appears often in Scripture.

🄲 Protecting the Heart (4:20–27)

SUPPORTING IDEA: *If the heart remains pure, the rest of the body will stay on course.*

4:20–22. In a third appeal to his son, the father calls once more for close attention to his important words. The message coming in the next few verses is crucial, so you should keep it central in your thoughts. Don't let it **out of your sight**; keep it **within your heart**, in the center of your soul. Solomon promised life in verses 4, 10, and 13, and he returns to the theme here. If you want life, pay attention to wisdom. And he promises that you will not only enjoy life, but you will flourish in your physical health. Like many other promises in Proverbs, this does not guarantee total immunity from illness, but it does reflect the fact that many maladies stem from foolish choices.

4:23. This verse contains the crucial concept of this section. **Above all else**, literally, "with all vigilance," keep **guard** over your **heart**. The heart in the Old Testament includes more than just the emotions; it can refer to the whole personality, the inner life of a person. And as such, it is the **wellspring of life**. As Jesus explained, the heart is the source of words and actions (Luke 6:45), so it is the key to controlling behavior. This verse may be the background for Christ's statement in John 7:38 about rivers of water flowing from one's innermost being. Solomon has been teaching on **life**, and the heart is the source from which life flows to all other parts of a person's being.

4:24. Once the heart is guarded, we can turn our attention to outward behavior. The remaining verses mention various parts of the body, beginning with the **mouth**. We must avoid speech that is distorted with falsehood or tainted with deviousness.

4:25. Returning to the imagery of walking down a path, the father implores his son to keep his **eyes** straight ahead. Do not allow your gaze to wander off to the side where temptations might lead you astray.

4:26–27. If the eyes wander, the **feet** soon go astray. The closing verses warn against walking in the way of the wicked. **Make level** can sometimes mean "take heed, consider," but either meaning can fit the picture of choosing our paths carefully. When we do, we can be confident that the pathway is solid. But if we wander carelessly off the main road **to the right or the left**, we will soon be in deep trouble. Nothing good lies there!

> **MAIN IDEA REVIEW:** *A father can give no greater gift than to pass on a thirst for wisdom, so his children can stay on the right path in life.*

III. CONCLUSION

It Won't Be Different with You!

Someone has said, "Learn from the mistakes of others. You don't have time to make them all yourself." That is the point Solomon is making in this chapter. "Listen to me, son. Take my advice. I've been around the block, and I can save you from a good deal of hardship if you will let me."

The problem is, of course, that young people don't believe it. They think they know better themselves. A young girl found a baby raccoon and was raising it as a pet. She was warned by a veterinarian that when the raccoon became an adult, it would become unpredictable and potentially violent. Her response was that her raccoon wouldn't do anything violent. Other raccoons might, but *it would be different with her.* Shortly afterward, the raccoon suddenly and viciously attacked her for no reason, leaving scars on her face that required plastic surgery. We are foolish to ignore the warnings of those who have gone before us, who have more experience, more knowledge, and more wisdom than we. When we ignore history, we are condemned to repeat it.

So, if we are on the teaching end, we must warn others and implore them to live a life of wisdom. If we are on the receiving end, we must heed the warning. It will not be different with us! Foolishness always extracts a severe price from those who court her.

PRINCIPLES

- Life comes with cause-and-effect consequences. Certain actions will bring about certain consequences.
- Wisdom can be learned by observing others. We don't have to experience everything ourselves.
- Wisdom is not automatic. It comes to those who commit to it and seek it.

APPLICATIONS

- Don't be a fool. Learn from the experience of others.
- Make the decision now to pursue wisdom.

- Guard what you allow into your mind. From this vigilance comes your ability to live a wise life.

IV. LIFE APPLICATION

When You Come to a Fork in the Road, Take It!

The venerable philosopher Yogi Berra (former New York Yankees Hall of Fame catcher, given to unlikely and sometimes bizarre misstatements) once said, "When you come to a fork in the road, take it!"

Yes, but which direction?

Solomon presents his son in this chapter with a fork in the road: the road to wisdom and a harmonious life or the road to foolishness and a life of self-destruction. He begs his son to take the right road. This option is before us through the entirety of life's journey, and we are continuously being forced to choose. Yet the reasonableness of the right choice is well explained by Solomon. When we choose wisdom, she will reward us with honor, blessing, and success.

To be free to sail the seven seas, you must make yourself a slave to the compass. The compass is the wisdom of God. If we make ourselves slaves to the wisdom of God, to his word, we will be free to sail the seven seas of life with the blessing of God. To ignore the law of wisdom is to run aground on the rocks of foolishness and bring unnecessary pain and hardship into our lives, as well as the lives of those whom we love and others whom our lives affect.

Another way of stating this principle is that you can be a slave to the toothbrush and free from cavities, or you can be free from the toothbrush and a slave to cavities. But you cannot be free from the toothbrush and free from cavities. That kind of absolute freedom doesn't exist. We cannot flaunt the laws of God and not pay a price. So seek wisdom. Choose wisdom. Make the conscious choice that you will walk the way of wisdom. The quality of your life and the lives of those whom you influence depend on it.

V. PRAYER

Father in heaven, by your grace, grant that we might become people of wisdom. Grant that we might have the grace to respond to wisdom and embrace it and live it, that you might be glorified, that we might be blessed, and that others might be instructed through us. Amen.

VI. DEEPER DISCOVERIES

A. The Heart

In English usage, the heart usually refers to either the physical organ that pumps our blood, or to the seat of our emotions. But in the Old Testament, "heart" covers a much wider range of meaning. The heart is linked with moods (Judg. 16:15) and emotions such as grief (Neh. 2:2), fear (Gen. 42:28), anger (Prov. 19:3), joy (1 Sam. 2:1), and peace (Gen. 34:3). The heart can also be the source of the will (Prov. 11:20; 14:14) and the conscience (Isa. 59:13). Even more frequently it is joined to the intellect (Prov. 3:3; 6:32; 7:7). Several verses mention a heart of wisdom (Prov. 10:8) or understanding (Deut. 29:4). The Hebrew concept of heart can actually refer to the whole inner man, the real "you." There are nearly fifty occurrences of the word *heart* in Proverbs, and Scripture contains a rich vocabulary of descriptions for the heart.

B. Life and Death

Many passages in Proverbs call the reader to look past immediate pleasure or pain and to see the ultimate consequences of his actions: life or death. At times the verses refer primarily to the length of physical life (4:10; 3:2; 9:11). But the language often goes beyond that concept, referring to a superior quality of life. It might be the social status and privilege that come with the favor of the king (16:15) or the financial stability that comes from avoiding greed (15:27). It might be the physical vitality and health that come from living according to the principles of wisdom (14:30). Or it might be the relationship with God that comes to the righteous (10:16).

Proverbs does not speak unmistakably about the eternal life that God promises to believers, but it leaves room for that truth. It emphasizes the benefits of wisdom for the present life, while other portions of Scripture explain God's plans for us in the life to come.

VII. TEACHING OUTLINE

A. INTRODUCTION
1. Lead Story: The Urgency of Wisdom
2. Context: Solomon describes a choice that everyone has—to choose wisdom or foolishness—and then describes what happens, depending on the choice.
3. Transition: Whether a person chooses wisdom or foolishness determines the quality of the rest of his life.

B. COMMENTARY
1. Passing Wisdom Down Generations (4:1–9)
2. Picking the Right Pathway (4:10–19)
3. Protecting the Heart (4:20–27)

C. CONCLUSION: IT WON'T BE DIFFERENT WITH YOU!

VIII. ISSUES FOR DISCUSSION

1. What are some experiences from your past in which you ignored wisdom and paid a price?
2. What are some experiences from your past in which you chose wisdom and benefited?
3. What decision are you facing now in which you are tempted to foolishness but called to wisdom?

Chapter 4

The Safety of Marriage

Proverbs 5:1–23; 6:20–35

I. **INTRODUCTION**
The Myth of Greener Grass

II. **COMMENTARY**
A verse-by-verse explanation of these verses.

III. **CONCLUSION**
Immediate Danger

An overview of the principles and applications from these verses.

IV. **LIFE APPLICATION**
Lead Me Not into Temptation

Melding these verses to life.

V. **PRAYER**
Tying these verses to life with God.

VI. **DEEPER DISCOVERIES**
Historical, geographical, and grammatical enrichment of the commentary.

VII. **TEACHING OUTLINE**
Suggested step-by-step group study of these verses.

VIII. **ISSUES FOR DISCUSSION**
Zeroing these verses in on daily life.

Q u o t e

"*Successful marriage is always a triangle:*

a man, a woman, and God."

C e c i l   M e y e r s

Proverbs

5:1–23; 6:20–35

 I N   A   N U T S H E L L

God has provided marriage as the fulfillment of earthly joys and the hedge against temptation to immorality. Feel free to enjoy fully the pleasures of marriage. Be sure to listen to your parents because they will save you from the disaster of sexual immorality.

The Safety of Marriage

I. INTRODUCTION

The Myth of Greener Grass

J. Allan Petersen wrote a book entitled *The Myth of the Greener Grass* (Wheaton, Ill.: Tyndale House, 1983). Though the book was written many years ago, it's conclusions are still up-to-date. Petersen wrote:

> Sex, sex, sex. Our culture is near the point of total saturation. The cesspool is running over. Books, magazines, billboards, movies shout it ceaselessly. TV, the most powerful and immediate medium, trumpets it in living color. Sex gets the ratings. It is the recurring theme in daytime soaps and talk shows, the inevitable subject in the nighttime interview. Every day, all day, the message bombards us like pellets from a brain-washing gun: "Get all the sex there is. . . . Don't miss out. There is no tomorrow" (Petersen, 15–16).

And because of this saturation, for many people the grass seems greener somewhere else. If they are single, the grass seems greener with premarital sex. If they are married, the grass seems greener with another person other than their present spouse. The world used to take adultery seriously, but things have changed. The tabloids and TV talk shows send the message that adultery is normal. "Everybody's doing it" becomes a moral guideline. And judging from the statistics, America is listening.

Therefore, the warnings against premarital sex and adultery given us by Solomon are even more relevant today than ever before. Yet the Scripture teaches, and observation demonstrates, that immorality is never a good answer—it always promises more than it can deliver. From Solomon's time until today, everyone would be wise to heed the warnings of Solomon.

II. COMMENTARY

The Safety of Marriage

> **MAIN IDEA:** *An illicit affair may provide short-term pleasure, but the long-range consequences will be disastrous. Stay faithful to your spouse, and you will experience genuine satisfaction—and God will be pleased. You cannot escape the painful results of immorality.*

A The Dangers of Adultery (5:1–14)

> **SUPPORTING IDEA:** *A man should beware of any involvement with an immoral woman because that path leads to death. At the end of the road, you will regret ignoring the advice that could have spared you from ruin.*

5:1. Maintaining moral purity is one of the premier challenges for a young man, and Solomon deals with this topic five times in the opening chapters (2:16–22; 5:3–23; 6:24–35; 7:5–27; 9:13–18). Like many of the discourses in Proverbs, this section begins with a call for the son's attention. This issue is vital, so it is important to **listen well** to the father's **insight**.

5:2. Heeding the advice in this chapter will enable you to **maintain discretion** in the face of temptation. Let your **lips** be filled with wise words, in contrast to flattery on the lips of the adulteress (v. 3). Knowledge of the truth helps guard you from seductive distortions of the truth.

5:3. Solomon moves without a pause into his warning against the wiles of an immoral woman. It is her words, not her physical attractiveness, that pose the greatest danger. Her lips **drip honey**, the sweetest substance in the ancient world, and her words are **smoother than oil**, the smoothest item in the Israelite household. Her flattery is designed to inflate the young man's ego and signal her availability, opening the way for him to turn his thoughts into action.

5:4–5. The encounter may seem sweet at first, but the end of the experience will leave you tasting **gall**, the bitterest item in the Jewish experience. Your encounter with this woman will feel like being slashed with a **double-edged sword**. Proverbs often warns us to judge things by their outcome, not their beginning (5:11; 14:12–13). Accepting the invitation to illicit lust will lead a person to **death** or **the grave** (Heb. *Sheol*), the place of the dead. This could be literally true or a metaphor for the death of a life of peace and harmony.

5:6. The subject of the Hebrew in this verse could be either "she" or "you," so it could be describing the moral confusion of the seductress or her victim. In either case, there is clearly one path that leads to **life**—God's design of commitment to one mate for life. But the **paths** of immorality **are crooked** (wandering, movable, slippery); people who take these paths are continually improvising their own rules for life, ignoring God's standard.

5:7–8. The father begins a new section with a fresh appeal to listen carefully. Do not turn away from my words, but do turn away from the immoral woman, he urges. If you put yourself in the course of temptation by loitering **near the door of her house**, you will surely fall. It is better to break off contact completely.

5:9–10. These verses list the losses that crouch in the path of those who toy with lust. They will lose their **strength**, a reference to their health, honor, or self-respect. They will lose their **years**, either by a shortened life or by one composed of wasted years. They will lose their **wealth** to others, whether through blackmail, judicial penalty, or heavy spending on the lover.

5:11. Solomon paints the scene at the end of a wasted life in verses 11–14. To sum it up, **you will groan**. You were so eager to placate the desires of your body, and now it has been consumed by your sin. Sexually transmitted diseases have probably hastened its deterioration.

5:12–13. As a wasted life winds down, the foolish man will look back with regret and admit his stubborn disregard of the advice that could have saved him from disaster. His conscience condemns him, as he admits that he **hated** every instance when others tried to correct him. He refused to accept any accountability and failed to heed his **teachers**. He failed to obey the father's instruction from Proverbs 5:1,7.

5:14. Where does the path of immorality lead? To public disgrace and **ruin**. Under the Mosaic law, adultery was an offense that could bring the death penalty (Deut. 22:22–24), though the **assembly** of elders could settle for a lesser penalty.

Ⓑ The Joys of Marriage (5:15–20)

> **SUPPORTING IDEA:** *Just as you drink from your own fountain, you should find your fulfillment in the love of your own wife.*

5:15. Water is precious, particularly in the arid climate of Palestine. Here Solomon makes an extended comparison between the water that supports physical life and the sexual intimacy that brings such zest to life. He speaks primarily of water in verses 15–16. A man who has his **own well** or **cistern** (storage chamber for rain water) would certainly want to drink from that personal supply rather than carrying water from a public stream.

5:16. Some have translated this verse as an exhortation, "Let your **springs overflow in the streets**." This would describe the way that good marriages produce a flow of blessings to everyone around. But the context supports the idea that verse 16 is a question, expecting a negative answer. If a person has a well, it would be ridiculous to let the water spill over and drain down the street.

5:17. This verse answers the question of verse 16. Your water sources should be for the exclusive use of your household, not open for foreigners to consume. In the same way, physical intimacy should be strictly for one's own spouse, not wasted on **strangers**. This verse forbids any form of marital infidelity.

5:18. Marital love is pictured as enjoying a **fountain** in Song of Songs 4:12,15, and this verse develops the same concept. God will bless physical intimacy between a husband and the **wife of your youth** but not in any other relationship.

5:19–20. No one can deny the excitement of physical attraction. Proverbs calls on the man to channel that excitement toward his wife. He should appreciate her beauty as if she were **a graceful deer** and be satisfied with her body and her love. He should love her "alone" (v. 17) and **always**. The word translated **captivated** is sometimes used to describe the effects of intoxication, to stagger or to be exhilarated (Prov. 20:1; Isa. 28:7). So God intends a man to be exhilarated with the affection of his own wife, not some other **man's wife**.

The Eyes of God (5:21–23)

SUPPORTING IDEA: *God knows all we do, and he will judge immorality.*

5:21. The first part of the chapter examined the natural consequences of immorality. This section turns to our accountability to God. The path a person takes is, literally, before the eyes of the Lord. Nothing can be hidden (see Gen. 16:13). **Paths** refers to the tracks made by the constant passing of wagons, making an apt reference to a man's habits.

5:22–23. Those who promote self-indulgence often proclaim their commitment to freedom, but sin takes away a person's freedom, trapping him and binding him to his vice. Because he refused discipline (v. 12), his pathway ends in death. He made the choice of short-term pleasure, too intoxicated (**led astray** is the same Hebrew word as "captivate," vv. 19–20) to realize his foolishness.

The Way to Avoid Disaster (6:20–35)

SUPPORTING IDEA: *We must pay close attention to the wisdom of parents who warn us that immorality leads to pain; the consequences are inescapable.*

6:20–22. The section beginning here runs through the end of chapter 7, and it gives guidelines to help a young person avoid the danger of sexual immorality. The father begins by pointing out that advice is available. He repeats a reference from Proverbs 1:8 to the **father's commands** and the

mother's teaching (Heb. "torah," often translated "law"). This parental guidance is the key to avoiding moral ruin.

These words of wisdom are so valuable that the young person should attach them permanently to his **heart** or inner being and make them a visible part of his life, like a pendant around one's neck. Once these maxims become a permanent part of your life, they (literally "it" or "she") will provide guidance, protection, and counsel wherever you are.

6:23. The **commands** and **teaching** of the parents, like the law of God, serve as a lamp and a **light** to illumine the pathway (cp. Ps. 119:105). Even the times when parents reprove their child are beneficial because they give instructions for staying on the path of **life**.

6:24. Specifically, the instructions of parents will prevent a son from becoming involved with an **immoral woman** (literally, "woman of evil"). The **wayward wife** is a woman with the loose morals associated with non-Jewish cultures (Prov. 2:16).

6:25–26. Verse 25 gives a warning, and verses 26–35 give the reason for the warning. It is forbidden to **lust** mentally for an attractive woman, just as Jesus said in Matthew 5:28. Even if she encourages attention by returning your glance, the desire for her is wrong.

The Hebrew of verse 26 is difficult because it gives no verb for the first half of the verse. The NIV translation warns that immorality will impoverish a man. Another possible rendering is, "Although a prostitute may cost as much as a **loaf of bread**, another man's wife hunts for a man's **very life**" (Garrett, 100). This translation points out that immorality with another man's wife is the ultimate foolishness, costing you everything for the momentary pleasure you could get cheaply from a **prostitute**.

6:27–29. Two rhetorical questions show that it is impossible to commit adultery without suffering the consequences. Just as it is impossible to **scoop** burning embers into your **lap** or **walk** barefooted on a bed of **hot coals** without being burned, the man who conducts an affair with a married woman cannot hope to escape unscathed. Pain is inevitable.

6:30–31. Even though theft is a serious crime, **a thief** will receive a certain degree of mercy, particularly if he steals because he lacks the necessities of life. If he is apprehended, he will have to pay the penalty, of course. Restitution may be expensive: though the law required as little as 20 percent penalty (Lev. 5:16), and Zacchaeus volunteered to repay 400 percent (Luke 19:8), a thief might be fined **sevenfold** what he stole, even though it would empty his resources.

6:32–35. But how can you make restitution for **adultery**? Committing such a deed shows a lack of **judgment**, a self-destructive urge. The **disgrace**

of his action can **never be wiped away**, and the injured husband becomes an implacable foe whom no payment will satisfy.

> **MAIN IDEA REVIEW:** *An illicit affair may provide short-term pleasure, but the long-range consequences will be disastrous. Stay faithful to your spouse, and you will experience genuine satisfaction—and God will be pleased. You cannot escape the painful results of immorality.*

III. CONCLUSION

Immediate Danger

It is vital that we read Proverbs as a book for today. We must not conclude because the history, culture, and location are different from ours that things are really different for us. We must resist the temptation to think that those people had a primitive culture, they would not understand what life is like today, and we cannot take the teachings of Proverbs straight across to our lives today.

To come to that conclusion would be a big mistake. Cecil Dickard once said, "Give me a Bible and a candle and shut me up in a dungeon, and I will tell you what the world is doing." Things have not changed since Bible times. That is why Solomon said, "There is nothing new under the sun." Our motivations, our desires, our weaknesses remain unchanged since the beginning of time. Proverbs is a warning to us. Today. We would be foolish not to hear its message.

PRINCIPLES

- Grass will often seem greener in the other pasture, and it will appear greener and greener the more we look.
- The devil will see to it that we don't get through life without temptation to immorality.
- God's avenues for fidelity are sufficient.

APPLICATIONS

- Always assume that you are vulnerable to sexual temptation, and take drastic measures to guard against it.
- Physical infidelity always begins with mental infidelity. Guard your mind! Don't feed it things that strengthen temptation; instead, occupy it with thoughts that strengthen holiness.
- If you feel yourself weakening, get help! Seek a pastor or a spiritual mentor. Don't fight a losing battle alone.

IV. LIFE APPLICATION

Lead Me Not into Temptation

In *The Myth of the Greener Grass*, J. Allan Petersen writes:

> When you were born, you were married—married to a companion who will walk the road of life with you until the end. You will never awaken any morning or retire any night without this companion's being right at your side. This companion will never leave you. Whether you like it or not, you and this partner will be together until death do you part. Temptation—your lifelong companion.

> Everyone is tempted. Temptation knows no strangers. Everyone is tempted, and always will be. It is like germs that we carry with us that attack us when our resistance is down. No isolation from people will isolate us from temptation. The priest in his secluded monastery, the hermit in his secret cave, the prisoner in his lonely cell, these all know temptation. . . . If you have a mind through which you think, you'll be tempted through that mind. If you have a body in which you live, you'll be tempted through that body. If you have a social nature by which you enjoy other people, you'll be tempted by other people. If you are a sexual being, you'll have sexual temptations (Petersen, 90–91).

What to do about it? Petersen suggests six things. First, develop a biblical conscience. Educate it with Scripture, and strengthen it through memorization and meditation. Second, defuse it by not fearing it. Every temptation is an opportunity to defeat the devil. Third, decide irrevocably if you want victory. If you don't want it badly and commit to it, you'll be in grave danger.

Fourth, determine your response ahead of time. Predetermine how you will react, before the pressure hits. Fifth, discipline your mind with counteraction. Don't leave your mind a vacuum, but fill it with things that encourage faithfulness. Sixth, follow Christ as your example. He was totally committed to doing his Father's will. He countered temptation by quoting Scripture that he had memorized. He guarded his mind from tempting thoughts and spent time cultivating an eternal perspective.

In the face of the kind of temptation we face today, and in light of the exhortations of Solomon, we would all do well to take the message of Proverbs to heart, realizing that each of us is vulnerable to temptation. If we accept our vulnerability ahead of time and put the safety measures into place up front, we'll be more secure from sexual temptation.

V. PRAYER

Father in heaven, rush to our aid, strengthen our hearts, purify our minds, intensify our resolve to live holy lives before you. Stand between us and the desire of the evil one to destroy us. May we always be spiritually faithful to you, and in doing so, always be physically faithful to our spouse. Amen.

VI. DEEPER DISCOVERIES

A. People with No Heart

The Book of Proverbs often speaks of people who "lack sense" or "lack judgment," as in the case of the adulterer in 6:32. In Hebrew, the phrase is literally one who "lacks heart." Heart (Heb. *leb*) can refer to the inner person, including intellect, emotions, and will. A person who "lacks heart" still has these faculties, but he is not using them—he may as well not have a mind if he doesn't use it!

Proverbs uses the phrase to describe people who linger near immoral women (7:7), despise their neighbors (11:12), waste time pursuing empty schemes rather than working (12:11), cosign for loans (17:18), or let their property deteriorate (24:30). A person whose heart is nonfunctional will not benefit from hearing wisdom (17:16); he responds only to sharp discipline (10:13). He actually enjoys folly (15:21) and is responsive to invitations to participate in it (9:16). Wisdom, however, also extends an invitation (9:4) for him to come and acquire understanding (15:32).

B. The Mother's Part in Proverbs

The father stands in the spotlight in most of the Book of Proverbs, but the book does not ignore the mother. A mother gives instruction to her children (1:8; 6:20), and her teaching provides light that enables them to avoid sin. A wise mother cherishes each child as if he were her only child and passes on what she has learned from her own parents (4:3). Even kings benefit from a mother's advice (31:1).

Proverbs actually focuses most frequently on how a child should treat a mother. Do not forsake her teaching (1:8), disobey her (30:17), or grieve her by becoming a fool (10:1; 15:20). Do not curse her (20:20; 30:11), rob her (28:24), or drive her away (19:26). Do not despise her, even when she becomes old (23:22). Instead, sons and daughters should listen to her (23:22) and observe her teaching (6:20) so they will become righteous and wise (23:23–25). In the end, they will bless her (30:11).

VII. TEACHING OUTLINE

A. INTRODUCTION

1. Lead Story: The Myth of Greener Grass
2. Context: Solomon describes the dangers of sexual immorality and the joys of marriage, and he appeals to the disciple to choose the way of joy and shun the way of pain.
3. Transition: If a person wants to maximize his joy and minimize his pain, he must be faithful to God's truth.

B. COMMENTARY

1. The Dangers of Adultery (5:1–14)
2. The Joys of Marriage (5:15–20)
3. The Eyes of God (5:21–23)
4. The Way to Avoid Disaster (6:20–35)

C. CONCLUSION: IMMEDIATE DANGER

VIII. ISSUES FOR DISCUSSION

1. Do you believe you are vulnerable to sexual immorality? Why or why not? If so, how vulnerable?
2. What steps have you taken to lessen your vulnerability? Are they sufficient? Is it working?
3. How is your example affecting your children? Your spiritual children?

Chapter 5

The Battle Against Sexual Temptation

Proverbs 7:1–27; 23:26–28; 22:14; 29:3

I. **INTRODUCTION**
Looking for God

II. **COMMENTARY**
A verse-by-verse explanation of these verses.

III. **CONCLUSION**
Swimming Upstream

An overview of the principles and applications from these verses.

IV. **LIFE APPLICATION**
Real and Virtual Purity

Melding these verses to life.

V. **PRAYER**
Tying these verses to life with God.

VI. **DEEPER DISCOVERIES**
Historical, geographical, and grammatical enrichment of the commentary.

VII. **TEACHING OUTLINE**
Suggested step-by-step group study of these verses.

VIII. **ISSUES FOR DISCUSSION**
Zeroing these verses in on daily life.

Quote

"*D*o not bite at the bait of pleasure 'til you know there

is no hook beneath it."

T h o m a s   J e f f e r s o n

Proverbs
7:1–27; 23:26–28;
22:14; 29:3

I N   A   N U T S H E L L

*S*exual temptation is a very real force in life, especially for young
men. When temptation comes looking for you, resist it. You will pay a
dreadful price if you don't. And forget about getting involved with a prostitute. There is a price to be paid here, too.

The Battle Against Sexual Temptation

I. INTRODUCTION

Looking for God

G. K. Chesterton once said that the man who knocks on the door of a brothel is knocking for God. What he meant, of course, is that God has placed longings in our soul for meaning, for purpose, for love. If we do not get those longings filled by following Christ, we go looking to get them filled elsewhere. This leads us to many false sources of fulfillment, such as workaholism, alcoholism, and illicit sexual activity. All are harmful and self-destructive. Yet, if a person will not be satisfied in Jesus, he will invariably seek satisfaction in one or more of the historic substitutes.

In this section, Solomon warns his son of the danger of giving in to sexual temptation, and he prepares him for resisting it when it comes. Evangelist Billy Graham once said that his grandchildren faced more moral temptation going to school on Monday mornings than he and his buddies could find in their non-Christian youth driving around on Friday nights looking for it. The warnings of Solomon are as relevant today as at any time in history. If a modern father or parent does not prepare his son or daughter to face sexual temptation, he is leaving his son or daughter exposed and unprepared for one of life's greatest dangers. A study of Proverbs is one of the most important and helpful steps that can be taken.

II. COMMENTARY

The Battle Against Sexual Temptation

> **MAIN IDEA:** *A young person must be convinced not only that marriage is good but that immorality is deadly, whether it involves another man's wife or a prostitute.*

A The Story of a Seduction (7:1–27)

> **SUPPORTING IDEA:** *In Proverbs 6, the father explained the importance of maintaining sexual purity. Now he dramatizes the story of a seduction, taking his son through a verbal role-playing scenario to prepare him for the real thing, explaining the specific details as a way to prepare his son to deal with such situations.*

7:1–2. This chapter opens with the father once again pleading for his son to heed the wisdom that follows (vv. 1–5). To underscore the point, he repeats the instruction to **keep**, to **store up**, to **guard**. This is a life-and-death matter; he cannot afford to ignore or forget it. In fact, the father is issuing **commands**, not just suggestions. The word for "command" is also used for the commands of God, reminding us that the father is transmitting God's standards. His purpose is not to restrict but to help the young man escape death.

The son should recognize that these teachings are so valuable that he must guard them like the **apple** (literally, the "little man," the center or pupil) of his **eye**. We generally take the greatest care to protect this sensitive organ (see Deut. 32:10; Ps. 17:8).

7:3. In Proverbs 3:3, Solomon instructs the son to bind his teaching on his neck like a necklace; here he tells him to place it on his **fingers** like a ring. Wisdom will serve as an adornment to make the wearer more attractive—but only if it is worn.

It is not enough simply to hear instructions and then forget; the young man should inscribe the words permanently on his **heart**. He should make them part of his internal values, not just an external set of rules. In Jeremiah 31:33, God promises to **write** his new covenant on the hearts of his people.

7:4. In Old Testament culture, **sister** was a term of endearment for a wife or lover (Song 4:9–10,12; 5:1–2). **Kinsman** (NIV, "relative") is used in Ruth 2:1 and in general refers to someone who knows you intimately. The writer exhorts the young man to love wisdom rather than an immoral woman.

7:5. Now the writer begins a transition to his cautionary story of seduction. The wisdom he dispenses will protect the son from the seductress. He uses the same words to describe the immoral woman in 2:16 and 6:24, referring to the loose morals of foreign women. The story that follows shows how easy it is to fall prey to the **seductive** (literally, "smooth") **words** of flattery.

7:6–7. The body of this chapter (vv. 6–23) tells the story of a young man's encounter with a married woman who lures him into a sexual encounter. The scene opens (vv. 6–9) with an account of the victim's naivete.

Solomon says, "I looked through the lattice of my window and saw a young man." There is some discussion about whether this is an actual event or just a composite account based on his knowledge of the typical patterns of such encounters. But a man with Solomon's insight could easily have watched such a scene and foreseen the outcome.

The victim was one of the crowd of **simple** young men loitering in the area. All were inexperienced and gullible, easy prey for anyone who wanted to exploit them. This fellow was not a confirmed rebel; he simply **lacked judgment.** Literally, he "lacked heart," failing to use his mind and will to avoid the danger.

7:8–9. He was in the wrong place. Whether deliberately or carelessly, he was **walking** near the home of a seductive woman. They evidently were acquainted with each other (v. 15), and it is likely that he realized she might be in the neighborhood.

He was there at the wrong time, at night when much immorality took place in the concealment of the dark. The Hebrew phrases describe ever-deepening darkness, moving from **twilight, as the day was fading,** to the middle of the **night,** to darkness.

7:10–12. Now the **woman** appears, and the next three verses describe her character. Her appearance was alluring, since she was dressed like a prostitute. Her attitude was **crafty** (wily, secretive), but her voice was **loud.** She seemed to have nothing to hide. She had an independent spirit, **defiant** toward the authority of God and her husband. Her independence also surfaced in her restless refusal to **stay at home.** She was evidently circulating constantly, looking for potential lovers.

7:13. The next section (vv. 13–20) provides a clear picture of sexual temptation at work. Once this naive young man reaches this point, his only hope of resisting is to run immediately; she is much too clever for him. She begins with an aggressive embrace, surprising him with a sudden kiss. The phrase **brazen face** suggests boldness, and its other use in 21:29 is connected with deceit. What she is about to tell him is unlikely to be true.

7:14. The woman claims that she has just made peace or **fellowship offerings** at the completion of a religious **vow.** Not only does she portray herself as a reasonably devout person, but she adds urgency to her plea. This is a special opportunity to enjoy a festive meal featuring the meat left over from the sacrifice.

7:15. Here we have a sample of the "smooth words" by which she flatters him. She exclaims, "You are the very one I was looking for!" This claim shows that there was some previous contact, so her excitement over finding him seems plausible.

7:16–17. Next she appeals to his senses by a description of the way in which she has prepared her bedroom for him. Clearly, this invitation involves more than just a meal! She has spread colorful, luxurious **linens** imported **from Egypt** across her **bed**. She has sprinkled fine fragrances there so he will smell the exotic blend of **myrrh, aloes and cinnamon.** She paints a word picture that leaves no sense untouched: the taste of the meat, the sound of her voice, the sight of the linens, the smell of the perfumes, and the promise of touching her body.

7:18. She concludes with an invitation to spend an evening in sexual pleasure, borrowing the imagery of **love** as drinking from a fountain. Solomon uses the same language to describe married love in Proverbs 5:18 and Song 4:12–15, which even mentions the same fragrances as verse 17.

7:19–20. At this point, the only thing restraining the young man is his fear of the consequences if they should be discovered. So the seductress assures him that her **husband** has left on an extended **journey.** He took a large amount of **money** with him for expenses because he did not plan to return until the **full moon,** probably several days away.

7:21. Solomon sums up the lengthy speech of 7:14–20 here and reports the victim's response in verses 21–23. She wears down his resistance with her **smooth** flow of **words,** until he can no longer see anything but the pleasure she offers.

7:22–23. His wall of resolve crumbles **all at once.** Surrendering to the temptation, he follows her to her house. The writer then uses a series of similes to describe the actual plight of this hapless victim. He is like an **ox** being led **to the slaughter,** totally unaware of the fate that will soon strike. The last phrase in verse 22 reads "like fetters for the correction of a fool" in Hebrew, an appropriate comparison for the young man who has been captured by the woman's words and will soon face the consequences of his choice.

The NIV has adopted a reading from the Septuagint and Syriac translations that compares him to **a deer stepping into a noose.** The young man's naivete blinds him to his danger until the moment that **an arrow pierces his liver,** ending his life. **Like a bird darting into a snare,** he is oblivious to his danger and is trapped before he realizes that death is inescapable.

7:24–25. The father concludes his account with a stern warning. First he commands his sons to **pay attention** to his words. Then he issues two prohibitions: **do not let your heart turn to her ways,** and do not **stray into her paths.** Both commands aim to help him avoid temptation before it gains momentum, by guarding the heart (4:23) from going astray and by keeping himself physically away from the place of danger. The young man in the story was doomed because he wandered too close to a temptation he did not have the strength to resist.

7:26–27. The section closes with a warning of the terrible danger of immorality. The woman may seem harmless and desirable, but she has been responsible for the deaths of innumerable victims. Solomon uses military terminology to describe her lethal effect. **Victims** can be translated "casualties," and **throng** may refer to armies. It is foolish to imagine that you can escape when so many others have been trapped. When you enter **her house**, you place yourself on the **highway to the grave**.

B The Peril of Prostitution (23:26–28; 22:14; 29:3)

SUPPORTING IDEA: *The man who visits prostitutes will be trapped in terrible trouble.*

23:26–28. Like many of the passages in Proverbs 1–9 that begin with a father's appeal to his **son**, this section asks the son to commit himself to his father's ways. First, the son must **give** his **heart** or inmost person to the father, committing himself to the attitudes and values passed on from his parents. Second, he must keep his **eyes** on the paths of righteousness that he has watched his father follow.

What would distract a young man from the paths of righteousness? A sensual woman, whether she is a married woman who chooses to be unfaithful to her husband, or a common **prostitute**. Proverbs 1–9 speak primarily of the danger of becoming involved with a married woman, but this passage warns that prostitutes are no safer. Either kind of involvement is like falling into a **deep pit** or **well**; there is no way to climb out once you have fallen in.

A prostitute looks for unwary men whom she may entrap, just as a **bandit** springs suddenly on unsuspecting victims. And her sinful activities drag down the moral level of society.

22:14. The writer uses the imagery of a **pit** again (see 23:27), here to remind us that the words of an **adulteress** may seem like harmless flirting, but they will leave you trapped in consequences that you cannot escape.

It is interesting to note that this wicked woman can serve as an instrument of God's judgment. When God's **wrath** is ready to fall on a man, he allows the sinner to stumble into her trap. As in Romans 1:18–32, God sometimes expresses his wrath toward sin by allowing the person to dive deeper into sin.

29:3. A comparison of the two parts of the proverb shows that **wisdom** will keep a person from adultery (see also Prov. 2:12,16; 5:1–3,7–11). And a wise son who avoids **prostitutes** will bring **joy to his father** (Prov. 10:1;

15:20; 23:15,24; 27:11). But a son who becomes involved with prostitutes will squander **his wealth** and that of his father.

> **MAIN IDEA REVIEW:** *A. young person must be convinced not only that marriage is good, but that immorality is deadly whether it involves another man's wife or a prostitute.*

III. CONCLUSION

Swimming Upstream

Beginning in the 1960s, a revolution began against biblical standards of sexuality. Now the traditional values of sexual fidelity within marriage have collapsed under the onslaught of personal desire. Before this there was a stigma against sexual immorality, and society in general supported traditional and biblical standards. Now society in general does not support traditional and biblical standards. From television and movies to public education to examples in business and government, the world is saying, "Do what you want to."

Whereas, in the early part of the twentieth century, the admonitions against sexual immorality in Proverbs seemed over the top—unnecessary, out of step with American culture—now they are right in step and never more relevant. A wise parent will be as proactive as Solomon was in teaching his children what the Bible says about sexual immorality and as urgent in calling his children to a life of biblical faithfulness.

PRINCIPLES

- Temptation to immoral behavior is one of life's constants. It will always be there.
- Sometimes the temptation comes looking for you; sometimes you are looking for it. A wise person will be alert to either situation.
- Parents can help prepare their children to resist temptation.

APPLICATIONS

- Be on your guard against temptation via television, movies, and the Internet, which are sources of "virtual temptation."
- Get a spiritual accountability partner with whom you will be open and honest if you are vulnerable in this area.
- If you are a parent, have a meeting with another set or two of parents to discuss ways in which you can protect your children from the dangers of electronic temptation.

IV. LIFE APPLICATION

Real and Virtual Purity

As life changes from one generation to the next, we are entering an era in which Jesus' words in Matthew 5:28 are becoming more and more important: "But I tell you that anyone who looks at a woman lustfully has already committed adultery with her in his heart." As we enter a "virtual" age, the opportunities for Christians to "look at a woman lustfully" are almost unlimited. In the old days, television and movies were the primary sources of temptation. The bad news is not only that those have not gotten any better, but an even more powerful and dangerous source is available: the Internet. While a Christian would have to sneak into an x-rated theater or video rental store, that same person can feed on x-rated pornography in the secrecy of his own home via the Internet. If a person is careful, no one else will ever know.

God knows, of course. And the Christian should not be deceived: God is not mocked. Whatever a person sows, that will he also reap (Gal. 6:7). And reap he will, from one of three categories.

First, there is the cause-effect consequence of sin (Prov. 6:27–28). Just as a person cannot shoot drugs into his veins in secret without it eventually being revealed in his physical health, so a person cannot shoot pornography into his soul without it eventually being revealed in his spiritual health. He will spiritually shrivel, deform, and eventually collapse. What further sin he might be led into is impossible to say.

Second, he will experience the chastening hand of God (Heb. 1:5–10). We have God's word on it that he loves us too much to allow us to continue in self-destructive behavior without his intervention. In 1 Corinthians 11:27–32, flagrantly unrepentant Christians experienced weakness, sickness, and even death as a result of divine discipline.

Third, he will experience the influence of spiritual attack from the forces of evil. Ephesians 4:26–27 and 6:13–18 teach us that unrepentant sin is an open door for spiritual attack.

All this to say that the dangers of virtual immorality are profound not only because pornography is so readily available and confidential on the Internet but also because of the consequences if a person should fall into its influence. Many more Christian men are likely to fall into virtual sexual immorality than would fall into actual physical immorality. Therefore, when considering the application of this subject from Proverbs, we must consider not only the face value of the warnings against physical immorality but also the related danger of virtual immorality.

V. PRAYER

Dear Father in heaven, may we leave behind the encumbrance and sin which so easily beset us, and may we run with endurance the race that is set before us. May we, by your grace, be satisfied with Jesus and not feel the pull to find our life satisfaction in counterfeits. May we be holy—in body and mind—as you are holy that you might be glorified in us and that we might be spared the ravages of sin and be given the joy of righteousness. Amen.

VI. DEEPER DISCOVERIES

A. Tablet of the Heart (7:3)

The word *tablet* here sometimes refers to wooden boards like the planks of a ship (Ezek. 27:5) or the planks used in the structure of the tabernacle (Exod. 27:8; 38:7). It also refers to the metal plates on the base of the lavers found in Solomon's temple (1 Kgs. 7:36) and the stone tablets on which God wrote the Ten Commandments (Exod. 24:12; 34:28).

The Jews usually wrote on leather or animal skins. A tablet would normally be used for messages of special significance, designed to be kept permanently. The father in Proverbs is asking his son to make a permanent mental record of his instructions, incorporating them in his moral makeup.

B. Peace Offerings (7:14)

Leviticus 3:1–17 and 7:11–38 give the instructions for offering peace (NIV "fellowship") offerings. A worshipper would bring an animal as a peace offering, and when the priest had slaughtered it, some of the flesh would be burned on the altar, some would be reserved for the priests to eat, and the rest would be returned to the person who had brought it. In many cases, the person would use the high quality meat as the basis of a festive banquet, inviting family and friends to share in a joyful occasion. This was usually done immediately while the meat was still fresh.

VII. TEACHING OUTLINE

A. INTRODUCTION

1. Lead Story: Looking for God
2. Context: Solomon describes the danger of adultery and prostitution and even presents a vivid, hypothetical example.

3. Transition: If a person wants to live a life that minimizes pain and maximizes joy, he must be sexually pure, and he must resist the temptation to sexual immorality.

B. COMMENTARY
1. The Story of a Seduction (7:1–27)
2. The Peril of Prostitution (23:26–28; 22:14; 29:5)

C. CONCLUSION: REAL AND VIRTUAL PURITY

VIII. ISSUES FOR DISCUSSION

1. On a scale of 1 to 5 (1 being not very cautious and 5 being extremely cautious), how cautious are you to the level of immorality you expose yourself to in television, movies, and the Internet?
2. What safeguards have you taken, or do you need to take, to protect your heart and mind from "virtual immorality"?
3. In what ways do you think failure in this area affects an individual? A spouse? A father? What steps have you taken, or should you take, to protect your children from the dangers of "virtual immorality"?

Chapter 6

The Call to Wisdom

Proverbs 8:1–36

| Q u o t e |

"*W*isdom is the right use of knowledge. To know is not to be wise. Many men know a great deal, and are all the greater fools for it. To know how to use knowledge is to have wisdom."

C h a r l e s   H a d d o n   S p u r g e o n

Proverbs
8:1–36

 I N   A   N U T S H E L L

*W*isdom calls to each human being to come to its safety and pleasure. It is within the reach of everyone, is more valuable than financial wealth, and calls us to high moral standards. God created wisdom, which should tell us how valuable and important it is. It is the doorway to happiness when we fall in love with "her."

The Call to Wisdom

I. INTRODUCTION

The Double Eagle II

*O*n August 11, 1978, the *Double Eagle II*, a large helium balloon, set sail from Maine for France. As the crew approached the continent six days later, they were losing altitude, and they had to lose weight or crash in the ocean. One of them wrote, "We have been expending ballast (weight) wisely, but as we neared land, not cheaply . . . over went such gear as tape recorders, radios, film magazines, sleeping beds, lawn chairs, most of our water, food, and the cooler it was in." They made their destination and enjoyed the feeling of satisfaction, plus the recognition of the world, and the financial rewards that went with it.

As we follow Christ, if there are things that are keeping us from following him fully, we need to throw them overboard. Like the *Double Eagle II*, it might not be cheap. But it is better to lose the things that weigh us down than for us to ditch in the ocean of failure. No price is too great to pay if God asks it of us.

That is the point that wisdom makes in this chapter. "Follow me," she calls. "Give everything you must, but follow me. Personal satisfaction and the full blessing of God are found only in me."

II. COMMENTARY

The Call to Wisdom

MAIN IDEA: *Solomon portrays Wisdom as a wonderful woman, extolling the value of pursuing her rather than wasting energy on fleeting romances.*

Wisdom's Call (8:1–5)

SUPPORTING IDEA: *Wisdom is available to everyone, particularly those who need it most.*

8:1. In the first three verses, Solomon introduces Wisdom, pictured as a gracious woman. Rather than giving counsel directly as he did in the earlier chapters, he allows Lady Wisdom to speak for herself for the rest of the chapter. He uses the literary device of personification elsewhere (1:20–33; 3:13–20; 4:5–9; 9:1–9) but develops it most fully here. The chapter makes a useful contrast to the description in chapter 7 of an immoral woman enticing a gullible young man to destruction.

8:2–3. Wisdom plants herself in the busiest public place, at the very entrance to the **city**, where all the roads **meet** and caravans funnel through the **gates**. Accessible to all, she issues a loud invitation to the crowds bustling past her.

8:4–5. What is the message of Wisdom? From this point on, Lady Wisdom is the speaker, and she begins by making a direct appeal addressed **to all mankind**. Whoever wants to gain wisdom can do so by coming to her. She addresses the invitation specifically to two groups badly in need of her help. To the **simple**, who are naive and gullible because of lack of experience, she offers to teach **prudence**, so they can avoid the pitfalls of life. To the **foolish**, she offers **understanding**. Solomon uses the word for a fool who chooses his own way rather than God's path but is not yet confirmed in rebellion.

𝔅 Wisdom's Value (8:6–11)

> **SUPPORTING IDEA:** *Wisdom's noble words are right and are much more valuable than financial wealth.*

8:6. How can a person gain these benefits? First, by listening to the words of Wisdom, which are characterized by several outstanding qualities. Wisdom's message consists of **worthy things**. Literally she says, "I speak princes" or "nobles"; her words are like the people who exemplify the highest levels of moral excellence. Wisdom speaks only **what is right**, upright or straight. The same word is translated "faultless" in verse 9.

8:7–9. What one hears from the lips of Wisdom is sure to be **true** because any sort of evil is abhorrent to her. Her speech stays consistently righteous, with no taint of **crooked** or crafty deceit or **perverse** distortions of truth. In fact, those who have walked the path of righteousness long enough to have a degree of discernment are the ones who recognize the merits of her counsel. Every word is **right**, upright and straight, and **faultless**, straightforward and honest.

8:10–11. Once again Wisdom issues a command. Verse 6 instructed people to listen, and verse 10 asks them to **choose**. Pick **wisdom**, not wealth, because wisdom possesses much greater value than treasures such as **silver**, refined or **choice gold**, and jewels (possibly **rubies** or coral). The writer weighs these costly commodities against **instruction**, **knowledge**, and **wisdom**, and urges, "Choose wisdom."

ℂ Wisdom and Righteousness (8:12–21)

> **SUPPORTING IDEA:** *Wisdom is linked to high standards of moral ethics. It is not just a set of clever ways to succeed.*

8:12. Wisdom, you might say, lives with a family of other wonderful virtues. **Prudence** can refer to trickery (Josh. 9:4), but in Proverbs it always means good, sensible behavior. **Knowledge** describes not just academic attainment but knowledge of truth. And **discretion** in Proverbs means the careful behavior that arises from clear thinking. It is the opposite of recklessness. All three words refer to the ability to form sound plans.

8:13. But wisdom is far more than shrewdness; the **fear** of **the LORD** is its foundation (Prov. 1:7; 9:10). Therefore, the wise person shares God's hatred for any form of **evil**. Knowledge alone can inflate a person's ego (1 Cor. 8:1), but wisdom hates **pride and arrogance** because they interfere with our relationship with the Lord.

8:14–16. Wisdom returns to the catalog of accompanying virtues begun in verse 12. She can provide people with direction because she has **counsel and sound judgment**; and she strengthens them to meet the challenges of life with **understanding and power**.

Verses 15–16 make the point that wisdom is indispensable for good leadership. **Kings**, **rulers**, **princes**, and **nobles**—all must have wisdom in order to rule with justice and righteousness. A wicked ruler may be able to seize power and wealth, but only the ruler who fears the Lord can maintain a righteous administration.

8:17. Although wisdom offers her services to everyone (Prov. 8:5), the only ones who actually receive the benefits are those who **love** and **seek** her. As James 1:5 promises, those who come to God seeking wisdom will receive it (see also Prov. 2:1–4).

8:18–21. In these verses, wisdom promises a lavish array of gifts for those who do carry out the search for her. Along with wisdom come **riches**, **honor**, **enduring wealth**, and **prosperity**. The word translated "prosperity" should be translated "righteousness," as in verse 20 and in most other passages. This list blends financial benefits with the honor that comes from righteous conduct and shows that wisdom can offer far more than money. Verse 19 repeats the claim of verses 10–11 that wisdom produces a **yield** better than riches.

Verses 20–21 sum up the main thought of the paragraph: the life of wisdom is all about living with **righteousness** and **justice**; spiritual prosperity is the result, and financial prosperity is a normal by-product.

Ⓓ Wisdom and the Creation (8:22–31)

SUPPORTING IDEA: *God used Wisdom when he created the world, so we should understand how vital it is for us to seek her.*

8:22–26. Here begins a new stanza of the description of Wisdom, reaching new poetic heights as it tells how she was involved in God's creation of the world. Verses 22–26 describe Wisdom's origin before creation, while verses 27–31 describe Wisdom's activities during creation.

The passage begins emphatically with God. He is the active agent in creation as well as the source of Wisdom. Many commentators believe this section of the chapter refers to Jesus Christ, but it seems likely that it actually continues the same literary device used in the rest of the chapter—Wisdom personified in the form of a woman (see "Deeper Discoveries").

Before God created the heavens and the earth, he brought forth Wisdom. The passage uses three different verbs to describe this action. First, Wisdom was **brought . . . forth** (v. 22), from a verb that occurs eighty-four times in the Old Testament, usually meaning "to get, acquire." In a few passages it is translated "to possess" or "to create." Second, Wisdom was **appointed** (v. 23) or installed in a prominent position. The verb appears in this sense elsewhere only in Psalm 2:6 to describe the Son's installation as king. It can also mean "to be woven" or "formed." Third, Wisdom was **given birth** (v. 24), from a verb meaning "to writhe or twist" with the pains of childbirth.

These verses emphasize the fact that Wisdom came forth from God before creation. She was the **first** (either earliest or foremost) **of his works**, existing before time or **the beginning** of earth's history. Wisdom was before the creation of the **world** in Genesis 1:1–3, the separation of the water into **oceans** in Genesis 1:6–8, or the emergence of dry land in Genesis 1:9–10.

8:27–29. Since Wisdom originated before creation, she was obviously present during the process of creation. These verses take us back through some of the same events described in Proverbs 8:22–26. Wisdom was involved when God **set the heavens** firmly in place and when he set out the circle or boundaries of the seas. She was there when the Lord installed the firmament or **clouds** in place and established the ocean beds on the second day of creation. When God caused the dry land to appear, she was present on the third day of creation.

8:30–31. Wisdom was not only an observer during creation but an active participant. God used Wisdom in creating the universe. And if God used Wisdom for such a task, surely we need his wisdom for the problems we face. We can also conclude that the principles of Wisdom are built into the very structure of the creation, so it would be foolish to ignore them.

At God's side, Wisdom participates in the role of a **craftsman**. The Hebrew word here can sometimes refer to a child, but the image of an artisan fits this context more readily. The shared task of creation was a delightful one. Wisdom was **rejoicing** in God's presence, God's universe, and God's people— all fitting sources of rejoicing for us as well.

Ⓔ Waiting Near Wisdom's Door (8:32–36)

> **SUPPORTING IDEA:** *The way to happiness is to fall in love with Wisdom, constantly turning your attention to that pursuit.*

8:32–34. Listen to Wisdom, and you will receive blessing! Wisdom closes her message with this appeal. The way to find blessing is to devote oneself to Wisdom. **Listen** to her words; **keep** her instructions; take every opportunity to spend time in her presence like a young man who devotes hours daily **waiting** near his loved one's **doors**—just to make sure he misses no opportunity to be in her presence.

8:35–36. Only two pathways stretch before you: the path to **life** and the pathway to **death**. And the only way to find life is to commit yourself to following Wisdom. With Wisdom comes life. The alternative is disaster and, ultimately, death.

> **MAIN IDEA REVIEW:** *Solomon portrays Wisdom as a wonderful woman, extolling the value of pursuing her rather than wasting energy on fleeting romances.*

III. CONCLUSION

Audubon's Commitment

John Audubon, well-known naturalist and artist, considered no personal sacrifice too great to learn about birds and to record that information for posterity. He would go into the swamps night after night to record observations about nighthawks. One summer Audubon repeatedly visited the bayous near New Orleans to observe a shy waterbird. He would stand neck deep in the stagnant waters, scarcely breathing, while poisonous water moccasins swam past his face. It was a great hardship, but he reported with enthusiasm that the pictures of the birds that he was able to paint as a result made it all worthwhile. If a person could be so disciplined for an earthly goal, how much more should a child of God be willing to sacrifice for following Christ.

The life wisdom calls us to is not necessarily an easy life. Many of the things we have to give up are things we want or things that make life easier. Many of the things we have to do are hard—perhaps physically, but maybe also spiritually or emotionally. But the result is worth it. The trophy at the end of a contest is won through hard work, but in the end, it is well worth it.

PRINCIPLES

- Wisdom does not come easily or cheaply. We have to pay a price for it.
- Wisdom gives her best to those who follow her most closely.

- The way of discipline (wisdom) is the way of freedom.

APPLICATIONS

- If your parents are still living, listen to them. If there are other mentors, counselors, or authorities in your life, listen to them. God often leads us through those whom he places over us.
- Ask God if there is any wisdom he wants you to acquire or foolishness he wants you to lose. It is a prayer that he will surely answer.
- Guard what you let into your mind. Allow only that which will nurture wisdom and not foolishness. You will become what you allow your mind to think about.

IV. LIFE APPLICATION

Burning the Ships Behind Them

Legend has it that when the Spanish explorer Cortez landed at Vera Cruz to begin his conquest of Mexico with his small force of seven hundred men, he set fire to his fleet of eleven ships. As his men watched the ships burn, they realized they had no hope of going back, and they had to make a success of their new life in the new world. All thoughts of going back were vanquished, and their minds were focused only on the future in this new world.

This kind of single-mindedness is required to meet the demands of the Christian life. We must not look back to the old life for cues on how to live. We must not harbor affection for things of the past. We must not keep a mental note of an avenue for going back. We have to make a break with the old life. We must realize that there is nothing about the old life that could be better than the new life Jesus calls us to.

That is the point Wisdom makes as she calls us to follow her. She is the path of new life in Christ. She is the avenue of peace, love, and joy. She is the secret to the fulfilled longings of our soul.

Like Cortez setting fire to his ships, we must mentally set fire to any thought we have about an old life being superior to the new one. We must make a clean break from a life of rebellion or carelessness or laziness. We must look ahead to the path of wisdom and let the past be a thing of the past.

V. PRAYER

Father in heaven, we pray that you would make us willing to pay the price for wisdom. Help us see that the price for foolishness is much greater than any price we may pay for wisdom. May our lives be pleasing to you as a result. Amen.

VI. DEEPER DISCOVERIES

A. Who Is Lady Wisdom?

The identity of Wisdom in Proverbs 8 has been a topic of lively discussion for centuries. Some writers, including contemporary feminists, have claimed that the chapter is a description of an Israelite or pagan goddess. However, this idea contradicts the monotheism of the Old Testament and the admonition of Proverbs to "fear the Lord" rather than any goddess.

Most writers have debated whether we should understand Wisdom as a personification (a figurative way to describe the attribute of wisdom) or an actual person (Jesus Christ as the Wisdom of God).

There are problems with the view that Wisdom here is a direct description of Christ, even though it has been a popular view. The verbs used in 8:22–25 seem to support the idea that Wisdom is a creation of God rather than an eternal part of the Godhead. The Arian heretics in the fourth and fifth century A.D. actually used this passage to argue against the deity of Christ.

Wisdom as a female personification of the attribute of wisdom escapes that doctrinal drawback and fits smoothly with the rest of Proverbs 1–9. Chapter 1 portrays Wisdom as a woman, and chapter 9 moves directly into a comparison of two women, Wisdom and Folly, calling simple young men to come to dinner with them. Almost all agree that the bulk of chapter 8 can be understood as a personification, so it seems reasonable to maintain that approach through verses 22–31.

The New Testament does present Jesus as God's Wisdom (Col. 2:3) and teaches that he participated with his father in creation (Col. 1:15–17; Rev. 3:14; John 1:3). Therefore we should not be surprised if many of the phrases in Proverbs 8 also serve as excellent descriptions of Christ. The chapter speaks of him indirectly but is not a direct description of him.

B. Does God Promise Money to the Wise?

Proverbs often promises that the wise and righteous will prosper (8:18–21, for example). Many have asked whether Christians today can expect to prosper financially when they follow God. Solomon himself experienced financial blessing as a by-product of God's blessing. When he asked for wisdom, God gave him wealth as well (1 Kgs. 3:5–15).

God had entered into a covenant with Israel, outlined in Deuteronomy 28, which involved specific promises of political and economic prosperity. He swore that he would bless them with land, crops, and wealth if they obeyed him. This covenant could serve as a basis for the Old Testament reader of Proverbs to expect such blessings. However, even in the Old Covenant, the promise was made to a nation. And if the nation as a whole was living in sin, then even the rare righteous person often suffered some of the consequences.

For example, during the reign of Hezekiah, the nation of Judah suffered as a result of the accumulating sin of the nation; and righteous people, such as Isaiah, also had to suffer some of those consequences. So the proverbial promise of wealth for wisdom is for an ideal situation for individuals living in a nation that is, as a whole, pursuing wisdom. Again, it is not a blanket promise but a general truth that if all Jews band together to live in wisdom, the result will be financial wealth.

Since the covenant was made specifically with the nation of Israel, modern believers cannot use it directly to claim a divine promise of wealth. The principles taught in Proverbs, however, are enduring guidelines that will enable us to avoid many of the pitfalls that trap people in poverty.

VII. TEACHING OUTLINE

A. INTRODUCTION

1. Lead Story: The Double Eagle II
2. Context: In chapter 8, Wisdom is a female personification of the attribute of wisdom. This observation fits smoothly with the rest of Proverbs 1–9. Chapter 1 portrays Wisdom as a woman, and chapter 9 moves directly into a comparison of two women, Wisdom and Folly, calling simple young men to come to dinner with them. After repeated practical warnings against sexual immorality and other common sins and indiscretions, this chapter presents a concentrated and compelling call to be wise—to accept the blessings of wisdom and refuse the curses of foolishness.
3. Transition: After starting the Book of Proverbs with a practical appeal to avoid specific sins, Solomon uses chapters 8 and 9 as a profound argument for embracing an overall commitment to following wisdom in life.

B. COMMENTARY

1. Wisdom's Call (8:1–5)
2. Wisdom's Value (8:6–11)
3. Wisdom and Righteousness (8:12–21)
4. Wisdom and the Creation (8:22–31)
5. Waiting Near Wisdom's Door (8:32–36)

C. CONCLUSION: AUDUBON'S COMMITMENT

VIII. ISSUES FOR DISCUSSION

1. What is the wisest thing you are committed to right now? What is the most foolish thing you are committed to right now?
2. What is the most important thing you could do right now to begin following wisdom more closely?
3. What is the impact of your life on your children? On others whose lives you influence? Are they learning how to live a life of wisdom by watching you?

Chapter 7

Competing Invitations from Wisdom and Folly

Proverbs 1:20–33; 9:1–6,10–18

"*The wise man learns from tragedy. The foolish man merely repeats it.*"

Michael Novak

Proverbs
1:20—33; 9:1—6; 10—18

IN A NUTSHELL

Wisdom and foolishness call us, appealing to us to enjoy their pleasures. There is joy in following wisdom and pain in following foolishness. Choose wisdom.

Competing Invitations from Wisdom and Folly

I. INTRODUCTION

The Angel on Your Shoulder

$\mathcal{T}$emptation has often been portrayed as an angel sitting on one shoulder and a devil sitting on the other, both whispering in the person's ear, trying to get him to follow their advice. The angel tries to get us to think of others and to delay immediate gratification and do what is right, while the devil tries to get us to listen to our own desires and get what we want right now. Who wins, of course, depends on which one of these the person listens to.

In this section in Proverbs, Solomon places the angel of wisdom on one of his listener's shoulders and the devil of foolishness on the other and lets them call to us. But then Solomon goes one step further. He shows us the consequences of listening to wisdom and the consequences of listening to foolishness. Then, after we have seen the results of our choice, he asks us to choose. Of course, the ability to see the results of our choices helps tremendously. Only a spiritually shortsighted person would listen to the devil's call to foolishness after seeing the consequences laid out before him.

II. COMMENTARY

Competing Invitations from Wisdom and Folly

MAIN IDEA: *God's wisdom is pictured as a gracious woman who invites everyone to come and learn from her. Even those who are naive can find life and escape disaster if they pay attention to her advice.*

A Accepting Wisdom's Reproof (1:20–33)

SUPPORTING IDEA: *Wisdom will rebuke you when you start heading into dangerous ground. He who is willing to accept her reproof will avoid disaster, but he who ignores her warnings cannot escape.*

Wisdom has appeared before in the chapters of this commentary as a gracious, almost regal woman (3:16–18; 4:3–6; 8:1–36). This passage introduces her for the first time in Proverbs. Such a literary device is a dramatic way to call young men to devote themselves to "Lady Wisdom" rather than becoming infatuated with the young women who would lead them astray.

1:20–21. Wisdom enters the scene by moving into the most public areas of the city, addressing those who pass by. She **calls aloud**, with a clear, piercing voice, so that everyone can hear her. She goes to the open air of **the street**, to **the public squares** crowded with markets. Rather than staying in the quiet halls of scholars, wisdom plunges into the **noisy** hubbub of the **streets** and takes up a position at **the gateways of the city** where all traffic must pass. No one can claim that Wisdom is inaccessible; she takes the initiative to offer her services.

1:22. Lady Wisdom is the speaker in the rest of the chapter. She begins with two rhetorical questions addressed to the classes of people who need her counsel most yet are most likely to disregard it. The **simple ones** are naive and gullible, not yet confirmed in foolishness (Prov. 1:4). The **mockers** reject truth, scorning anyone who presents it (cp. Ps. 1:1). The **fools** (Heb. *kesiyl*) have moved further from God than the simple ones but are not as rebellious as the mockers. All three categories are moving along a pathway of spiritual stupidity, but they are foolish enough to be happy with their course.

1:23. All these people are going down the wrong path, so Wisdom's words to them will be a **rebuke**. Proverbs reminds us often that it is vital to welcome reproof, not reject it (1:23,25,30; 3:11; 9:8; 13:1; 15:31; 17:10; 19:25; 25:12; 30:6). The fool needs to turn from his self-destructive ways and place himself under Wisdom's tutelage. When he does, Wisdom will pour out her **heart** (literally "spirit") and make known her **thoughts** (literally "words").

1:24–25. Both of these verses use the phrase **since you**. Because the hearers have chosen to ignore wisdom's advice, they miss out on all the benefits that were promised. Wisdom has **called** and beckoned, but they have refused to **heed** any of her **advice**. They **ignored** all her counsel, dismissing it as irrelevant, and they refused to **accept** correction or **rebuke**.

1:26–28. These verses form the climax of the passage, the moment when Wisdom's warnings come true. Just as she had warned, the fools are suddenly blasted by the consequences of their stubborn rebellion. **Calamity** will hit them like a storm; **disaster** will sweep over them like a whirlwind; **distress and trouble** will come upon them.

And when this catastrophe strikes, it will be too late to get any help from Wisdom. They laughed and mocked at her, and now she will turn the tables and **mock** them. Even if they cry for rescue, they will find no way of escape.

Wisdom's laughter might seem heartless, but Wisdom is not a true "person." It is a force which carries with it natural cause-and-effect consequences. Therefore, the laughter simply shows that we cannot escape the consequences of rejecting rebuke. In verse 24, Wisdom called and they refused; now they call and she refuses. It appears that Wisdom's primary contribution is to help us avoid trouble. It does not keep us from pain after we have gotten into it, or necessarily make it easy to extricate ourselves from it.

1:29–30. These verses are similar to verses 24–25. Both begin with **since they** and explain the reasons the fools are in such trouble. They have rejected the help God has made available. The problem is that they refuse to **fear the LORD** and reject the knowledge that he gives (1:7; contrast 2:5). Based on that attitude, they ignored Wisdom's rebuke when it came.

1:31. The doom that comes to the foolish is simply the **fruit** of their choice to pursue their own paths and devise their own **schemes**. As Galatians 6:7 points out, we reap what we sow.

1:32–33. The passage concludes by picturing the ultimate result of ignoring Wisdom or heeding her. The **simple** are wayward, turning away from the advice that would save them. And the **fools** are complacent, plodding down the path to death, unaware of their danger. The wise man, however, will **live in safety**, able to enjoy a quiet, restful life. The foolish are at ease out of carelessness, but the wise are at ease because they have genuine security.

Solomon intends this passage as a call for his readers to devote themselves to the pursuit of wisdom, heeding the advice of parents and wise teachers.

B Choosing Between Two Invitations (9:1–6,10–18)

> **SUPPORTING IDEA:** *Lady Wisdom and Lady Folly are both inviting passersby to their homes for a feast. The choice is critical because the path leads to life or death, and only those who fear the Lord will make the right choice.*

This chapter is divided evenly into three sections. First, Wisdom invites people to her feast (vv. 1–6). Second, Solomon discusses the underlying causes that motivate people to choose Wisdom or Folly (vv. 7–12). Finally, Folly in the form of a harlot invites people to her feast (vv. 13–18). The scenes of the two women form a striking conclusion to the discourses found in the first nine chapters and follow naturally the portraits of the prostitute in chapter 7 and of Wisdom in chapter 8.

9:1–2. Wisdom has provided a spacious setting for the feast, a **house** large and grand enough to feature **seven pillars**. In addition, she has prepared a lavish meal, which features **meat** and **wine**. She has butchered the animals and cooked the meat, and the wine is carefully **mixed**; everything is ready for the table.

9:3. Now it is time to gather the guests, so Wisdom sends **out her maids** to invite people to attend. And she herself goes to **the highest point of the city**, where many can hear her call out an invitation. The scene reminds one of Jesus' parable in Luke 14:15–24.

9:4–6. Wisdom's words are recorded in verses 4–6 and possibly in verses 7–12. This feast is not reserved for the elite. It is intended specifically for the

simple and for **those who lack judgment** (literally "heart") or sense—the ones who need help most. Her invitation to "**come, eat,** and **drink,**" refers on the surface to sharing the meal she has prepared. Literally, this is a plea to acquire wisdom and enjoy its benefits. The needy are asked to leave behind their naivete and learn from her to **walk** in the path of **understanding.** By doing so, they will find life.

Similar language appears in Isaiah 55:1–2, and Jesus used similar imagery in John 6:51–56. **Simple ways** in Proverbs 9:6 could be translated "simple ones," but the latter half of the verse shows that the subject is pathways.

9:10. The discussion comes full circle here and restates the theme of the book from 1:7, placing the same theme at the beginning and end of chapters 1–9. Solomon uses a different word for **beginning,** meaning "turning point" or "first step," and substitutes **wisdom** for "knowledge" in 1:7. **Holy One** actually has a plural ending here and in 30:3, emphasizing the fullness of God's holiness. The verse makes clear that wisdom apart from God is impossible.

9:11–12. Wisdom promises that she will reward her followers with **long life** and adds a strong statement on our individual responsibility before God. A **wise** man gains reward through his own wisdom, not that of anyone else. And **a mocker** suffers for his own stubbornness, not that of anyone else. A similar truth is explained in Ezekiel 18.

9:13. The third portion of the chapter introduces **Folly** as a **woman** who attempts to lure passersby to her "feast." She **is loud,** like the adulteress in Proverbs 7:11. She is **undisciplined,** literally naive and gullible like her simpleminded guests. And she is ignorant, **without knowledge.**

9:14–15. Like Wisdom, Folly takes her position on **the highest point** where many people can hear her. Rather than taking the trouble to send out maids with invitations, she sits by her doorway, calling to those who are near. Folly shouts to those who **pass by** the **door of her house,** who are heading **straight** down the path, probably a reference to those who are leading upright lives (cp. Prov. 4:25–27).

9:16–17. Folly deliberately uses the same words as Wisdom to get the attention of her intended victims. But the menu offered is quite different: bread and water rather than meat and wine. Proverbs 5:15–16 compares married love to a drink of water from one's own fountain, and it is likely that **stolen water** here is an allusion to illicit sex. **Food eaten in secret** may be a reminder of the criminal conspiracies described in Proverbs 1:11–14; 4:14–17; 6:12–15.

9:18. Folly's invitation may sound attractive, but the reality is that death lies behind the door. All of Proverbs 1–9 presents the two paths: the path of wisdom leading to life, and the path of folly leading to death. The rest of Proverbs explains these paths and their consequences.

> **MAIN IDEA REVIEW:** *God's wisdom is pictured as a gracious woman who invites everyone to come and learn from her. Even those who are naive can find life and escape disaster if they pay attention to her advice.*

III. CONCLUSION

Playing with Fire

The American proverb says, "If you play with fire, you'll get burned." The biblical proverb asks, "Can a man scoop fire into his lap without his clothes being burned? Can a man walk on hot coals without his feet being scorched?" (Prov. 6:27–28). Of course, the answer is no. If a person does something dangerous, he pays a price. Flirting with sexual immorality is dangerous. It can burn you in three ways.

First, the cause-effect consequences of sin kick in. You can contract a sexually transmitted disease; you can be emotionally riddled with guilt; you can get caught and ruin your reputation or family. Second, there is the consequence of the discipline from God. As a loving father, he loves us too much to allow us to engage in self-destructive behavior without disciplining us for it (Heb. 12:5–12). Third, it opens the door to spiritual attack. When we do not repent of sin, it gives the devil an opportunity to begin working in our lives (Eph. 4:27).

So don't play with fire. Don't toy with sexual immorality. You will pay a terrible price if you do!

PRINCIPLES

- Sin has automatic consequences.
- The worse the sin, the worse the consequences.
- A word to the wise is sufficient. If an activity is morally dangerous, a wise person will not flirt with it. If a person flirts with it, he is being foolish and may become a fool.

APPLICATIONS

- If you are toying with immorality, think through the potential consequences of your actions. Are you willing to pay that price?
- Reflect on others who have gotten caught in immorality. Assess if you think their lives are better because of it. Decide if you want to end up like them.

- Guard what you let into your mind. If you feed your mind on sensual images and stories from television, movies, and the Internet, it will only weaken your resistance to immorality.

IV. LIFE APPLICATION

Sailing the Seven Seas

If you want to be free to sail the seven seas, you must make yourself a slave to the compass. All of life involves balancing our freedoms and our bondages. We can be free from the toothbrush and a slave to cavities, or we can be a slave to the toothbrush and free from cavities. We cannot be free from the toothbrush and free from cavities. That kind of absolute freedom does not exist. We may wish it did, and we may act for a time as though it does. But it doesn't, and eventually we pay the price for both our freedoms and our bondages.

If we want the freedom of a good reputation, if we want the freedom of guilt-free living, if we want the freedom of emotional peace, if we want the freedom of moral authority, of a strong and happy family and physical health, we must make ourselves slaves to sexual purity.

We can choose the freedom of sexual immorality if we want. But then we become slaves to all the consequences. Decide in advance what you want from the rest of your life. Then ask yourself if you are willing to pay the price. You have a freedom and a corresponding bondage. You can get a bondage and a corresponding freedom. Choose wisely.

V. PRAYER

Father in heaven, help us to see that our freedom lies in discipline and that to experience the joy of your blessings we must make ourselves a slave to your truth. Amen.

VI. DEEPER DISCOVERIES

A. Seven Pillars

Many have speculated about the possible significance of the seven pillars mentioned in 9:1. Solomon's temple had two pillars in front (1 Kgs. 7:15), and archaeologists have found shrines with seven pillars, so some interpreters have thought this represents a genuine sanctuary in contrast to idol shrines. Some have suggested that the pillars correspond to the seven days of creation in Genesis 1–2, while others have seen a reference to the sun, the moon, and the five planets that were visible in Old Testament times. It is difficult to establish any of these interpretations definitely. The verse may simply mean that the house was spacious and impressive.

B. Mixed Wine

The reference to mixing wine in 9:2 may refer to diluting it with water. The Jews considered undiluted wine distasteful. Passover wine was mixed with three parts of water to one part of wine. The verse might also refer to the custom of mixing spices into the wine to enhance its flavor (Ps. 75:8). Or perhaps Wisdom may have done both forms of mixing.

VII. TEACHING OUTLINE

A. INTRODUCTION

1. Lead Story: The Angel on Your Shoulder
2. Context: In Proverbs 1:20–33, Lady Wisdom calls passersby to follow her. She promises them good things if they do and warns them of bad things if they don't. In Proverbs 9:1–18, both Lady Wisdom and Lady Folly invite passersby to their homes for a feast. The choice is critical because the path leads to life or death. And only those who fear the Lord will make the right choice.
3. Transition: Look at Lady Wisdom as the angel on one shoulder and Lady Folly as the devil on the other. Listen to what both of them have to say, and pay special attention to the consequences of obeying. The choice will be clear.

B. COMMENTARY

1. Accepting Wisdom's Reproof (1:20–33)
2. Choosing Between Two Invitations (9:1–6,10–18)

C. CONCLUSION: PLAYING WITH FIRE

VIII. ISSUES FOR DISCUSSION

1. Are you toying with sexual immorality? How about your TV, movie, and Internet habits? Any other way? What do you think the consequences will be if you don't deal with it?
2. What is the most important thing you could do right now to begin following wisdom more closely?
3. What is the impact of your life on your children? On others whose lives you influence? Are they learning how to live a life of wisdom by watching you?

Chapter 8

Giving God Control

Proverbs 3:5–8; 10:27; 14:2,12,26–27; 15:3,33; 16:1,3–4,9,20,25,33; 18:2,4,10; 19:3,21,23; 20:24; 21:22,30–31; 22:12; 26:12; 27:1; 28:14,26; 29:25

I. INTRODUCTION
God Isn't Safe

II. COMMENTARY
A verse-by-verse explanation of these verses.

III. CONCLUSION
My Way or the Highway

An overview of the principles and applications from these verses.

IV. LIFE APPLICATION
Garbage Mary

Melding these verses to life.

V. PRAYER
Tying these verses to life with God.

VI. DEEPER DISCOVERIES
Historical, geographical, and grammatical enrichment of the commentary.

VII. TEACHING OUTLINE
Suggested step-by-step group study of these verses.

VIII. ISSUES FOR DISCUSSION
Zeroing these verses in on daily life.

Quote

"*I*f God maintains sun and planets in bright and

ordered beauty, he can keep us."

F .   B .   M e y e r

Proverbs

13:5-6; 14:27; 14:2,12,21-27;
15:3,33; 16:1,3-4,9,20,25,33;
18:2,4,10; 19:3,21,23; 20:24;
21:22,30-31; 22:12; 26:12;
27:1; 28:14,26; 29:25

I   N   A   N   U   T   S   H   E   L   L

*G*od is Lord of creation, source of all laws. He has told us how to live, what to do, and what not to do. Blessing follows wisdom; trouble follows foolishness. The sooner we realize this and chose the path of wisdom, the better off we will be.

Giving God Control

I. INTRODUCTION

God Isn't Safe

In The Lion, the Witch, and the Wardrobe, a novel in the allegorical series The Chronicles of Narnia by C. S. Lewis, two young girls, Susan and Lucy, are getting ready to meet Aslan the lion, who is a figure of Christ. Mr. and Mrs. Beaver, two animal guides who can speak, get the children ready for the encounter.

> "Ooh," said Susan, "I thought he was a man. Is he quite safe? I shall feel rather nervous about meeting a lion."
>
> "That you will, dearie," said Mrs. Beaver. "And make no mistake, if there's anyone who can appear before Aslan without their knees knocking, they're either braver than most or else just silly."
>
> "Then isn't he safe?" said Lucy.
>
> "Safe?" said Mr. Beaver. "Don't you hear what Mrs. Beaver tells you? Who said anything about safe? Of course he isn't safe. But he's good."

What a brilliant insight. God, safe? No. But good? Yes. That is why God has given us the Book of Proverbs: because he is good. He wants us to understand the right way to live, the safe way to live. But it is not safe to ignore God's instructions about wisdom. You do so at your peril. As Galatians 6:7 says, "Do not be deceived: God cannot be mocked. A man reaps what he sows."

God must be respected, or the price for disrespect will be paid. Either through cause-and-effect consequences or through divine discipline, if someone disobeys God or flouts his wisdom, he will pay a price. That is the warning of Proverbs.

II. COMMENTARY

Giving God Control

> **MAIN IDEA:** *God is in charge of the universe, and we are not. The sooner we realize this, the better.*

A Fear of the Lord (10:27; 14:2,26–27; 15:33; 19:23; 28:14)

> **SUPPORTING IDEA:** *The starting point for wisdom and blessing is to recognize that God is God and to treat him with the awe and respect he deserves.*

The fear of the Lord stands at the focal point of the key verse of Proverbs (1:7), as well as the climax of the opening nine chapters of the book (9:10). The fear of God provides the foundation for gaining wisdom because reverence for God motivates us to heed his words. These crucial passages make clear that the wisdom of Proverbs is not merely a set of clever instructions for earthly success; it rests on a commitment to trust and obey God.

10:27. This proverb states the general principle that **fear of the LORD** adds to the length of physical **life**, while the **wicked** often die young (3:2,16; 4:10; 9:11; 14:27; 15:24). Though there are exceptions to this dictum, Proverbs clearly teaches that death comes sooner to the foolish—either because of divine judgment or the natural consequences of sin.

14:2. Attitude produces acts, and acts reveal character. A person who acts in an **upright** manner demonstrates a heart that **fears** God, but **devious** behavior shows that the person thinks so little of God that he feels free to pit his will against him.

14:26–27. Fearing the Lord provides security from all attacks, including temptations, as effectively as the walls of a stout **fortress**. And this protection extends to a person's family. A second metaphor portrays the fear of the Lord as a **fountain of life** (10:11; 13:14; 16:22), which lengthens one's life by revealing the moral traps that lead to premature death.

15:33. This verse runs parallel to 1:7, proclaiming that **the fear of the LORD** is not only the first step toward **wisdom** but the continuing instructor in wise behavior. In addition, **humility** springing from the fear of God will produce the wise behavior that brings **honor** (cp. 22:4).

19:23. The **fear of the LORD** provides the basis for the good **life**. Not only does obedience to God produce greater length of life; it also grants a superior quality of life. When we fear God, we need not fear people or events; we can enjoy peace because we have learned to be **content**.

28:14. Here we find one of the several verses in Proverbs that promise blessing or happiness, much like the Beatitudes of Matthew 5. The path to genuine prosperity is a constant attitude of fear. The phrase "the LORD" does not appear in the Hebrew text, probably indicating that we must maintain a proper respect not only toward God but also toward the authorities he has put in place, such as government officials. The second line shows that the opposite of fearing God is to harden one's heart.

B Trust in God or Self (3:5–8; 14:12; 16:3,20,25; 18:2,4,10; 19:3; 20:24; 21:22; 26:12; 28:26; 29:25)

> **SUPPORTING IDEA:** *We instinctively assume that we can figure out how to handle the issues of life, but we eventually discover that we must trust the Lord rather than our own resources.*

3:5–8. The first twelve verses of Proverbs 3 form a series of commands and consequences. If we obey the command, we will receive the benefit. And in these verses, the command is to **trust** God rather than our own wisdom. The word *trust* is used in Psalm 22:9 to describe a baby resting peacefully in its mother's bosom and in Jeremiah 12:5 for a person who has fallen helpless on the ground. Obviously, it requires that we trust ourselves completely to the Lord, a concept reinforced by the phrase **all your heart**, including emotions, mind, and will.

When we rely completely on God, we will not **lean** on our own intellect or sense of right and wrong. God's ways are often beyond our comprehension (Isa. 55:8–9; Rom. 11:33–34). Instead, we will **acknowledge him** by (literally) knowing him intimately and recognizing him in every aspect of life. When we do, his wisdom will clear the obstacles from our paths.

The second set of commands shows the contradiction between humility and arrogance. A person who **fears the LORD** will not be impressed with his own wisdom; he will avoid **evil**. And as a result he will enjoy the physical health that comes from a well-ordered life submitted to God. Living by God's wisdom brings **health to your body** (literally, the *navel* as a symbol of the entire body) and to the **bones** (a concept repeated in Prov. 12:4; 14:30; 15:30; 16:24; 17:22).

14:12; 16:25. These two verses are identical, probably to emphasize the importance of the concept. It pictures a person standing at the beginning of a path that seems to be level and straight. **Right** sometimes means "upright," as in Proverbs 14:11; the path may seem to be morally legitimate to the person. But our vision is too limited to foresee the end—a **death** trap. Here is a graphic reminder of the limits of human foresight.

16:3. We cannot expect success in our **plans** unless we **commit** them, or roll them over on to, the Lord (see Ps. 37:5). God does not promise to bless every plan, but no plan can succeed without his blessing.

16:20. Trusting God translates into attentiveness to his words. The two parts of this verse make clear that the person **who trusts in the L**ORD is the one who ponders or takes note of the word of **instruction** which God gives.

18:2. In contrast, a fool refuses to listen. He shows no interest in gaining **understanding** but loves to vent his own views. The phrase **airing his own opinions** means literally "to uncover," a verb used in Genesis 9:21 to describe Noah's shameful nakedness. The fool is unaware that he is putting his ignorance on display (see Prov. 17:28).

18:4. But is not in the Hebrew, and the two halves of the verse may not be a contrast. The **words** of the wise are like water—**deep** in its profound insights, yet **bubbling** forth like a **brook** to refresh others.

18:10. True safety is found by taking refuge in the **name of the L**ORD, in his revealed character. The **righteous** will turn to him, while the rich (18:11) imagine that their wealth will protect them.

19:3. How often a person ignores God's warnings and ruins his own **life** yet blames God for his trouble!

20:24. Human discernment is limited. We do not **understand** all that takes place and we certainly cannot predict its outcome because life is under God's control, not ours. Trusting God is the only reasonable response.

21:22. God's wisdom is mightier than human strength. The **stronghold** of one who has military protection may seem impregnable, but the **wise man** can conquer it. The New Testament makes similar promises in the spiritual realm (Matt. 16:18; 2 Cor. 10:3–4).

26:12. A **fool** may eventually realize his need for instruction, but a person who is **wise in his own eyes** is unteachable. There is no **hope** for him to change until he admits his need for help.

28:26. Proverbs 28:25 states that "he who trusts in the L**ORD** will prosper." In contrast, **he who trusts in himself is a fool.** The sole source of safety is to walk in God-taught **wisdom.**

29:25. The writer uses a word for **fear** that means "trembling, terror," unlike the term for reverent awe found in 1:7. When we are terrified by a person, we are easily trapped or controlled. But when we overcome fear of man by trusting in God, we will be **kept safe.** The word used means "to be set inaccessibly high, to be exalted"—lifted to safety above the reach of human threats.

🄲 Divine Providence (15:3; 16:1,4,9,33; 19:21; 21:30–31; 22:12; 27:1)

SUPPORTING IDEA: *God controls every detail of life, and none of our plans can succeed apart from his purpose.*

15:3. God's sovereign control of the universe is based on his omniscience. Like 2 Chronicles 16:9, this verse pictures God as a watchman with his **eyes** on everyone—a warning to **the wicked** and a comfort to **the good**.

16:1,4,9. The opening section of Proverbs 16 focuses on God's control of events. A person can make plans in his heart, like a general setting up a battle (Gen. 14:8), but the Lord guides even the words that are said. Proverbs 16:9 echoes the thought, substituting man's steps for his tongue. Finally, verse 4 shows that God controls even the wicked person, using his evil actions to bring about divine purposes (Rom. 8:28).

16:33. Casting lots may seem to be mere chance, like flipping a coin. But the practice of casting lots was one way Old Testament believers sought God's direction. And even the apparent luck of **the lot** was sovereignly controlled by the Lord.

19:21. We make **plans** instinctively and continually. But planning does not guarantee success; God's **purpose** determines the outcome.

21:30–31. Do not fight against God and do not fight without him. No human wisdom can thwart God's plan. And nothing, not even the superior military might of cavalry, can guarantee victory without his pleasure.

22:12. God promises to guard truth like a sentinel. But he **frustrates** or overturns the words of the treacherous.

27:1. James 4:13–16 enlarges on this verse. It is foolish to **boast** about the future because God determines the outcome. The course of wisdom is to embrace God's will, whatever it may be.

MAIN IDEA REVIEW: *God is in charge of the universe, and we are not. The sooner we realize this, the better.*

III. CONCLUSION

My Way or the Highway

We are familiar with people who have the attitude "my way or the highway." They are arbitrary and dictatorial—hard to work with and impossible to please. Yet that is not what God is like. God does not place whimsical demands on us. He only asks us to do those things that are good for us, and he asks us not to do those things that are bad for us. Knowing God's attitude usually makes all the difference for us. If we accept that his commands and instructions always come from a heart that loves us, we are much more open and responsive to him. So, must things be done God's way? Yes. Is he being arbitrary and unreasonable? No. He only requires what is best for us.

PRINCIPLES

- God's way is always best, regardless of whether it seems so to us at the time.
- God's character can be trusted. Bad advice does not come from a good heart and mind.
- To pay the price for righteousness is to save the price of sin.

APPLICATIONS

- Trust God's wisdom. He created you. He surely knows what is best for you.
- Pay the price to do what is right. In the end, it's far cheaper than doing what is wrong.
- Don't put your own opinion above the Word of God. It is inspired. You aren't.

IV. LIFE APPLICATION

Garbage Mary

"Woman in Rags Revealed as Heiress." So read the headline of the *San Francisco Chronicle* I was reading one day while sitting in the San Francisco airport, waiting to fly back to Atlanta where I lived at the time. A lady who was picked up in a shopping mall in Delray Beach, Florida, appeared to be just another derelict whose mind had faded. Neighbors told of her scrounging around through garbage cans for food, which she hoarded in her car and her two-room apartment. There were mounds of stinking stuff packed in the refrigerator, the stove, the sink, the cabinets, the bathtub. Other than the kitchen, there were no chairs to sit on because stuff was piled up on every-thing else.

Police finally identified her as the daughter of a well-to-do lawyer and bank director from Illinois who had died several years earlier. In addition to the garbage, police found Mobil Oil stock worth more than $400,000; documents indicating ownership of oil fields in Kansas; stock from such firms as U.S. Steel, Uniroyal, and Squibb; as well as passbooks for eight large bank accounts.

Garbage Mary was a millionaire who lived like a pauper. And so are we: spiritual millionaires who ignore the wealth of the Word of God and scrounge around in the squalor of our own making, charting our own course while ignoring the wisdom and counsel of the Creator of the universe. How foolish. How much wiser to go to our riches and draw on them for a life of joy.

V. PRAYER

Heavenly Father, help us to see that faith produces obedience, that if we truly believe your way is the right way, it will spur us to obedience, knowing that sin is self-destructive. May our faith in you and your truth run deep, and may our obedience, as a result, be complete. Amen.

VI. DEEPER DISCOVERIES

A. Beatitudes

Proverbs contains at least eight verses that begin, "Blessed be." Like the Beatitudes of Matthew 5:3–12, these passages list the people who can be described as truly happy.

> He who finds wisdom (Prov. 3:13)
> He who keeps the ways of wisdom (Prov. 8:32)
> He who listens to wisdom, watching daily at her gates (Prov. 8:34)
> He who is gracious to the poor (Prov. 14:21)
> He who trusts in the Lord (Prov. 16:20)
> He whose father walks in integrity (Prov. 20:7)
> He who always fears the Lord (Prov. 28:14)
> He who keeps the law (Prov. 29:18)

B. Citadels

In Solomon's day, a well-constructed tower or fortress could be nearly invulnerable. Many cities took advantage of steep-sided heights to enhance the effectiveness of their defenses. A broken-down fortification was cause for Nehemiah to go into mourning (Neh. 1:4), but the defenses of a city like Jerusalem could frustrate the attacks of the Babylonians for over two years (2 Kgs. 25:1–2). When the righteous take refuge in the tower of God's name, they cannot be touched by the enemy.

C. Casting Lots

Casting lots in the Old Testament was much more important than just flipping a coin. The Israelites used lots for many important decisions. The land allotments for each tribe after the conquest of Canaan were determined by lot (Josh. 14:1–2), and the schedule of service for the priests was set up by drawing lots (1 Chr. 25:8). Pagan peoples also cast lots to select auspicious days for activity (Esth. 3:7). But the early church used this method to choose between the two finalists for a vacancy in the apostolic group (Acts 1:26). Two special stones called the Urim and the Thummim were kept by the high priest for use in determining God's will.

VII. TEACHING OUTLINE

A. INTRODUCTION
1. Lead Story: God Isn't Safe
2. Context: God is in charge of the universe, and we are not. The sooner we realize this, the better. God's wisdom is given to us not to lord it over us but to save us from the pain of foolish decisions.
3. Transition: If you want to maximize your pleasure in life and minimize your pain, follow the path of wisdom.

B. COMMENTARY
1. Fear of the Lord (10:27; 14:2,26–27; 15:33; 19:23; 28:14)
2. Trust in God or Self (3:5–8; 14:12; 16:3,20,25; 18:2,4,10; 19:3; 20:24; 21:22; 26:12; 28:26; 29:25)
3. Divine Providence (15:3; 16:1,4,9,33; 19:21; 21:30–31; 22:12; 27:1)

C. CONCLUSION: MY WAY OR THE HIGHWAY

VIII. ISSUES FOR DISCUSSION
1. Who is the wisest person you know? Why do you think you consider him or her so wise?
2. What are the consequences of his or her lifestyle that cause you to desire wisdom?
3. If that person were suddenly in your shoes, what do you think he or she would do differently than you are doing?

Chapter 9

Trusting God's Guidance

Proverbs 10:13–14,23; 13:14–16; 14:6,8,15,18, 24,33; 15:14,21,24; 16:16,22; 17:12,24; 18:15; 19:2,8; 20:5,12,15; 21:11; 23:12; 24:3–4,7,13–14; 26:4–11; 27:22; 29:9

"*All* I have seen teaches me to trust in the Creator for

all I have not seen."

R . W . E m e r s o n

Proverbs

10:13–14,23; 13:14–16;
14:6,8,15,18,24,33;
15:14,21,24; 16:16,22;
17:12,24; 18:15; 19:2,8;
20:5,12,15; 21:11; 23:12;
24:3–4,7,13–14; 26:4–11;
27:22; 29:9

I N   A   N U T S H E L L

When we see the dreadful consequences of foolishness and the wonderful consequences of wisdom, it is only reasonable to place our complete confidence in God and follow his instructions in life.

Trusting God's Guidance

I. INTRODUCTION

Trust Is Dangerous

Trust is a dangerous thing. It means placing our welfare, our well-being, in the hands of another. Therefore, trust is only as safe as the thing or person we're trusting in. Sometimes we don't have any option. For example, if we must have emergency surgery in a hospital, we must trust the doctor or die. Other times we do have options. We might decide not to invest our money with a given person because we don't trust him to look out for our best interests.

We must make the choice of whether to trust. In those situations, we look at the past to guide us in the future. If the person or thing has demonstrated trustworthiness in the past, we are comfortable trusting him or it for the future. If the person or thing has not demonstrated trustworthiness in the past, we are not comfortable trusting him or it for the future. It is as simple as that. That is why Solomon spends so much time telling us the results of wisdom and the results of foolishness. When we see how consistently foolishness produces pain and how consistently wisdom produces joy, there is every reason to trust God and follow his principles of wisdom in life.

The fool is blind to such insight and charges ahead in his foolishness, proving himself to be a fool in the process. But when wisdom calls out in the streets, she doesn't know who will respond in wisdom and who will respond in foolishness. The old proverb says, "A word to the wise is sufficient." And so it is. If there is any capacity for wisdom in the heart of the hearer, he or she will respond in faith and obedience to God.

II. COMMENTARY

Trusting God's Guidance

MAIN IDEA: *We easily make the foolish assumption that we can unravel all of life's difficulties ourselves simply by using our heads. But the demands of life often outstrip our capabilities. We desperately need God's help to make the right moves.*

A Wisdom and Folly (13:14; 14:24; 15:24; 16:22; 17:12; 24:7,13–14)

SUPPORTING IDEA: *With God's wisdom, life is good. However, nothing but trouble lies ahead if we are foolish enough to ignore him.*

13:14; 16:22. In an arid climate like Palestine, nothing could be more refreshing than a **fountain**. In fact, a traveler's **life** could depend on it! In the same way, the law (*torah*) or **teaching of the wise** not only refreshes your soul, but it preserves your life by guiding you around the **snares** that would trap you like an animal, unable to escape the inevitable **death** that would follow. In 16:22, **understanding** (good sense, insight) is also described as a **fountain of life**. But **fools** lack it and learn only from the **punishment** that hits as a consequence of their behavior.

14:24. Living according to God's wisdom brings practical benefits. When a person follows God's principles of diligence and honesty, financial success often follows; for him, **wealth** is an external symbol of God's blessing like a **crown**. But the person who foolishly ignores God produces nothing but more foolishness.

15:24. The theme of the two paths runs throughout Proverbs, and this verse reminds us that the wise person is on an **upward** path to **life**; his wisdom will prevent a premature descent to the **grave** (Heb. *sheol*).

17:12. What could be more dangerous than facing a mother **bear** defending **her cubs**? According to Proverbs, a **fool** on the prowl can be even more perilous. The bear will only launch a direct attack, but a fool can destroy you in a dozen different ways.

24:7. The word **wisdom** is plural, emphasizing its importance. It is over the head of a **fool**; he cannot appreciate or comprehend it. The **gate** of a city is the place where city leaders met to judge disputes and decide the affairs of the town. The fool **has nothing** worthwhile to contribute to these serious discussions.

24:13–14. Honey was the sweetest substance known in the Old Testament world, and the father encourages his **son** to **eat** it in order to enjoy its sweetness. In the same way, **wisdom** provides **sweet** delight because it gives **hope** for the **future**. A second command urges the son to seek wisdom—not only because it is right but because it is the shortest route to genuine joy.

Ⓑ Dealing with Fools (26:4–11; 27:22; 29:9)

SUPPORTING IDEA: *Anyone foolish enough to think he has all the answers causes trouble not only for himself but for everyone whom he encounters.*

26:4–11. This sequence of verses warns of the risks involved in dealing with a fool. Verses 4 and 5 seem to be contradictory at first glance, but they simply present the two sides of dealing with fools. Sometimes it is best to argue on the fool's terms (v. 4), and sometimes it is better to avoid such a conflict (v. 5); it takes wisdom to know which verse applies to a given situation. The danger in descending to the level of the fool is that you may pick up his bad attitudes. But there are times when it is necessary to **answer** fools with arguments they understand because the rebuke won't be received in any other way. Paul used such "foolish" arguments in 2 Corinthians 11 and 12.

Proverbs 26:6–11 forms a series of analogies, explaining how aggravating a fool can be. In verses 6 and 10, the writer warns that fools are unreliable. **Sending a message** by such a person is foolish; it is unlikely to arrive. His progress is blocked by his folly as effectively as if his **feet** had been amputated. Choosing such a person to carry out an important trust is self-defeating; one might as well be **drinking violence**—both are damaging. The Hebrew text of verse 10 is difficult, and more than one translation has been suggested. But the idea is clear: don't give an important task to a fool.

Verses 7 and 9 show that a fool does not know what to do with a wise saying or **proverb**. The **legs** of a **lame man** are ineffective; they dangle uselessly. In the same way, a fool cannot use a proverb properly. Verse 9 may picture a **drunkard's hand** waving thorny branches around and endangering people, or it may refer to a man so drunk that he doesn't notice the thorns pricking him. Similarly, a fool may grab a proverb to use in an argument but never notice that it condemns him.

Honoring a fool is as unwise as **tying a stone in a sling**. Such a move makes the sling useless, and the stone may slip out and hurt you. So giving **honor to a fool** is senseless and may damage your reputation.

Verse 11 shows that a fool does not learn from his mistakes. Just as a **dog returns to its vomit** (quoted in 2 Pet. 2:22), a fool reverts to his level, even when exposed to something better.

27:22. A **fool** and his **folly** are inseparable. Even if he is punished repeatedly, pounding **him like grain** in **a mortar**, he will still be a fool. Folly is the essence of a fool's being.

29:9. A dispute with a fool soon descends into an emotional brawl, even when it takes place in a court case. There is no objective, calm discussion but an emotional outburst.

Discernment and Understanding (10:13,23; 13:15; 14:6,8,15,33; 15:21; 16:16; 17:24; 19:8; 20:5,12)

SUPPORTING IDEA: *God's wisdom gives us the ability to see danger ahead and sidestep it, as well as the understanding to analyze each situation we enter.*

10:13. The first verses selected for this section deal with discernment, the ability to distinguish between truth and error, wisdom and folly. First, Solomon contrasts the person who has discernment and the person who lacks it. He who has discernment will become wise, and the words that come from his **lips** will help others. But he who **lacks judgment** (literally, heart) has no capacity for learning wisdom. He will face punishment because he learns in no other way.

14:6. In an unexpected turn, this verse pictures a **mocker** who is looking for **wisdom**. Even a hardened sinner sometimes wants wisdom to escape an unpleasant situation, but he looks in the wrong place. A **discerning** person, however, gains knowledge **easily** because he knows the source to consult.

14:33. Wisdom is pictured here as a woman, just as in earlier chapters. Her normal residence is in the heart of a discerning person, even though she offers her counsel to the foolish who pass by (see 1:20–33; 9:1–5).

17:24. Literally, "wisdom is in front of a man of discernment." He sets his sights on **wisdom** and finds that it is clearly visible. A fool, on the other hand, is continually distracted by temptations so that he misses the truth at hand.

14:8,15. Discernment goes with prudence, the good sort of shrewdness that thinks things through before walking into trouble. Fools, on the other hand, are easily deceived; the simple, gullible person is easily influenced. Both will stumble into trouble.

10:23. **Understanding**, like discernment, leads a person in the path of truth, wisdom, and righteousness. A fool enjoys **evil conduct**, leading to the accusation that the godly person is a killjoy. But the closing line of the verse answers that objection.

13:15. **Good understanding** is associated with **favor** (also in 3:4), sometimes translated "grace" or "graciousness." This may refer to God's grace or man's favor. An unfaithful person, in contrast, finds that life is **hard**. This word is used to describe something permanent like a rock (Num. 24:21), ever-flowing or perennial like a stream (Ps. 74:15), or enduring like a nation (Jer. 5:15). Perhaps it depicts the calloused heart of the wicked, so hardened that it cannot change.

15:21. When a person **lacks judgment** (literally, lacks heart), he derives pleasure from foolishness. **Understanding**, however, keeps a person on a **straight course**, one that has been cleared of obstructions.

16:16; 19:8. Once again the writer compares the relative values of wisdom and wealth. **Understanding** is more valuable than **silver**. The person who chooses **wisdom** is acting in his best interest, out of genuine concern for his destiny. And he who **cherishes** or guards and preserves understanding will reap ample benefits.

20:5. People can conceal their real **purposes** just as **deep waters** hide objects. But the person who has the **understanding** offered in Proverbs is able to bring even those hidden thoughts to the surface.

20:12. Our **eyes** and **ears** must be used to evaluate each person or situation that we encounter. But the God who **made them both** is the ultimate source of wisdom, more reliable than any of his creations.

Knowledge (10:14; 13:16; 14:18; 15:14; 18:15; 19:2; 20:15; 21:11; 23:12; 24:3–4)

> **SUPPORTING IDEA:** *Knowledge is power—not to dominate others but to approach life from God's perspective.*

23:12. **Knowledge** is vitally important, so Proverbs commands us to **apply** ourselves to the task of gaining it. Here is the key to true education: use not only your **ears** but your **heart**, receptive to be changed by what you hear.

20:15; 24:3–4. **Knowledge** is also valuable. These verses compare it to the costliest treasures. We normally think of **gold** and gems as valuable because of their scarcity as well as their beauty. But the ability to **speak** words of knowledge appropriate for the occasion is an even rarer treasure.

Broadening the imagery, the writer tells how **wisdom** builds a **house**, **understanding** provides the foundation, and **knowledge** fills its **rooms** with **rare and beautiful treasures**. Though these statements could apply to a person's literal house, they refer more directly to a person's character, life, or family.

10:14; 13:16. Like wisdom and prudence, **knowledge** stands in stark contrast to the behavior of a fool. **Wise men** reserve their knowledge to use at the proper time, while a **fool** spouts off without thinking and gets himself in trouble.

A **prudent** person uses his **knowledge** to foresee and avoid danger, but a **fool exposes his folly** like a peddler spreading his wares in the marketplace.

14:18; 15:14. Both the gullible simpleton and the talkative **fool** are unable to gain wisdom for themselves. The fool **feeds**, or grazes randomly like cattle, nibbling on his own brand of **folly**. But the **prudent** or **discerning** man carries on a search for **knowledge** that is well rewarded.

18:15. He who has knowledge knows how little he knows, so he constantly seeks more. The NIV obscures the fact that the Hebrew mentions **knowledge** in both lines, emphasizing its value. Knowledge is so precious, in fact, that the wise person not only listens for it with his **ears** but folds it into his **heart**, or inward self.

19:2. A person may have **zeal** (literally, Heb. *nephesh,* soul) with a strong inner drive for success. But if this motivation is not directed by **knowledge**, it can lead to **hasty** blunders. Many people act hurriedly, then blame God for their mistakes.

21:11. This verse discusses three mental attitudes. First, the **mocker** has a closed mind; even when he is **punished**, he learns nothing. Second, the **simple** person has an empty mind; he can be startled into attention by a vivid lesson like the penalty inflicted on the scoffer. Third, the **wise** man has an open mind and will learn simply from instruction.

> **MAIN IDEA REVIEW:** *We easily make the foolish assumption that we can unravel all of life's difficulties ourselves simply by using our heads. But the demands of life often outstrip our capabilities. We desperately need God's help to make the right moves.*

III. CONCLUSION

Wisdom Is Increased by Knowledge

A two-year-old is not wise for two reasons. First, because he is emotionally immature. Second, because he does not know enough to draw reliable conclusions. One can have great knowledge without wisdom. But the capacity for wisdom is increased by knowledge. By this we don't mean academic knowledge but the knowledge based on accurate observations of life.

Someone once asked, "How do you get an archeology major (or history major, or medieval literature major) off your front porch?" The answer is, "Pay for the pizza!" This joke recognizes the fact that even though some people may possess specialized knowledge, they might end up delivering pizza for a living because their knowledge doesn't translate into anything that you can make a living at. The same principle is true for the living of life. Often, the knowledge we have doesn't translate into the effective living of life.

Solomon makes the point in these passages that wisdom is increased by knowledge. If we keep our eyes and ears open and our lips closed, taking in what is happening around us and processing it accurately, it will increase our wisdom, decrease our suffering, and increase our joy.

PRINCIPLES

- Foolishness produces a world of pain, both for the fool and for those people whom he influences.
- Our attitude toward life determines whether we can learn from our own mistakes and the mistakes of others.
- Fools resist wisdom. Wise people soak it in.

APPLICATIONS

- Make the decision to become a wise person. You will probably not achieve the level of wisdom you wish for, but you will be better off for trying and failing than if you do not try at all.
- Do not try to deal with a fool on his level. Although you must sometimes deal with fools, never descend to their level.
- When you are confronted with the inescapable fact that you have acted or are acting foolishly, repent and choose to act wisely.

IV. LIFE APPLICATION

The Great Blondin

One day in 1860, a famous tight-rope walker, the Great Blondin, walked across Niagara Falls as a huge crowd looked on. He crossed many times on a 1,000-foot cable stretched 160 feet above the water. Not only did he walk across by himself, but he also pushed a wheelbarrow across. After he walked across and back with the wheelbarrow, he asked a little boy who was watching him in amazement if the boy believed Blondin could take a person across in the wheelbarrow without falling. "Yes sir, I do," replied the boy. "Well, then, get in," shouted the Great Blondin. The boy didn't get in.

Ah, that's the test of faith, isn't it? Action. Obedience. If we truly believe, into the wheelbarrow we go. If we have major doubts, we stay on the ground. The same is true with all faith. If we believe—truly believe—we act. If we don't act, it is because we don't truly believe.

This observation can be applied to many areas of life, including wisdom. When we read Proverbs, if we truly believe the warnings against foolishness and if we truly believe the promises of blessing that come with wisdom, then we will commit ourselves to wisdom. We are rational creatures who tend to act in our own best interest if we truly believe that something is, in fact, in our best interest. But too often we doubt—like Eve, who took the devil's bait—because we are not persuaded of God's wisdom and goodness.

We must come to grips with God's wisdom and goodness and bring ourselves to a point of actively believing the warnings and promises in Proverbs. When we do, we will act accordingly.

This is something we can pray for. Even the disciples prayed, "Increase our faith" (Luke 17:5). We can pray, "Lord, please increase my ability to believe the warnings of Proverbs, as well as the promises, so that I may act more consistently wisely." The reason we need such a prayer is that we sometimes find ourselves in a state of half belief. We pretty much believe the warnings and promises, and we particularly believe them for other people. But we deceive ourselves into thinking that we can play fast and loose with them and not get hurt, not pay too high a price.

This is delusion and self-destruction. Only a clear conviction of right and wrong will give us the resolve to act consistently wisely. So, believe. Believe. You will be rewarded if you do and spared much grief.

V. PRAYER

Father in heaven, thank you for creating within us the capacity for wisdom. Keep us ever mindful of our need for you and the wisdom you so generously offer so that we may approach each situation you bring us with the mind of Christ. Amen.

VI. DEEPER DISCOVERIES

A. Honey

In Old Testament times, the only sweet foods available were honey and fruits like dates, apricots, and grapes, so honey was the sweetest substance normally available. It was therefore used as the standard of comparison for pleasant things, either good or bad (Prov. 5:3; Song 4:11; 5:1; Ezek. 3:3). It was an indication of abundance, so that the land of Canaan was described as "flowing with milk and honey" (Exod. 3:8). Honey was recommended as food but only in moderation (Prov. 25:16,27).

B. Discernment and Understanding

In these verses (10:13; 14:6,33; 17:24), the word *discernment* comes from the Hebrew *biyn*, used nearly 250 times in the Old Testament. It is related to the Hebrew word for "between," and it reflects the ability to tell the difference between two opposites: good and evil, wisdom and foolishness. It is a crucial element in the Book of Proverbs, where so much of the material consists of such contrasts.

Though *biyn* is frequently translated as "understanding," a different word for understanding is used in Proverbs 13:15 and 16:22. This word, *sekel*, refers to good common sense, the ability to think through a complex set of factors and reach a wise conclusion.

VII. TEACHING OUTLINE

A. INTRODUCTION

1. Lead Story: Trust Is Dangerous

2. Context: We must learn to trust God's warnings against foolishness and to believe his promises about wisdom. Otherwise, we might act against our best interest.
3. Transition: When it comes to trusting God, we must rest in his character. If we believe he is trustworthy, we place our trust in him. If we don't, we don't.

B. COMMENTARY
1. Wisdom and Folly
2. Dealing with Fools
3. Discernment and Understanding
4. Knowledge

C. CONCLUSION: WISDOM IS INCREASED BY KNOWLEDGE

VIII. ISSUES FOR DISCUSSION

1. If we truly believe that God's will is the source and center of joy, we will obey him in all things. If you are not obeying him in an area of your life, what do you think it is that you are not believing? What truth of Scripture have you not yet accepted?
2. As you analyze the things in your life that might not be going well, do you think there is an area of wisdom that you have not yet gained? What might you need to change in order to help that area go better?
3. If it is true that wisdom is increased by knowledge, is there an area of knowledge that you would benefit from having? How might you get that knowledge?

Chapter 10

Giving and Taking Advice

Proverbs 3:1–2; 9:7–9; 10:8; 11:14; 12:15;
13:1,13; 15:22,31; 17:10; 19:16,20,25,27; 20:18;
23:9; 24:5–6; 25:12; 27:5–6,17; 29:1

I. INTRODUCTION
Two Heads Are Better Than One

II. COMMENTARY
A verse-by-verse explanation of these verses.

III. CONCLUSION
We're Not Home Yet

An overview of the principles and applications from these verses.

IV. LIFE APPLICATION
Heed the Warnings!

Melding these verses to life.

V. PRAYER
Tying these verses to life with God.

VI. DEEPER DISCOVERIES
Historical, geographical, and grammatical enrichment of the commentary.

VII. TEACHING OUTLINE
Suggested step-by-step group study of these verses.

VIII. ISSUES FOR DISCUSSION
Zeroing these verses in on daily life.

Quote

"*I* not only use all the brains I have, but all I can borrow."

W o o d r o w   W i l s o n

Proverbs
3:1–2; 9:7–9; 10:8; 11:14;
12:15; 13:1,13; 15:22,31;
17:10; 19:16,20,25,27;
20:18; 23:9; 24:5–6; 25:12;
27:5–6;17; 29:1

I N   A   N U T S H E L L

*I*f we are wise, we will seek counsel from others and listen to good counsel, even if it means we have to correct our own behavior. A wise person listens to a rebuke. A fool resents it. Whether or not we listen to wisdom, even when it hurts, often makes the difference between success and failure in life.

Giving and Taking Advice

I. INTRODUCTION

Two Heads Are Better Than One

*P*roverbs: 24:6 (KJV) says, "In multitude of counsellors there is safety." A person does not even have to have a high view of Scripture to see that that is right. Presidents have a cabinet, businesses have boards of directors, and churches have elders, all so we can have the best advice possible.

When we come to hard places in life, we might even wish we could have God's counsel. How many times I have heard people say, "I just wish God would write me a note or give me a vision or something." While God may not come to earth to tell us personally what college to attend or which car to buy, he has given us a vast body of truth to help guide us. The Bible is a God-given counselor, giving us the best advice possible. Our job is to learn the Word as well as we can, being careful to do everything we read in it. When we are in the center of God's will morally, he will surely lead us into his circumstantial will.

The Book of Proverbs is specific to many situations in life. In this selection of passages, Solomon urges us to surround ourselves with wise people and to listen carefully to them. He promises to guide us carefully in that way.

II. COMMENTARY

Giving and Taking Advice

> **MAIN IDEA:** *One of the key lessons of Proverbs is the truth that we cannot make it through life unaided. The sensible person seeks to learn from others, even if advice comes cloaked in the form of a correction.*

Learning from Good Advice (3:1–2; 10:8; 12:15; 19:16,20,27; 19:27; 23:9; 27:17)

> **SUPPORTING IDEA:** *The wise person never stops learning, reaping the benefits of being teachable. But the self-satisfied person who thinks he knows it all is destined to miss many blessings.*

3:1–2. Solomon opens several chapters in Proverbs with a strong appeal to his son to pay attention to the invaluable counsel he is receiving. Don't take these words lightly, but store them away in your **heart**. They are more than mere suggestions: **teaching** comes from the Hebrew *torah,* often used as a description of God's "law"; and the word **commands** implies an authority that demands attention.

These words of wisdom bring wonderful benefits. The fifth commandment promises prolonged life to those who honor their parents, and Proverbs frequently links longevity with heeding the advice of parents (Prov. 3:16; 4:10; 9:11). This advice also leads to *shalom*, a word much deeper than mere peace or **prosperity**; it also includes wholeness, health, and harmony in all areas of life.

10:8. When you are talking, you are not learning. We gain wisdom by listening to **commands**, accepting them, and acting on them. But the opinionated **fool** is full of his own ideas, too busy **chattering** to learn anything. So he eventually runs into disaster.

12:15. What makes the difference between a wise man and a fool? The **fool** thinks he knows what is **right**, so he sees no need to learn from advice. He is the only one who does not see his deficiencies. A **wise** person, on the other hand, is never so sure of himself that he ignores **advice**. He realizes that he may still have a blind spot.

19:16. In Hebrew, this verse contains a play on words: literally, "He who keeps instructions keeps his life." Keeping God's commands is the best way to preserve your **life**. But a **contemptuous** attitude that disregards the instructions of wisdom will end in death. The phrase **his ways** could refer to God's ways or to the hearer's path.

19:20. Wisdom pays off in the **end**. A person who is humble enough to listen to **instruction** (Heb. *musar,* moral correction and discipline) will eventually reach the place where he reaps the benefit of wisdom.

19:27. This verse gives the opposite side of 19:20. The father issues a slightly sarcastic command: "Go ahead and **stop listening to instruction!**" But when you do, you will wander without guidance.

23:9. A **fool** (*kesiyl,* thick-headed, dull) is unresponsive to truth. No matter how sensible your words are, they will be wasted on this scorner. Jesus used a similar concept in Matthew 7:6 when he warned against casting pearls before swine.

27:17. When two pieces of **iron** are rubbed together, one shapes and **sharpens** the other. In the same way, interaction between people keeps us sharp. This principle operates in almost every area of life—business, intellectual, physical, and spiritual. In fact, the Hebrew literally says that **one man sharpens** the *face* of **another**; the benefit can even show up in their appearance!

🅱 Learning from Firm Correction (9:7–9; 13:1,13; 15:31; 17:10; 19:25; 25:12; 27:5–6; 29:1)

SUPPORTING IDEA: *When we are headed toward trouble, a friend will correct us. A wise person will welcome the rebuke, but a stubborn person will only get angry.*

9:7–9. Criticism is one of wisdom's prime teaching methods, but not everyone appreciates it. A **mocker** (vv. 7–8a) will explode if you correct him, lashing out with an **insult**, slandering you with **abuse** (literally a blotch or defect), and hating you. Solomon parallels the **mocker** with the **wicked**, showing that a defiant attitude goes with moral depravity.

Verses 8b–9 depict the wise man's different response. He will **love you** for trying to help him, and he will end by being **wiser** because he will **add** your insight **to his learning**. Here Solomon links the **wise** man with the **righteous** because the two traits go hand in hand.

13:1. The first line in Hebrew contains no verbs, so it reads, "A wise son, a father's instruction." Where you see a **wise son**, you know that a **father's instruction** lies behind him. A **mocker**, on the other hand, is in the last stages of foolishness. A son who can't stand hearing his father's counsel is on the way to becoming insufferable.

13:13. No one can avoid the consequences of his choices. If a person **scorns** (despises, holds in contempt, ridicules) **instruction**, he will **pay** the price of guilt and misery. But if he **respects** a **command** enough to act on it, he will receive the reward that is attached.

15:31. How can a person enter the ranks of the wise? One of the most direct routes is learning to pay attention to a **rebuke**. Proverbs 1:33 explains that reproof can turn you from a path that leads to death, so it does indeed give life. All wise people welcome correction, so you will **be at home** among them when you have learned to submit to wisdom's unflattering instruction.

17:10. A wise person is instantly responsive to a **rebuke**; it sinks deeply into his soul, and he evaluates his actions to look for ways to improve. But a stubborn **fool** ignores words. In fact, even extreme measures like beating often make no impression. The law normally permitted no more than forty lashes, so the mention of **a hundred lashes** suggests that the fool will not change no matter what you do to him.

19:25. This verse mentions three types of people: the **mocker** who has a closed mind, the **simple** who has an empty mind, and the **discerning** man who has an open mind. Even a flogging will do nothing to change a defiant mocker, but observing the flogging may startle the simpleton into learning a lesson in **prudence**. For the person of discernment, a verbal **rebuke** is enough to teach him the needed lesson.

25:12. A **rebuke** does not sound like anything attractive, but Proverbs here compares it to a gold **earring** or some other piece of jewelry. When a **wise** person offers you correction, he gives you advice that will enrich your life if you pay attention to it. His advice will enhance the attractiveness of your life. Paul urged Christians to behave in such a way that their lives would adorn the gospel of Christ (Titus 2:10). Peter told women to focus on the adornment of a meek and quiet spirit (1 Pet. 3:3–4).

27:5–6. In one of the nineteen proverbs that identifies one thing as "better than" another, verse 5 expresses the need for communication and expression of love. A **rebuke** may be painful, but healthy reproof is a way to express love. Even uncomfortable contact is preferable to no contact or to **love** that is **hidden** (closed up or withdrawn).

Verse 6 compares genuine and false love. A reproof that **wounds** your feelings may seem like the work of an enemy. But you can trust a rebuke from a person who loves you. On the other hand, a person who **multiplies kisses** may seem like a friend. But these kisses may mean no more than Judas's kiss if they come from a person who hates you.

29:1. One day the wicked really will fall though justice may seem silent now. A person who is **stiff-necked** and hardened, so that he refuses to repent even in the face of repeated rebukes, will eventually reap the consequences of his actions. When the judgment hits, it will come abruptly, and there will be no **remedy** that can reverse it.

🅲 Valuing the Help of Advisors (11:14; 15:22; 20:18; 24:5–6)

> **SUPPORTING IDEA:** Getting good advice makes the difference between success and failure in any area of life.

11:14. On a national level, bad decisions can produce havoc overnight. So it is extremely important to obtain good advice. The word used for **guidance** sometimes served as a nautical term, describing the steering of a ship. If no one is steering the ship of state, it will soon sink. To be safe, a leader should use the wisdom of **many advisers**, to prevent the mistakes that can allow **victory** to slip away.

15:22. Even on a personal lever, the same principle operates. When we seek no **counsel**, our purposes will be disappointed. But when we seek much counsel, our purposes will be established.

20:18. Proverbs speaks often about kings, so the references to war should be taken literally. Plans will be more likely to succeed if we seek advice. But if you become involved in warfare (**wage war**), the stakes are too high to take a chance on poor preparation. You must obtain the best counsel you can find.

Jesus expressed a similar idea in Luke 14:31, and Christians can profitably apply this principle to spiritual warfare (Eph. 6:10–13).

24:5–6. These verses make the point that raw **strength** is insufficient to give **victory** in combat. History is filled with battles where shrewd strategy overcame superior forces. A wise commander never underestimates the importance of knowledgeable **advisers**.

> **MAIN IDEA REVIEW:** *One of the key lessons of Proverbs is the truth that we cannot make it through life unaided. The sensible person seeks to learn from others, even if advice comes cloaked in the form of a correction.*

III. CONCLUSION

We're Not Home Yet

Sometimes a single sentence can clear our mind, give us balance, set our spinning heads straight. You have perhaps heard a well-known story that illustrates the power of simple truth. A missionary couple was returning from Africa after spending a lifetime ministering there among the nationals. They had retired and were coming back to live out their days. Theodore Roosevelt was also on their ship. He was coming back from a hunting trip, and a band was on the dock playing "Hail to the Chief." Many dignitaries and a huge public audience were there to welcome him back.

"It's not fair," said the husband. "Here he goes to Africa for a silly hunting trip, and the world welcomes him back with all this fanfare. But we gave our lives for the cause of Christ in Africa, and when we come home, there is no one to welcome us and no big fanfare."

But his words were put into proper perspective when his wife turned to him and said, "Yes, I know dear, but just think: you are not home yet."

That is the power of wise counselors. They can make sense out of chaos, bring perspective from confusion, and put one's feet on solid ground. The wise person looks for wise counselors and then listens to what they say.

PRINCIPLES

- No person has enough wisdom to make all his own decisions and get them right every time.
- Sometimes wisdom hurts, but it must be followed if it's right.
- Wisdom will never violate Scripture.

APPLICATIONS

- Look for counselors when you need them. Don't wait for them to come to you.
- Listen to your parents if they are still living. Except in rare cases, they have your best interest in mind and will give you good advice.
- Steep your mind in Scripture so that you can give good counsel to those who ask you.

IV. LIFE APPLICATION

Heed the Warnings!

One of the best things we can do is to keep ourselves open to the wisdom God has for us in his Word and in the counsel of persons he has sent into our lives. Sometimes this wise counsel will come from people that the world might overlook. We should value and stay close to persons who are honest with us, who hold us accountable, and who warn us when we are off the right path.

In 1889, a corps of civil engineers inspected a dam on a river above Johnstown, Pennsylvania, and warned the town that the dam was unsafe. The dam had been poorly maintained, and every spring there was talk that the dam might not hold. But it always had, and the supposed threat became something of a standing joke around town. The warning was ignored. At 4:07 p.m. on the cold, wet afternoon of May 31, the dam broke, sending twenty million tons of water crashing down the narrow valley leading from the dam to the town. Boiling with huge chunks of debris, the wall of floodwater grew at times to sixty feet high, thundering downhill at forty miles per hour, destroying everything in its path. In less than thirty minutes, Johnstown was leveled, and 2,209 people were dead. They thought it wouldn't happen to them, so they ignored the warnings.

The dangers Solomon is warning young people about are just as devastating on an individual level. Criticisms and warnings from those who really care about us may sting at the time, but they will save us from disaster and put our feet back on the path of life.

V. PRAYER

Father in heaven, may we trust you in all things: your warnings, your encouragement, your commandments. May we compare your teachings with "life" and see that you are accurate and true in all you say. And may we be strengthened to follow you completely in all things. Amen.

VI. DEEPER DISCOVERIES

A. The End

Proverbs 19:20 promises that the teachable person will be wise "in the end." The Hebrew word *acheriym* appears often in Proverbs, with various translations. It can refer to physical death (14:12; 16:25) or to the closing days of life when an adulterer regrets his ruined health (5:11). But more often it refers to the outcome of a choice or experience, whenever it occurs.

Proverbs 25:8 warns against suing a neighbor because you might lose the case in the end. Pampering a servant from youth produces grief in the end (29:21), and gaining wealth too quickly brings no blessing when all is said and done (20:21). In any situation, present joy may turn to grief later (14:13). Wine may seem enjoyable at the moment, but it will bite like a snake in the long run (23:32).

Finally, one group of passages renders it as "a future hope" (23:18; 24:14,20). The common thread running through all the passages is the importance of considering the long-term consequences of each action.

B. Beating

The Jewish nation, as well as other cultures of the ancient world, used beating as one of the more common punishments for crimes. The Jews were to stretch the criminal on the ground and apply no more than forty blows to his back, always in the presence of a judge (Deut. 25:2–3). To assure compliance with this regulation, the Jews in the New Testament limited the punishment to thirty-nine lashes (2 Cor. 11:24).

VII. TEACHING OUTLINE

A. INTRODUCTION

1. Lead Story: Two Heads Are Better Than One
2. Context: Throughout the Book of Proverbs, Solomon implores his son to listen to him—or to wisdom—to observe the consequences of wisdom and foolishness, and to choose wisdom.
3. Transition: A wise person will seek counsel from others and will listen to it. A fool resents it. Our response will often spell the difference between success and failure, between joy and misery in life.

B. COMMENTARY
1. Learning from Good Advice
2. Learning from Firm Correction
3. Valuing the Help of Advisors

C. CONCLUSION: WE'RE NOT HOME YET

VIII. ISSUES FOR DISCUSSION

1. Do you remember a time when you faced an important decision and you rejected wisdom? How did it turn out?
2. Do you remember a time when you faced an important decision and you acted wisely? How did it turn out?
3. Who is the wisest person you know personally? Why do you value his or her advice?

Chapter 11

Growth Through Discipline

Proverbs 3:11–12; 10:17; 12:1; 13:18,24; 14:9; 15:5,10,12,32; 19:18; 20:30; 22:6,15; 23:13–14; 28:4,7,9,13; 29:15,17–19,21

| Q u o t e |

"Discipline is the basic set of tools we require to solve life's problems."

M . S . P e c k

Proverbs
3:11–12; 10:17; 12:1; 13:18,24;
14:9; 15:5,10,12,32; 19:18;
20:30; 22:6,15; 23:13–14;
28:4,7,9,13; 29:15,17–19,21

I N A N U T S H E L L

Parents must discipline their children to save them from harm and to build into them self-discipline for the future. Children must chose to respond well to the loving discipline of parents and learn to obey God as they obey their parents.

Growth Through Discipline

I. INTRODUCTION

Tiger

As the twenty-first century opened, Tiger Woods was demonstrating himself to be the best golfer in the world. He won twenty of the first fifty tournaments he entered, meaning he was batting .400 in a sport where most others were happy to bat .040. There are others who are as physically gifted as Tiger. The secret to his success lay in his mental toughness. His success is 1 percent inspiration and 99 percent perspiration. The key is good old-fashioned hard work. The same was true with basketball greats Michael Jordan and Larry Bird. They worked harder than most others. The great athletes press through the boredom to achieve a level of habitual performance that surpasses those they are playing against.

Many of us want freedom: freedom to excel, freedom to achieve, freedom to succeed. But the price of that freedom is discipline and hard work.

The same is true spiritually. Many of us want to excel, to achieve, to succeed spiritually. But spiritual excellence is not an accident. It is the result of hard work. God does not reward the halfhearted. Halfhearted measures yield halfhearted results. God asks for everything and in return promises great blessing. Solomon makes this very clear in his call for discipline—both external, from others, and internal, from ourselves. Self-discipline is a key to freedom and success in life.

II. COMMENTARY

Growth Through Discipline

> **MAIN IDEA:** *Every parent realizes that children do not become mature and godly accidentally. Successful adults generally look back to firm, loving parents who took the initiative to discipline them in the early years.*

A Giving Discipline (13:24; 19:18; 20:30; 22:6,15; 23:13–14; 29:15,17,19,21)

> **SUPPORTING IDEA:** *You may feel that good parents simply let their kids follow their natural inclinations. But children enter the world with a bent toward selfishness and sin. So mom and dad must take the time to teach them what's right and discipline them for doing wrong.*

13:24. Fathers sometimes instinctively feel that love is incompatible with physical punishment. Proverbs declares that the opposite is true. A parent who genuinely cares for his son will be faithful in using **the rod** to punish misbehavior. In fact, he will be **careful**, literally, to "seek him early or earnestly with discipline."

The father who **spares** his child from discipline at the proper time shows hate for him in reality because he does not care enough to teach him how to avoid dangerous behavior.

Proverbs does not endorse cruelty; it emphasizes tenderness and instruction (Prov. 4:3,4,11). And the expansion of this principle in Hebrews 12:5–11 makes clear that proper discipline comes from a heart of love. Human parents maintain this ideal imperfectly, but God always disciplines perfectly.

19:18. This verse is a command, unlike the majority of proverbs, which are simply statements of principles. The Lord commands parents to instruct and **discipline** their **son**. There is no place for a passive parent, particularly in the early years when harmful attitudes have not become hardened patterns. Early correction holds high **hope** for success. Withholding discipline may seem to be the act of a kind parent, but it can actually lead to **death**, either from capital punishment (Deut. 21:18–21) or from the natural consequences of folly, if not curbed.

20:30. A parent does not spank a child to produce pain but to steer him away from sin, and a son with a sluggish conscience may need such a stimulus to spur him in the right direction. The Hebrew here pictures a severe beating, literally "strokes of bruising or cutting." The context mentions the judicial punishment of criminals (Prov. 20:26), and that may well be the meaning here, so that a parent administering a mild spanking may save his child from harsher punishment later in life.

22:6. Christians have explained this verse in various ways (see "Deeper Discoveries"), but the central point is clear: parents are responsible to invest their energy in the instruction and discipline of their children so that they will ultimately follow the pattern learned in their formative years. The word for **train** is usually translated "dedicate," suggesting that we should set aside each son and daughter for God, channeling them toward holiness. Proverbs speaks often of the **way** of life and the way of death, and this verse probably refers to the path that leads to life.

Faithful, skillful training in the early years will normally produce results in adulthood. This is not an ironclad guarantee, however; each adult must choose whether to follow the wisdom presented in his home.

22:15. Since Adam's fall, every **child** has entered the world with a willful, selfish streak. The behavior of an arrogant fool comes naturally to youngsters, and it will not go away automatically. Parents must take the initiative to discourage such **folly** whenever it surfaces.

23:13–14. Discipline includes more than just verbal instruction; corporal punishment is a necessary ingredient in the process. The verse gives a direct command not to omit the rod from our parenting. The latter half of verse 13 may be taken in two ways: (1) the child will survive the spanking; or (2) the child will survive *because of* the spanking. Verse 14 expands on the second of these concepts.

29:15. Here the passage views the need for discipline from the mother's viewpoint. **Correction**, even if it requires a spanking, helps a child develop **wisdom**, the trait that will ultimately cause a mother to be proud of her children. But a **child** who is **left to himself** and allowed to develop however he wishes will become a fool who will cause his **mother** to be disgraced.

29:17. A parent who makes the effort to restrain and train his **son** will reap two benefits. First, your son will give you the **peace** of being able to relax, knowing that you need not worry about what he will do next. Wisdom itself will guide him well. Second, your son will give you joy. The Hebrew literally says, "dainties for your soul," a metaphor for the joyful satisfaction that comes from watching one's offspring prosper and mature in the ways of God.

29:19,21. The principle of discipline for a son applies to a **servant** as well. In the Old Testament culture, many families had slaves or servants who were part of the household. The family head was responsible for helping these family members develop character as well. **Words** alone are not effective; we must follow up with action (v. 19). And a person who **pampers** a servant produces poor results in the long run (v. 21). The meaning of the Hebrew word for **grief** is uncertain.

🅑 Receiving Discipline (3:11–12; 10:17; 12:1; 13:18; 14:9; 15:5,10,12,32; 28:13)

SUPPORTING IDEA: *Once a father corrects his child, the son or daughter faces a choice. How will they respond to the reprimand: by resistance or by repentance?*

3:11–12. God demonstrates his love by disciplining his children. The word for **discipline** in Hebrew is *musar,* which primarily refers to teaching or training rather than punishment for wrongdoing. As in military training, severe treatment is intended to help a person progress, not take retribution for an offense.

When God chastens us, we must not **despise** (reject or take lightly) his correction. In addition, we should not **resent** (loathe or shrink from) his rebuke. This verse is cited in Hebrews 12:5–6, where the writer expands on the idea that divine discipline is evidence of divine love.

10:17. Our response to **discipline** affects others who see our example. If a person maintains a teachable spirit and chooses to pay attention to discipline, he will show others how to stay on the path that leads to **life**. But if he refuses to learn, he will lead **others astray**, with disastrous results.

12:1. Discipline always pinches our pride, and most people instinctively shrink from it. But this proverb calls on us to love **discipline**, willingly accepting it as a gift, an opportunity to learn. The attitude adopted leads either to **knowledge** or stupidity, a dull-minded state like that of an animal.

13:18. The writer offers another contrast, showing the results of heeding or ignoring the voice of reproof. A person without self-discipline is lazy, and he ends in **shame** and **poverty**. But a person who is willing to take the opposite course ends with opposite results: honor and prosperity.

15:5. When a person refuses to learn from **his father's discipline**, he shows that he is a **fool** (*ewiyl,* a coarse, hardened fool). On the other hand, anyone who pays attention to a parent's **correction** shows that he is well on the way to becoming prudent or shrewd in a good sense so that he can avoid the pitfalls along the path of life.

15:10,12. A person who is keeping to the right path will experience **discipline** as a mild corrective, but a person who forsakes the **path** will be hit by severe or grievous discipline. And if he refuses to respond to that **correction**, the end of the road is death, physical or spiritual.

Proverbs uses the term **mocker** to describe such a hardened rebel. The scoffer rejects any attempt to correct him. He is sure that he knows what is best, so he never seeks counsel from **the wise**.

15:32. Spurning instruction is a form of self-hatred. When we ignore criticism, we only hurt ourselves.

14:9. The word for **sin** here refers to the kind of offense that required a trespass offering in the Old Testament system, generally involving some form of restitution. Rebellious fools scoff at the idea of **making amends** for the harm they have done, but an **upright** person is careful to do what is right. For that reason, the upright experience **good will**, acceptance, and approval.

28:13. It is a rule in all relationships, either with God or with people, that confession strengthens the bond of friendship and trust. We instinctively try to hide or cover our **sins**, but unconfessed sin brings misery. When we choose to acknowledge the wrong we have done and renounce it, we will always find **mercy** with God and usually from people as well. David provides a classic expression of this principle in Psalms 32 and 51.

🄲 Keeping the Law (28:4,7,9; 29:18)

> **SUPPORTING IDEA:** *Getting the word from your parent is essential to grow up well, but it is even more important to get God's view by committing ourselves to obey his law.*

28:4,7,9. Each of these verses speaks of **the law**, referring to the law of Moses. There is a logical progression in the trio of verses. First, those who **forsake** God's **law** will usually begin to side with the **wicked**. Lawkeepers, on the other hand, will **resist** lawbreakers (v. 4). Second, those who side with the wicked soon pick up their habits and become **disgraces** to their parents. Lawkeepers, on the other hand, have enough discernment to avoid gluttony and other such vices (v. 7). Third, those who constantly associate with bad companions soon lose the companionship of God, who refuses to hear their **prayers**. If a man does not listen to God, God will eventually stop listening to him (v. 9).

29:18. The King James translation of "vision" here is often misunderstood. The Hebrew word consistently refers to the visions in which prophets receive a **revelation** from God (Dan. 8:13; Nah. 1:1). When people have no revealed word from God, they will **cast off restraint**, running wild as they please. The word means to let loose or to let one's hair down (Lev. 13:45) and was used to describe Israel's reveling with the golden calf (Exod. 32:25). In contrast, the person who **keeps** God's **law** will be **blessed**.

> **MAIN IDEA REVIEW:** *Every parent realizes that children do not become mature and godly accidentally. Successful adults generally look back to firm, loving parents who took the initiative to discipline them in the early years.*

III. CONCLUSION

You Cannot Break the Laws of God

About a year before writing this commentary, I bought a used car. It is a car with one of the most reliable records ever. It rarely needs repairs, and the car can be expected to last for 200,000 miles or more. About a year after buying it, the engine blew. As the mechanic inspected it in the process of putting a new engine in the car, it turned out that the engine was completely impacted with sludge, an oatmeal-like substance that builds up inside the engine if you fail to change the oil. It seems likely, from what the mechanic said, that in several years of driving, the oil had never been changed.

Someone has said you cannot break the laws of God; you can only break yourself against them when you violate them. There are natural consequences that come to us when we break God's laws. Just as a car owner cannot ignore or violate the owner's manual, so a person cannot ignore or violate the Bible, God's owner's manual. All the instructions in it are for the good of the vehicle, or the person, as the case may be. The manufacturer/creator knows how the car/human was made, how it runs, and what must be done to it to care for its welfare. Car owners, and humans, ignore this information at their peril. Solomon makes clear that external discipline, leading to self-discipline, is necessary for the proper functioning of the human spirit.

PRINCIPLES

- Humans are naturally self-willed.
- Self-will must be curbed or we will self-destruct.
- Self-discipline is gained first of all by external discipline.

APPLICATIONS

- Accept the "bent" of your flesh to self-will and self-destruction.
- Place yourself under the spiritual authority of others whom you trust: your parents, the church, a spiritual accountability group, and such.
- Cultivate a tender and obedient heart. You will save yourself much pain in life if you do.

IV. LIFE APPLICATION

How People Grow

One of the most difficult challenges in the Christian life is "how to get self-discipline." You cannot go out and get self-discipline. If you are not disciplined enough, you cannot become more disciplined so that you will be more disciplined. Life doesn't work like that. So if we need more self-discipline, how do we get it? Proverbs shows us a pattern. The easiest way to get self-discipline is to be lovingly and skillfully disciplined by our parents. However, most people reading this were not so disciplined, as I was not. But Proverbs makes several points for us.

First, we are to love discipline. Solomon writes, "Whoever loves discipline loves knowledge, but he who hates correction is stupid" (Prov. 12:1). We must see life clearly enough to know that we need discipline—that it is the path to freedom and success and that we must be willing to pay whatever price we must for it. You must ask yourself what you want out of life. Then ask yourself if you are willing to pay the price. If you are not willing to pay the price, then scratch off your list what you said you wanted out of life because you will not get it.

Next, you must place yourself under the discipline of God (Prov. 3:11–12). As a father loves his son, so God loves you; he will bring discipline into the life of a believer for the purpose of helping him become more like Christ (Heb. 12:5–11). Next, respond to the work of God in your life. Philippians 2:13 says, "For it is God who works in you to will and to act according to his good purpose." God works in you to will something; then you must act. Paul writes, "Do you not know that in a race all the runners run, but only one gets the prize? Run in such a way as to get the prize. . . . Therefore I do not run like a man running aimlessly; I do not fight like a man beating the air. No, I beat my body and make it my slave so that after I have preached to others, I myself will not be disqualified for the prize" (1 Cor. 9:24,26–27).

If you find that you do not yet have the discipline to respond to God at this point, then you must place yourself under the spiritual accountability of others. You must call on friends and spiritual authorities in your life to walk with you through the challenge and hold you accountable to your responsibilities. The Lord never intended us to be able to make it alone. We can only grow normally when we are properly integrated with the lives of other believers, who give us what we need to help us grow, including support and accountability (Eph. 4:11–16).

It is a delicate balancing act. We cannot do it without the work of God in our lives, but neither can we be passive. Our activity takes the form of responding to God's work by repenting of sin when we should, being as faithful as we can at the spiritual disciplines (such as reading the Bible, praying, worshipping, etc.), being obedient to the degree that we are able to all that God asks of us, and placing ourselves under the spiritual accountability of others who will help us grow.

Finally, we must wait for God to bring us the growth as a fruit of the Spirit (Gal. 5:22–23). There are books on spiritual growth that provide broader and deeper help, but this is a general pattern on how God causes us to grow.

I read one time how workmen used to put bridges over deep canyons and gorges. We are told that they would shoot an arrow across the canyon. To the arrow was tied a very light thread. Tied to the thread on the original side of the canyon was a light cord, so they pulled the cord across the canyon with the thread. Then they pulled a rope across with the light cord. The rope was tied to a chain, and finally the chain was hooked to a cable. When they pulled the cable across, they were able to erect the bridge with the cable.

The construction workers started with something weak and gradually built up to something very strong. That is how discipline is developed. We become faithful on a level that we are able (even if that level is only to place ourselves under the spiritual accountability of others who will shepherd us through the process), and God increases our ability. We are faithful at this new level, then God increases our ability again, and so on until we become mature. As we are faithful with a little, God gives us a lot (Matt. 25:14–23).

V. PRAYER

Father in heaven, we humans are naturally self-willed, and if this self-will is not curbed, we self-destruct. We pray you will work powerfully in our hearts to help us lay down our self-will in favor of your will. Amen.

VI. DEEPER DISCOVERIES

A. Instruction

The word translated "discipline" in many of these passages is *musar*, also rendered "instruction, training." Like the word *paideia* in Greek, it emphasizes teaching rather than just punishment for wrongdoing. It can include great tenderness and affection (Prov. 4:1) but usually has a tone of sternness, ranging from a simple warning (24:32) to chastening by the Lord (3:11) or by a rod (23:13). The severity involved in our discipline is not primarily intended as retribution for our wrongs but as a means of toughening and maturing us.

B. Training a Child

Proverb 22:6 is one of the best-known verses in Proverbs, but it has generated a considerable amount of controversy.

The word "train" in Hebrew is *chanak*, which is generally translated "to dedicate." It is used for dedicating a house (Deut. 20:5), a temple (1 Kgs. 8:63; 2 Chr. 7:5), or an image (Dan. 3:2). The corresponding noun is used to describe the dedication of an altar (Num. 7:10; 2 Chron. 7:9) and the walls of Jerusalem (Neh. 12:27). It includes the idea of using something for the first time or making someone accustomed to something. It may be related to a word in Egyptian that means "give to the gods, set up something for divine service."

"In the way he should go" is literally, "upon the mouth of his way," a Hebrew idiom for "according to his way." This has been explained as (1) in accordance with his nature, taking his individual characteristics into account;

or (2) in the way he *should* go, vocationally or morally; or (3) in a manner befitting a child, geared for his level of understanding. Elsewhere in Proverbs, there is extensive discussion of the way that leads to life and the way that ends in death. This lends credence to the second alternative.

"He will not turn from it" has been explained as a promise that (1) he will never stray from the right way; or (2) he will return to the right way, even though he may wander for a time in his youth. The overall thrust of Proverbs favors the concept that faithful parental training will normally produce results, and the young man will build his life on the principles he learned as a child. There are exceptions, of course, and these are apparent in Proverbs 22:3–4,9,11,16,29.

VII. TEACHING OUTLINE

A. INTRODUCTION
1. Lead Story: Tiger
2. Context: Parents can have a profound influence on their children's lives, especially as it relates to self-control. The key to developing self-control is to be wisely guided and disciplined by our parents. But the day comes when children accept the responsibility to govern themselves.
3. Transition: This chapter begins with proverbs that challenge and instruct parents to bring up their children wisely. Then, it transitions into challenging and instructing children to heed their parents. Finally, it moves into counsel for individuals to transfer their spirit of faithful obedience from their parents to God.

B. COMMENTARY
1. Giving Discipline
2. Receiving Discipline
3. Keeping the Law

C. CONCLUSION: YOU CANNOT BREAK THE LAWS OF GOD

VIII. ISSUES FOR DISCUSSION

1. How well do you think your parents brought you up, in light of the instructions to parents in Proverbs? How do you think their performance helped you or hurt you?

2. How well are you doing in rearing your children? Are there adjustments you need to make?
3. How well have you transferred a spirit of faithful obedience to following God?

Chapter 12

Strength Through
Righteous Living

Proverbs 10:6–7,16,28–30; 11:5–10,18–20,23;
12:2–3,5–8,12,21,28; 13:9,21,25; 14:11,19,34;
15:6,9; 20:7; 21:18; 24:15–16; 28:12,28; 29:2,16,27

I. INTRODUCTION
You Can't Buy Wisdom

II. COMMENTARY
A verse-by-verse explanation of these verses.

III. CONCLUSION
Responding to the Light
An overview of the principles and applications from these verses.

IV. LIFE APPLICATION
How the Barber Found God
Melding these verses to life.

V. PRAYER
Tying these verses to life with God.

VI. DEEPER DISCOVERIES
Historical, geographical, and grammatical enrichment of the commentary.

VII. TEACHING OUTLINE
Suggested step-by-step group study of these verses.

VIII. ISSUES FOR DISCUSSION
Zeroing these verses in on daily life.

Quote

"God permits the wicked, but not forever."

S i r   T h o m a s   F u l l e r

(1 6 0 8 – 1 6 6 1)

Proverbs
10:6–7,16,28–30; 11:5–10,
18–20,23; 12:2–3,5–8,12,21,28;
13:9,21,25; 14:11,19,34;
15:6,9; 20:7; 21:18; 24:15–16;
28:12,28; 29:2,16,27

 I N   A   N U T S H E L L

Righteousness and wickedness are two paths in life that lead to dramatically different ends. The path of the righteous leads to what is good, while the path of wickedness leads to what is bad. This is true not only on a personal level but also on a societal level. As righteousness dominates a society, it results in great good for those who are part of it, and as wickedness dominates a society, it results in great harm.

Strength Through Righteous Living

I. INTRODUCTION

You Can't Buy Wisdom

The IRS has a conscience fund which receives anonymous contributions from people who have cheated the government out of money in the past and who want to make up for it to clear their consciences but don't want to risk criminal prosecution. The conscience fund received a check for $500 from a man who included the following note: "I have not been able to sleep ever since I cheated you out of some money, so here is a check for $500. If I still can't sleep, I'll send you the rest."

The guy was headed in the right direction, but he fell short. Wisdom does not belong to the halfhearted. It belongs to those who have given themselves fully to it. Proverbs says, "The fear of the Lord is the beginning of wisdom" (Prov. 9:10). When a person fears the Lord, he doesn't send in half the money; he sends in all of it. He doesn't look for ways to cut corners; he dedicates himself to doing things right. He doesn't go halfway with the Lord. He goes all the way.

In this chapter, Solomon presents a continuous succession of choices that a person has to make between right and wrong, good and bad, true and false. The wise person sets his life to choose consistently the right, the good, and the true.

II. COMMENTARY

Strength Through Righteous Living

MAIN IDEA: *Wisdom is far more than just cleverness; it is linked inextricably with righteousness. And folly in Proverbs is far more a matter of morals than of mental capacity; the fool chooses his own path rather than God's way, and ends in wickedness.*

A Righteous and Wicked Individuals (10:6–7,16,28–30; 11:5–9,18–20,23; 12:2–3,5–8,12,21,28; 13:9,21,25; 14:11,19; 15:6,9; 20:7; 21:18; 24:15–16; 29:27)

SUPPORTING IDEA: *Everyone chooses whether to live a righteous life according to God's standards or to make his own moral choices. God promises great rewards for those who commit themselves to doing right, but he warns that wickedness doesn't pay in the long run.*

10:6–7. Most of the sayings in Proverbs 10–15 are devoted to the contrast between righteousness and wickedness, and most of the verses in this section are drawn from those chapters. In most of these verses, the word *but* connects the two halves of the verse, highlighting the contrast between good and evil.

God gives his **blessings** to the **righteous**, either as his direct gift or as the natural consequence of acting wisely. They are as conspicuous as a **crown** to those around him, and even the **memory** of a godly person will pass on more blessings to those who cherish him. The **wicked**, on the other hand, are characterized by **violence**, and after they are gone, their **memory** will **rot** like a corpse.

10:16. Money alone does not guarantee happiness; one's character determines how we use our money and what we gain in the end. The return for **righteous** living is a rich, meaningful **life**, while the **wicked** earn only **punishment** (cp. Gal. 6:7).

10:28–30. What does a person have to look forward to? The **righteous** can look forward to **joy**, to the fulfillment of their fondest hopes. The **wicked** may have high **hopes**, but they will come to **nothing** in the end.

The Lord has marked out a path for his people, and it is a place of safety and security for those who follow it. But **those who do evil** show that they have chosen another path, one that leads to their **ruin**.

For the Israelites, having a place **in the land** was a mark of security. They were not homeless aliens but people with roots, a sense of belonging, and a refuge. **The righteous** have a permanent place in the land, but the **wicked** will have no such security (cp. Prov. 2:21–22).

11:5–9. Verses 5 and 6 show how different life is for the righteous and the wicked. **The righteousness** of those who are **blameless** or without moral blemish leads to a **straight** path in life, one where many of the obstacles have been removed. It enables them to escape from many pitfalls. But wickedness trips a person and brings them crashing **down**. The **evil desires** of those who are **unfaithful** or treacherous will lead them into a treacherous trap of sin, and then to death (Jas. 1:14–15).

Some people choose to do evil because they believe they can gain **power** that will protect them from unpleasant consequences. But like Haman in the Book of Esther, such people find that God turns the tables on them, and they have no power to prevent it from happening.

A **godless**, morally polluted person may try to destroy his neighbor's character by slander, but a **righteous** person will **escape** destruction by a **knowledge** of God's truth that enables him to live above reproach and respond wisely to the attacks.

11:18–20. A wicked person may be deceived into thinking that he is gaining what he wants, but he will eventually find that he has been deceived. His wallet is simply full of air. But he who **sows** or invests in **righteousness** will reap a **reward** that is secure.

What does the righteous reap? **Life**! And the mention of **sure** or permanent **reward** in verse 18 suggests that this may extend to eternal life. The wicked, in contrast, **goes to his death**. The verbs used here are interesting. The wicked pursues his goal like a hunter seeking a quick kill, while the righteous sows like a farmer who takes the slow but sure route of planting a crop.

God has an opinion about the righteous and the wicked. He **detests** the person who is **perverse**, twisted, or crooked, while he **delights** in the straightforward truth of the **blameless**.

11:23. Starting out with high hopes is good, but the end of the path is what really counts. Along the way, everyone hits high and low moments, but the hand of God determines the final outcome: totally good for the righteous and totally bad for the wicked.

12:2–3. A **crafty** or deceptively shrewd person generally tries to maintain control of his own fate, **but the LORD** ultimately decides our fate. He **condemns** the crafty person but bestows his **favor** on the **good**, as a mark of his pleasure.

Jews valued the stability of being settled in the land of Palestine, just as we value financial security. But this verse points out that we cannot become **established** by illicit methods. We can too easily be **uprooted** like a tree torn up by the roots. The **righteous**, however, cannot be uprooted (Ps. 1:3–5).

12:5–8. The **plans** of a **righteous** man proceed from unselfish motives, and they can be trusted. But a **wicked** person's **advice** cannot be trusted, even when it seems plausible, because it comes from a **deceitful**, self-serving source.

In fact, a **wicked** person lays traps with his **words**, like a murderous ambush. The righteous person gives counsel that **rescues** us from such snares. Truly, words can either be lethal or liberating.

The wicked may try to overthrow innocent victims (v. 6), but God will ensure that they themselves are **overthrown**. **The righteous**, however, are secure. Their **house** or family **stands firm**, a concept expanded by Jesus in Matthew 7:24–27.

Even public opinion generally respects wisdom. **Wisdom** here is the word used of Abigail in 1 Samuel 25:3, and it means sound judgment with integrity, the capacity to deal with the problems in life. People look down on persons with **warped minds**, the wrong-headed inability to think straight.

12:12. Wicked people want the **plunder** (literally, the net) of evil. They enjoy the thrill of trapping some innocent person and defrauding him of his money. The **righteous**, on the other hand, allow their prosperity to grow gradually from deep, firm roots.

12:21. God gives his protection to the godly. The verse promises that **no harm** is allowed to happen to **the righteous**, while the wicked will **have their fill of trouble**. Job's friends misapplied this principle, but Paul (Rom. 8:28,36–37) and Joseph (Gen. 50:20) understood it.

12:28. Although the second line of this verse is difficult to translate, the first line makes the idea clear. **Righteousness** leads to **life**; and though the Old Testament normally speaks of blessings in this life, the verse seems to move beyond to the promise of **immortality** or eternal life.

13:9. Light is used frequently as a metaphor for physical life (Prov. 6:23; 20:20; 21:4; 24:20; Job 18:5–6; Ps. 119:105) and describes here the life that can be expected by the righteous and the wicked. For the **righteous** life is a light that **shines** (literally, rejoices) **brightly**, a fire burning merrily to cheer us. For **the wicked**, life is like **the lamp** in a tent that has gone out; the darkness is so deep that it feels like death.

13:21. Trouble **pursues the sinner** as an animal pursues its prey; you can't escape it. **But prosperity** is the normal **reward of the righteous**. There are exceptions, of course, but a person who follows the principles of Proverbs is on the surest road to prosperity. And spiritual prosperity is guaranteed.

13:25. Food is one of God's tools for showing his approval or disapproval. He supplies not only the minimal needs of the **righteous** but provides as much food as they can eat. Hunger is sometimes the result of sin in a society rather than in the individual (Prov. 13:23), but many families have experienced the effects of alcoholism, addictions, laziness, or irresponsibility.

14:11. The righteous and the wicked have different destinies. **The wicked** may seem to have a solid **house**, while the righteous have merely a **tent**. But all that the wicked has built up **will be destroyed**, while the household of the righteous will **flourish** like a tree ready to break out into buds.

14:19. It often seems that reality contradicts this verse. Too often upright people must deal with wicked leaders, and evil people seem to prosper. But men and women of godly character do win grudging or unconscious respect. And Scripture promises that good will be recognized in the end. When Christ returns, everything will be set right.

15:6. God promises **great treasure** to the **righteous**, as in other verses in Proverbs. But for the **wicked**, their wealth **brings** nothing but **trouble**. The word *trouble* is related to the name Achan, who serves as a vivid illustration of the truth in this verse (Josh. 7:25–26).

15:9. God **detests** the path followed by **the wicked**, but **he loves those who pursue righteousness**. "Pursue" is an intensive form of the Hebrew verb, implying a strong purposefulness, a commitment to follow righteousness.

20:7. A **righteous** man can leave a precious heritage for his children. When they see his example of consistently behaving with integrity, they will be motivated to do the same. And when they do, they will enjoy the consequences of wisdom.

21:18. This verse sounds strange when compared to the New Testament because ransom or redemption there is Christ's payment to atone for our sin. We do not and cannot be redeemed by the wicked. In this context, the thought is more likely that God punishes the wicked for their sin and allows the righteous to go free, no longer suffering at the hands of the evildoers or falling under God's judgment.

24:15–16. These verses warn against trying to destroy the righteous. It simply won't work. The good are resilient, and they will always bounce back. Those who hatch schemes against them will find that trouble boomerangs back to hit them. Proverbs says, "Don't do it; it will backfire!" And such an appeal to self-interest is often the only argument a wicked person will hear.

29:27. Proverbs offers a surprisingly graphic description of the antagonism between the righteous and the wicked. The word **detest** means to consider abominable, to abhor, and is used to describe God's attitude toward idolatry and child sacrifice (Deut. 12:31). No verse more clearly expresses the truth that life is a choice between two paths. A person chooses for God or against him, and there will always be conflict between those two alternatives.

Ⓑ Righteous and Wicked Society (11:10; 14:34; 28:12,28; 29:2,16)

SUPPORTING IDEA: *Like individuals, societies reap the harvest of their moral choices. When morally upright people take the lead, the society will thrive; when leadership is immoral, chaos breaks loose.*

11:10. When **righteous** citizens move into leadership in a city, and **the wicked** who have been dominant fall out of power, there is much reason to be joyful. Commitment to standards of right and wrong provides the best basis for good political life.

14:34. A rise in the general level of **righteousness** causes a **nation** to be exalted or lifted up. This is true directly in the moral sense but also impacts the nation's political life. Pervasive **sin**, on the other hand, brings **disgrace**, a strong word for shame. The only other occurrence of this noun, in Leviticus 20:17, describes sexual sin.

28:12,28; 29:2. All three of these verses describe the impact of morality in national leadership. When people in authority are **righteous**, others have every reason to **rejoice**. Those who are godly can **thrive** (literally, become great). But when the **wicked** rise to power, people **groan** and **go into hiding**, withdrawing to a safer place on the outskirts of social life. The ablest men and women will surface when their quality of life is appreciated, not persecuted.

29:16. When **the wicked** become great and move into power, **sin** and rebellion also increase. But sin is inherently unstable, and the **righteous** will eventually live to **see** the **downfall** of this wicked regime.

> **MAIN IDEA REVIEW:** *Wisdom is far more than just cleverness; it is linked inextricably with righteousness. And folly in Proverbs is far more a matter of morals than of mental capacity; the fool chooses his own path rather than God's way and ends in wickedness.*

III. CONCLUSION

Responding to the Light

The foolish person has the ability to look good and evil straight in the eye and choose evil. It is often impossible to reason with a foolish person because he has already set his mind to reject truth, goodness, and wisdom. Therefore, when truth, goodness, and wisdom are presented, he must reject them or repent. And having already made the decision not to repent, he must come up with whatever excuse or rationale he can in order to maintain his position.

I have never understood this. When I was a teenager, my older brother had rejected the church and Christianity. I asked him why. He replied that it was because of all the hypocrites in the church. I thought to myself what a self-destructive decision that was. My response to the hypocrites in the church was: "I'm not going to let a hypocrite keep me from God." Later in life, he changed his outlook and became a Christian. But his first choice to reject the Lord because of the hypocrites was not a rational answer.

Because the fool often has his mind made up and does not want to be confused by the facts, the Book of Proverbs is written not for the confirmed fool because the confirmed fool will not listen to wisdom. It is written for the wise person, to guide him into fruitful living. And it is written for the person who is hanging in the balance. He may be acting foolishly, but he is not a confirmed fool. He can still be reached. Solomon begs and pleads for such a person to respond to wisdom.

The Christian must tune his heart to hear the Holy Spirit speaking through the Scriptures, convicting of sin and calling to righteousness. To hear truth and reject it brings greater darkness. To hear truth and accept it brings greater light.

PRINCIPLES

- Wise choices bring good consequences while foolish and wicked choices bring bad consequences.
- The choices that individuals make affect society as a whole.
- The choices a society makes also affect individuals. It is either a downward or an upward spiral, each affecting the other.

APPLICATIONS

- Learn a lesson from those around you. Seeing the outcome of their actions, choose wisdom.
- Resist the influence of society to pull you in the direction of foolish and wicked behavior.
- Ponder the influence your choices have on your children and others. Don't lead anyone astray.

IV. LIFE APPLICATION

How the Barber Found God

For the fool, the beginning of wisdom is repentance. Proverbs says that the fear of the Lord is the beginning, but for the fool, he must repent of his lack of fear, his rejection of God. In his book *Release from Phoniness* (Dallas, Tex.: Word Books, 1968), Arnold Prater wrote:

A man I knew who stood behind the second chair in the barber shop was a friend of mine, but this fellow in the second chair, a man about 65 years of age, was about the vilest, most vulgar, profane, wicked-talking man I had ever known. He must have had some kind of fixation on preachers, because it seemed to me that every time I came in the shop, he doubled his output. One day when I went in, he was gone. I asked my barber friend where he was, and he said, "Oh, he's been desperately ill. For a while, they despaired of his life."

Perhaps six weeks later, I was entering the post office when I heard my name, and I turned and saw the profane man. He was seated in a car so that he could see the people walking in and out of the post office. He was a mere shadow of a man, and his face was the color of death itself. He crooked a long bony finger at me, and I walked over to where he was. He said in a voice so weak I had to lean over to hear it, "Preacher, I want to tell you something. I was in a coma down at the hospital. And I could hear the doctor tell my wife, 'I don't think he can last another hour.'" Then his voice trembled and it was a moment before he could continue. Then he said, "Preacher, I ain't never prayed in my entire life . . . but I prayed then. I said, 'Oh, God, if there is a God, I need you now.' And when I said that . . . I don't know how to put it into words . . . but He was there. He came."

Then tears welled up in his reddened eyes, and then he said, "Just think, Preacher, I kicked Him in the face every day of my life for sixty years, and the first time I called His name, He came."

God does not come into a life uninvited, but once invited, he does not have to be asked twice. Repentance is the key that converts a fool into a wise person.

V. PRAYER

Father in heaven, give us grace to repent—to repent of the big sins in our lives, and to repent of the accumulated little sins in our lives—that we may walk in wisdom and not be confirmed and self-condemned to walk in this world as fools. Amen.

VI. DEEPER DISCOVERIES

A. What God Detests
No sensible person wants to practice the things that God detests. Such things are bad for us, and they put us in line for God's discipline. Proverbs gives a veritable catalog of qualities that God dislikes: crooked living (3:32; 11:20), lying (12:22), hypocrisy (15:8), wicked conduct (15:9), wicked thoughts (15:26), pride (16:5), injustice (17:15), dishonesty in business (20:10,13), and a well-known list of seven abominations (6:16–19).

B. Old Testament Immortality
The Old Testament does not speak as often or as clearly about life after death as the New Testament. Some liberal scholars have claimed that immortality was a concept unknown to the Old Testament Jews. There are, however, several passages that intimate the reality of life after death. Job declared his confidence that after his physical body was destroyed, in his flesh he would

see God (Job 19:25–27). In Psalm 16:10, David not only predicted that the Messiah's body would not decay but also rejoiced that God would not leave his (David's) soul in Sheol, or the grave. And Isaiah 25:8 predicted that God would swallow up death forever, a promise cited in 1 Corinthians 15.

VII. TEACHING OUTLINE

A. INTRODUCTION
1. Lead Story: You Can't Buy Wisdom
2. Context: The final consequences of wise choices compared to foolish choices reveal the stark difference between the two. Solomon reveals the difference for the individual between wise and foolish choices, as well as for a society.
3. Transition: If you watch someone else touch a hot iron and get burned, surely that would teach you not to touch the iron yourself. That principle is what Solomon uses to get us to choose wisdom rather than foolishness.

B. COMMENTARY
1. Righteous and Wicked Individuals
2. Righteous and Wicked Society

C. CONCLUSION: RESPONDING TO THE LIGHT

VIII. ISSUES FOR DISCUSSION
1. What choices are being made now by our society that are foolish and wicked?
2. How do these choices affect our society as a whole?
3. How do they affect you as an individual?

Chapter 13

Lives of Integrity

Proverbs 3:33–35; 10:3,9,22,24–25;
11:21,27,30–31; 13:6; 14:14,22; 15:26; 16:7; 17:13;
18:3; 19:29; 21:8,12,16,21; 22:8; 24:8–9; 26:1,3,27;
28:18; 29:10

I. **INTRODUCTION**
Forty-five Seconds to Integrity

II. **COMMENTARY**
A verse-by-verse explanation of these verses.

III. **CONCLUSION**
Rickenbacker's Test of Integrity

An overview of the principles and applications from
these verses.

IV. **LIFE APPLICATION**
Riding the Right Horse

Melding these verses to life.

V. **PRAYER**
Tying these verses to life with God.

VI. **DEEPER DISCOVERIES**
Historical, geographical, and grammatical enrichment of the commentary.

VII. **TEACHING OUTLINE**
Suggested step-by-step group study of these verses.

VIII. **ISSUES FOR DISCUSSION**
Zeroing these verses in on daily life.

Quote

"*It* is never 'do, do' with the Lord, but 'be, be,' and he will 'do' through you."

Oswald Chambers

Proverbs
3:33; 37; 10:7,9,22,24–25;
11:3,4,6,7; 3:1–3; 13:6;
14:4,22; 15:26; 16:7; 17:15; 18:5;
19:29; 21:8,12,16,21; 22:8;
24:8–9; 26:1,3,27;
28:18; 29:10

IN A NUTSHELL

We are continuously confronted with the choice to be whole and upright or to lead a double life concealing a lack of integrity. If we are people of integrity, we will reap the reward of God's blessing. If we are not, our false appearance of integrity will be exposed for what it is.

Lives of Integrity

I. INTRODUCTION

Forty-five Seconds to Integrity

*S*ome years ago, Cleveland Stroud, coach of the Bulldogs of Conyers, Georgia, led his team to a championship season with a record of twenty-one wins and five losses. In their final game in March, they won a dramatic, come-from-behind win that gave them the state championship. But a short time later, a confession was made that stripped them of the trophy. It was not a revelation of wrongdoing but a revelation of right-doing.

In the first of the school's five post-season games, an ineligible player had played forty-five seconds of one game. No one knew at the time that he was ineligible. When it was discovered, the coach voluntarily reported it to the Georgia High School Athletic Association, which deprived them of their trophy. Coach Stroud was widely quoted when he said:

> We didn't know he was ineligible at the time; we didn't know it until a few weeks ago. Some people said we should have just kept quiet about it, that it was just 45 seconds and the player wasn't even an impact player. But you've got to do what's honest and right and what the rules say. I told my team that people forget the scores of basketball games; they don't ever forget what you're made of.

Now, that's integrity. Not only doing what is right but doing what is right even if you don't have to. That is the level of integrity the Bible calls us to—being like Jesus, even when no one is looking.

II. COMMENTARY

Lives of Integrity

MAIN IDEA: *Only God is absolutely perfect, and we will fall short of his perfection in this life. But he does call us to be people of integrity who are whole and complete, yielding every part of our life to him.*

Ⓐ Integrity and Perversion (10:9; 13:6; 15:26; 21:8; 24:8–9; 28:18; 29:10)

SUPPORTING IDEA: *At the root of life lies a basic choice: the decision either to be a whole person who seeks to be consistently upright, or to lead a double life, with a moral shell that conceals a twisted inner self.*

10:9; 28:18. When a person's **walk** or daily conduct displays **integrity** (wholeness, completeness), he or she will have nothing to hide and nothing to fear. He can maintain a carefree, confident state of mind, with a clear conscience. The person whose **paths** or behavior are **crooked** or twisted may succeed temporarily, but his true nature will eventually be **found out**, and he will fall into calamity.

13:6. To a wicked person, sin seems to be the safest course. But the truth is precisely the opposite. A person of **integrity**, without moral blemish (Job 1:1; Prov. 11:20), finds that righteous living is his greatest protection (Prov. 2:11; 4:6; 12:21; 13:3).

15:26. The LORD **detests** evil **thoughts** even before they are carried into action; the plan is as bad as the deed itself. But the plans of **the pure** are his delight. This verse underscores the omniscience of God, who knows our inmost thoughts. It also indicates that justice is not just a matter of natural consequences; God is involved in seeing that justice is ultimately done.

21:8. Here we find a contrast between those laden with guilt and those living in godliness. There is a deeply rooted crookedness about the guilty, while the **innocent** are straightforward and upright. You can trust what you see about a pure person, but the outward appearance of the wicked is always deceiving.

24:8–9. Schemes are the stock in trade of the **evil** person. Verse 8 shows that he purposely devises **plots**, and everyone soon figures out that he is not to be trusted—he is, literally, "the possessor of evil plans." He will lose his good name, and a reputation once lost is hard to regain. And once a person starts down this road, he gets worse. **Schemes** in verse 9 is often translated "outrage, lewdness" (Lev. 18:17; Judg. 20:6). He soon becomes a **mocker**, confirmed in his defiance, and public opinion turns against him.

29:10. Jesus told his disciples that the world would hate them (John 17:14), confirming this proverb. Unprincipled people **hate** the righteous, whose pure lives constitute an unspoken rebuke of the evil around them. They can even resort to violence. The second line is literally, "to seek the soul," a phrase normally used in a hostile sense. Some commentators believe the phrase should be translated, "But the upright seek his soul," in the sense of wanting to avenge the victims.

Ⓑ Reaping the Results of Our Character (3:33–35; 10:3,22,24–25; 11:21,27,30–31; 14:14,22; 16:7; 17:13; 18:3; 19:29; 21:12,16,21; 22:8; 26:1,3,27)

SUPPORTING IDEA: *When we bring our lives into line with God's standards, we will reap the benefits of that commitment. But a false appearance of piety will eventually be exposed as a sham.*

3:33–35. In this section, the writer gives three reasons we should not envy the **wicked**, even though they may seem to prosper.

First, God will **curse** their house while he **blesses** the house of the righteous. **House** here probably refers to their family or household. Second, God **mocks proud mockers**, causing their actions to boomerang back on them. The New Testament quotes the Greek Septuagint version of this verse in James 4:6 and 1 Peter 5:5, promising that God resists the proud but gives grace to the humble. And third, God exposes the fools to **shame**, while he brings honor to the wise. **Honor** in this verse is the Hebrew *kabodh*, which can refer to human honor but also appears as a description of the "glory" of God. The wise not only earn the respect of their contemporaries but will ultimately share in the glory of God.

10:3. Proverbs speaks often of the general truth that **righteous** people tend to be secure and prosperous. Natural consequences serve to explain this truth to a certain point, but godly people know that many circumstances go far beyond their control. This promise depends on God's care, not just our diligence. The first line literally reads, "the soul of the righteous," including not only physical appetite but the entire person and his needs.

10:22. The Hebrew here adds the word *it* for emphasis: "The blessing of the LORD, it brings wealth." Rich people know that wealth often brings complications: taxes, legal wrangling, and newfound "friends" with urgent needs for help. When we build a fortune of our own, all the problems seem to be attached. But when God blesses us with wealth, he doesn't send all the extra entanglements that suck the joy out of the situation.

10:24–25. A wicked person is never secure because his hopes are limited to this life. He must always live with the fear of losing what he has gained. And in the end, he will be brought down by the disaster he fears. On the other hand, the righteous look forward to the future and finally gain what they have hoped for. In the final analysis, what the wicked fear is God himself, and he is what the righteous desire. Both inevitably meet him.

As C. S. Lewis observed, "In the end, that Face which is the delight or the terror of the universe must be turned upon each of us either with one expression or the other, either conferring glory inexpressible or inflicting shame that can never be cured or disguised" ("The Weight of Glory," *Transposition* [1949], p. 28, cited in Kidner [1964], p. 89).

Verse 25 may lie behind Christ's parable of the wise man and the foolish man in Matthew 7:24–27. The image of a **storm** that wipes out the wicked appears in Proverbs 1:27; 6:15; 29:1.

11:21. The verse begins with a Hebrew idiom (literally, "hand to hand") well translated by **Be sure of this**. It is probably based on the shaking of hands to close an agreement. Simply stated, the verse warns that sinners will be punished while the righteous will not. The descriptions have a ring of the courtroom about them: to **go free** or acquit, **not** to **go unpunished** or to be convicted. Literally, the second line reads "the seed of the righteous," broadening the principle to include influence on succeeding generations.

11:27. The key thought here is searching. The verb means to pursue, look early or eagerly for, like a person looking for the dawn. Anyone who **seeks** that diligently for **good** will find acceptance and favor from God and others. And anyone who **searches** for **evil** can find it. We get what we look for.

11:30–31. A tree produces **fruit**, which in turn can produce trees that bear even more fruit. In the same way, a person's **righteousness** can become **a tree of life** (3:18; 13:12; 15:4), a source of righteousness and life for many others.

The verb **wins** generally means to attract or take, but the phrase "wins souls" often means to take a life (1 Kgs. 19:4) or to capture people with ideas in a bad sense (Prov. 6:25; 2 Sam. 15:6). In the context of Proverbs, it would not refer to the type of soul-winning or evangelism that modern Christians speak of. But it could be used to describe the process of luring people into the path of life and wisdom.

In Proverbs 11:31, the righteous will receive their due, a phrase that can sound like a promise or a threat. First Peter 4:18 quotes the Septuagint and uses it as a warning that even a Moses or a David will be judged when they sin. And if the godly face chastisement, how much more will God judge the wicked?

14:14. Once again, both the godly and the wicked will receive what is due them. The **faithless** are literally "the backsliders in heart," who will not get away with their faithlessness.

14:22. Plot and **plan** both come from the same Hebrew word, which means "to plow." Perhaps it pictures a person turning over ideas like a plow turns over the soil as it cuts furrows in the field. The misguided plans of the wicked go astray, but those who plot good will find **love** and **faithfulness** coming back to them.

16:7. Although Jesus told his disciples that they would face hatred from the world (John 15:18–20), the person who pleases the Lord can move through life without fear because God can even bring **peace** with our enemies.

17:13. This proverb portrays the very opposite of forgiveness. Instead of doing good to one's enemies, this person does **evil** to those who have offered him only **good**. Such behavior reveals a wicked heart, and such a person will face God's judgment, so that calamity will persistently plague his household. David and Bathsheba both violated this principle in their treatment of Uriah, and the consequences for David's family continued for years.

18:3. A wicked or evil person soon finds himself locked into an unpleasant chain reaction. He faces **contempt** from others, which produces **shame** and ends in utter **disgrace**. Shame was one of the first results of the first sin (Gen. 3:7). Holiness, on the other hand, is linked with glory in Isaiah 6:3 and Romans 8:30.

19:29. Confirmed **fools** and **mockers** will not respond to verbal reproof, so they inevitably suffer harsh **penalties** (see Prov. 19:25; 26:3). It was for such people that **beatings** were devised.

21:12. **The Righteous One** may refer to God or to a righteous leader, but either meaning leads to the truth that God (directly or indirectly) knows the wicked exhaustively and is able to overthrow them with calamity.

21:16. A person **who strays from the path of understanding**, deliberately turning his back on righteous living, will soon be lost. Ironically, he who wants to roam freely eventually loses his mobility (**comes to rest**), his independence (**in the company**), and his life (**of the dead**). The word for "stray" is used for wandering in the sense of being lost or searching for a place (Gen. 21:14; Exod. 23:4; Isa. 53:6).

21:21. The person who seeks **righteousness** and the steadfast **love** shown by God in his covenant will find what he seeks, plus far more. The idea is similar to Christ's statement in Matthew 6:33. Such a person **finds life** (Prov. 3:18,22; 4:13,22; 8:35), righteousness (3:2,16; 8:18; 13:21; 15:6; 28:25), and **honor** (3:16,35; 4:8; 8:18). **Prosperity** in the second line is substituted by the NIV for the actual Hebrew "righteousness," probably for stylistic reasons to avoid repeating the word.

22:8. The oppressed may be suffering now, but they can take courage in the fact that harvest time will come for the wicked. Those who sow seeds of **wickedness** and injustice will reap a harvest of **trouble** and sorrow. Their overflowing rage will be turned back upon them.

26:1. **Snow** makes no sense in **summer**; it is surprising and inappropriate. But **rain in harvest** is not only unusual but damaging to the crops. Honoring a fool is similarly inappropriate, and it may be harmful to those who take him as a model. He may even believe the compliments and be encouraged to try to take charge, with disastrous results!

26:3. A **horse** and a **donkey** do not respond to the logical pleas of wisdom. You can only spur them to action with a **whip**, and only a bridle can direct their course. In the same way, *fools* only pay attention to force (cp. Ps. 32:9).

26:27. The Old Testament speaks repeatedly of the way deceit boomerangs on the plotter. He who tries to lay a trap for others **will fall** into it himself (cp. Pss. 7:15; 9:15; 35:8; 57:6; Eccl. 10:8).

> **MAIN IDEA REVIEW:** *Only God is absolutely perfect, and we will fall short of his perfection in this life. But he does call us to be people of integrity who are whole and complete, yielding every part of our life to him.*

III. CONCLUSION

Rickenbacker's Test of Integrity

Years ago, Douglas Aircraft was competing with Boeing Aircraft to sell Eastern Airlines its first big jets. Former World War II Ace Eddie Rickenbacker, then president of Eastern Airlines, reportedly told Donald Douglas that the specifications and the claims made by Douglas Company for the DC-8s were close to Boeing's on everything except the noise suppression. Rickenbacker then gave Douglas one last chance to outpromise Boeing on this feature. After consulting with his engineers, Mr. Douglas reported back that he did not feel he could make such a promise.

Rickenbacker smiled and replied, "Oh, I know you can't. I just wanted to know if you were still honest. You've got yourself an order for $135 million. Now go home and silence those jets!"

Now, that's integrity. If we take care of our integrity, our integrity will take care of us. We will not always win since there are people who will take advantage of us when we exhibit integrity, but in the end, God will vindicate and reward us, as will others in this life who respect integrity.

PRINCIPLES

- Integrity, or lack of it, will always be found out.
- Integrity will impact our lives tremendously, sometimes in ways we learn about and other times in ways we cannot know.
- Both God and others will come to our aid if we live lives of integrity.

APPLICATIONS

- What is your greatest area of temptation to cheat on integrity?
- What is the most important step you can take to strengthen yourself in that area?
- In what ways have you seen integrity help you in your own life? In what ways have you seen a lack of it hurt you?

IV. LIFE APPLICATION

Riding the Right Horse

It is no secret that our nation and the American church are in a crisis of integrity. We all tend to conform to society around us. That is the way God made us. This can work for us when those around us have integrity, but it works against us when they don't. One hundred years ago, if we conformed to society around us, we did not live in violation of the Ten Commandments. Today, if we conform to society around us, we violate all of them!

A hundred years ago we could be like the circus performer who rides around the ring standing on the backs of two horses, going the same direction at the same speed. He could do this because the horses were hooked together. If the horses became unhooked, the rider would quickly have to choose which horse he was going to ride.

In principle, the same is true with us. It used to be that we could stand with one foot on the horse of American culture and the other foot on the horse of Christianity because they were traveling in the same direction at the same speed. But about midway through the last century, they became unhooked, and now we must choose which horse we are going to ride. Unfortunately, too many Christians are choosing, either knowingly or unknowingly, to ride the horse of American culture rather than Christianity.

No one seems to notice that as our culture becomes more calloused and aggressive, Christians are becoming more calloused and aggressive; as the culture becomes more tolerant of sexual immorality, Christians become more tolerant of sexual immorality; as the culture becomes less honest and ethical, Christians are becoming less honest and ethical. We drift down at the same angle and speed as the culture around us, and no one seems to notice or care.

Yet, Paul said in 1 Corinthians, "Do not be deceived: 'Bad company corrupts good morals'" (1 Cor. 15:33 NASB). We are keeping company with the world—to a great extent through indiscriminate exposure to electronic entertainment—and as a result, we watch the same television and movies as the world, listen to the same music, laugh at the same jokes, vote for the same reasons (economic prosperity rather than justice and righteousness), and are largely indistinguishable from the world.

It is a terrible mistake, succumbing to the external pressure from the world. Our integrity crumbles when we do. We are no longer what we claim to be—devoted followers of Jesus. Rather, we are halfhearted creatures, as C. S. Lewis said, "fooling about with drink and sex, and ambition, when infinite joy is offered us." Christians must keep a keen eye on the Bible and see cultural drift for what it is, choosing not to go down with the ship, living lives of spiritual integrity.

V. PRAYER

Father in heaven, speak to us through your Word and Holy Spirit to reveal those areas we hold on to in our hearts that do not align with your character and Word, those areas in which we do not have integrity. Strengthen our desire for holiness and our ability to live out those things that you reveal to us. Amen.

VI. DEEPER DISCOVERIES

A. Integrity

The Hebrew word for "integrity" in Proverbs 10:9; 13:6; and 29:10 is *tom*, which stems from a verb meaning "complete." This word and others in the same group describe that which is ethically sound or upright. Psalm 78:72 speaks of the integrity of King David's heart, and he makes this claim for himself in other passages like Psalms 7:8; 18:20; 101:2. It does not imply absolute sinlessness but definitely lays a claim to be on the path of righteousness rather than choosing the way of the wicked.

Job was the preeminent example of integrity in the Old Testament (Job 1:1,8; 2:3,9; 9:21–22; 12:4; 27:5; 31:6). In 1 Kings 22:34, a soldier is described as loosing an arrow "in his integrity or simplicity," or "at random," without harmful intent.

B. Rain in Harvest

The references to unusual weather in Proverbs 26:1 would be familiar to a Palestinian farmer. Israelites started the farming year by plowing their fields when the rainy season began, usually around September or early October. The early rains provided moisture to help the wheat and barley sprout and become established quickly. During the winter months, rain diminished and crops grew more slowly. But a renewed season of rain in late spring brought the barley, then the wheat to readiness for harvest. The actual harvest was timed for the beginning of the dry season, leading into summer. Heavy rain at harvest time could cause the crops to mildew or rot, and the loss could be catastrophic.

Laws of the Harvest

1. We reap what we sow.
2. We reap more than we sow.
3. We reap at a later time than we sow.
4. We must sow and reap at the right times (Prov. 6:8).
5. We must often labor in difficult circumstances (Prov. 10:5; 20:4; 2 Sam. 23:13).
6. Crops first, comfort later (Prov. 24:27).
7. We must keep an eye on the crop.
8. We should use the growing season to prepare for harvest.
9. God causes the growth (Deut. 11:10–14), but we must plant the seed (1 Cor. 3:6).
10. We must focus on the crucial task at harvest time (Ruth 2:21,23).
11. We should diversify (Eccl. 11:6).
12. We must process what we gather (Prov. 6:8).
13. We can rejoice at harvest time (Isa. 9:3).
14. We must share our harvest with God and others (Lev. 23:10,22).

VII. TEACHING OUTLINE

A. INTRODUCTION

1. Lead Story: Forty-five Seconds to Integrity
2. Context: In the verses in this chapter, Solomon contrasts integrity with perversion and calls on the child of God to be whole before him, to be as God is.
3. Transition: Integrity is noble and good, while perversion is callous and bad. We must commit to being people of integrity not only because of our personal peace but also because of the negative consequences that come into our lives when we play fast and loose with life.

B. COMMENTARY

1. Integrity and Perversion
2. Reaping the Results of Our Character

C. CONCLUSION: RICKENBACKER'S TEST OF INTEGRITY

VIII. ISSUES FOR DISCUSSION

1. On a scale of 1 to 10, how high do you think you would rate on the scale of integrity? How do you think others would rate you? What are the areas of integrity that could be improved in your life?

2. What are the sources of negative influence from society that you find most difficult to resist?

3. What actions could you take to strengthen your resistance in those areas?

Chapter 14

Serving with Sincerity

Proverbs 6:12–15; 10:10; 11:3; 15:8,11,29; 16:2,30; 17:3; 20:11,14,27; 21:2–3,27; 23:6–8; 26:23–26; 27:19

I. **INTRODUCTION**
Sing Sing Shenanigans

II. **COMMENTARY**
A verse-by-verse explanation of these verses.

III. **CONCLUSION**
Fingers on the Scales

An overview of the principles and applications from these verses.

IV. **LIFE APPLICATION**
The Cat's Reward

Melding these verses to life.

V. **PRAYER**
Tying these verses to life with God.

VI. **DEEPER DISCOVERIES**
Historical, geographical, and grammatical enrichment of the commentary.

VII. **TEACHING OUTLINE**
Suggested step-by-step group study of these verses.

VIII. **ISSUES FOR DISCUSSION**
Zeroing these verses in on daily life.

Quote

"*Sincerity has an openness of heart;*

we find it in very few people."

Francois de la Rochefoucauld

Proverbs
6:12–15; 10:10; 11:3;
15:8,11,29; 16:2,30; 17:3;
20:11,14,27; 21:2–3,27;
23:6–8; 26:23–26; 27:19

IN A NUTSHELL

God wants us to be authentic, sincere, to serve him and others truthfully, and he frowns on hypocrisy and deceit. We must be alert to insincerity in ourselves and others.

Serving with Sincerity

I. INTRODUCTION

Sing Sing Shenanigans

*O*ne time a lady who had acquired wealth and social prominence decided to have a book written about her genealogy. The well-known author she contracted for the project discovered that her grandfather was a murderer who had been electrocuted in Sing Sing, the famous maximum-security federal prison. He knew that the grandfather could not be left out of the book, so with rose-colored glasses on, he wrote: "One of her grandfathers occupied the chair of applied electricity in one of America's best-known institutions. He was very much attached to his position, and literally died in harness."

We all are tempted to put the best possible spin on things related to us, but Solomon teaches us that sincerity—genuineness, all the way down—is important. God knows what we are like on the inside, and people will find out. These verses in Proverbs show us that God sees below the surface, that he sees through feigned sacrifice, and therefore, the wise will see through duplicity.

II. COMMENTARY

Serving with Sincerity

> **MAIN IDEA:** *Beauty is only skin deep, and so is honesty in some cases. People claim to have our best interests at heart, and they appear to be honoring God, but not all are sincere. God sees the true condition of the heart, and we need to look closely to see whether the exterior matches the interior.*

God Sees Below the Surface (15:11; 16:2; 17:3; 20:11,27; 21:2; 27:19)

> **SUPPORTING IDEA:** *Sincerity means that the truth about our hidden, internal motives matches the impression we try to give to the world. When we realize that our heart is an open book to the Lord, we will realize that we must approach him with sincerity.*

15:11. The Hebrew words rendered **Death** and **Destruction** are *Sheol* and *Abaddon*. In the Old Testament, *Sheol* is the grave, the place of the dead. *Abaddon* comes from a verb meaning "perish, die," and the name itself means "destruction." It is probably another name for the fate of the dead, describing a little of the character of the place. Revelation 9:11 uses it as a title of the devil, and the two words occur together in Proverbs 27:20 and Job 26:6. What is the point of the proverb? If God can see what happens in the realm of the dead, surely he can see what goes on in the hidden recesses of our heart!

16:2; 21:2. Most people think their actions are **right**; we see ourselves as **innocent**. But the Lord **weighs** or tests (same word in Hebrew) our inmost being. He judges on the basis of **motives**: not just what we do but why. As he told Samuel, "Man looks at the outer appearance, but the LORD looks at the heart" (1 Sam. 16:7). He unmasks not only those who fool others but also those who fool themselves.

17:3. The writer uses the metaphor of refining precious metals to show how God tests the heart. The **crucible** and **furnace** purify **gold** and **silver** through extreme heat, and God uses the heat of difficult circumstances to reveal the true condition of our soul. The test may be hard, but it is for our good (Jas. 1:2–3; 1 Pet. 1:7).

20:11. God's rules of life apply even to **a child**. At the earliest age we reveal our character not by our words but by our **actions**. And children can demonstrate purity and righteousness on their own level just as surely as adults can.

20:27. This verse pictures the LORD carrying a **lamp** from room to room as he searches through the **spirit** of a person so that no corner is hidden from his sight. **Inmost being** is sometimes translated "heart" and refers to the whole inner person—mind, emotions, will. The Hebrew word for "man" here is *adam*, and the word for "spirit" is also translated "breath," a fascinating parallel to Genesis 2:7, which describes God breathing the breath of life into Adam.

27:19. The original wording of this verse is somewhat difficult because it contains no verb. But the addition of the word **reflects** seems to be justified by the context. When we bend over a pool of water and view our reflection, the image in the water matches our actual face. And in the same way, our inner self (heart) corresponds to our total self (the man). If a person is good, he will be good all the way through—inside and outside.

Ⓑ God Sees Through Feigned Sacrifice (15:8,29; 21:3,27)

SUPPORTING IDEA: *People have gone through rituals for centuries, appearing to worship God. But he knows whether we are coming to him with a loyal heart or just going through the motions of respectable religion.*

15:8. The Old Testament prophets unite in warning that God **detests** those hypocrites who pretend to worship him but nurture evil in their hearts (Amos 5:21–24; Mic. 6:6–8). Even a **sacrifice** is not enough to win his favor. But when a person has an **upright** heart, a simple **prayer** is enough to please the Lord.

15:29. Because God hates wickedness (Prov. 15:8–9,26), he distances himself from evil people. In effect, he stays so far away that he will not hear their prayers. But he comes near to the **righteous**, near enough to hear and answer their whispered **prayer** (Ps. 34:15,17; 1 Pet. 3:12).

21:3. The Lord prefers obedience to sacrifices (1 Sam. 15:22; Hos. 6:6), and we cannot buy his favor with offerings. Of course, ceremonies of worship are legitimate in themselves, but they are no substitute for the loyal heart that chooses to **do what is right and just**.

21:27. This verse repeats the theme of God's distaste for sacrifices brought by unrepentant worshippers, offerings that mask a person's hypocrisy. But he finds their gifts even more **detestable** when they are deliberately offered with **evil intent**. We are not told precisely what evil motives are in view, perhaps to leave room for several types. Perhaps the person is trying to impress others with his generosity. Perhaps he hopes to bribe God into blessing one of his **wicked** projects!

C The Wise Person Sees the Danger of Duplicity (6:12–15; 10:10; 11:3; 16:30; 20:14; 23:6–8,23–26)

SUPPORTING IDEA: *The wise person is careful to be sincere because God hates hypocrisy and deceit. And the prudent person keeps a wary eye open to detect those who would take advantage of him by false pretenses.*

6:12–15. This paragraph provides a six-part description of a scoundrel or **villain**. **Scoundrel** is literally "man of Belial," a description of a worthless man (1 Sam. 2:12; 1 Kgs. 21:10). The word can refer to a person's destructiveness (Nah. 1:11,15; Ps. 18:4) and was later used as a name for the devil (2 Cor. 6:15). What are the marks of such a man? He is known for having a **corrupt** or twisted **mouth**, full of deceptive words.

He uses his body language liberally; he **winks with his eye** (Prov. 10:10; 16:30; Ps. 35:19), **signals with his feet**, and **motions with his fingers**. These gestures are probably ways to signal his fellow plotters.

But underneath the sleight-of-hand trickery, the man of Belial has a heart bubbling with deceit. His **heart** is brimming with **plots**, even though his external actions may give no clue of the treachery under the surface. Wherever he passes, he leaves **dissension** in his wake, pulling other people into angry quarrels.

And even though the scoundrel may seem to succeed, we may be sure that God will eventually bring disaster that strikes unexpectedly (**in an instant**), quickly (**suddenly**), and with no way to offset the loss (**without remedy**). Whether the verse is speaking of natural consequences or the direct act of God in judgment, we can be sure that judgment will eventually hit the wicked.

10:10. The phrase **winks maliciously** suggests a deceitful person who pretends friendship but intends harm, signaling his accomplices covertly (Prov. 6:13; 16:30; Ps. 35:19). He can cause much trouble unless a person listens with discernment. Such a talkative **fool** (see also Prov. 10:8) will eventually get the grief he deserves.

11:3. This verse continues the emphasis in Proverbs on the consequences of moral behavior. The person with **integrity** who is whole, without moral blemish, is pursuing a way of life that will guide him as a shepherd leads his sheep. Honesty by definition is the wisest choice, as demonstrated in the life of Joseph. Those who are **unfaithful**, on the other hand, are ruined by their own **duplicity** or deceit. This noun is used only here and in Proverbs 15:4 and comes from a verb that means "to pervert, overturn, or overthrow."

16:30. A prudent person observes nonverbal clues very carefully before trusting someone. The words you hear may be a tempting offer, but a wink of the **eye** or a tightening of the **lips** can be a clue that the person is getting ready to trap you with a clever scam.

20:14. Pay careful attention when people are bargaining, and you will soon see that people will say whatever is to their advantage at the moment. The **buyer** will downplay the worth of an item in order to get a lower price, then go home and brag about the wonderful deal he made. This verse is a warning that applies to spiritual treasures as well. Esau's exchange of his birthright for a serving of stew illustrates the point.

23:6–8. The opening section of Proverbs 23 warns against seeking the favor of a ruler or a wealthy man. These verses explain the foolishness of socializing with a **stingy man** in an attempt to share in his **delicacies**. If a man is stingy (literally "has an evil eye" as in 28:22, NASB), he will not change character simply because you manage to get a dinner invitation. He is greedy to the core and is calculating **the cost** of your food, not preparing to lavish any gifts on you. He may outwardly follow the rules of hospitality, but there is no genuine love for you. If you knew what he was really thinking, it would make you want to **vomit**. The **compliments** and flattery you have expended will be **wasted** because he is a taker, not a giver.

26:23–26. Verse 23 packages a warning in the shape of an analogy, and then verses 24–26 expand the concept. At a potter's stall, one might pick up a beautiful jar with a smooth, shining finish. But closer examination will show that it is just a cheap clay pot with a thin **glaze** covering the **earthenware**. In the same way, a person may seem very attractive at first acquaintance, with **fervent** or burning **lips**. His enthusiastic, passionate speech threatens to sweep aside our caution, but the fine words may hide a wicked **heart**.

Verses 24–25 explain that the person is actually **malicious** at **heart** but covers his wickedness with smooth speech. His words may be **charming**, but a person cannot put any confidence in him; the reality of his inner self is filled with **abominations**, detestable traits (cp. 6:16–19).

Such a person is full of **malice** or hate. He may be able to hide his feelings for a time, but they will eventually surface. Then he will find himself exposed before the **assembly**—probably the Jewish assembly that gathered to administer justice.

MAIN IDEA REVIEW: *Beauty is only skin deep, and so is honesty in some cases. People claim to have our best interests at heart, and they appear to be honoring God, but not all are sincere. God sees the true condition of the heart, and we need to look closely to see whether the exterior matches the interior.*

III. CONCLUSION

Fingers on the Scales

Many years ago on the cover of *The Saturday Evening Post*, the famous American illustrator Norman Rockwell painted a picture of an elderly lady buying a Thanksgiving turkey. The turkey was on the scales, and the butcher was standing behind the counter. The customer, a lady of about sixty, stood watching the weigh-in. The focal point of the painting is on the faces, as each has a pleased look. Nothing unusual seems to be going on.

A closer look, however, reveals the butcher pressing down on the scales with a thumb while the woman is pushing up with her finger. We smile because the little tug-of-war seems harmless on that level. We get the impression that they "break even" on the deal, and no one is out. But if we truly use that tactic to gain an advantage over another, it is a clear sin that God frowns on. Honesty is the best policy.

PRINCIPLES

- You can't fool God.
- You can't fool others for very long. Sooner or later, who you truly are will be known by everyone. It cannot be hidden because it is revealed not only by what we say and do but by what we don't say and don't do.
- Honest people must be alert to the possibility that other people may be dishonest.

APPLICATIONS

- Be honest with God, others, and yourself. Truth is the only avenue for happiness in life.

- Serve God with sincerity. Sham and brokenness are the only fruits of duplicity, and how you treat God will determine how you treat others.
- Don't let others take advantage of you. Runaway dishonesty in a society harms everyone.

IV. LIFE APPLICATION

The Cat's Reward

Haddon Robinson tells the story in his book *What Jesus Said About Successful Living* (Grand Rapids: Discovery House Publishers, 1991) about a man in New York City who met and married a woman who had a cat. Actually, the cat had her. She loved the cat. She stroked it, combed its fur, fed it, and pampered it. The man detested the cat. He was allergic to cat hair, he hated the smell of the litter box, he couldn't stand the scratching on the furniture, and he couldn't get a good night's sleep because the cat kept jumping on the bed. When his wife was out of town for the weekend, he put the cat in a bag with some rocks, dumped it in the Hudson River, and uttered a joyful good-bye to the cat. When his wife returned and could not find her cat, she was overwhelmed with grief.

Her husband said, "Look, Honey, I know how much that cat meant to you. I'm going to put an ad in the paper and give a reward of five hundred dollars to anyone who finds the cat."

No cat showed up, so a few days later he said, "Honey, you mean more to me than anything else on earth. If that cat is precious to you, it is precious to me. I'll tell you what I'll do. I'll buy another ad and raise the ante. We'll increase the reward to one thousand dollars."

A friend saw the ad and exclaimed, "You must be nuts; there isn't a cat on earth that is worth a thousand dollars."

The husband replied, "Well, when you know what I know, you can afford to be generous."

Of course, the story is probably not true, but it illustrates the spirit of deception that is the opposite of sincerity. When we feel free to hide the truth, fiddle with circumstance, and manipulate people, we drive a wedge between us and all that makes life meaningful. We cannot have intimacy with people we are deceiving, we may get caught in our duplicity, we must carry around the guilt, and we break fellowship with God. Sincerity—authenticity—is the crucial character trait for God's children, as well as for an orderly society.

V. PRAYER

Father in heaven, help us to maintain conscious awareness of your presence at all times. Help us understand that we cannot play games with you and should not try. Help us to realize the awfulness of duplicity and insincerity with you and with others. May we be honest before you and trustworthy before others.

VI. DEEPER DISCOVERIES

A. Son of Belial

The word translated "scoundrel" in Proverbs 6:12 is literally "son of Belial." Belial comes from two Hebrew words meaning "not" and "worth, profit," signifying worthlessness or uselessness. The word is used several times in the Old Testament. Four passages appear to have the idea of destruction (Pss. 18:4; 41:8; Nah. 1:11,15). In various writings between the Old and New Testament, the word took on the meaning of a proper name for Satan, the most wicked and worthless of all. This usage appears in 2 Corinthians 6:15 and 2 Thessalonians 2:3.

B. Abaddon

This word is translated "Destruction" in Proverbs 15:11 and occurs five other times in the Old Testament (Job 26:6; 28:22; 31:12; Ps. 88:11; Prov. 27:20). It means a place of destruction or ruin and appears only in the Wisdom books as a description of the utter ruin reserved for the wicked in Sheol, the abode of the dead. In Revelation 9:11, it is used as a name for the devil ("Apollyon" in Greek), who is the ultimate source of destruction.

VII. TEACHING OUTLINE

A. INTRODUCTION
1. Lead Story: Sing Sing Shenanigans
2. Context: Solomon warns of the dangers of duplicity and urges sincere service toward God and others.
3. Transition: If you want to have a meaningful relationship with God and others, it must be based on truth—not just on the surface but through and through.

B. COMMENTARY
1. God Sees Below the Surface
2. God Sees Through Feigned Sacrifice
3. The Wise Person Sees the Danger of Duplicity

C. CONCLUSION: FINGERS ON THE SCALES

VIII. ISSUES FOR DISCUSSION

1. God sometimes brings suffering into our lives to purify our motives and bring our lives into conformity with his will. Is there anything going on in your life right now that, as you ponder it, gives you greater insight into how you might serve the Lord more faithfully?

2. God went on record as "detesting" the hypocritical worship of Old Testament pseudo-saints—their sacrifices and offerings, etc. What do you think God hates today when our worship is not sincere?

3. How do you think Christians can help society as a whole be more honest and trustworthy?

Chapter 15

Love and Friendship

Proverbs 3:3–4; 10:12; 11:16–17; 12:10,25–26; 13:20; 14:7; 15:17; 16:6; 17:5,17; 18:24; 20:6; 21:10; 24:1–2,17–18; 25:16–17,19,21–22; 27:8–10; 29:24

I. **INTRODUCTION**
Friendly Paul

II. **COMMENTARY**
A verse-by-verse explanation of these verses.

III. **CONCLUSION**
Choosing a Friend over the President

An overview of the principles and applications from these verses.

IV. **LIFE APPLICATION**
POW Friendship

Melding these verses to life.

V. **PRAYER**
Tying these verses to life with God.

VI. **DEEPER DISCOVERIES**
Historical, geographical, and grammatical enrichment of the commentary.

VII. **TEACHING OUTLINE**
Suggested step-by-step group study of these verses.

VIII. **ISSUES FOR DISCUSSION**
Zeroing these verses in on daily life.

Quote

"*If* a man does not make new acquaintances as he advances through life, he will soon find himself alone. A man, sir, must keep his friendships in constant repair."

S a m u e l   J o h n s o n

Proverbs

3:3–4; 10:12; 11:16–17;
12:10, 25–26; 13:20; 14:7;
15:17; 16:6; 17:5,17; 18:24;
20:6; 21:10; 24:1–2,17–18;
25:16–17,19,21–22;
27:8–10; 29:24

IN A NUTSHELL

Love is the essential ingredient of any good relationship—with God, with family, or with friends. Genuine love is demonstrated in the practical, everyday interactions between people. Be sure you don't get taken in by those who are not truly your friends.

Love and Friendship

I. INTRODUCTION

Friendly Paul

*W*hen we think about the apostle Paul, we usually think of him as hard-driving, no-nonsense, independent, and self-sufficient. Perhaps those are accurate qualities, but he was also a very good cultivator of friends. In his book *Restoring Your Spiritual Passion* (Nashville: Oliver-Nelson Books, 1986), Gordon MacDonald points out that Paul had a great capacity for friendship. He writes:

> The apostle Paul was clearly a man committed to raising up a band of special friends. He knew who they were, and he regularly recognized them for their contribution to his spiritual passion. His friends were a resource upon which he obviously depended and without which he would not have survived.
>
> His address book of special friends would have included Aquila and Priscilla, with whom he occasionally worked and lived (Acts 18:3), Onesiphorus ("for he often refreshed me," 2 Tim. 1:16 NASB), Philemon ("I have derived much joy and comfort from your love," Phlm. 1:7), Luke, and a host of others. Paul's friends came in all ages and backgrounds, and he seems to have taken great care to cultivate them (MacDonald, 176–77).

To hear how affectionately Paul addresses his friends compared to how we address our friends reveals how stilted and reserved we often are about friends. Paul was generous with his praise, affirmation, and affection. The result was that he had a lot of good friends. If we would have many friends, we must take Paul's example to heart.

In this chapter, Solomon's wisdom helps us do just that—cultivate good friends—and not be taken in by those who are not true friends.

II. COMMENTARY

Love and Friendship

> **MAIN IDEA:** *The New Testament tells us that love is the greatest virtue. And even though Proverbs centers on wisdom, it gives love its rightful place as the bedrock of any good relationship—with God, with family, or with friends.*

Love: Foundation for Friendship (3:3–4; 10:12; 11:16–17; 12:10,25; 15:17; 16:6; 17:5; 20:6; 21:10; 24:17–18; 25:19,21–22)

> **SUPPORTING IDEA:** *Some relationships are based on convenience, on shared goals, or on business interests. But the only way to have a truly satisfying relationship is to develop the qualities of love and faithfulness.*

3:3–4. Proverbs 3 begins with a series of command-promise connections. One verse issues an instruction, then the next explains the reward that a person receives for following it. First, the writer speaks literally, "Never let love or faithfulness leave you." **Love** is *chesed*, the loyal love that keeps the covenant or commitment that has been made. And **faithfulness** refers to dependability. These two cardinal virtues of the Old Testament are linked in Proverbs 14:22; 16:6; and 20:28, and both are vital attributes of God himself.

The next lines underscore the urgency of this command in figurative language. Like Deuteronomy 6:8–9, this verse calls on the reader to attach love and faithfulness permanently to his life, attaching them securely around the throat, engraving them on the **heart** like writing on a stone **tablet**.

If love and faithfulness become permanent features of a person's life, the reward will be favor and a good name. **Favor** is sometimes translated as "grace" or "kindness," and **a good name** is literally the word for shrewdness or competence. We will enjoy a good reputation among men, and **God** himself will recognize these character qualities.

10:12. When a person's heart is full of hate, **dissension** is inevitable. He will be unable to stand the other person's company, and the slightest offense will cause a blow-up. In contrast, **love covers over all wrongs**, not in the sense of pretending they do not exist, but by choosing not to let them push you into an angry argument. The idea of covering or hiding is used in Proverbs 11:13 as the opposite of revealing secrets and in Proverbs 17:9 as the contrast to harping on a matter. As 1 Corinthians 13 expands the idea, love does not dwell on faults but bears all things. This verse is alluded to in James 5:20 and 1 Peter 4:8. To balance this truth, Proverbs 28:13 warns against covering up one's own sins, and Proverbs 27:5–6 shows that there are proper times to rebuke a person.

11:16–17. Some people believe that hard-nosed, intimidating ruthlessness is the only path to success, and it may enable them to **gain only wealth**. But that's where their success hits the wall and eventually backfires because they never gain respect from others. But a **kindhearted** or gracious **woman** earns the **respect** that the bully never enjoys, even though she may seem defenseless to protect her interests.

In the same way, a **man** characterized by *chesed* or covenant love will find that his loyalty brings him the **benefits** of loyalty and respect in return. The **cruel man** will find his cruelty coming back to bring him **trouble**. The same word is used to describe the disastrous trouble caused by Achan (Josh. 7:25–26) and Ahab (1 Kgs. 18:17–18).

12:10. Sympathy goes with righteousness. The godly man **cares for the needs** (literally, "knows the soul") **of his animal** and surely does the same for the people in his care. He has received mercy from God, so he shows mercy to others. **The wicked**, on the other hand, exploit those under them. Even the **kindest** deeds they perform are done for their own selfish motives.

12:25. All of us suffer from anxiety at times. Worry can burden us, causing us to bend low, perhaps in depression. Our whole inward self can scarcely stand the stress. But it is amazing how a **kind** (literally, *good*) **word** can cheer us and give us courage to face the next situation.

15:17. This verse is one of a cluster of comparisons that help us appreciate what is truly good (15:16–17; 16:8). If you had to choose between good meals and good relationships, which would you pick? Proverbs points out that the diet of **vegetables** of a poor family is tolerable if the home is filled with **love**. But a home full of **hatred** undoes all the enjoyment that you would normally get from a **fattened calf**, the kind of food normally found only at the feast of a wealthy man.

16:6. Here we find **love** (*chesed*) and **faithfulness** linked again as in 3:3. At first glance, this verse seems to present a strange concept of having one's sins **atoned for** by doing good works, an idea contradicted by the New Testament. The first line could be talking about God's love and faithfulness that atone for **sin**. But the second line seems to be talking about human character traits. Probably the verse as a whole means that God expects spiritual fruit after a person has placed his faith in God. And certainly love and faithfulness, similar to the fruit of the Spirit in Galatians 5:22–23, would be a typical evidence that a person's sins have been atoned for and forgiven.

17:5. We find here a frightening portrait of the person who persists in selfishness rather than love. He **mocks the poor**, forgetting that they are also made in God's image. When you mock them, you mock **their Maker** (14:31; 18:23). In fact, God promises to judge anyone who **gloats over** another person's **disaster**.

20:6. Proverbs draws a bold line between those who claim to have **unfailing love** and those who actually have it. The twin virtues of loyal love and faithfulness are joined here again (3:3; 16:6). Both words imply steadfastness, but love includes overtones of a covenant relationship that drives the loyalty. It is difficult to find a person who genuinely has such qualities.

21:10. Not all evil is just a slip into sin in a moment of weakness. Proverbs shows that people sometimes sin eagerly and ruthlessly. They crave it; it functions like an addiction and causes them to refuse **mercy** even to those who are closest to them.

24:17–18. In Proverbs 17:5, God warns against gloating over the poor. This verse broadens the command, forbidding us to **gloat** even over an **enemy**. Gloating implies an attitude of superiority, and God hates such pride. When he sees it, he may relent and lift his judgment of wrath against the enemy. In fact, he may turn against you!

25:19,21–22. Love is faithful, and you can trust a person who loves you. But nothing but disappointment comes from relying on someone who is not trustworthy in a time of crisis. We rely on our teeth when we eat and on our feet when we walk, but you cannot rely on an **unfaithful** person.

Verse 21 deals with the responsibility of love toward our enemies, an early version of Christ's command to love our enemies (Matt. 5:43–47). We are told to treat our enemy with practical kindness, meeting his needs for food and water.

When we take the initiative to meet an enemy's needs, two things result. We **heap burning coals on his head**, and we receive our **reward** from God, whether or not we ever receive anything from our enemy. Traditionally, this verse has been explained as a description of the intense humbling that our enemy will suffer when he must receive help from those he despises. Some recent scholars have linked it to the custom of graciously giving a neighbor some burning coals from the cooking fire so that they could light their own. Either explanation clearly promotes the need for us to treat our enemies with kindness and consideration.

Ⓑ Friendship: Daily Practice of Love (12:26; 13:20; 14:7; 17:17; 18:24; 24:1–2; 25:16–17; 27:8–10; 29:24)

SUPPORTING IDEA: *Where does love show itself? Genuine love comes into play in the practical, everyday interactions between people. A good friendship is the best proving ground for love.*

12:26. Friendships are wonderful, but it is vital to be **cautious** in choosing friends, searching out (Deut. 1:33) or investigating (Eccl. 7:25) them. If you choose a **wicked** friend and follow his ways, he will lead you **astray**.

13:20. We must choose our friends wisely because their influence on us is powerful. The person who habitually **walks with the wise** will become more **wise**, but the person who associates with **fools** will grow like them and share the trouble that comes their way. Proverbs speaks frequently about the crucial influence of others (1:10–11; 2:12; 4:14–17; 16:29; 22:24–25; 23:20–21; 28:7).

14:7. There is no point in building a close relationship with a **foolish man** because he has nothing worthwhile to offer. **You will not find knowledge** or wise advice **on his lips**. It is better to **stay away** from him.

17:17. Some translations connect the two lines of this verse with "but," contrasting friends with brothers. But the point is evidently that both a **friend** and a **brother** are valuable supports because they will remain faithful even in a crisis.

18:24. The first line of this verse is difficult to translate, but a literal rendering is "a man of friends [is] to be shattered or broken in pieces." In other words, a person who has chosen a wide circle of friends indiscriminately will eventually get in trouble, and his many acquaintances will do nothing to rescue him. But in the second line the writer uses a more intimate word for friend—literally, one who loves. It is better to have one true friend than a dozen disloyal companions.

24:1–2. Proverbs elsewhere warns against **envy** of the **wicked** (23:17; 24:19). Here the command is not based on the harmful consequences; we should avoid it simply because it is wrong. The writer offers a close-up view of the sinner, obsessed with evil. Such a person has a heart that is continually plotting **violence**, and his conversation never strays far from plans to make **trouble** for others.

25:16–17. Proverbs in these verses gives the same advice about honey and friends; both are wonderful, but too much of a good thing makes you sick. God has created sweet delicacies like **honey** for his people to enjoy, but in moderation. Eat **too much**, and you won't want to see any more.

The same principle applies to friendship. Visits from friends are a pleasure, but if you are always at the **neighbor's house**, he will soon **hate** to see you coming.

27:8–10. A mother **bird** and her babies belong in the nest until they have grown mature enough to survive on their own. If the mother **strays**, the young will be unprotected; if the baby birds leave, they will be unable to fend for themselves. In the same way, a father and his children should not wander from the home. A father who does so abandons his responsibilities. The prodigal son learned that independent living was harder than he expected (Luke 15:11–32).

Perfume and incense were often used for festive occasions, for times of joyful celebration (Eccl. 2:10). In the same way, a **friend** who gives good **counsel** is just as pleasant and satisfying.

Proverbs 27:10 is not a slap at family members but an exaltation of friends. Citizens of Israel maintained close family ties, so a person would normally go to a relative in a time of **disaster**. But this verse instructs the reader to seek help from a neighbor instead. The third line explains the rationale: a brother may be too **far away** to help, so it is legitimate and wise to **go** to a **neighbor** instead.

29:24. According to Leviticus 5:1, if a person has direct knowledge of a crime and hears a public call to come to testify about the matter, he is obligated to do so. If he fails to come forward, he is guilty before God and the court. A curse is pronounced on such a person. Being an **accomplice of a thief** would put a person in a terrible predicament: he does not dare **testify** because he will incriminate himself, but he falls under a curse if he refuses to tell the truth. How much better to avoid friendships with criminals so we can avoid such dilemmas!

> **MAIN IDEA REVIEW:** *The New Testament tells us that love is the greatest virtue. And even though Proverbs centers on wisdom, it gives love its rightful place as the bedrock of any good relationship—with God, with family, or with friends.*

III. CONCLUSION

Choosing a Friend over the President

Sam Rayburn, Speaker of the House of Representatives longer than any other man in history in the middle part of the twentieth century, was a man of clear priorities. The teenage daughter of a friend of his died suddenly one night. Early the next morning the man heard a knock on his door, and when he opened it, there was Mr. Rayburn standing outside.

The speaker said, "I just came by to see what I could do to help."

The father replied in his deep grief, "I don't think there is anything you can do, Mr. Speaker. We are making all the arrangements."

"Well," Mr. Rayburn said, "have you had your coffee this morning?"

The man replied that they had not taken time for breakfast. So Mr. Rayburn said that he could at least make the coffee. While he was working in the kitchen, the man came in and said, "Mr. Speaker, I thought you were supposed to be having breakfast at the White House this morning."

"I was," he said, "but I called the President and told him I had a friend who was in trouble, and I couldn't come."

When Solomon said, "A friend loves at all times" (Prov. 17:17), this is exactly the type of thing he was talking about. Someone said, "A friend is one who walks in when others are walking out." To be a true friend, we've got to be prepared to walk into another person's life when he needs a friend.

PRINCIPLES

- As honey attracts bees, so genuine, biblical love attracts friends.
- Selfishness destroys friends.
- No person will be totally happy, fulfilled, or successful without good friends.

APPLICATIONS

- Your spouse is your potential best friend. Cultivate him or her. Your life will be immeasurably enriched if you do.
- Plan a first step to take in cultivating the welfare of old friends.
- Plan a first step to take in cultivating new friends.

IV. LIFE APPLICATION

POW Friendship

We all need friends if we are to have joy and achieve success in life. However, we often don't realize it, or we are not willing to pay the price of vulnerability—for a person must be vulnerable if he is to have friends. But prisoners of war are placed in circumstances so demanding that they must either cultivate friends or die. As a result, we can often learn from them the fine art of friendship. In a book, *Winning Life's Toughest Battles* (New York: McGraw Hill, 1986), author Julius Segal writes of the experience of Vice Admiral James B. Stockdale, a heroic survivor of 2,714 days as a POW in Vietnam.

On one occasion, Stockdale was handcuffed with his arms behind his back with his legs in irons and was taken out into the bright sunlight of the courtyard so other prisoners could see what happened to those who did not cooperate with the enemy.

The heat sapped his strength as he lay there for three days, but whenever he tried to sleep, the guards beat him mercilessly. As Stockdale neared his breaking point, he heard a towel snapping out in a prison code the letters: GBUJS. It stood for, "God bless you, Jim Stockdale." It was a message he would never forget, and it gave him renewed strength to endure.

Segal writes:

In every episode of captivity in recent American history, POWs and hostages have been sustained by ingeniously improvised lifelines of communication. In Vietnam, a clever tap code, in which the number and sequence of taps spelled out letters of the alphabet, became the prisoners' chief means of communication. It was this code that sustained Jim Stockdale.

Companionship, human friendship, is necessary for survival when circumstances are severe. Segal reports a study of over two thousand people who survived trauma, including physical abuse, rape, or the death of a loved one. Survivors were healthier if they managed to confide in someone about the event. Those who hadn't discussed their experiences developed more illness of various sorts, from headaches to lung disease.

Yet, in the face of this truth, Christians are often friendless. Chuck Swindoll tells the story of a recent convert to Christianity who said something to the effect of: "You know, the only thing I miss [from my former life] is the fellowship I used to have with all the guys down at the tavern. We used to sit around, laugh, and drink a pitcher of beer, tell stories, and let our hair down. I can't find fellowship like that with Christians."

There is something that seems to stifle Christians, especially men. Whether it is the fear of being condemned by others or of taking ourselves too seriously, we often don't enjoy the friendship of others the way we might. Like the apostle Paul, we would benefit from working at it harder.

V. PRAYER

Father in heaven, help us to be the kind of people who have friends because we are a friend. Help us to so encourage and affirm others that their lives will be deeply enriched and that friendship will naturally return to us from them. May our lives be enriched through our friends, and may our friends be enriched through us. Amen.

VI. DEEPER DISCOVERIES

A. Love

Proverbs generally uses two different words for love. *Chesed* appears in 3:3; 16:6; and 20:6. It refers to love, mercy, or kindness either from man to man or from God to man. It is used to describe Ruth (Ruth 1:8–9; 2:11–12; 3:10), Rahab (Josh. 2:12), and David (2 Sam. 9:1,3,7). It may be given freely because of the merciful nature of the giver, but it is often connected with covenants such as the agreement between David and Jonathan (1 Sam. 20:8,14–15). When the word is applied to God, it often appears in connection with his covenants. The Lord shows his love to his people because he has made a covenant with them (Exod. 20:6; 34:6–7; Deut. 5:10).

The other word for love is *'ahab*, which means "to breathe after, to lust, to be attached, to delight, to love." It is used in Proverbs 10:12 and 15:17. The range of meaning is broad and may cover anything from God's love toward his people to the carnal appetites of a lazy glutton. The great commandment of Deuteronomy 6:5 asks Israel to love God using this word, and a form of it is used when 2 Chronicles 20:7 calls Abraham the "friend" of God.

B. Friend

The Hebrew word *re'a* is the most common word for friend, used 187 times in the Old Testament. It is translated both "friend" and "neighbor," appearing in Proverbs 12:26; 17:17; and 27:9–10. It can refer to a wide range of levels of intimacy, from Job's three friends or a chance acquaintance (Exod. 2:13; Judg. 7:13) to a much closer friend, though the word is not used to describe David and Jonathan's friendship. This is the word used in Leviticus 19:18, which Christ quoted in Matthew 22:39, "Love your neighbor as yourself."

VII. TEACHING OUTLINE

A. INTRODUCTION

1. Lead Story: Friendly Paul
2. Context: Friends enrich life immeasurably. Good friends must be cultivated, and bad people don't make good friends. So choose wisely and work hard at making friends.
3. Transition: The key to being a friend is love. Love is "the steadfast direction of my will toward the good of another." If we are prepared to do that, we will not lack for friends.

B. COMMENTARY

1. Love: Foundation for Friendship
2. Friendship: Daily Practice of Love

C. CONCLUSION: CHOOSING A FRIEND OVER THE PRESIDENT

VIII. ISSUES FOR DISCUSSION

1. How many good friends do you have? How many casual friends do you have? Do you wish you had more?
2. If you have all you need or want, why do you think you do? If you don't have all you want, why do you think you do not?
3. Do you have old friendships that you need to keep in better repair? How could you do that? Do you have new friendships you need to make? How could you do that?

Chapter 16

Selfish Self-Destruction

Proverbs 11:2; 12:9; 13:7,10; 14:30; 15:25; 16:5,18–19; 18:1,12; 19:10; 20:9; 21:4,24; 22:4; 24:19–20; 25:27; 26:16; 27:2,4,21; 28:25; 29:23

I. **INTRODUCTION**
Uncle Zeke's Horseshoe

II. **COMMENTARY**
A verse-by-verse explanation of these verses.

III. **CONCLUSION**
Killed by Envy

An overview of the principles and applications from these verses.

IV. **LIFE APPLICATION**
Selfish from Birth

Melding these verses to life.

V. **PRAYER**
Tying these verses to life with God.

VI. **DEEPER DISCOVERIES**
Historical, geographical, and grammatical enrichment of the commentary.

VII. **TEACHING OUTLINE**
Suggested step-by-step group study of these verses.

VIII. **ISSUES FOR DISCUSSION**
Zeroing these verses in on daily life.

Quote

"*Pride is the mother hen under which all other sins*

are hatched."

C .   S .   L e w i s

Proverbs
11:2; 12:9; 13:7,10; 14:30;
15:25; 16:5,18–19; 18:1,12;
19:10; 20:9; 21:4,24; 22:4;
24:19–20; 25:27; 26:16;
27:2,4,21; 28:25; 29:23

I N   A   N U T S H E L L

Pride is the root of our conflicts with the Lord and with others. When we put self rather than God at the center of our lives, we condemn ourselves to conflict with others and opposition to God.

Selfish Self-Destruction

I. INTRODUCTION

Uncle Zeke's Horseshoe

*P*ride is a subtle sin. In fact, it has been said it is the only disease that makes everyone sick except the person who has it. Vance Havner, a well-known preacher of years ago, said, "An egotist is a person who talks so much about himself that you don't have a chance to talk about yourself." Yes, pride is a subtle sin.

And those infected with it have difficulty admitting it. Jess Moody, in his book *A Drink at Joel's Place* (Waco, Tex.: Word Books, 1967), told the story of his Uncle Zeke, who could never admit he was wrong, no matter what.

One day, Uncle Zeke was walking along the street, and he happened to shuffle into the blacksmith's shop, sawdust all over the floor. What he didn't know was, just before he got there, the blacksmith had been working with an uncooperative horseshoe and beat on it until it was black. It was still hot, but it wouldn't cooperate, so he tossed it over in the sawdust. Zeke walked in, looked down and saw that black horseshoe. He picked it up, not knowing it was still hot. Naturally he dropped it very fast. The old blacksmith looked over his glasses and said, "Kinda hot, ain't it, Zeke?" Zeke replied, "Nope, just don't take me long to look at a horseshoe."

Yet, subtle as it is and difficult to admit as it is, pride can be a damaging and even deadly sin. Solomon warns us about pride and its cousins: jealously, greed, and envy. He gives us ample reason to conclude that they are devastating sins that we would do well to repent of.

II. COMMENTARY

Selfish Self-Destruction

> **MAIN IDEA:** *The core attitude of sin is self-centeredness. We choose to put ourselves in the center of the universe, to seat ourselves on the throne of our lives. And when we do, we ruin our chances for healthy relationships with other people and place ourselves in the crosshairs of God's judgment.*

Pride and Humility (11:2; 12:9; 13:7,10; 15:25; 16:5,18–19; 18:12; 19:10; 20:9; 21:4,24; 22:4; 25:27; 26:16; 27:2,21; 29:23)

> **SUPPORTING IDEA:** *Pride was the keynote of Satan's original rebellion against God, and it is the root of our conflicts with the Lord and with others. You might say that pride is self-centeredness turned outward.*

11:2. **Pride** ultimately loses what it seeks. The arrogant person seeks honor, but he eventually stumbles into **disgrace**. But the person with **humility** is blessed not only with the glory that we might expect to see mentioned but with **wisdom** itself.

12:9. This is the first of nineteen verses in Proverbs that draw a contrast by declaring that one thing is **better** than another. A person filled with himself may put on a show of prosperity even though he has no income to back his flashy lifestyle. But it is far better to keep a low profile yet be prosperous enough to afford a servant. Pick reality over appearance every time!

13:7. Another proverb reminds us that appearances are deceiving. Conceit will motivate a person to adopt a lavish lifestyle, even though he actually has **nothing**. The word **pretends** probably refers not to playacting the part of a **rich** person but actually to adopting a rich man's pattern of life. This was harder to do before credit cards were introduced. Other people, wiser people, adopt a frugal lifestyle even though they have **great wealth**.

13:10. The word for **pride** in this verse is related to the word "to boil or cook." It involves an unyielding arrogance, an inflated opinion of oneself that claims to know it all. It appears as an ingredient in all **quarrels**. The wise person is humble and teachable enough to **take advice**, and his actions show up by contrast the closed mind of the egotist.

15:25. The word for **proud** here means "to be lifted up," a fitting description of a person who rises by pushing others down. An unprotected person, like an orphan or a widow, is their natural prey. They accumulate possessions by infringing on a widow's property. However, God declares himself to be the protector of the helpless; he **tears down** the oppressor's **house** but preserves the **boundaries** of the widow's land. Land in ancient Israel was a precious commodity with carefully marked boundary lines to ensure that the property would remain permanently in the hands of the original owner.

16:5. Pride is a serious evil, not just an inconvenient imperfection. It stands high in the list of things that the Almighty **detests** (see Prov. 6:17). **Be sure of this** is literally "hand to hand," a reference to the practice of clasping hands to seal a deal. God has committed himself to bring judgment on the proud, right alongside more noticeable sinners like adulterers (6:29) and perjurers (19:5).

16:18–19. This is undoubtedly the most commonly (and inaccurately) quoted verse on pride. The words used for **pride** and **haughty spirit** both carry the concept of height, of lifting ourselves up. But in the moral realm, what goes up does come down. The Lord warns that the prideful path will end in **destruction** or downfall.

In fact, the fate of the proud is so fearful that it is **better** to avoid it, even if that means taking a place among the **lowly** and **oppressed**. This verse links pride with robbery, a self-centered act that ignores the rights of others. But it points out that even if you **share** the **plunder** temporarily, your gains will be short-lived.

18:12. Even though God has warned the proud person that judgment is coming, the arrogant man assumes he is invulnerable. But disaster is likely to strike at the moment of apparent security, and all the glory will be gone. The humble person, on the other hand, can be assured that **honor** will eventually be his reward.

19:10. Pride often arises when a person is promoted beyond what he deserves. He is unworthy of the power he wields, and the situation is inappropriate. Neither **luxury** nor honor (26:1) is fitting for a **fool**. And it is even worse to install a **slave** as ruler over those who deserve to rule. He is unqualified to lead (cp. 17:2; Eccl. 10:7).

20:9. In various psalms in the Book of Psalms, David claimed to be innocent. But the full record of his experience shows that he realized the truth of this proverb. No one can truthfully claim to have kept a completely **pure** heart, totally **clean** and free from **sin**. As Romans 3:23 points out, everyone has sinned. This proverb serves as a warning not to trust others naively, as well as a reminder that we need to be aware of our own sinfulness.

21:4. An arrogant person may justify his pride by declaring that a person needs to be proud in order to make it through life. For him, **haughty eyes and a proud heart** are the very things that serve as a **lamp** through the darkness. In other passages, "lamp" serves as a metaphor for physical life (6:23; 21:4; 20:20; 24:20) and the hope that goes with life. But what the **wicked** calls life, God calls **sin**!

21:24. When we pile up the synonyms for **pride** and watch them combined in one person, we will describe that person as the worst kind of fool

("**Mocker**" is his name). By definition, he is verbally offensive, aggressive, and insolent. And his words show his attitude toward God.

22:4. The good things in this life proceed from **humility** toward God, which leads to the **fear of the LORD**. A person who fears God cannot be full of selfish pride at the same time. He is in precisely the state that God can bless. **Wealth**, prosperity, and **life** are also described as the results of righteousness (21:21), showing the close connection between humility, fear of the Lord, and righteousness.

25:27. Though the Hebrew in the second line is difficult, the main thought of this verse is clear. **Honey** is sweet, but **too much** honey is not good (25:16; 27:7). And seeking to exalt yourself too much is also unhealthy. Self-promotion is seldom convincing; it may produce notoriety but not honor.

26:16. Pride goes with laziness, for the sluggard thinks that avoiding work is the surest proof of his wisdom. **Seven men** is a figurative way to say "anyone"; the sluggard considers himself the wisest of all. To the discerning listener, however, it is clear that his answers lack discretion (literally, taste).

27:2. Praise here comes from the Hebrew *hallel,* from which we get "hallelujah." When we regularly sing our own praises, we are motivated by pride (or insecurity) and obviously feel the need to make sure everyone else recognizes our excellence. If there is real merit, others will notice and carry the word for you. John 12:43 explains that we should seek God's praise, not the adulation of men.

27:21. The heat of a **crucible** both tests and refines the **silver** or **gold** subjected to it. In the same way, we are tested when we receive **praise**: gloating reveals an arrogant spirit, but a humble spirit will accept the praise modestly, giving credit to others who have made success possible. This principle is illustrated by the reactions of Saul and David when they heard the songs about their exploits in 1 Samuel 18:7.

29:23. God consistently operates on the principle that the first shall be last and the last first (Matt. 19:30), even in the Old Testament. The proud man tries to elevate himself, but God **brings him low**. The one with a **lowly** (same word used in the first line) **spirit** will be raised to a position of **honor**. One reason God chooses to break down pride is that it motivates a person to live independently of him.

🅱 Other Offspring of Selfishness (14:30; 18:1; 24:19–20; 27:4; 28:25)

SUPPORTING IDEA: *When we adopt the humanistic philosophy that puts man rather than God at the center of things, we doom ourselves to a life characterized by jealousy, envy, and greed. Even our charitable deeds will be tainted because they are done with self-centered motives.*

14:30. Corrosive attitudes will eventually eat away at physical health, ruining both soul and body (15:13,30; 17:22; 18:14). A **heart at peace** renews physical well-being, but the **envy** that churns with the urge to have what you see in others will cause harm to the body, even to the point of deteriorating **bones** (3:8; 12:4; 14:30; 15:30; 16:24; 17:22). Surely it is no sacrifice to relinquish our envious spirit.

18:1. The **unfriendly man** is more than merely withdrawn; he is a divisive person who splits up relationships. The term *unfriendly* comes from a verb meaning "to separate." He pursues his own **selfish** agenda, rather than thinking of the good of the whole group, and he **defies** or mocks (1:26; 17:5; 30:17) those who present more sensible plans.

24:19–20. It is natural for lovers of truth to be disturbed when they see wicked people thumbing their nose at God and his laws—and apparently getting away with it! But Scripture consistently warns us not to envy or **fret** over the **wicked** (Ps. 37:1,7–8; Prov. 23:17; 24:1). The word *fret* comes from the verb "to burn" and means to be infuriated, to burn with resentment. Believers are tempted not only to rage but also to be **envious**, secretly wishing to enjoy them.

The antidote to anger or envy is trust in God and confidence in what he says about the fate of the wicked. Their lives will be **snuffed out**, just as a person extinguishes a **lamp**. And since the wicked have **no future hope** beyond this life, death ends any good they may appear to have. By implication, we can see that the righteous have hope beyond the grave as receivers of eternal life.

27:4. Jealousy in Scripture is usually a good thing, an appropriate intolerance of anything that would disrupt an intimate relationship. It is a mark of love, the opposite of indifference. But this verse describes jealousy that has turned into an intense form of anger. **Anger** can be **cruel**, and **fury** can cause you to cower in fear. But when jealousy is added to anger, there is little hope of appeasing it with apologies or appeals to reason (Prov. 6:32–35; Song 8:6–7).

28:25. A **greedy** person is literally "large of soul," with an uncontrolled appetite for more and more things. Such a selfish attitude inevitably leads to **dissension** and strife as people compete for everything. A person **who trusts in the LORD**, on the other hand, can wait for God to satisfy his desires. He does not need to cause discord and will eventually find that God richly meets his needs (Matt. 6:19–34).

MAIN IDEA REVIEW: *The core attitude of sin is self-centeredness. We choose to put ourselves in the center of the universe, to seat ourselves on the throne of our life. And when we do, we ruin our chances for healthy relationships with other people and place ourselves in the crosshairs of God's judgment.*

III. CONCLUSION

Killed by Envy

James Packer once said, "Envy is one of the most cancerous and soul-destroying vices there is. . . . It is terribly potent, for it feeds and is fed by pride, the taproot of our fallen nature." Billy Graham once observed that envy can ruin reputations, split churches, and cause murders. Envy can shrink our circle of friends, ruin our business, and dwarf our souls. It is poisonous to the heart and damaging to relationships. It is a sin we should forsake because it can destroy the sinner.

According to an ancient Greek legend, a certain athlete ran well but placed second in the race. The winner was encompassed with praise, and eventually a statue was erected in his honor. Envy ate away at the second-place runner who deeply resented the winner and could think of little else. Eventually, he decided to destroy the statue of the winner.

Night after night, he went to the statue under cover of darkness, chiseling away at the base to weaken the foundation. But one night as he chiseled in violent anger, he went too far. The heavy marble statue teetered on its base and crashed down on the disgruntled athlete. He died beneath the weight of the marble replica of the man he had grown to hate.

While it is not a true story, it illustrates the self-destructive nature of envy, jealousy, and hate. Left unchecked, they can destroy the person who harbors them. Solomon makes the case against such attitudes very admirably. The person who has ears to hear will abandon these self-destructive sins.

PRINCIPLES

- Pride ultimately loses what it seeks. We want to look good in the eyes of others, but pride always makes us look small.
- Pride, unchecked, leads to a multitude of other sins that are necessary to feed its demands.
- Jealousy and envy eat a person up from within, while pride can eat a person up from without, from circumstances that backfire on him.

APPLICATIONS

- Be alert to the green-eyed monster of jealousy. When you see it, call it what it is—sin.
- Recognize that Solomon is talking about the danger of pride for all of us in this selection of passages, not just the other person who irritates us.

- Calculate the price of pride, jealousy, envy, and greed. Aware of their self-destructive nature, give them up. Be as drastic as necessary.

IV. LIFE APPLICATION

Selfish from Birth

Pride and selfishness are built into us from birth. From the earliest days of our lives, we calculate how we can maneuver to put ourselves in the number one place. I read one time of a mother who was preparing pancakes for her sons, Kevin, five, and Ryan, three. The boys began to argue over who would get the first pancake. Their mother saw the opportunity for a moral lesson. "If Jesus were sitting here, he would say, 'Let my brother have the first pancake; I can wait." Kevin turned to his younger brother and said, "Ryan, you be Jesus!"

And as we get older, our scheming becomes more sophisticated, but at the heart, they are exactly the same as when we were children—finding ways to put ourselves in the number one place. It is a tendency that we will always struggle with, but in order to master it, we must be as drastic as necessary.

For many years Sir Walter Scott was the leading literary figure in the British Empire. No one could write as well as he. Then the works of Lord Byron began to appear, and their greatness was immediately evident. Soon an anonymous critic praised his poems in a London newspaper. He declared that in the presence of these brilliant works of poetic genius, Scott could no longer be considered the leading poet of England. It was later discovered that the unnamed reviewer had been none other than Sir Walter Scott himself! Although we may not need to go to such dramatic ends to do it, we must all, like Sir Walter Scott, find ways of admitting to ourselves and to the world that we are not the greatest and that we were put here on earth to serve.

Solomon makes clear that pride, selfishness, jealousy, and greed are self-destructive sins. If we would reduce our pain in life and increase our joy, we must repent of those sins of self-destruction and follow the way of wisdom, which is the way of love and service.

V. PRAYER

Lord, help me to see myself as you see me: worth no less than any other human ever born but worth no more. When I see myself as you see me, I will have the security not to need pride. Deliver me from that sin so I may rest in my position in Christ and from there be used to help others. Amen.

VI. DEEPER DISCOVERIES

A. Pride

Proverbs uses four different groups of words to describe pride.

1. Several passages (11:2; 13:10; 21:24 twice) use a term derived from a verb meaning "to boil." It refers to the sense of self-importance that seethes inside a person, leading to such problems as presumption, rebellion, and willful disobedience. David prayed to be kept from "presumptuous sins" in Psalm 19:13 (NASB).

2. Another cluster of words (15:25; 16:18a,19; 29:23) relates to a verb meaning "to rise" like an ascending column of smoke. It describes God's legitimate majesty or excellence (Isa. 24:14; 26:10; Deut. 33:26) but more often speaks negatively of the attitude and conduct of those who trust themselves rather than God.

3. Other verses (16:5; 16:18b; 18:12) use a word derived from the verb for "to be high or lofty." Saul was described as physically taller than his countrymen (1 Sam. 10:23), and God's ways are higher than our ways (Isa. 55:9). But the word usually describes those who lift themselves haughtily above others. Uzziah (2 Chr. 26:16), Hezekiah (2 Chr. 32:25–26), and the prince of Tyre (Ezek. 28:2,17) are specifically charged with this sin.

4. Proverbs 21:24 uses a word for pride that occurs only there and in Habakkuk 2:5, referring to an egocentric, arrogant person.

B. Jealousy

Jealousy in the Old Testament is a strong emotional desire for someone or something, either envy, which desires another person's possession, or true jealousy, which zealously guards its own. It most often describes the legitimate exclusiveness that refuses to tolerate adultery or any other disloyalty to the marriage vows. God himself is described as a jealous God (Exod. 20:5) who will not tolerate the spiritual adultery of idolatry. In Proverbs 27:4, it refers to the implacable desire for revenge of a wronged husband toward the person who has violated his marriage.

VII. TEACHING OUTLINE

A. INTRODUCTION

1. Lead Story: Uncle Zeke's Horseshoe
2. Context: Pride, envy, jealousy, and greed are self-destructive sins that are hard to resist.

3. Transition: Notice how much you dislike those sins in others, and then transpose that to yourself. Others will dislike them just as much in you as you do in others. Give them up before they destroy you.

B. COMMENTARY
1. Pride and Humility
2. Other Offspring of Selfishness

C. CONCLUSION: KILLED BY ENVY

VIII. ISSUES FOR DISCUSSION

1. Why do you think we sometimes resent it when we hear of others' good fortune, especially if it is a classmate, neighbor, or fellow professional?
2. What truth from Scripture do you think we are failing to embrace that makes us resent success and good fortune in others?
3. How do you think we can gain the ability to rejoice with others' good fortune?

Chapter 17

Freedom Through Self-Control

Proverbs 12:16; 14:16–17,29; 15:18; 16:32; 19:11,19; 20:1,25; 21:5; 22:24–25; 23:19–21,29–35; 25:8,28; 29:8,11,20,22

Quote

"*You* can tell the size of a man by the size of the thing

that makes him angry."

J .   K .   M o r l e y

Proverbs
12:16; 14:16–17,29; 15:18;
16:32; 19:11,19; 20:1,25; 21:5;
22:24–25; 23:19–21,29–35;
25:8,28; 29:8,11,20,22

IN A NUTSHELL

There are several self-destructive things that will damage our lives if we're not self-controlled. First is acting on impulse. Our first impulses are often wrong and need to be controlled. Second is anger, which unleashes a torrent of harmful consequences if not brought under dominion. Third is appetite. We can become addicted to food and drink and cause untold misery in life.

Freedom Through Self-Control

I. INTRODUCTION

Self-Control: Game, Set, Match!

In 1975, tennis great Arthur Ashe was playing the arrogant and rude Ilie Nastase, nicknamed "Nasty" Nastase because he was so volatile on the tennis court. It was the Masters Tournament in Stockholm, Sweden. Nastase was at his worst this day, stalling, cursing, taunting, and acting like a madman. Finally, Ashe put down his racket and walked off the court, saying, "I've had enough. I'm at the point where I'm afraid I'll lose control."

The umpire yelled, "If you leave the court, you'll forfeit the match."

Ashe replied, "I don't care. I'd rather lose that than my self-respect."

The next day the tournament committee came to a surprising solution. Refusing to condone Nastase's bullying tactics, they insisted that Nastase default the match for his unsportsman-like conduct.

That day, Ashe won not only in the game of tennis but also in the game of life.

How many of us would have had the self-respect and guts to forfeit a match when you were in the right and the other person was clearly in the wrong? How many of us would have been willing to lose money and improvement in the tennis ratings when it was the other guy who was at fault? Ashe demonstrated, in that gesture, a towering character and dedication to integrity. At the same time, Nastase was demonstrating the devastation that occurs among people when their actions are unrestrained.

All of this sets the stage for Solomon's teachings on the subject of self-control. As he said, "Like a city whose walls are broken down is a man who lacks self-control." Few things demonstrate that like the contrast between Ashe and Nastase.

II. COMMENTARY

Freedom Through Self-Control

MAIN IDEA: *Few paths lead to disaster more surely than lack of self-control. The person who cannot tame his emotions and discipline his desires soon finds himself mired in predicaments he never expected.*

Impulsiveness and Haste (20:25; 21:5; 25:8; 29:20)

SUPPORTING IDEA: *Men and women with self-control think before they speak or act. When we leap before we look, we seldom have a soft landing!*

20:25. The law of Moses warned against making a casual vow, declaring that no one is required to make a vow to God, but once made, a vow may not be broken (Deut. 23:21–23). So the wise person thinks it through carefully before he utters a vow. Like an animal who steps into a **trap**, the person who vows thoughtlessly cannot get out of the obligation he has assumed. Better not to vow than to fail to carry through (Eccl. 5:4–6).

21:5. One person tries to get rich quickly (Prov. 20:21; 21:6), taking shortcuts and making hasty decisions. Eventually, his thoughtless plunge into these schemes will impoverish him. The **diligent** man, however, carefully **plans** his work, then works his plans. This methodical approach takes longer but leads more surely to success.

25:8. Some translations connect the first phrase of this verse with verse 7 instead. But the main idea of this verse remains intact either way: Do not be too quick to file a lawsuit against someone. The **court** might be a single judge or a judicial council. Jesus himself advised his followers to settle disputes with adversaries personally, before a case could come to court (Matt. 18:15; Luke 12:57–59). Always try to resolve such problems on the basis of personal relationship; use the legal system as a last resort. After all, you may lose the case!

29:20. The **man** who **speaks** before he thinks causes problems wherever he goes (Prov. 17:19–20; 18:6–7). His impulsive words stir up disputes so quickly that there is virtually no **hope** of keeping him out of trouble. James 1:19 (NASB) provides a concise summary of this topic, advising us to be "quick to hear, slow to speak and slow to anger."

Impatience and Anger (12:16; 14:16–17,29; 15:18; 16:32; 19:11,19; 22:24–25; 25:28; 29:8,11,22)

SUPPORTING IDEA: *A quick temper ignites conflict even in situations that could have been easily reconciled. A person without patience misses many opportunities that would have opened up if he had controlled his urge to take matters into his own hands.*

12:16. A hardheaded, stubborn **fool** (Heb. *ewiyl*) reacts without restraint, showing **his annoyance** instantly when he encounters a real or imagined insult. The **prudent man**, in contrast, shows patience in the face of **insult** or disgrace (11:2). He not only ignores the slander but consciously chooses not to respond in kind. The verb **overlooks** used here is translated "covers" in Proverbs 10:12.

14:16–17. The first line in Hebrew does not contain the words "the LORD"; it simply tells us that a **wise man** is afraid to do **evil**, lest he suffer the consequences. This, of course, implies the need to fear the Lord since he is the one who administers judgment for sin. A **fool**, on the other hand, is driven by his **hotheaded**, impetuous nature. He is wild and **reckless**. And his overconfidence leads him into disaster.

One man thinks too little. The flare of anger overrides his judgment, and he does things he would never consider in a calmer moment. Another man thinks too much because anger is simmering inside him. He is crafty and underhanded, scheming to take advantage of others. Naturally, he is hated by his victims.

14:29. This verse extols the value of patience. It is one of the evidences of a person of **understanding**, one who realizes that it is always wise to control his temper. A **quick-tempered** person may think that he is defending his honor or proving his strength, but his inability to harness his emotions puts his **folly** on public display (literally, "exalt, lift up for show.").

15:18. A **hot-tempered** man (Heb. "a man of rage") constantly **stirs up** quarrels and **dissension** (see Prov. 6:14,19; 10:12; 16:28; 28:25; 29:22). But a **patient man**, one who is slow to anger, **calms** a disagreement. Derek Kidner (*Proverbs*, 115) quotes a description by R. T. Archibald of peacemakers as ones "who carry about with them an atmosphere in which quarrels die a natural death." In reality, many arguments stem from personality rather than from objective issues.

16:32. In the culture of Israel, a soldier was highly respected as a necessary defense against foreign foes. But Proverbs points out that conquering oneself deserves even more honor than taking **a city** in battle. Power and aggression have their place, but a humble position can be even **better**.

19:11. The patient person knows how to avoid quarrels and stay out of trouble (14:29; 15:18; 16:32; 25:15) because he is not easily offended. Such longsuffering is a mark of **wisdom**; it has practical value. And when he chooses to **overlook an offense** rather than retaliating, his forbearance is **his glory**. Patience often goes unnoticed, but it is actually one of the most glorious adornments of a godly character.

19:19. A **hot-tempered** man will repeatedly end up in trouble. He does not learn from his experiences, so it does little good to **rescue him**. He will only lose control again and **pay the penalty** despite your best efforts to help him.

22:24–25. A hot-tempered man is literally a "possessor of anger," a "lord of rage." The **one easily angered** in Hebrew is a "man of wrath." Both descriptions picture a person for whom anger is a built-in part of his character, not just an occasional problem. Proverbs warns us not to **associate** with such a person because we are liable to develop a similar problem with anger. One who learns the **ways** of an angry man will be **ensnared**, sharing the trouble he has stirred up.

25:28. When you won't control your emotions, you will be vulnerable to an enemy who can control his. This verse compares the **man who lacks self-control** to a **city** that cannot be defended because its **walls** have been **broken**. And by implication, it makes clear that self-discipline is one of our chief defenses against calamity.

29:8. Mockers are full of unprincipled arrogance, and they can **stir up** or inflame an entire **city**. History is full of uprisings resulting from a few people who incited others to rebellion. The **wise**, on the other hand, will help calm a city and **turn away anger** and its disruptive results.

29:11. One of the characteristics of a **fool** is his inability to hold back his **anger** (literally, his spirit). A **wise man**, on the other hand, keeps his temper **under control**, even in a confrontation. The Hebrew for keeping oneself under control is literally "to calm it back"; the same word is used in Psalms 65:7 and 89:9 to describe the stilling of a storm. What a perfect picture of a godly response when we are tempted to blow up!

29:22. Anyone who can be described as **angry** or **hot-tempered** (literally, "lord of rage") has a spiritual problem that goes deep into the heart. It is not a temporary lapse. And it not only **stirs up** trouble among people; it also produces **many sins**. It spoils one's relationship to God, not just people.

C Intoxication and Gluttony (20:1; 23:19–21,29–35)

SUPPORTING IDEA: *Hunger and thirst are wholesome physical urges given to us by God. But when we don't know where to stop, they can turn into addictions that blight our lives.*

20:1. The writer personifies wine and strong drink. **Wine**, made from fermented grapes, is pictured as a **mocker**, scoffing at the person foolish enough to drink it. **Beer** or strong drink was made from barley, dates, or pomegranates and is portrayed as a **brawler**. It not only bullies the drinker but turns him into an aggressive fool. Alcohol will lead you **astray**, causing you to play the part of a fool. A wise person stays clear of drunkenness.

23:19–21. Like many other passages in Proverbs, this verse calls on the young man to **listen** to his father's instruction. And in this case, the father is warning him not to **join** in drunkenness or gluttony. Modern Christians often focus on alcohol, forgetting verses like these that speak against gluttons who lack self-control and **gorge themselves on meat**. In each case, the problem is the urge to indulge in too much!

Either problem leads to the same result. The alcoholic pours all his resources into his drinking habit and eventually lands in poverty. The laziness and **drowsiness** that accompany such behavior lead inevitably to financial embarrassment.

23:29–35. These verses provide the Bible's longest and most eloquent argument against drinking. It is a combination of satire and sermon. Verse 30 states the problem: a preoccupation with wine that motivates a person to **linger over** the glass or to take the trouble to **go** out **to sample bowls of mixed wine**. This pictures the person who has gone beyond the occasional social drink, and it pronounces the litany of problems that will result.

The drunkard has emotional problems: **woe** and **sorrow**. He has social problems: **strife** and **complaints**. Alcohol leads to physical problems: **bruises** from beatings or from injuries suffered while staggering under the influence; **bloodshot** or blackened **eyes**, perhaps the blurred vision of a drunken stupor.

Wine appeals to the senses of sight (it is **red**, and it **sparkles**) and taste (it **goes down smoothly**). But the immediate pleasure cannot compensate for the bitter reality revealed **in the end**. It **bites like a snake** and **poisons** you **like a viper**.

Eventually the alcoholic develops hallucinations and other mental problems. He will be unable to trust his senses because his **mind** is filled with **confusing**, perverse images. He will be as unsteady as a person **sleeping** high in the rigging of a sailing ship, weaving back and forth. He has reached the place where he is in a stupor so deep that he cannot even feel pain.

And in the end, all he can think of is getting **another drink**.

MAIN IDEA REVIEW: *Few paths lead to disaster more surely than lack of self-control. The person who cannot tame his emotions and discipline his desires soon finds himself mired in predicaments he never expected.*

III. CONCLUSION

D. L. Moody's Repentance

Evangelist D. L. Moody was the "Billy Graham" of the nineteenth century. He had a quick temper, which was something he continually had to guard against. One evening he was conducting two evangelistic services, one right after the other. In between the services, Moody was standing near the door, welcoming people as they came in. A man approached him and said something to Moody that was offensive and deeply insulting. Moody never repeated to anyone what the man had said. But in a sudden fit of anger, Moody shoved the man, sending him head over heels down a short flight of steps.

The man was not injured, but those who saw it wondered how Moody could possibly recover to preach another evangelistic service after such an alarming lapse of control. All the people who saw it would have trouble listening to anything Moody might say.

But Moody recovered his composure, called the meeting to order, and with a trembling voice said:

> Friends, before the meeting tonight I want to confess that I yielded just now to my temper, out in the hall, and have done wrong. Just as I was coming in here tonight, I lost my temper with a man and I want to confess my wrong before you all, and if that man is present here whom I thrust away in anger, I want to ask his forgiveness and God's. Let's pray (William R. Moody, *The Life of Dwight L. Moody*, Fredonia, N.Y.: Fredonia Books, 2001, pp. 110–11).

Instead of a lost cause, the meeting seemed unusually touched that night with the power of the Holy Spirit, and many people came to Christ.

This story tells us many things. First, it tells us that we must always be on guard against a loss of self-control. Second, it tells us how quickly we can lose our reputation and our platform for ministry if we do lose our self-control. Third, it tells us that the only thing to do after such an incident is to repent before God and others. Finally, it tells us that God can always use anyone who has repented of any sin and experienced his forgiveness.

PRINCIPLES

- Those who leap before they look will always have bad landings.
- It takes a big person not to get angry at little things.
- We are a slave to food and drink if we cannot control them.

APPLICATIONS

- Analyze your decision-making style. If you tend to speak or act before you have thought things through, embark on a plan to be more controlled in your approach to life.
- Think of the last time you got angry. Consider whether your anger was justified or your response was appropriate. If not, commit to the Lord to become a more patient person, and get a spiritual accountability partner, if necessary, to encourage growth in the area of inappropriate anger.

- If you do not exercise appropriate self-control over food and drink, decide on a plan to exercise moderation. Get a spiritual accountability partner if you need help.

IV. LIFE APPLICATION

Problem or Inconvenience?

In his book, *Uh-Oh* (New York: Ballantine Books, 1993), author Robert Fulghum wrote of the time he was a young man, just out of college, working at the Feather River Inn in the Sierra Nevada Mountains of California. One week he became angry because all the workers had been served the same thing for lunch every day: two wieners, sauerkraut, and stale rolls. On top of the terrible menu, the food was being deducted from his checks. One Friday night he learned that the same thing was going to be served for the next two days.

Fulghum lost it and vented his frustration to the night auditor, Sigmund Wollman. He declared that he had had it up to here with that garbage, that human life could not be sustained on such rubbish, and that for two cents he would go wake up the owner and throw it on him. To take the money for such trash out of his wages only added insult to injury. On and on he went, proclaiming that the whole hotel stank, that the horses were nags, that the guests were idiots, that the owner was a moron, that he was too good for this kind of treatment, and that he had a good mind to pack his bags and head for Montana where they had never heard of sauerkraut and wieners and wouldn't feed it to the pigs. He ran on for about twenty minutes at the top of his lungs, lacing his tirade with much profanity.

Sigmund Wollman, who had spent three years in a German death camp during World War II, just sat, watching and listening. Finally, he said, "Fulghum, are you finished?"

"No, why?"

"Lissen, Fulghum. Lissen me, lissen me. You know what's wrong with you? It's not the wieners and kraut and it's not the boss and it's not the chef and it's not this job."

"So, what's wrong with me?"

"Fulghum, you think you know everything, but you don't know the difference between an inconvenience and a problem. If you break your neck, if you have nothing to eat, if your house is on fire—then you got a problem. Everything else is an inconvenience. Life *is* inconvenient. Life *is* lumpy. Learn to separate the inconveniences from the real problems. You will live longer. And will not annoy people like me so much. Good night."

And with those words, he waved young Fulghum off to bed (Fulghum, 143–46).

What wisdom poured from those lips. People with anger problems have not learned to tell the difference between inconveniences and real problems. The same is true with those people who are jealous and greedy. They haven't learned what life is really about, and they destroy themselves and those with whom they have relationships by their constant demand to have life go their way. Solomon warns us that selfishness will destroy us and those around us if we do not learn to control it.

V. PRAYER

Father in heaven, help us to discern our hearts, to know when we are being selfish, demanding, and self-destructive. Keep us from damaging those we love. Enable us not to bring embarrassment to your name. Strengthen us to give up a demanding heart, to be willing to serve you and others because of all you have done for us. Amen.

VI. DEEPER DISCOVERIES

A. Patience

The word translated "patient" (14:29; 15:18; 16:32; 25:15) comes from a Hebrew phrase that literally means "long of nose or nostril." This picturesque description refers to the way people often show anger by dilating their nostrils and breathing heavily through them. We would say someone is "long of anger"; in other words, he takes a long, deep breath before allowing himself to get angry. This phrase is used, much like "longsuffering" in the New Testament, as a rich description of God's forbearance and slowness to judge.

B. Alcoholic Beverages

Wine, as used in Proverbs, is the Hebrew word *yayin*, which describes the fermented juice of grapes. Grapes were one of the main crops in Palestine, and the main harvest took place in August and September. Laborers would put the grapes in winepresses, large vats where barefoot men would crush the grapes and allow the juice to drain out into a basin. The juice was placed in earthenware pots or leather wineskins until fermentation was complete. Since distillation had not yet been developed, neither wine nor beer had an alcohol content of more than 7 to 10 percent—much less than today's liquor but still enough to cause drunkenness.

VII. TEACHING OUTLINE

A. INTRODUCTION
1. Lead Story: Self-Control: Game, Set, Match!
2. Context: Selfishness is self-destructive. Whether it is anger or jealousy or greed, we damage ourselves and those around us when we have no control in these areas.
3. Transition: Solomon presents the dangers of the three I's: impulsiveness, impatience, and intoxication.

B. COMMENTARY
1. Impulsiveness and Haste
2. Impatience and Anger
3. Intoxication and Gluttony

C. CONCLUSION: D. L. MOODY'S REPENTANCE

VIII. ISSUES FOR DISCUSSION
1. Which area of your life is the hardest for you to exercise patience? Why do you think that is? What do you think you could do to increase your patience?
2. Would your family say that you have an anger problem? What would those at work say? What do you think God says? Are there any steps you think you ought to take to deal with anger?
3. Are you addicted to alcohol or food? Do you need help overcoming an addiction? Are you willing to pay the necessary price to be free from anything that controls you? Is there something you think you should do?

Chapter 18

The Gift of Gracious Speech

Proverbs 10:19–21,31–32; 11:11; 12:13–14,23; 13:2–3; 14:3; 15:1–2,7,23,28; 16:21,23–24; 17:4,27–28; 18:6–7,13; 19:1; 21:23; 23:15–16; 25:11,15; 27:14

"*The* great test of a man's character is his tongue."

O s w a l d   C h a m b e r s

Proverbs

10:19–21,31–32; 11:11;
12:13–14,23; 13:2–3; 14:3
15:1–2,7,23,28; 16:21,23–24;
17:4,27–28; 18:6–7,13;
19:1; 21:23; 23:15–16;
25:11,15; 27:14

I N   A   N U T S H E L L

The tongue reveals what is in the heart: wise heart, wise words; foolish heart, foolish words. The wise person is committed to doing right in words and deeds, he studies how to say the right thing at the right time, and he controls his anger so that he does not say harmful things that cannot be taken back.

The Gift of
Gracious Speech

I. INTRODUCTION

Yogi's Verbal Genius

*S*ometimes the words that come out of our mouths aren't what we would choose if we could have them back. No one knows this more than Yogi Berra, who has received national acclaim for his verbal missteps. Yogi is a Hall of Fame baseball player who played for the world series champion New York Yankees in the 1950s and 1960s and was one of the best catchers ever to play the game. Yet, if there were a Hall of Fame for saying unexpected and unusual things, he would be a charter member. Out of his mouth have come some of the most dazzling incoherencies ever uttered by man.

One time, in preseason, when asked what size hat he wore, he said, "I don't know, I'm not in shape yet." Speaking of the intellectual side of baseball, he said, "Ninety percent of this game is half mental." Concerning a restaurant in his hometown, he said, "Nobody goes there any more. It's too crowded." Commenting on golf, he mangled another statistic when he said, "Ninety percent of short shots don't go in." Then, there are: "a nickel ain't worth a dime any more; if I didn't wake up, I'd still be asleep; the future ain't what it used to be; always go to people's funerals, otherwise they won't go to yours; when you come to a fork in the road, take it"; and the most famous Yogi-ism, "It's *déjà vu* all over again."

Well, there is nothing to do but chuckle and shake your head at the magnitude of this gift. It's harmless and entertaining. But other verbal missteps are neither harmless nor entertaining. There is speaking that takes on important proportions in our lives—speaking that reflects good and bad, right and wrong, encouraging and discouraging. There is a dimension to our speech that reflects the heart and, as such, impacts our relationships and our reputations, and it either enriches or diminishes our lives.

Solomon challenges us to use our tongues to encourage and improve our lives and warns us that foolish or corrupt speech will damage us and people around us.

II. COMMENTARY

The Gift of Gracious Speech

MAIN IDEA: *When James devoted the third chapter of his letter to the power of the tongue, he drew on ideas that had already appeared in Proverbs. Our words not only make a tremendous impact on others; they also reveal the condition of our hearts.*

🅰 Wise and Foolish Words (14:3; 15:2,7; 16:23; 18:6–7; 19:1; 23:15–16)

SUPPORTING IDEA: *When the heart is filled with wisdom, it will spill over into our words. But the speech of a fool exposes his empty-headed stubbornness.*

14:3. The Hebrew text actually declares that a **fool's talk** brings a "**rod** of pride." Anyone can hear the evidence of pride just by listening to him, and most will welcome the chance to "take him down a notch." Such haughty speech will inevitably bring pain, but the *ewiyl*, or arrogant fool, pays no attention. On the other hand, a **wise** person's speech will **protect** him from such a reaction.

15:2. A **wise** person's speech **commends knowledge**, literally "uses it skillfully or handsomely" (see Prov. 30:29; Ezek. 33:32). His skillful use of knowledge shows the value of knowledge and motivates others to want it for themselves. A **fool**, however, **gushes** (Prov. 15:28) or "bubbles forth" foolishness like water from a spring. His words reveal his foolish heart.

15:7. Notice the way this verse contrasts the **lips of the wise** with the **hearts of fools.** Scripture consistently teaches that mouth and mind go together; what the mouth says simply reveals what the heart feels. A wise man shares helpful words that increase **knowledge**, but the fool does no such thing.

16:23. A wise teacher chooses his words carefully. His **wise** mind **guides his mouth**, literally, "causes his mouth to be prudent." As a result, his words will help and heal, not hurt. Listening to such a person makes you want to learn.

18:6–7. Lips and **mouth** refer to a person's speech, and these verses describe the trouble that appears when a fool opens his mouth. His words lead to **strife** and trouble; his remarks are so out of place that others beat him; his speech is his **undoing** or downfall; it traps him.

19:1. Here is another of the proverbs that compare God's values with those of the world. No one wants to be **poor**, but honest poverty is **better** than being a **fool**. The verse contrasts a **blameless** or morally whole lifestyle with the **perverse** or twisted utterances of a fool.

23:15–16. This proverb offers an additional motivation for seeking wisdom. Not only will it help you live more effectively; it will also bring great joy to your parents. It is an attractive picture of warm affection, pairing love for wisdom with love for the people closest to you. The **inmost being** here is literally "the kidneys," often seen as the seat of emotions. A dad's heart will be encouraged when he hears his son say something that shows he has committed himself to righteousness.

🅱 Righteous and Wicked Words (10:20–21,31–32; 11:11; 12:13–14; 13:2; 15:28; 17:4)

SUPPORTING IDEA: *In Proverbs, wisdom and righteousness go together. The wise person is committed to doing what is right, even in the words he says. But a fool cannot be trusted; his speech is a ruse to get what he wants.*

10:20–21. Verse 20 announces the value of a **righteous** person's speech, and verse 21 explains why it is so precious. Like fine **silver**, words that come from a righteous heart are a scarce treasure, and we feel a deep sense of satisfaction when we listen to such a person. A **wicked** person, on the other hand, is so worthless that not even his thoughts have **value**, let alone his words.

Words can **nourish** the soul, and a strengthened soul helps the body as well. The righteous person provides nourishment enough for himself and for many others, but a fool does not even have enough to sustain himself. He will eventually **die** because he will **lack** the **judgment** to turn from his folly.

10:31–32. Both of these verses declare that a **righteous** person knows what to say. His mouth **brings forth** (literally, "bears fruit of") **wisdom** as a natural result of inner righteousness. He knows what is **fitting** or pleasant. A **wicked** person, on the other hand, produces only **perverse** words, the expression of a crooked nature that twists normal meanings into evil sayings. Such a person will receive the severest punishment, though the threat of having one's tongue **cut out** is probably figurative. Old Testament law never incorporated such a penalty.

11:11. The people of a **city** benefit from having an upright neighbor. The godly person may ask God to bless his neighbors, or they may enjoy the side effects when God blesses his servant (Gen. 30:27; 39:5). But when **wicked** people poison the atmosphere with their words, a society is in danger of economic and moral destruction.

12:13–14; 13:2. These verses explain the consequences of good or bad speech. The **evil** are **trapped** by their **sinful talk** because their words give them away. But the **righteous** person **escapes** such snares.

The **fruit** of one's **lips** refers to his words and their results. Words can bring a bountiful harvest of **good things** just **as surely as** deeds. They can establish relationships and plant helpful ideas for the future.

Helpful words, like loving deeds, produce blessing. Proverbs promises that a person who ministers to others by his speech enjoys **good things**. The unfaithful or treacherous, however, have an appetite (Heb. *nephesh,* usually translated "soul"), or a deep-seated **craving, for violence**, and their words are intended to hurt.

15:28. One way to distinguish a righteous person from a wicked person is to listen to him speak. A **righteous** person **weighs** his answers. The word originally meant "to mumble" and eventually came to mean "meditate deeply" (Pss. 1:2; 63:6). The good person thinks carefully before he speaks, so his words are more appropriate. A wicked man, on the other hand, **gushes** (literally, bubbles forth) **evil** words like water from a spring.

17:4. A person **listens to** people who resonate to the same tune, so a **wicked man** pays special attention to those who share his **evil** motives. He is happy to hear gossip or anything else that tears down another person maliciously.

Appropriate Words (15:23; 16:21,24; 25:11; 27:14)

SUPPORTING IDEA: *It is not enough just to say the right thing. We must be able to size up the situation and say the right thing at the right time.*

15:23. The ability to give a wise, timely **reply** is highly valued in the Wisdom Books of the Old Testament. Saying the right thing at the right time is an art, and it gives us pleasure to see an artist at work. Ecclesiastes tells us that there is a time for everything, and it takes wisdom to recognize when to encourage and when to rebuke.

16:21. A **wise** person is known for her discernment, the ability to see to the heart of an issue. And such a person's words are **pleasant** (from a word meaning "sweetness"); they make **instruction** attractive. Students will *want* to show up for their lessons.

16:24. Pleasant or delightful **words are** as **sweet** and desirable as **a honeycomb**. Honey was the sweetest substance available in the ancient world, so this imagery was powerful. Such conversation is not only healthy for **the soul**, but it can have a **healing** effect on the body as well.

25:11. An appropriate, well-timed saying can be as attractive and valuable as a fine piece of metalwork, **apples of gold in settings of silver**. Note that the apples are enhanced by the fine setting, just as the saying is "apt" precisely because it comes in the right context, carefully timed for the situation.

27:14. As a humorous example of poor timing, this verse points out the trouble you can get into if you say the right thing at the wrong time. Surely there can be nothing wrong with blessing or praising a **neighbor**! But loudly disturbing your friend's sleep **early in the morning** will feel more like a **curse** than a blessing.

ⅅ A Time for Silence (10:19; 12:23; 13:3; 17:28; 18:13; 21:23)

> **SUPPORTING IDEA:** *Sometimes the only thing we think about is what we can say; we assume that we need to say something. But there are times when the wisest course of action is to say nothing at all.*

10:19. Use words sparingly because the more you talk, the more likely you are to stumble into something foolish. Constant chattering eventually leads to **sin**, but a **wise** person knows when to remain silent.

12:23. **A prudent man**, one who is shrewd in a good sense, is cautious in giving out information. He thinks before he speaks, so that his words will be understood, not twisted; helpful, not wasted. A fool, however, has no valve to stem the flow of words; the **folly** in his **heart** spills out in his speech.

13:3; 21:23. Place a guard at the door of your mouth, and you preserve your **life** (Heb. "soul"). You can avoid immense **calamity** by choosing your words carefully. But the person who **speaks rashly** ends in **ruin**. He hastily makes promises he cannot keep, thoughtlessly divulges private information, offends others, misrepresents the truth. No wonder he is destined for trouble!

17:28. A fool's speech reveals the emptiness of his character, but even a hardened **fool** (Heb. *ewiyl*) can maintain a reputation for wisdom and discernment if he just **keeps silent**. Unfortunately, most fools find this almost impossible to do.

18:13. Jumping to conclusions is a special temptation for the self-important. They announce the solution before they have fully heard the problem. This is often a symptom of people who are arrogant, unteachable, or prejudiced. They have no interest in hearing the facts or anything else that might contradict their opinions.

ⅇ Words Under Control (15:1; 17:27; 25:15)

> **SUPPORTING IDEA:** *When we are angry, it's easy to let fly a sentence that we wish we could pull back. But it's too late. The only way we can avoid such blunders is to exercise self-control before the words leave our mouths.*

15:1. How can we handle an angry person? Our instinctive response is to come back with a **harsh**, hurtful retort—a tactic that just escalates the level of rage. The other option is a **gentle**, soft **answer**. The wise person can avoid needless quarrels by defusing a tense situation. Such tact requires forethought, patience, self-control, and kindness.

17:27. A person with **knowledge** and **understanding** is cautious in speaking, and he weighs his words carefully. He is **even-tempered** (literally, "cool in spirit"), so that his mind is not clouded by a storm of emotion.

25:15. Here is a tribute to the power of a persistent, controlled tongue. Persuading an authority to follow a particular course is one of the most difficult of assignments, and you cannot do it by threatening. **Patience** that refuses to be provoked is the only weapon that can succeed. And it can produce surprising results. Just as a **gentle tongue can break a bone**, the most rigid part of the body, soft words can break down the deepest, most hardened resistance to an idea.

> **MAIN IDEA REVIEW:** *When James devoted the third chapter of his letter to the power of the tongue, he drew on ideas that had already appeared in Proverbs. Our words not only make a tremendous impact on others; they also reveal the condition of our hearts.*

III. CONCLUSION

The Power of Encouragement

There are many ways our words can be pleasant—like apples of gold in settings of silver is a word aptly spoken. For example, we can encourage one another. It has been said that a compliment is verbal sunshine. Gerhard Frost said, "We blossom under praise like flowers in sun and dew; we open, we reach, we grow." Mark Twain once said, "I can go for two months on one good compliment." First Thessalonians 5:11 (NASB) says, "Therefore encourage one another and build up one another."

There are a number of ways we can encourage one another. First, keep it simple. Most people can spot a fake a mile away, and we all know when encouragement is overdone or insincere. But if it's sincere, a little goes a long way. I remember a time in seminary when a professor of mine simply waited for me as I was walking up to him, and together we walked into the classroom together. I felt wonderfully affirmed and deeply encouraged.

Second, we can look for special times to encourage. During one of the last major offensives of World War II, General Dwight Eisenhower was walking near the Rhine River and came upon a soldier who seemed depressed.

"How are you feeling, son?" he asked.

"Well, sir, I'm awfully nervous."

To which Eisenhower replied, "Well, you and I are a good pair, then, because I'm nervous, too. Maybe if we just walk along together, we'll be good for each other."

There was no sermon, no orders to "buck up," no special advice. Just a few choice words that showed the soldier that he mattered and that he was important.

One time, the legendary Vince Lombardi reprimanded a player in practice for missing several blocking assignments. After practice, Lombardi went into the locker room where the player was sitting, head down, dejected. Lombardi mussed his hair, patted him on the shoulder, and said, "One day you are going to be the best guard in the NFL." And it turned out he was: Jerry Kramer went on to the Hall of Fame. If you think something good and important about a person, tell him. He may not know it; he may not believe it, but it may help him become all he can be.

If you hear something good about a person, pass it along to him. He may not know it; he may not have heard it. Compliment persons in public when others can hear. Instead of saying something to the person in private, wait until there are others around to hear it. Write them notes of appreciation, send them an e-mail of congratulations. It's like water to a thirsty soul, like sunshine to flowers.

We have great power in our words, power to help people reach their potential, to become all that God gifted them to be. It is easy and inexpensive. All it takes is our own vision for how God might want to use us in the lives of other people.

PRINCIPLES

- Wise speech comes from a wise heart. It is futile to work on speech unless you realize you are really working on your heart.
- Encouragement is one of the most powerful forces on earth.
- Sometimes silence is, in fact, golden, and the most appropriate response.

APPLICATIONS

- Think about encouraging at least one person a day. Think ahead of time what you might say to encourage him or her, and then do it.
- Memorize one passage of Scripture that will help you become a person of more wise speech.
- If you have hurt someone with your speech, go to him or her and ask for forgiveness. It is the right thing to do this time and will help you hold your tongue next time.

IV. LIFE APPLICATION

Corrie's Wise Father

Step number one in Proverbs is to stop saying foolish and harmful things. Step number two is to say encouraging things. Step number three is to say wise things. Proverbs 16:23 says, "A wise man's heart guides his mouth, and his lips promote instruction." Our hearts are to be wise, and they should instruct our mouths.

This takes hard work and attention. Proverbs 15:28 says, "The heart of the righteous weighs its answers." That is, the righteous heart thinks about how best to answer a situation. It doesn't just pop off the top of his head all the time. Sometimes the righteous heart has to think and pray about a matter for a time. And then the righteous heart ponders how to say something in such a way as to help the listener embrace the wisdom behind it. Proverbs 16:21 says, "The wise in heart are called discerning, and pleasant words promote instruction."

What a challenge this is! How do we gain this kind of wisdom, and how do we cultivate this kind of speech? First, by working hard to learn God's truth and being obedient to it. Scripture says, "Do your best to present yourself to God as one approved, a workman who does not need to be ashamed and who correctly handles the word of truth" (2 Tim. 2:15). That is, work hard at mastering the Word, so that the Word will in turn master you. Second, combine that hard work with an attitude of obedience to God. Only as we are obedient do we learn what the Holy Spirit has for us through Scripture.

Notable examples of wisdom are encouraging. In Corrie ten Boom's book *The Hiding Place* (Carmel, N.Y.: Guideposts Associates, 1971), she tells the story of her father's remarkable wisdom. When Corrie was a little girl, preadolescent, she was traveling with her father on the train to Amsterdam from their home in Haarlem, in the Netherlands. Her father was a watchmaker, and he traveled once a week for repair parts, for new watches that he sold in his store, and to get the accurate time from a special clock in Amsterdam so he could be assured all his clocks and watches in Haarlem were accurate. He carried with him a large, heavy briefcase with spare parts and tools. Corrie had read the word "sex" some time before, and could not imagine what it meant. So she asked her father on the train.

"Father, what is sex?"

He turned to look at me, as he always did when answering a question, but to my surprise he said nothing. At last he stood up, lifted his traveling case from the rack over our heads, and set it on the floor.

"Will you carry it off the train, Corrie?" he said.

"It's too heavy," I said.

"Yes," he said. "And it would be a pretty poor father who would ask his little girl to carry such a load. It's the same way, Corrie, with knowledge. Some knowledge is too heavy for children. When you are older and stronger you can bear it. For now you must trust me to carry it for you" (the allusion is on pp. 29–31; the quote is on p. 31).

I stand in awe of that kind of wisdom. It's almost as though the answer came from another world. Then I think of the kind of man he was. A faithful man. A man of the Word. A man of prayer. A man of obedience. A wise man. His wisdom and his articulate speech were an outgrowth of his close walk with the Lord. That is how such wisdom comes. It is available to all of us but only when we give ourselves completely to it.

V. PRAYER

Father in heaven, change our hearts, and in so doing, change our speech. Make us wise and obedient and also faithful. And may our words help others in their walk with you. Amen.

VI. DEEPER DISCOVERIES

A. Cutting Out a Tongue (10:31)

When Proverbs warns that a perverse tongue will be cut out, it is speaking of a rare, drastic occurrence. Under the Mosaic law, criminal penalties included execution, scourging, and fines or restitution. The principle of "eye for eye, tooth for tooth" (Exod. 21:24–25) could require the cutting off of some part of the body. But there is no provision in Old Testament law for cutting out the tongue. This penalty was, however, practiced in some surrounding nations.

B. Prudent (12:23)

Two different words are commonly translated "prudence" in the Book of Proverbs. The most common is *sakal,* which occurs at least eighteen times, all describing a positive character quality. The person with this kind of prudence can think through a complex situation and determine a course that displays practical common sense. In Proverbs 12:23, however, a less common word for prudence, *'arum,* is used. It appears in Proverbs 12:16,23; 13:16; 14:8,15,18; 22:3; 27:12, always with a good connotation. In other parts of Scripture, this word group usually refers to the shrewd or crafty behavior of a person who schemes to harm others. The best-known usage is Genesis 3:1, which describes the serpent as more crafty than any other animal.

VII. TEACHING OUTLINE

A. INTRODUCTION

1. Lead Story: Yogi's Verbal Genius
2. Context: The tongue is a reflection of the heart. It reveals what is within. We must groom and cultivate our hearts so that our speech is wise, helpful, and encouraging.
3. Transition: The wise person studies how and when to say encouraging things, and he guards his tongue so he will not say harmful things.

B. COMMENTARY

1. Wise and Foolish Words
2. Righteous and Wicked Words
3. Appropriate Words
4. A Time for Silence
5. Words Under Control

C. CONCLUSION: THE POWER OF ENCOURAGEMENT

VIII. ISSUES FOR DISCUSSION

1. Do you remember a time when you were especially encouraged by something someone said to you? Why do you think you were so encouraged? Do you try to encourage others in the same way? If you don't, why not?
2. Do you remember a time when you said something and you wished you could take it back? Why did you say it? Do you say such things often? Are you working hard to become a person who says helpful things and not harmful things?
3. Do you talk too much? Have you ever tried to cultivate the art of effective silence? Are you known as a person of prudent speech? If you are not, what do you think you would have to do to change?

Chapter 19

When Talk Turns Malicious

Proverbs 10:18; 11:12–13; 12:18–19,22; 15:4;
16:27–28; 17:9,14,19–20; 18:8,20–21; 19:5,22; 20:3,19;
21:6; 22:10; 25:23; 26:2,20–22,28; 28:23; 29:5

Quote

"A slip of the foot you may soon recover, but a slip of the tongue you may never get over."

Benjamin Franklin

Proverbs
10:18; 11:12–13; 12:18–19,22;
15:4; 16:27–28; 17:9,14,19–20;
18:8,20–21; 19:5,22;
20:3,19; 21:6; 22:10; 25:23;
26:2,20–22,28;
28:23; 29:5

 IN A NUTSHELL

What we say makes a lasting impact. It can produce great good, but it can also hurt others deeply. Don't flatter or trust a flatterer. Never attack someone's reputation. Never lie.

When Talk Turns Malicious

I. INTRODUCTION

Words in the Headlines

*A*t the time of this writing, in the current news headlines a high-powered defunct oil company executive is charged with lying and cover-up and is jockeying for a reduced prison sentence, the national security advisor is being challenged on whether sufficient attention was paid to intelligence information before the 9/11 attack on the World Trade Center, a clear channel radio consortium yanks a notorious shock-disk jockey from its airwaves, accusations of misjudgment and misrepresentation are being hurled against the President, a conservative radio talk-show host blasts his liberal detractors, while his liberal detractors are making a clumsy attempt to start their own liberal talk show to offset him. Hot words fired across cultural divides are the order of the day. Words, words, words!

The tongue is a fire, the apostle James says—a world of iniquity which is set on fire by hell (Jas. 3:6). We see this world of iniquity every day in the newspapers. Hatred, anger, gossip, slander, and cover-ups are front-page items nearly every day. It is difficult to calculate the personal pain, the broken relationships, the devastating circumstances that can be traced back to the malicious use of the tongue.

In this chapter, we see the world of iniquity in all its horror presented by Solomon. From curses, death, and a crushed spirit, to flattery, slander, and lies, the tongue wreaks havoc from the beginning of the Book of Proverbs until the end.

Solomon's goal is to help us see the devastating consequences of the malicious use of the tongue so that we will be warned against it. As the son of the great king of Israel, as the brother in a bevy of selfish siblings, as the father of his own sons, Solomon has the background and the vested interest to give cold, clear truth on the subject of the tongue. The warning: when talk turns malicious, bad things happen. Be on your guard against others, and be on your guard against yourself!

II. COMMENTARY

When Talk Turns Malicious

> **MAIN IDEA:** *The old nursery rhyme "Sticks and stones may break my bones, but words will never hurt me" is far from true. We can unleash incredible destruction in our lives, as well as in the lives of others, through our words. Thoughtless words can lead to quarrels, and quarrels, once started, are difficult to contain.*

A Power of the Tongue (11:12; 12:18; 15:4; 16:27; 18:20–21; 25:23; 26:2)

> **SUPPORTING IDEA:** *What we say makes a lasting impact. It can produce great good, but it can also hurt others deeply.*

18:20–21. These verses use the picture of fruit and harvest to dramatize the power of the tongue for good or for evil. The **fruit** of the **mouth** and the **harvest** of the **lips** (see 12:14; 13:2) refer to the consequences of our words. As literal fruit satisfies the appetite, wise words will produce satisfying results.

On the other hand, the **tongue** has great potential for **death** as well as **life**. And those who **love** to talk will experience the consequences of their words, for better or worse.

11:12. Sometimes we are tempted to deride a **neighbor**, to belittle him or hold him in contempt. But such a verbal attack shows that the speaker **lacks judgment**, literally that he lacks heart. Something is malfunctioning at the core of his soul, even though he obviously feels superior to his target. **A man** with **understanding** has the wisdom to restrain his words at such a time.

12:18; 15:4. Fools hurt others with **reckless words**, but the **wise** person heals others with carefully chosen words. In this case, the speaker may not intend to cause harm, but he blurts out his mind without thinking through the consequences. The verb from which "reckless" is derived is used to describe the hasty words that cost Moses his entrance to the land of Canaan (Ps. 106:33). And though there may be no malice, the damage can be as searing as a **sword** thrust. A wise person has the chance to come along afterwards and use his **tongue** to help heal the wound.

Such a person is like **a tree of life** (Prov. 3:18; 11:30; 13:12), a solid source of strength and growth. He or she lifts the spirits and brings not just relief for the immediate pain but **healing** in the sense of overall health and wholeness. In contrast, a deceitful tongue **crushes** a person's **spirit**. The Hebrew word for **deceitful** refers to a twisted, treacherous person (11:3).

16:27. This verse is part of a short section (16:27–30) explaining the danger of various kinds of evil people. The **scoundrel** is literally a "man of Belial"—a worthless, morally degraded person (6:12). Such a person **plots**

schemes to harm the innocent just as a hunter digs a pit to trap his prey (1:10–14; 6:14; 12:20; 14:22; 24:2,8). The writer, like James in the New Testament (Jas. 3:5–6), describes his **speech** as a destructive, **scorching fire**.

25:23. Bible scholars have debated the meaning of this verse because the **north wind** in Israel is normally dry. But the point of the passage is quite clear. The Hebrew literally says that the north wind has the birth pangs or **brings** forth **rain**. Anyone familiar with the weather knows the results of a north wind. In the same way, we know the results of a **sly**, secretive **tongue**. Slandering a person behind his back will lead inevitably to an **angry** response.

26:2. There is a limit to the power of words. Even if a person pronounces a **curse** on someone, the words will be without effect. An innocent person need not be afraid; such a curse is ineffective because like a little **sparrow** it never lands and has no impact. This truth was dramatically illustrated by the experience of Balaam (Num. 23:8).

Flattery (26:28; 28:23; 29:5)

> **SUPPORTING IDEA:** *You cannot trust a person who flatters you with compliments that go beyond the truth. It is merely a smoke screen for deceit.*

26:28. Hate expresses itself in a variety of ways. Sometimes it makes a direct attack, spreading lies to hurt or oppress a person. In other cases, it resorts to flattery, exaggerating praise beyond the bounds of truth. The velvet words are intended to lull the victim into complacency just before the trap is sprung. Either tactic uses falsehood as a weapon to express hatred.

28:23. Flattery seems to be the easy way to win friends and **gain more favor**, the approval and acceptance that all of us desire. But **in the end**, the wise person will speak the hard truth. Anyone who **rebukes** a person takes a chance on losing the friendship, but the person who risks losing is the one who ultimately gains. It is a hint of the principle that Jesus taught in Matthew 10:39.

29:5. The person who **flatters his neighbor** is literally seducing him with smooth words, deceiving him for some malicious purpose. He is **spreading a net** designed to entangle the victim by appealing to his vanity and lowering his guard. When a person listens to flattery, it is only a matter of time before he makes foolish decisions and ends up mired in problems.

Slander and Gossip (10:18; 11:13; 16:28; 17:9; 18:8; 20:19; 26:20,22)

> **SUPPORTING IDEA:** *Never attack a person's reputation behind his back. Such slander reveals an attitude of hatred and jealousy in the speaker, and it spreads discord among the hearers.*

10:18. Proverbs 10:18–21 forms a section devoted to speech, and verse 18 explains that **slander** is actually camouflaged hatred. Open **hatred**

explodes with anger, but when a person chooses to hide his hate, he resorts to lies about the opponent. He may think that his whispering campaign is clever, but Scripture identifies him correctly as **a fool**.

11:13; 20:19. A **gossip** in Proverbs is literally a babbler, a person who goes about spreading harmful information about another person. His stories are lies, or twisted versions of truth at best. Such a person is too indiscreet to keep **a confidence**. He **talks too much**, and you should **avoid** entrusting private information to him. In fact, other passages show that a gossip is not just careless but malicious. He is deliberately out to hurt you. **A trustworthy man**, on the other hand, will keep your **secret**. Nothing inappropriate will escape his lips.

16:28. Gossip may spring from a **perverse**, twisted personality. This wicked person spreads **dissension**, just as Samson released foxes in the Philistine fields to spread fire among their crops (Judg. 15:5). And by his words he **separates close friends** by causing them to doubt and distrust each other. Such sabotage of relationships is a serious offense in the eyes of God (Prov. 6:14,19).

17:9. When someone has committed an **offense** against you or some third party, you have two options available: cover it **over** by a discreet silence or publicize it through gossip and complaint. Your choice affects more than just yourself. Covering the offense **promotes love** by maintaining an atmosphere of trust; the person who **repeats the matter** stirs up suspicion, even among **close friends**.

18:8; 26:22. These two verses are identical, and each forms part of a larger collection of proverbs about gossip and the tongue. In either case, the verse points out how strongly people are attracted to gossip. Hearing **gossip** is like eating **choice morsels**, literally, "things greedily devoured." Too many of us snap up the latest tidbit of news, just as a glutton devours the latest delicacy. And when the gossip is received, it takes up a permanent place in the **inmost parts**, lodging in the memory and corrupting the soul.

26:20. Gossip is the fuel that feeds the **fire** of a quarrel. Just as the flame dies out without wood to burn, a **quarrel** that is not fed by fresh reports of offenses can be set aside to die a natural death. A similar concept is repeated in verse 21.

Quarreling (17:14,19; 20:3; 22:10; 26:21)

SUPPORTING IDEA: *Thoughtless words lead to quarrels, and quarrels, once started, are difficult to contain.*

17:14. Proverbs uses dramatic pictures from nature to describe the nature of quarrels. Here, for instance, **a quarrel** is similar to **breaching a dam**; once the water begins to spill through a small opening, it carves a bigger channel until the dam gives way. Once the process starts, it is almost irreversible. And once a **dispute** begins, it escalates quickly. The only solution is to **drop the matter** before things get out of hand. "Dispute" here can refer to a court case; a personal disagreement can end in a costly lawsuit.

17:19. A person who **loves a quarrel** also **loves sin** because you cannot quarrel without sin. There is also an inseparable link between building **a high gate** and inviting **destruction** or breakup. Some have taken the high gate as a literal, impressive entranceway constructed as a display of wealth. It seems more likely that it is a figurative description of pride that walls itself off—a defensive isolation. In this case, both aggression and withdrawal are self-centered and lead to trouble.

20:3. In some periods of history, men would fight duels to defend their **honor**. Our world is still full of people who will lash out when they think they have been slighted. But Proverbs says that only a **fool** is **quick to quarrel**. The person who deserves highest honor is the one who can **avoid** a fight whenever possible.

22:10. In a situation where conflict rages, we instinctively try to deal with the problem by changing the situation. But there are times when the problem is not policies; it is the presence of a **mocker**. Remove the person, and the other problems fall into place. A troublemaker produces **strife**, **quarrels**, and **insults**.

26:21. Men use **wood** to feed a **fire**, and **charcoal** to keep **embers** burning. Without the fuel, a fire dies. In the same way, a **quarrelsome man** keeps a dispute going. He kindles or heats up **strife**, refashioning the facts into more fuel.

🄴 Lying (12:19,22; 17:20; 19:5,22; 21:6)

> **SUPPORTING IDEA:** *God is a God of absolute truth, and he despises lying. We dare not allow ourselves to become accustomed to falsehood.*

12:19. It may seem that a falsehood is the only way out of a tight situation, but a **lying tongue** produces results that last only **a moment** (Job 20:5). **Truthful** words seem to leave you open to trouble, but only truth produces permanent success and endures **forever**.

12:22. Why is it important to tell the truth? Not merely because lies will get you in trouble but because God hates them. He **detests lying** because he is the standard of absolute truth. Because his nature is truth, he commands truth for his people (Prov. 12:17,19; 14:5,25).

17:20. A twisted **heart** or mind eventually surfaces in **deceitful** speech, and both lead to divine judgment. Such a person will not be blessed by God, so he cannot fully **prosper**. He will fall into **trouble** of some kind.

19:5. The Old Testament law contained a stiff penalty for perjury (Deut. 19:18–21), but it was not always enforced. This verse warns the **false witness**

that God will always judge sin, even though human courts may allow him to **go unpunished**, as in the case of the accusations against Naboth or Jesus. The person who **pours out**, or spews out, **lies** will not escape.

19:22. Our deepest desire is not only to experience **unfailing**, loyal **love** but to display it ourselves. We can do without money more easily than we can live without character. **A liar** shows the lack of unfailing love, and it is **better to be poor** than to be known as a person without integrity.

21:6. Is it possible to become wealthy by dishonesty? Yes, but the **fortune** will fade as quickly as a **fleeting vapor**. And dishonesty ultimately becomes a **deadly snare**.

> **MAIN IDEA REVIEW:** *The old nursery rhyme, "Sticks and stones may break my bones, but words will never hurt me," is far from true. We can unleash incredible destruction in our lives, as well as in the lives of others, by means of our words. Thoughtless words lead to quarrels, and quarrels, once started, are difficult to contain.*

III. CONCLUSION

Verbal Battles

The great Puritan preacher Richard Baxter wrote a pamphlet in which he lumped the Quakers with "drunkards, swearers, whoremongers, and sensual wretches" and other "miserable creatures." And then—just in case he had not yet insulted them enough—he insisted that Quakers are no better than "Papists." The Quaker leader James Naylor announced that he was compelled "by the Spirit of Jesus Christ" to respond to those harsh accusations. He proceeded to characterize his Puritan opponent as a "Serpent," a "Liar," and "Child of the Devil," a "Cursed Hypocrite," and a "Dumb Dog."

Even God's children are tempted, when we think the situation calls for it, to use language that ought not to be used. From our perspective hundreds of years later, Baxter's and Naylor's words seem over the top. But what words have we spoken in our daily lives—perhaps to our spouse or children or coworkers—which, if given the advantage of time, might seem inappropriate? It is important for God's children to use Scripture, rather than a personal assessment of circumstances, as our guide for what words are appropriate and what are not. May we let Solomon's warnings take root in our hearts. When talk turns malicious, nothing good happens.

PRINCIPLES

- The tongue has great power for good or evil.
- The words from the tongue reflect the condition of the heart.

- Words always boomerang. We get back from others what we give out.

APPLICATIONS

- Analyze your words, and gain insight on the condition of your heart.
- Read other people's reactions to your speech. Do you win them and draw them? Or do you put them off?
- Ponder the times when people have said encouraging things to you. Compare that with the times people have hurt you with words. Seeing the difference, commit yourself to being lavish with helpful and encouraging words.

IV. LIFE APPLICATION

The High Gate

There are many potential applications of the many truths presented in this chapter. One important one relates to the idea of the "high gate" in Proverbs 17:19. The high gate is a good picture of pride that walls itself off from other people. In his book *Disciplines of a Godly Man* (Wheaton, Ill.: Crossway Books, 1991), Kent Hughes has written:

> There has been an interesting development in suburban architecture. Long gone are the days when homes all had large front porches, with easy access to the front door, enabling one to become quickly acquainted with others in the neighborhood.
>
> In the 1990s we have architecture which speaks more directly to our current values. The most prominent part of a house seems to be the two- or three-car garage. Inside are huge bathrooms with skylights and walk-in closets larger than the bedroom I grew up in. Modern architecture employs small living and dining rooms and now smaller kitchens as well, because entertaining is no longer a priority. Today's homes boast smaller yards and an increasing incidence of high fences.
>
> The old adage that "a man's house is his castle" is coming true today. His castle's moat is his front lawn, the drawbridge his driveway, and the portcullis his automatic garage door through which he passes with electronic heraldry. Once inside, he removes his armor and attends to house and hearth until daybreak, when he assumes his executive armament and, briefcase in hand, mounts his steed—

perhaps a Bronco or a Mustang—presses the button, and rides off to the wars.

Today's homes reflect our modern values of individualism, isolation and privatization (p. 57).

This may not always be a result of pride. Sometimes there are legitimate safety issues involved. Other times we may like to have a different kind of living arrangement, but there are none available. Nevertheless, each of us needs to be sure that prevailing modern culture does not reflect the attitude of our heart. The Lord calls us to reach out to others—to be servant hearted, not prideful—rather than living in isolation. Our words, which reflect our heart, are critical to overcoming barriers to other people, including the potential barrier of modern architecture.

V. PRAYER

Father in heaven, help us to hear our words as you hear them, to use our lips to minister to people, to extend grace to others, and to reflect your heart to our world. May our words always pass through the grid of Scripture and your Holy Spirit, and may they be pleasing to you. Amen.

VI. DEEPER DISCOVERIES

A. The North Wind

Proverbs 25:23 says that the north wind brings rain. In reality, the north wind blows chiefly in October and normally brings a dry cold (Job 37:9). Rain in Palestine most often comes from the west, off the Mediterranean Sea. Some scholars have suggested that the proverb may have been written in Egypt, where the sea is to the north, so that rain often comes from that direction. It may also be that a northwest wind is in view, which would bring moisture to the land.

B. The Mocker

The scorner is one of the most hardened types of fool in Proverbs. The word comes from a root that can mean "to speak boastfully, to talk big." The scorner takes prideful satisfaction in sarcasm and cutting remarks (Prov. 1:22). He ignores verbal rebukes (9:7–8; 13:1; 15:12), and physical punishment is often necessary—as a punishment and as a warning to less entrenched fools (19:25,29).

VII. TEACHING OUTLINE

A. INTRODUCTION

1. Lead Story: Words in the Headlines
2. Context: There are many ways words can turn malicious. Flattery, gossip, slander, quarreling, and lying are ways, Solomon tells us, that words can hurt.
3. Transition: If we want our lives to go as smoothly as possible, we must learn to control our speech. We must come to grips with the damage that hurtful words can do not only to others but also to ourselves.

B. COMMENTARY

1. Power of the Tongue
2. Flattery
3. Slander and Gossip
4. Quarreling
5. Lying

C. CONCLUSION: VERBAL BATTLES

VIII. ISSUES FOR DISCUSSION

1. On a scale of 1 to 10, with 10 being the best, how would you rate yourself on the subject of malicious talk? What is the greatest area you need improvement in? What first step do you believe you could take to begin improving?
2. Think back on a time when someone said something hurtful to you. Do you want to be that kind of memory to others? Are you willing to commit yourself to giving up hurtful speech?
3. Think back on a time when someone said something helpful and encouraging to you. Would you not like to be that kind of memory for someone else? Are you prepared to begin using your speech to increase your helpful impact on others? How might you begin?

Chapter 20

Stirring Up Trouble

Proverbs 1:10–19; 3:29–32; 6:16–19; 16:29; 17:1;
18:18–19; 20:22; 21:7,29; 24:28–29; 26:17; 25:26;
27:3; 28:10,17

I. **INTRODUCTION**
People I'm Going to Bite

II. **COMMENTARY**
A verse-by-verse explanation of these verses.

III. **CONCLUSION**
Wedding Dress for Sale

An overview of the principles and applications from these verses.

IV. **LIFE APPLICATION**
The Skeleton at the Feast

Melding these verses to life.

V. **PRAYER**
Tying these verses to life with God.

VI. **DEEPER DISCOVERIES**
Historical, geographical, and grammatical enrichment of the commentary.

VII. **TEACHING OUTLINE**
Suggested step-by-step group study of these verses.

VIII. **ISSUES FOR DISCUSSION**
Zeroing these verses in on daily life.

| Q u o t e |

"When we 'get even' with someone, that is literally

what we are doing—becoming even with them, that is,

descending to their level in vengeance and losing whatever

moral advantage we may have had."

S y d n e y   J .   H a r r i s

Proverbs

1:10–19; 3:29:32; 6:16–19; 16:29

17:1; 18:18–19; 20:22; 21:7,29;

24:28–29; 26:17; 25:26;

27:3; 28:10,17

I N   A   N U T S H E L L

It is best to resolve discord before trouble breaks out. If we wait for trouble to break out, revenge is always a knee-jerk reaction when we feel we have been offended, but it is a pathway to disaster. We must be careful not to allow others to sway us to act harmfully toward those we feel have hurt us. Violence takes its worst form when lawless people join together as a criminal gang. They incite one another to robbery and murder, more dangerous as a group than the individuals would be separately. Nothing can ruin a young person's life more decisively than becoming involved in such a gang.

Stirring Up Trouble

I. INTRODUCTION

People I'm Going to Bite

*P*erhaps you have heard of the man who went to the doctor and discovered that he had rabies. The man immediately took out a pen and began to write.

The doctor thought the man was making out his last will and testament, so he said, "Listen, this doesn't mean you are going to die. There's a cure for rabies."

"I know that," said the man. "I'm making a list of people I'm going to bite."

We smile at that, and yet the impulse for revenge can be almost that strong. When we feel someone has wronged us, it makes our blood boil, and if we do not respond biblically, we can find ourselves doing and saying things that we have no business doing or saying. Solomon warns us against the impulse for revenge and all forms of violence. We dare not give in to such harmful impulses. We pay a terrible price when we do.

II. COMMENTARY

Stirring Up Trouble

> **MAIN IDEA:** *Headlines are full of violence, and our society seems full of people who are ready to let their disagreements escalate out of control. Proverbs warns us that the best place to tackle the problem is at the very beginning: resolving discord before hurt feelings turn into angry actions.*

Dissension and Strife (6:16–19; 17:1; 18:18–19; 26:17)

> **SUPPORTING IDEA:** *Arguments annoy us, but we don't usually consider them all that bad. God, however, takes them very seriously. According to Proverbs, stirring up dissension holds a place on his "Most Hated Sins" list.*

6:16–19. You might call this passage the "Seven Deadly Sins" of the Old Testament. Starting a list with **six** and then **seven** may seem unusual, but it was a common literary device in Hebrew (see Prov. 30:15–16,18–19,21–31). It makes clear that this list is not exhaustive, but it does include specific things that God **hates**. The first five items are connected with various body parts, moving from the head downward; the last two are specific types of people. All are **detestable** to the Lord because they are corruptions of God's original intention for us.

A person with **haughty eyes** refuses to drop his gaze, even out of humility and respect for God. He recognizes no other as his superior.

The man or woman with **a lying tongue** not only refuses to submit to God's norms of right and wrong but also tries to distort reality for his or her own purposes.

Hands that shed innocent blood belong to a person who cannot control his anger and has so little regard for human life that he will kill for no good reason.

The con artist whose **heart**, or mind, occupies itself with devising **wicked schemes** is a danger to those around him. All he wants is an edge, a situation he can turn to his own advantage. And he obeys laws only when it is convenient.

A person whose **feet** are **quick to rush into evil** shows that he has plunged deep into depravity. This person greets any opportunity for sin with joyful enthusiasm. He is motivated not by tangible benefit so much as by the sheer pleasure of wickedness.

A **false witness** is probably a person who perjures himself in a court case, while the **man who stirs up dissension among brothers** is causing trouble in private life among family and friends.

17:1. Given a choice between poverty and wealth, who would hesitate? But the writer of Proverbs adds a factor to the question. Suppose one household is so poor that they have only a **dry crust** to eat, yet the home is a place of **peace and quiet**. And the alternative is a household affluent enough to afford a feast, but those who eat it are in a battle with one another. While most feasts were connected to a peace offering (Deut. 12:11–12,21), this family's feast is literally a sacrifice of **strife**. Now the answer is clear, even though it goes against the trends of society. Pick the peaceful home!

18:18–19. Casting the lot may sound to us like an unusual way to settle **disputes**, but for the Jewish people it was a method of leaving the choice to God. If the two sides were willing to accept the outcome graciously, they could avoid damaging conflict or litigation between **strong opponents**.

It was important to settle disputes in the early stage, before they escalated into full-scale battle. As verse 19 points out, once you have **offended** a **brother** (whether a friend or a relative), it is difficult to win him back. His defenses are as **unyielding** as a **fortified city** or the **barred gates of a citadel**. Such fortresses seldom fell to direct attack; a conqueror could only besiege them and wait for the defenders to surrender.

26:17. It is easy to predict what will happen if you grab a stray **dog by the ears**. You can expect to be bitten! And in the same way, there is little doubt about the outcome if you meddle in someone else's **quarrel**. The word med-

dles means "to excite oneself," a risky act when you are interfering in a situation you do not fully understand.

B Desire for Revenge (20:22; 24:28–29)

> **SUPPORTING IDEA:** *Dissension soon produces such strained feelings that people start to see themselves as the injured party. They think they have been wronged, and they begin to look for ways to make the other person pay for his insensitivity. This is a danger sign; when you feel it happening to you, back off!*

20:22. The desire to **pay back** the one who has harmed you is instinctive for most people. But Proverbs forbids us from taking that matter into our own hands. Rather than avenge a wrong, we can choose to **wait for the LORD** to take care of it. This verse promises that God **will deliver** us, so we don't have to take that responsibility ourselves. This concept is expanded in Romans 12:17–13:4, which explains that vengeance is God's prerogative. We can trust him to do what is right about our enemy.

24:28–29. In some societies, people have resorted to duels or murder to avenge themselves against wrongs. In other settings, the duel takes place in the courtroom, where a person gives false testimony to get back at someone who has lied about him. But the principle remains the same, whether it shows itself as a physical assault or a legal assault. We do not have the option of doing evil just because someone has done evil to us.

C Plotting to Harm (3:29–30; 16:29)

> **SUPPORTING IDEA:** *You can see how easy it is to crave revenge because there are people who scheme against those who have done nothing to deserve such treatment. We must carefully avoid joining the ranks of such sinners.*

3:29–30. It is wrong to **plot harm against your neighbor**, violating his trust in your good will. *Plot* can mean to plow furrows in a field or to devise plans, and Hosea 10:13 combines the two ideas nicely when it speaks of people who plant wickedness and reap evil. Such deceit can take the form of various schemes (Prov. 3:29) or a malicious lawsuit (3:30). The classic Old Testament example is Jezebel's fraudulent accusation against Naboth (1 Kgs. 21:1–27).

16:29. **A violent man** can be persuasive, enticing **his neighbor** to follow him **down a path** to disaster. This could refer to luring his victim into a trap or to recruiting an unwary soul into joining his life of crime.

D Violence and Murder (3:31–32; 21:7,29; 25:26; 27:3; 28:10,17)

SUPPORTING IDEA: *Jesus said that the person who hates another is actually guilty of murder. He may not have touched the other person, but the resentment seething inside him will eventually erupt into violence. Aggravate him at the wrong moment, and all the emotions will turn into actions.*

3:31–32. The person who uses violence to get what he wants may seem to have found the easy avenue to money and pleasure, and it can be tempting to **envy** his criminal success, but God warns against it. Envy leads eventually to imitation, and we dare not **choose any** of such a person's **ways**.

Why? Because **the LORD detests** a person who is so twisted and devious. The criminal not only faces the natural consequences of his behavior; he also faces the anger of a God who chooses to become personally involved. On the other hand, the **upright** can enjoy personal intimacy with God.

21:7. Violence boomerangs on those who use it. Eventually they will be caught and dragged away like fish in a net. They have refused **to do what is right**, even though they knew what it was.

21:29. A **wicked** person usually **puts** forward **a bold front**, bluffing to get his way. As a result, he gives few clues to his real thoughts. **An upright man**, on the other hand, makes the effort to devote careful **thought**, to go beneath the surface. The wording could refer either to the righteous man analyzing his own ways or the ways of the wicked.

25:26. In an arid climate like Palestine, sources of water are matters of life and death, and few disappointments are more intense than a thirsty man who finds a **spring** or **well**, only to discover that the water is **polluted** and undrinkable. In the same way, **a righteous man** can be a source of life for many others, but when he compromises with evil, he disappoints those who relied on him.

27:3. Stone and **sand** are very heavy, so that even a relatively small amount is a **burden** hard to carry. But that load is just a physical drag. It is even more difficult to carry the **heavier** weight of being provoked **by a fool**. The exact nature of the **provocation** is not given, but it is clear that we must not allow the fool to irritate us to the point where we react thoughtlessly.

28:10. Wickedness is bad in itself, but it becomes worse when it seeks to lead good people into the same sin. God promises that such a person will **fall into his own trap** and die. **The blameless**, on the other hand, **will receive** divine blessing, not only of deliverance from the wicked, but of a lavish **inheritance**.

28:17. A murderer may escape from the law, but he will not escape punishment. He will be **tormented**, or oppressed, by his conscience; he will be a **fugitive** on the run. And **death** will be his only escape. Proverbs 24:11–12 tells us to help the innocent, but this verse warns us not to interfere with God's justice, even by helping the criminal feel better about what he has done.

🅔 Criminal Gangs (1:10–19)

SUPPORTING IDEA: *Violence takes its most horrifying forms when lawless people join together as a criminal gang. They incite one another to robbery and murder, more dangerous as a group than the individuals would be separately. Nothing can ruin a young person's life more decisively than becoming involved in such a gang.*

1:10. Proverbs opens with this warning to a son about the dangers of becoming involved with a gang. The opening statement gives a preview of the discussion that follows. First, he raises the danger: **If sinners entice you,** expanded in verses 11–14. Then he gives the instruction: **Do not give in to them,** expanded in verses 15–18.

1:11–14. This sales pitch is crafted to catch the curiosity of an unwary young man. The gang offers excitement, lying **in wait** to **waylay** or ambush some unsuspecting victim. It promises success with no thought of danger, as the plotters **swallow** up their victims like an open **grave** receiving a corpse. The gang holds out the hope of easy wealth. And the constant repetition of **we** and **us** promises acceptance as one of a group of partners.

1:15–18. The father warns the young man to "Just say no!" It is imperative not to **go along** with such men, not even to **set foot on their paths,** because it is almost impossible to turn back once you begin such a course. These men **rush into sin,** and they **shed blood** without even hesitating. But they will meet disaster in the end. Even a bird is smart enough to avoid a **net** when the hunter has left it in full sight. But these foolish criminals are not as smart as a bird. They plan to **lie in wait,** but they have set their trap for themselves. They talk of ambushes, but they are the ones who will be ambushed.

1:19. In conclusion, the father points out that a universal principle lies beneath his warning. Not just this gang, but everyone who pursues **ill-gotten gain** will lose his life in the process.

MAIN IDEA REVIEW: *Headlines are full of violence, and our society seems full of people who are ready to let their disagreements escalate out of control. Proverbs warns us that the best place to tackle the problem is at the very beginning: resolving discord before hurt feelings turn into angry actions.*

III. CONCLUSION

Wedding Dress for Sale

In the newspaper was the following classified ad: *Wedding dress for sale, never worn. Will trade for .38 caliber pistol.*

This is the very spirit Solomon is warning us against, the spirit of anger, of revenge, of retaliation, of violence and murder, of doing whatever we need to do to satisfy our longing for retribution. But such unbridled anger is never the answer. It moves us to harm others and ourselves. It induces a sort of temporary insanity in which we are fully prepared to do wildly destructive and self-destructive things just to satisfy the craving for justice. Yet the Bible enjoins us never to seek justice on a personal level. The Bible says, "'It is mine to avenge; I will repay,' says the Lord" (Rom. 12:19).

We must heed Solomon's warnings. Nothing good can possibly come from revenge, from hate and anger, from plotting harm. Solomon watched his brother kill his other brother and try to kill their father. He had seen first-hand the destructive force of the spirit of revenge, like a tornado, whirling destruction and misery for everything in its path. In his wisdom, Solomon urges us to let go of the spirit of revenge before it takes hold of our heart. It is easier to prevent it from lodging in our heart than to let it lodge and then try to dislodge it.

PRINCIPLES

- Our thoughts are rehearsal for our actions.
- Violence starts out as hate.
- Unprincipled friends will encourage us to be unprincipled.

APPLICATIONS

- If you would not want the Lord to exact revenge on you for your actions, you should not exact revenge on others. Forgive, and leave vengeance with the Lord.

- Don't let revenge find a home in your heart. It is easier not to let revenge have a home than it is to kick it out after it finds a home.

- Choose your friends wisely. Do not be close friends with those whose attitudes, values, and behavior would entice you away from devotion to the Lord.

IV. LIFE APPLICATION

The Skeleton at the Feast

The uncontrolled anger that spurs us on to revenge cuts both ways, destroying others and destroying self. The story is told of Alexander the Great whose dear friend, a general in his army, became intoxicated and began to ridicule the emperor in front of his men. Blinded by anger and quick as lightning, Alexander grabbed a spear from the hand of a soldier and hurled it at his friend. Although he only intended to scare the drunken general, his aim was true and the spear took the life of his childhood friend. Alexander's revenge destroyed his friend.

Yet the anger cuts toward the self, as well. Deep remorse followed his outburst. Overcome with guilt, Alexander attempted to take his own life with the same spear, but he was stopped by his men. For days he lay sick, calling for his friend and chiding himself as a murderer.

Frederick Buechner, in his book, *Wishful Thinking* (San Francisco: HarperSanFrancisco, Revised/expanded edition, 1993), wrote:

> Of the seven deadly sins, anger is possibly the most fun. To lick your wounds, to smack your lips over grievances long past, to roll over your tongue the prospect of bitter confrontations still to come, to savor to the last toothsome morsel both the pain you are given and the pain you are giving back, in many ways it is a feast for a king. The chief drawback is that what you are wolfing down is yourself. The skeleton at the feast is you.

Before we wolf down our own carcasses in bitter anger and revenge, before we can hurl a spear, literal or figurative, let us lay down our right for revenge. Let us determine that we will leave vengeance with the Lord. As Jesus forgave those who crucified him, may we forgive those who wrong us. May we give up our desire for revenge.

V. PRAYER

Father in heaven, help us to have a heart of forgiveness for the wrongs people commit against us. May we forgive quickly. May we do unto others as we would have others do unto us. May we never allow revenge to find a home in our hearts. May we never plot violence and harm toward others. And may we never run with those who do. Amen.

VI. DEEPER DISCOVERIES

A. Feasts and Peace Offerings (17:1)

The Jewish people enjoyed feasts on a variety of occasions like weddings, the weaning of a child, sheep-shearing time, or birthdays. One distinctive feature of feasts under the Mosaic law was the feast connected with a peace offering. An Israelite could bring an animal and declare his intention to sacrifice it as a peace offering (Lev. 3). Unlike other offerings, this one was followed by a meal. Except for certain parts of the animal burned on the altar or assigned to the priest, the body was returned to the one who brought it, to be the centerpiece of a family celebration.

B. Casting Lots (18:18)

The Bible does not specify exactly what method was used to cast lots, but it was a fairly common way to seek God's will in important decisions. The high priest on the Day of Atonement would cast lots to choose which goat would be sacrificed and which would be sent into the wilderness (Lev. 16:7–10). After Joshua's conquest, lots were used to divide the land between tribes (Josh. 14:2). Lots were cast to decide the rotation of service for workers at the temple (1 Chr. 25:7–8). Some have suggested that the Urim and Thummim in the high priest's breastplate functioned like lots (Exod. 28:30).

C. Besieging a City (18:19)

Conquering an opposing army in the open field was always easier than gaining a fortified city. In fact, one reason Joshua asked God to lengthen the day during the battle at Gibeon was to enable him to destroy the enemy armies before they could reach the safety of their home cities (Josh. 10:11). An invading army could try to climb the walls, demolish the walls or gates with a battering ram, build a ramp to the top, or dig tunnels underneath. If such efforts failed, the enemy would simply surround the city and wait for water and food supplies to run out. This, however, could take years. The Assyrians besieged Samaria for three years (2 Kgs. 17:5), and the Babylonians camped around Jerusalem for eighteen months (Jer. 52:4).

VII. TEACHING OUTLINE

A. INTRODUCTION

1. Lead Story: People I'm Going to Bite
2. Context: Anger leads to revenge, which leads to violence if not checked. There is nothing but heartache when people stir up trouble.

3. Transition: Don't let revenge or unbridled anger find a home in your heart. Don't let unscrupulous people entice you to violent behavior. Let it all go before it builds up and causes you to do something awful.

B. COMMENTARY
1. Dissension and Strife
2. Desire for Revenge
3. Plotting to Harm
4. Violence and Murder
5. Criminal Gangs

C. CONCLUSION: WEDDING DRESS FOR SALE

VIII. ISSUES FOR DISCUSSION

1. What was the worst thing that ever happened to you that made you most desirous of revenge? Did you take revenge or not? Why or why not?
2. Is there anything in your thought life now that, left unchecked, would cause you eventually to do something you would regret? How do you think you can get rid of it?
3. Have you ever had friends who enticed you to do things you would never have done without them? Now that you have had time to think about it, what would you have done, if you could do it all over again, so that they did not influence you?

Chapter 21

Old-Fashioned Honesty

Proverbs 10:2; 11:1; 12:20; 13:5,11; 15:27; 16:11; 17:8,23; 20:10,17,21,23; 21:14; 22:28; 23:10–11; 24:26; 26:18–19

I. **INTRODUCTION**
Life Is a Two-Way Mirror

II. **COMMENTARY**
A verse-by-verse explanation of these verses.

III. **CONCLUSION**
Kids Know Honesty When They See It

An overview of the principles and applications from these verses.

IV. **LIFE APPLICATION**
Our Nose Is Growing

Melding these verses to life.

V. **PRAYER**
Tying these verses to life with God.

VI. **DEEPER DISCOVERIES**
Historical, geographical, and grammatical enrichment of the commentary.

VII. **TEACHING OUTLINE**
Suggested step-by-step group study of these verses.

VIII. **ISSUES FOR DISCUSSION**
Zeroing these verses in on daily life.

"*I* hope I shall always possess firmness and virtue enough to maintain what I consider the most enviable of all titles, the character of an honest man."

George Washington

Proverbs

10:2; 11:1; 12:20; 13:5,11;
15:27; 16:11; 17:8,23;
20:10,17,21,23; 21:14; 22:28;
23:10–11; 24:26; 26:18–19

IN A NUTSHELL

*H*onesty is a bedrock value of any good society. Deceit and lies are the marks of a wicked person. Dishonesty in the marketplace includes using false weights to cheat a customer, or moving boundary markers in order to gain a slice of one's neighbor's real estate. Bribes are also dishonest; they may work, but they are wrong. These and other forms of dishonesty are sin. They often backfire on us. In addition, God will judge the perpetrator.

Old-Fashioned Honesty

I. INTRODUCTION

Life Is a Two-Way Mirror

$\mathcal{P}$salm 51:6 (NASB) says, "Behold, You desire truth in the innermost being." God wants us to be honest toward him. And why not? It is very difficult to pull the wool over the eyes of One who is omniscient. Why be dishonest with God when he knows everything anyway?

When I was in seminary, I taught at a clinic that provided remedial therapy for children with learning disabilities. Part of the protocol was basic instruction in reading. We had a classroom with a two-way mirror in it. Behind the mirror was a small lounge where teachers and parents could observe what was going on in the classroom. We told the students that the mirror was two-way. We told them that their parents were back there and that from time to time we would leave them alone and we would go back there.

In spite of all that information and warning, when the instructors did go to the lounge behind the mirror, before long, some of the students would—I don't know—forget? They would lose sight of the fact that we were back there and would begin goofing around, not studying, annoying their neighbors, pushing their noses up in the mirror, and in general, acting as though there were no two-way mirror and that we were not watching.

We would have to go back into the room and say, "Now Billy, you were supposed to be studying, not bothering your neighbor." You think: *Can't they keep it in their mind for a half an hour and live in our absence as though we were present because in a sense we are?*

Then you think about the Christian life. We're the same way. Life is a two-way mirror. We can't see God, but he can see us. He tells us that he can see us, that we should live as though he were present with us, because he is. Psalm 139:1–4 (NASB) says:

> O LORD, You have searched me and known me. You know when I
>   sit down and when I rise up;
> You understand my thought from afar.
> You scrutinize my path and my lying down,
> and are intimately acquainted with all my ways.
> Even before there is a word on my tongue,
> Behold, O LORD, you know it all."

When we lie, he knows. When we look, he knows. When we cheat, he knows. When we are being dishonest, he knows. When we are being selfish or greedy or prideful or materialistic or lustful, he knows. He knows it all. So Solomon's teachings on honesty in Proverbs make all kinds of sense. And not to be honest doesn't make any sense. The wise person will heed Solomon's teaching.

II. COMMENTARY

Old-Fashioned Honesty

MAIN IDEA: *In our society, a person can be applauded for "honesty" when he acknowledges an extramarital affair on a TV talk show, with no sense of remorse or moral scruples. But Proverbs uses an older concept of honesty: maintaining truth and moral integrity in every aspect of life.*

Truthfulness (12:20; 13:5; 24:26; 26:18–19)

SUPPORTING IDEA: *No moral principle is clearer than the necessity for truthfulness. Regardless of society's opinion, a good person is honest. Deceit and lies are the marks of a wicked person.*

12:20. We would normally contrast **deceit** with *truth*, but this verse contrasts it with **joy**. But the statement is accurate. When you spend life plotting against others, a habit of deceit will embed itself in your heart. The word **plot** is sometimes translated "plow." Just as a farmer plows furrows as the first step toward a crop, the criminal plants thoughts that lead to a horrible crop. On the other hand, the person who promotes **peace** and prosperity for others will enjoy the blessing of **joy** himself.

13:5. If you fear God, you will **hate** what God hates. And God hates falsehood (Prov. 12:22). So the **righteous** person will pull away with disgust from anything that is **false**. The **wicked**, however, are characterized by dishonesty. As a result, they bring **shame** (literally, cause a stench) **and disgrace** on themselves, as well as others around them.

24:26. No one finds it hard to see that **a kiss on the lips** is desirable if it springs from sincere affection or respect. In ancient settings, kisses were not always romantic. Pharaoh declared that all the Egyptians would kiss, or make obeisance to, Joseph (Gen. 41:40). In the same way, everyone appreciates **an honest** or upright **answer**. When we say what is right, we show concern and respect for the other person.

26:18–19. Some people try to cover up malicious deception by pretending that their actions were just in fun. More than mere practical jokes are involved here; the activity is hurtful, damaging people like a berserk archer (Prov. 26:10) **shooting firebrands or deadly arrows**. This verse shows that God holds people responsible to think ahead about the implications of their actions. Playful motives are no excuse for wounding others.

⑤ Accurate Weights and Boundaries (11:1; 16:11; 20:10,23; 22:28; 23:10–11)

SUPPORTING IDEA: *Fraud takes many forms. In Israel, a con artist might use false weights to cheat his customers in commercial transactions. Or he might move the boundary markers in order to gain a slice of his neighbor's real estate. These and other forms of larceny are sin, and God will judge the perpetrator.*

11:1; 16:11; 20:10,23. Before the introduction of coins, a person would pay for a purchase by weighing out a prescribed weight of gold or silver. Unscrupulous merchants would cheat their customers by using **differing** sets of **weights** to squeeze out an extra margin of profit. The references to **dishonest scales** (literally, balances of deceit) and differing weights refer to the same type of fraud. To the merchant, it may have seemed to be a simple case of clever business practices. But each reference in Proverbs links such dishonesty to a higher set of issues. Deception is an affront to God. **Honest scales and balances are from the LORD;** he is the source of all standards of right and wrong, and we measure everything against his absolute truth and holiness. The **weights** in a trader's **bag** are used in a similar way, to ensure honesty in business dealings. And when anyone claims the right to redefine weights for their own advantage, they are disregarding God. No wonder he **detests** such cheaters!

22:28; 23:10–11. Property boundaries in Israel were marked by stones, and surreptitiously moving the stones was an easy way to increase your acreage at a neighbor's expense. The stones were **ancient**, marking boundaries set back at the time of Joshua, when each family received a land grant that would be their permanent possession. When a greedy neighbor rolled the **stone** a few yards to one side, he was ignoring legal boundaries set by their **forefathers**.

Stealing from a neighbor was bad, but encroaching **on the fields** of a defenseless widow or orphan was even worse. God cares for the **fatherless** in special ways (Deut. 10:18; Pss. 10:14,17–18; 68:5; 82:3; 146:9) and steps in as the **Defender** of those who cannot protect themselves. The word "defender" (Heb. *goel*) is often translated "redeemer," and it referred to a near kinsman who would come to the rescue of a person who had fallen on hard times (Lev. 25:25; Ruth 3:12–13; 4:1). And when anyone tries to cheat an orphan, God himself will step in to plead **their case**. When God is the opposing attorney, a crooked lawyer has no chance!

C Cutting Ethical Corners (10:2; 13:11; 20:17,21)

SUPPORTING IDEA: *A person can get cash quickly by cheating others, but he earns nothing but trouble in the end.*

10:2. It may seem contradictory to speak of **treasures** that are of **no value**, but when they have been obtained by theft or deceit, their value soon fades. They cannot preserve a person's life. **Righteousness**, however, can deliver you **from death**. Not only will it open the way to a longer life and a secure family, but it also gives the confidence of a relationship with God that will outlast death.

13:11. **Dishonest money** is literally "wealth from nothing." Such gain could involve dishonesty but would also include any wealth that was not produced by diligent work. Whether a man becomes rich through an inheritance or a lottery, he will soon lose his fortune if he has not learned the financial disciplines necessary to keep it. On the other hand, a person who has taken a slower route, gathering money **little by little**, will conserve his wealth and watch **it grow**.

20:17. A con artist can often get what he wants by **fraud**, and it is gratifying in the short run. He eats **food** bought with illicit funds, and the experience **tastes sweet** to him. But in the end, such a man will come to grief. The sweet taste will turn to **gravel** in his **mouth**, as he suffers the consequences of his crimes.

20:21. A son may be able to get his **inheritance** prematurely, like the prodigal in Luke 15, or he may gain it **quickly** through dishonesty (Prov. 19:26). Whether or not he receives it honestly, such a windfall will not bring blessing **at the end**. Humanly speaking, those who get money easily do not know how to keep it. And if they indulge in laziness or dishonesty, they will forfeit the blessing of God.

D Bribery (15:27; 17:8,23; 21:14)

SUPPORTING IDEA: *Bribery is a prevalent form of corruption, almost a requirement of doing business in many countries. The practice produces results but at the cost of moral integrity.*

17:8; 21:14. These two proverbs speak from the purely human viewpoint, making the observation that bribes can be very effective. We might say that a bribe "works like a charm." **Charm** here is literally "a stone of favor," a tool that a person can trust to bring results. A gift can be a legitimate way to calm someone's anger, perhaps to settle a dispute out of court. It is so effective that in can pacify even great wrath. But there is a fine line between justifiable gifts and an attempt to subvert justice.

15:27; 17:23. These verses give God's view of bribes as an evil practice. **A greedy man** will willingly accept **bribes** as a way to gain wealth quickly, but his practice eventually **brings trouble to his family. He who hates bribes**, in contrast, will prolong his life and avoid trouble.

Giving and receiving bribes are morally suspect. **A wicked man** will accept cash under the table in exchange for twisting or perverting **the course of justice**. The Bible clearly teaches that bribes will debase a person's values (Exod. 23:8; Deut. 16:19; Eccl. 7:7), threaten his home and soul, and cause him to disregard God (Eph. 5:5).

MAIN IDEA REVIEW: *In our society, a person can be applauded for "honesty" when he acknowledges an extramarital affair on a TV talk show, with no sense of remorse or moral scruples. But Proverbs uses an older concept of honesty: maintaining truth and moral integrity in every aspect of life.*

III. CONCLUSION

Kids Know Honesty When They See It

In ancient days when things were weighed on a scale, the merchant put a weight that said "one pound" on one side of a scale, then he weighed onto the other side of the scale a pound of wheat, or a pound of butter. Unscrupulous merchants might shave off an eighth of an inch from the bottom of the one pound weight, which would make it weigh less than one pound. Therefore, when he put on a pound of wheat or a pound of butter, it took less than a pound to make the weight balance. The buyer might never know.

The Bible says that is wrong. It is wrong to cheat, to be dishonest in our actions as well as in our words. Whether it is at work, or at church, or at home, we must be honest in our actions. In the book *Chicken Soup for the Soul* (Deerfield Beach, Fla.: HCI Books, Revised edition, 1993), we find the following story by Patricia Fripp.

It was a sunny Saturday afternoon in Oklahoma City. My friend and proud father Bobby Lewis was taking his two little boys to play miniature golf. He walked up to the fellow at the ticket counter and said, "How much is it to get in?"

The young man replied, "$3.00 for you and $3.00 for any kid who is older than six. We let them in free if they are six or younger. How old are they?"

Bobby replied, "The lawyer's three and the doctor is seven, so I guess I owe you $6.00."

The man at the ticket counter said, "You could have saved yourself three bucks. You could have told me that the older one was six; I wouldn't have known the difference."

Bobby replied, "Yes, that may be true, but the kids would have known the difference."

Whether in our relationship with God, in our words with others, or in our actions with others, God calls us to be truthful and honest in all we do. Whether it is in giving credit to others when we cite them in a paper or making sure the details of a contract are accurate or not exaggerating the claims in our sales pitch, we must be honest and truthful in our words and actions.

PRINCIPLES

- Truthfulness is a building block of society. Without it, life degenerates into the law of the jungle.
- Dishonesty in business is self-destructive, and while someone might win in the short run, we all lose in the long run.
- Bribes may work in an isolated situation, but a society that accepts bribery is a lawless society in which the strong prey on the weak.

APPLICATIONS

- Determine to live a life of honesty. Govern your life so that if everyone acted as you did, all would be well.
- If you don't want to be cheated by others, don't cheat them—in any area of life.
- Vote for government officials who will help establish justice and righteousness in our country so that we do not degenerate into a nation that accepts graft, corruption, and bribery as a way of life.

IV. LIFE APPLICATION

Our Nose Is Growing

We are seeing a decline in honesty in all sectors of life in America. A school principle in Maryland was forced to resign because he coached children to give the right answers on a test that reflected on his job as a principle. Teachers in a school in Ohio cheated by raising the test scores of their students. In New York City, more than four dozen teachers and administrators from thirty schools were accused of urging their students to cheat on various standardized city and state tests. It's bad enough when kids get kicked out for cheating, but an alarming number of teachers and principals are being found guilty.

Education is certainly not the only sector affected. We read of government officials who stretch the truth, of scientists who falsify research, of workers who alter career credentials to get jobs.

Our economy has been rocked by scandals in the banking sector, in high-profile businesses, and in investment companies. The whole fabric of society has loosened a great deal in the last several decades, and there is consequently more dishonesty of all kinds. There is an attitude prevalent today that if you can get away with it, go ahead and lie.

Like Pinocchio, whose nose grew each time he told a lie, our collective national nose has grown to grotesque proportions. From the office of a U.S. president who confessed to lying under oath, down to the elementary schoolchildren who lie about cheating on tests, our culture has been permeated with a loss of commitment to honesty. We think it is important in others, and we want others to be honest, but we want the freedom to manipulate the truth ourselves when it is to our advantage. No one wants to live in a world where everyone is dishonest; we just want to reserve the right for ourselves.

This is not good news. Furthermore, whatever affects society at large also affects the church. So, if lying is on the increase in the world, it is also, inevitably, on the increase in the church. In the face of these facts, the Bible still says, "Lying lips are an abomination to the LORD, but those who deal faithfully are His delight" (Prov. 12:22 NASB). So we in the church have to choose who we are going to be like: the world or Jesus. And if we decide on Jesus, many of us may have some cleanup work to do in the area of honesty.

V. PRAYER

Father in heaven, help us to carry in our hearts the conscious awareness of your presence—of the fact that you are always with us and you know everything we think and do. May that awareness help us be always honest with you and with others. May you use that awareness to conform us into the image of Jesus. Amen.

VI. DEEPER DISCOVERIES

A. Weights and Scales

The people of Palestine did not begin using coins until the Persian period, at the very end of the Old Testament narrative. Instead they bartered, or else they paid with a certain weight of gold or silver. They would use a small scale consisting of a balance beam mounted on an upright support or hung from a cord held in the hand. People would use stones of standard weight, usually kept in a bag, placing stones on one side of the scales until the weight balanced the silver or other commodity on the other side of the scale. The Old Testament frequently warns against using dishonest weights, suggesting that it was a common problem.

B. Boundary Markers

A man's livelihood in Israel often depended on his land, so tampering with property lines was a serious offense. The Jews used various kinds of markers to indicate the property line: a stake, a stone (often inscribed), or other monument. Moving a boundary stone was a crime in Babylonia, Egypt, and Greece, and the Romans took this offense so seriously that it was punished by death. The Mosaic law also warned against doing it (Deut. 19:14; 27:17).

C. The Redeemer

The word *goel* is sometimes translated "redeemer," but it also carries the idea of nearest kinsman because that relative was obligated to carry out various duties to help family members in distress. Kinsman-redeemers might be called on to avenge the murder of a relative (Num. 35:12) or to marry the widow of a brother (Deut. 25:5–10). But the primary function of the redeemer was to buy back land for a brother in distress (Lev. 25:25–28). Based on those human responsibilities, Scripture frequently describes God as the redeemer of his people, standing up for them and defending them (especially in the Book of Isaiah).

VII. TEACHING OUTLINE

A. INTRODUCTION

1. Lead Story: Life Is a Two-Way Mirror
2. Context: Dishonesty, theft, cutting ethical corners, and bribery are all marks of a degenerating society. They are marks of having forgotten God.
3. Transition: We must understand that if we are not part of the solution to these moral shortcomings, we are part of the problem. Christians ought to be like Christ rather than like the world in these matters.

B. COMMENTARY

1. Truthfulness
2. Accurate Weights and Boundaries
3. Cutting Ethical Corners
4. Bribery

C. CONCLUSION: KIDS KNOW HONESTY WHEN THEY SEE IT

VIII. ISSUES FOR DISCUSSION

1. On a scale of 1 to 10, how honest do you believe you are? Is there an area in your life that you believe needs improvement? What should you do?
2. Stealing goes both ways: a customer may shoplift, or a retailer may falsely represent his products or overcharge for them. Have you ever been guilty of stealing from someone? Did you make it right? Have you committed yourself never to do it again?
3. If you are in another country where bribes are required to do business, do you think it is wrong to provide one?

Chapter 22

In Search of Justice

Proverbs 12:17; 14:5,25; 17:15,26; 18:5,17;
19:9,28; 21:15,28; 24:11–12,23–25; 25:18;
28:5; 29:26

I. INTRODUCTION
I Want Justice!

II. COMMENTARY
A verse-by-verse explanation of these verses.

III. CONCLUSION
Justice Instructing the Judges

An overview of the principles and applications from these verses.

IV. LIFE APPLICATION
Justice, Mercy, and Grace

Melding these verses to life.

V. PRAYER
Tying these verses to life with God.

VI. DEEPER DISCOVERIES
Historical, geographical, and grammatical enrichment of the commentary.

VII. TEACHING OUTLINE
Suggested step-by-step group study of these verses.

VIII. ISSUES FOR DISCUSSION
Zeroing these verses in on daily life.

Q u o t e

"Justice is truth in action."

B e n j a m i n   D i s r a e l i

Proverbs
12:17; 14:5,25; 17:15,26;
18:5,17; 19:9,28; 21:15,28;
24:11–12,23–25; 25:18;
28:5; 29:26

I N   A   N U T S H E L L

God despises malicious false witnesses. Judges and those in authority in other places must see that innocent people are acquitted and the guilty are condemned. It takes great wisdom to be just in God's eyes. We must work to help those who are being mistreated, remembering that justice ultimately comes from God, not man.

In Search of Justice

I. INTRODUCTION

I Want Justice!

We all want justice in life, we think—but we don't really. What we want is mercy. A monk in the male counterpart to Mother Teresa's order came to the saintly leader and said, "Mother Teresa, one of my colleagues is spreading things around about me that are not true. I demand justice." To which Mother Teresa replied, "Oh just forget it. Think of what he would say if he knew the truth!"

Ah, how true. Montaigne said that there is not a man alive who, if his innermost thoughts were made public, would not deserve hanging ten times.

So the brother in Mother Teresa's order did not want justice; he wanted mercy. Nevertheless, for an orderly society to function, we must have justice. Justice is the equitable application of moral standards to everyone. If laws are not just, if judges are not just, then life is a wild foray into the unknown and the unpredictable. Chuck Colson once said, "The Christian's goal is not power but justice. We are to seek to make the institutions of power just, without being corrupted by the process necessary to do this."

Justice is found in the character of God. If laws and decisions do not reflect the character of God—the love of God—they cannot be just. George MacDonald wrote, "Justice, to be justice, must be much more than justice. Love is the law of our condition, without which we can no more render justice than a man can keep a straight line, walking in the dark."

In this chapter, Solomon urges all people to be just and all judges to judge justly. He also instructs everyone to look to God and his character for the standard of justice.

II. COMMENTARY

In Search of Justice

MAIN IDEA: *Most of us go through life with only a mild interest in the judicial system, but Proverbs reminds us that the courtroom is a place where lives and fortunes are affected. God cares what happens in court, and he intends that the courtroom be an instrument for rescuing the innocent and convicting the guilty.*

A The Crime of Perjury (12:17; 14:5,25; 19:9,28; 21:28; 25:18)

SUPPORTING IDEA: *Good decisions depend on accurate evidence, so truthful testimony is indispensable. Proverbs warns repeatedly that God despises malicious false witness.*

12:17; 14:5,25. These three verses highlight the difference between **a truthful witness** and **a false witness**. The setting is a judicial hearing where the stakes are high. False testimony can send a person to his death, while truthful testimony can save his life (see also Prov. 6:17,19).

The truthful witness in 12:17 **gives** (literally, bursts forth, breaks out) **honest testimony**. He is honest in character, so his words flow with truth. The false witness, on the other hand, is **deceitful** by nature, and he breathes out carefully prepared **lies**.

19:9; 21:28. Both of these verses warn that perjury will be punished by God. Proverbs 19:9 is virtually identical to 19:5, a double warning because of the seriousness of the offense. Solomon had certainly heard many false witnesses, and he declares that they will not escape punishment. Such a person breathes out **lies** and **will** surely **perish**. In addition, he will bring destruction on any judge who cooperates with his schemes to pervert justice. Both judge and witnesses are accountable for truth.

19:28. The **corrupt witness** is literally "belial," meaning "worthless and wicked." He **mocks at justice**, rather than having respect for the law. Instead, he **gulps down evil**; his appetite for sin is insatiable.

25:18. A perjurer is a dangerous weapon; his testimony can destroy a life or a reputation as effectively as weapons. The Hebrew text in the first line reads "one scattering," but a slight change of vowels allows the translation "club." **False testimony** against a neighbor can crush **like a club**, divide like a **sword**, or pierce like an **arrow**.

🄱 The Burden of Judges (17:15,26; 18:5,17; 21:15; 24:23–25)

SUPPORTING IDEA: *Those who make judicial decisions carry a weighty responsibility for ensuring that the innocent are acquitted and the guilty are condemned. It takes great wisdom to render verdicts in a way that reflects God's concern for justice.*

17:15. God hates injustice in all its forms—whether it involves **acquitting the guilty** or **condemning the innocent**. The law says that God will not let the guilty go unpunished (Exod. 34:7) because his very character demands justice. This is the reason Christ's death for our sins was necessary to provide a way that our sins could be forgiven (Rom. 3:24–27).

17:26; 18:5. These two proverbs identify acts that are **not good** (cp. Prov. 19:2; 24:23; 25:27; 28:21). First, it is wrong to **punish an innocent man** so that he loses a lawsuit he should have won. Second, it is even worse to **flog** a noble or official for carrying out his duties with **integrity**. Third, it is also wrong to be **partial to the wicked** (17:15,26; 24:23; 28:21) or to take their side in a dispute. The word for **wicked** here implies disloyalty to God, rebellion against his law, and total disregard for fellow citizens. Fourth, it is wrong to **deprive the innocent of justice**, either in a court case or in the other daily affairs of life.

18:17. In order to procure justice, a judge must hear both sides of a dispute before rendering a decision. The plaintiff would usually speak first in an Israelite hearing, followed by the defendant. This principle applies to many situations, such as a parent who must referee an argument between two children. The **first** to speak **seems right**, but further **questions** may reveal a different side to the story.

21:15. Justice is necessary if society is to function properly, and those who are **righteous** will always rejoice when justice is done. They have nothing to fear (Rom. 13:1–7), but **evildoers** are in terror of true justice. This **terror** involves dismay over their ruin or undoing.

24:23–25. Scripture consistently condemns any show of **partiality** toward the wicked. Not only does God hate it, but even society despises a corrupt judge. When a ruler gets a reputation for declaring the guilty **innocent**, even the Gentile **nations** who do not have the advantage of the Scriptures will denounce him. It is a universally recognized sin. On the other hand, when a judge becomes known as one who will **convict the guilty**, he will receive **rich blessing** along with respect and appreciation.

The Source of Justice (24:11–12; 28:5; 29:26)

SUPPORTING IDEA: *Human authorities are flawed and sometimes malicious. Sometimes governments oppress the innocent. When such things happen, we must work to help those who are being mistreated, always remembering that justice ultimately comes from God, not man.*

24:11–12. We sometimes speak of "sins of omission," where we fail to do what we know to be our duty. And Proverbs warns that we have the responsibility to take action to **rescue those** who are **being** taken to their **death**. It is unlikely that this refers to the legitimate execution of a murderer but to people who are being oppressed unjustly. They are **staggering toward** their own **slaughter** and desperately need someone to **hold** them **back** from destruction.

The verse condemns the willful ignorance that claims, **We knew nothing about this**. God, who **weighs** our hearts and our motives, knows whether we were genuinely unaware of the injustice, or whether we chose to close our eyes to it out of fear or selfishness. The Lord watches over each person's soul, both to safeguard and to inspect. And he will take both the heart and the deed into account when he renders his judgment.

28:5. A person's behavior determines his ability to understand God's justice. When an **evil** person habitually disobeys the law, he will be less and less able to think straight about moral issues. But the person who seeks **the LORD** will find that (as Prov. 1:7 teaches) he is increasingly able to **understand** moral issues of right and wrong. The New Testament also teaches that rejection of God's standards leads to moral blindness (Rom. 1:21,28), but obedience produces knowledge (John 7:17).

29:26. When we confront injustice, it seems natural to turn to the government for help. We assume that we can receive help if we can get an **audience** (literally, the face) of **a ruler**. But human leaders are not a reliable source of justice. **The LORD** is the ultimate source of **justice**, and we can be confident that he will make things right in the end.

MAIN IDEA REVIEW: *Most of us go through life with only a mild interest in the judicial system, but Proverbs reminds us that the courtroom is a place where lives and fortunes are affected. God cares what happens in court, and he intends the courtroom to be an instrument for rescuing the innocent and convicting the guilty.*

III. CONCLUSION

Justice Instructing the Judges

The traditional symbol for justice is the figure of a woman who is blind-folded, with a scale in one hand and a sword in the other. The blindfolded woman represents the Greek goddess Themis, the goddess of law, custom, and ethics. The idea is that, without regard for who is standing before her, she will mete out justice fairly to all.

In the Supreme Court Building in Bern, Switzerland, however, there is a unique painting by the Christian painter Paul Robert that gives a much more accurate picture of justice. The painting is hanging above the stairway leading to the Supreme Court offices. It is entitled *Justice Instructing the Judges*. In the foreground of the painting are all forms of litigation—the wife against her husband, the architect against the builder, and others arguing among them-selves. Above them stand the Swiss judges with their little white dickies. How will they judge the people before them? Roberts has painted Justice, but this time the woman is not blindfolded. She stands with her sword pointing downward toward a book, on which is written "The Word of God."

God alone is just, and it is only through his Word that we learn what justice is. It is only through his guidance that people will rule in justice. This represents the message Solomon is giving to us in these verses. Only as we represent God's truth can we dispense true justice.

PRINCIPLES

- God's character is the standard for all true justice.
- Only love can administer justice the way God would.
- If we are ever involved in a court trial, we must be faithful to the standards of justice.

APPLICATIONS

- Commit yourself to justice not only in courts of law but also in the home, church, and workplace.
- Judge others the way you would want to be judged.
- Look to God's Word to guide you in furthering justice and righteousness in your world.

IV. LIFE APPLICATION

Justice, Mercy, and Grace

A man stole a loaf of bread. He was caught and taken before the court. It was learned that he had, indeed, stolen the bread, so he was guilty. But the judge learned that the man had no job, and his family was hungry. He had tried to find work but was unsuccessful. Finally, to keep his family from starving, he was reduced to stealing.

The judge rendered his verdict. He said, "You stole the bread, and you are guilty. The law is unambiguous. I order you to pay a fine of ten dollars. However, I realize you do not have ten dollars, so I will pay the fine myself." The judge pulled out a ten-dollar bill and handed it to the man.

As the man took the money, the judge said, "Now I also want to remit the fine." That meant the man did not actually have to pay the fine. He could keep the money. The judge continued, "Furthermore, I am going to instruct the bailiff to pass around a hat to everyone in this courtroom, and I am fining everyone in this courtroom fifty cents for living in a city where a man has to steal in order to have bread to eat." The money was collected and given to the defendant.

Was justice meted out? Indeed. But so also were grace and mercy.

We don't know if this story is true, or true in all its details, but it does represent the kind of justice that God offers. Justice is always tempered with God's mercy and grace. This is an excellent illustration of the fact that only love is capable of delivering true justice.

V. PRAYER

Father in heaven, how grateful we are that your justice is tempered by your mercy and grace. Yes, the demands of justice must be met. But in your grace and mercy, you meet them in Jesus and then offer his righteousness to us by faith. There is no other solution for us. We are sorry that it cost you so much to be able to offer mercy and grace to us, but we take great joy in the fact that when we get to heaven, justice will look on us and smile. It will have been satisfied fully in Jesus. Again, Father, thank you. Amen.

VI. DEEPER DISCOVERIES

Going to Court in Israel

When Moses led the nation of Israel out of Egypt, he served as judge, settling disputes among the people. But when the caseload became too great, he appointed several levels of officials to act as judges in routine matters. Difficult cases were brought to Moses (Exod. 18:19–26). Once the Israelites settled in their land, each town had its own set of local officials to serve as a judicial body (Deut. 16:18). Once again, complex cases could be appealed to a court of priests at the tabernacle (Deut. 17:8; 19:16–17).

When the monarchy was instituted, the king took on the role of judge, though the system of local court sessions still functioned. Solomon was famous for the wisdom he showed in his role as judge over Israel.

The procedures in a court proceeding were very simple. The local officials designated to hear disputes usually met in an open square near the city gate; proceedings were open to the public (Deut. 21:19,22). Solomon erected a "porch of judgment" as a location for his hearings (1 Kgs. 7:7 KJV). The parties in the lawsuit would appear before the judges, and each in turn would present his arguments orally (Deut. 1:16; 21:19). The evidence required might involve a simple oath (Exod. 22:11) or the word of the accuser (Exod. 21:18). Generally the testimony of witnesses was required, and two or three witnesses were necessary to make the testimony valid (Deut. 19:15). Accurate testimony was so important to a fair trial that the law included a provision that any false witness would receive the punishment that would have been meted out to the person he accused (Deut. 19:18–19).

VII. TEACHING OUTLINE

A. INTRODUCTION

1. Lead Story: I Want Justice!
2. Context: Solomon warns us that God despises false witnesses and unjust judges.
3. Transition: God's justice demands that we be just. We must protect the innocent and condemn the guilty because that is what God does. We must look to him as the author and sustainer of all true justice.

B. COMMENTARY

1. The Crime of Perjury
2. The Burden of Judges
3. The Source of Justice

C. CONCLUSION: JUSTICE INSTRUCTING THE JUDGES

VIII. ISSUES FOR DISCUSSION

1. We would all think twice about perjuring ourselves in a court of law, but are you equally careful about truth and justice in the everyday affairs of life? How careful are you always to be truthful in your speech?

2. Probably the most frequent and common demand for Christians is in the home. If you are a parent—or even a roommate or spouse—do you work hard at being just in your dealings with others? Do you draw on the Scriptures to mete out justice for your children?

3. Do you care about the same injustices God cares about? Or do you get more upset about someone cutting in front of you in traffic than you do the inequitable distribution of wealth in the world? Do you think you have some adjustments to make in your life in this area?

Chapter 23

Money: A Trivial Pursuit

Proverbs 3:9–10; 10:15; 11:4,28; 13:8; 14:20; 15:16; 17:16; 18:11,23; 19:4,6–7; 22:2,7; 23:4–5; 27:7; 28:6,8,11,20–22

I. **INTRODUCTION**
Money Is a Terrible Master

II. **COMMENTARY**
A verse-by-verse explanation of these verses.

III. **CONCLUSION**
Money Will Not Make You Content

An overview of the principles and applications from these verses.

IV. **LIFE APPLICATION**
You Can't Take It with You

Melding these verses to life.

V. **PRAYER**
Tying these verses to life with God.

VI. **DEEPER DISCOVERIES**
Historical, geographical, and grammatical enrichment of the commentary.

VII. **TEACHING OUTLINE**
Suggested step-by-step group study of these verses.

VIII. **ISSUES FOR DISCUSSION**
Zeroing these verses in on daily life.

Q u o t e

"*M*oney never made a man happy yet, nor will it. There is nothing in its nature to produce happiness. The more a man has, the more he wants. Instead of its filling a vacuum, it makes one. If it satisfies one want, it doubles and triples that want another way."

B e n j a m i n   F r a n k l i n

Proverbs
3:9–10; 10:15; 11:4,28; 13:8;
14:20; 15:16; 17:16; 18:11,23;
19:4,6–7; 22:2,7; 23:4–5;
27:7; 28:6,8,11,20–22

I N   A   N U T S H E L L

*M*oney can be used to provide for our needs and to honor God, but it cannot make us happy or save our souls. In fact, wealth often leads to destructive attitudes.

Money: A Trivial Pursuit

I. INTRODUCTION

Money Is a Terrible Master

*I*n a church in the deep South, the preacher was moving toward the end of his sermon, and with growing crescendo he said, "This church, like the crippled man, has got to get up and walk."

And the congregation responded, "That's right, preacher. Let it walk."

And he added, "This church, like Elijah on Mount Carmel, has got to run."

"Run, let it run, preacher. Let it run."

"This church has got to mount up on wings like eagles and fly."

"Let it fly, preacher. Let it fly."

Then he added, "Now if this church is going to fly, it's gonna take money!"

"Let it walk, preacher. Let it walk."

That is similar to the story of a man who was standing at the door of the church on his way out after a Sunday morning service, talking to the pastor. He said, "Pastor, I'm glad you said you didn't know where the money was going to come from to operate this church. I was afraid you were going to ask us for it."

We all tend to live pretty close to our money. We have the instinctive perspective that more money will make us happy, and less money will make us less happy. Yet Solomon gives us a biblical perspective on money that helps us see money as God sees it. He admits that it takes money to live, but if you live for money, you will never have enough. Instead of living for money, Solomon teaches us to keep money in its proper perspective—an excellent servant but a terrible master.

II. COMMENTARY

Money: A Trivial Pursuit

MAIN IDEA: *It takes money to live. But that's much different than living for money. We readily appreciate the benefits of an ample income, and we are grateful for what we can earn, but we must also recognize the limitations and risks of wealth. Cash cannot meet our spiritual needs, and it can warp our character if we focus on it too much.*

What Money Can Do (3:9–10; 10:15; 13:8; 14:20; 18:11; 19:4,6–7)

SUPPORTING IDEA: *No one can deny the benefits of financial resources. When the old car dies, it's nice to have the cash to replace it. And wealth makes it easier to cope with a myriad of life's other problems. We can even use it to honor God.*

10:15; 18:11. Wealth does provide a certain amount of protection. In fact, the first line of both these verses acknowledges that **the rich** look to their treasures like a **fortified city**. And **poverty** is nothing to romanticize; it brings ruin to those who suffer its results. Of the several Hebrew words for **poor**, the one used here can also mean "feeble, weak, helpless."

The potency of money is easily overestimated, however. The rich **imagine** that it erects **an unscalable wall** between them and danger. But the only impregnable protection is the Lord, whose name serves as a strong tower for the righteous (18:10).

13:8. A rich man in Israel might face the danger of being kidnapped and held for **ransom**, and he would take comfort in knowing that he had enough resources to pay the price asked. The **poor** person, on the other hand, never needed to fear such a **threat** because no one would expect to gain much from kidnapping him. In many ways, the wealthy man spends his money protecting himself from dangers for which a poor man offers too small a target.

14:20; 19:4. Money also helps a person avoid isolation; **the rich** man always has **friends**, though their motives could be questionable. Unfortunately, **the poor** find that not even **their neighbors** or friends wish to associate with them, despite the statement in Proverbs 14:21 that such behavior is wrong. Poverty is bad enough in itself, but it becomes even more painful when it causes you to lose friends.

19:6–7. These verses expand the truth in the two verses just discussed. Verse 6 explains the great influence of the rich. **Many curry favor** (literally, "stroke the face") **with a ruler**, loading the leader with insincere flattery in order to take advantage of his wealth and power. **A poor man**, on the other hand, has no way to buy friendship. His perpetual needs embarrass and annoy even **his relatives**. People **avoid** him because he needs help they are unwilling to give.

3:9–10. Riches can also be used as a way to **honor the LORD**. These verses give the command, then provide the promise of reward for obedience. The godly person was to use his **wealth** to honor God by giving the first part of each harvest to him as an offering. This was prescribed in the law (Deut. 26:1–3,9–11), and this is the only place in Proverbs that mentions the ceremonial system of the Old Testament. Giving God **the firstfruits** of the **crops** was an expression of faith as well as worship because it would certainly have been useful to keep it for oneself.

God promises that he will bless such a person with lavish harvests, to the point that his **barns will be filled** to overflowing and his wine **vats** will be filled with ample supplies of **new** (fresh) **wine**. In a similar vein, Philippians 4:19 promises that God will supply all the needs of those who are faithful in giving to God's purposes.

Ⓑ What Money Cannot Do (11:4,28; 15:16; 17:16; 22:2; 28:6,11)

> **SUPPORTING IDEA:** *It is easy to overestimate the potency of wealth; it can only take a person so far. Money does not improve a person's standing with God, and it cannot save you from his judgment. It does not enhance one's character or wisdom, and it will not compensate for a life filled with turmoil.*

11:4. Money cannot buy a longer life; only **righteousness** can do that (10:2b). In fact, the way to live longer is not by stockpiling money but by living in the fear of the Lord. We have all observed that **wealth is worthless** in **the day** when God's **wrath** breaks loose, either the day of death or the day of one of *his* judgments.

11:28. Having money is legitimate, but trusting money is foolish. The writer uses the imagery of a tree to make this point. The person who **trusts in his riches** is like a decayed tree leaning precariously to one side; it will not take much to make it **fall**. Scripture teaches frequently that money can easily disappear (Ps. 62:10; Prov. 23:5; 27:24; Jas. 1:11). On the other hand, the **righteous** person is **like a** healthy **green leaf**, a concept repeated in Psalms 1:3–4; 92:12–15; Jeremiah 17:7–8.

15:16. This is one of the numerous sayings in Proverbs that compares two alternatives and tells which is better. Most people would agree that wealth is better than poverty. But let's go a step further. What if the **wealth** comes wrapped in a life of **turmoil**, confusion, and panic? And what if poverty is counterbalanced by a deep **fear of the LORD**? The choice is obvious.

17:16. Wealth will not make a person wise. A **fool** cannot buy **wisdom**, no matter how great the price. He has no **desire** (literally, "no heart") for it;

he simply does not have the capacity to become wise, even if he could pay for the best instruction.

22:2. Wealth does not give you special status in God's scheme of things. The **rich** and the **poor** have one thing **in common**—literally, they meet at this one point. Both are creatures from the hand of God. He is the **Maker** of us all. So there is no reason either to gloat or to despair; each of us should be humbled when we remember how we compare to the Creator, and any of us can have hope because God cares for all his creatures.

28:6. Wealth will not compensate for twisted morals. This is the last of nineteen proverbs that declare one thing **better** than another. Here the writer compares a righteous but **poor man** with a wicked **rich man**. One person has an empty purse but maintains a daily **walk** or practice of **blameless** integrity (cp. 2:7,21; 11:5; 28:10,18). The other person is **rich**, but his **ways are perverse** or twisted, so that he calls good evil and evil good. The verse makes clear that holiness is not always rewarded by earthly riches, but it is still the better path.

28:11. Some wealthy people think their money proves them superior in intelligence or ethics. They are **wise** in their **own eyes**; they think they know it all. But a **poor** person who has insight or **discernment** can see through the facade, recognizing the rich man's true character. Psalm 139:23 prays that God would search the psalmist's heart; at times he may do so through the painful evaluation of an onlooker.

Attitudes About Money (18:23; 22:7; 23:4–5; 27:7; 28:8,20–22)

SUPPORTING IDEA: *Money does not automatically make a person either happy or good. In fact, wealth often leads to destructive attitudes like pride, stinginess, and discontent.*

18:23. A poor person is in no position to demand fair treatment, so he often fails to get it. When he **pleads for mercy**, the **rich man** feels no obligation to show mercy. Instead, he **answers harshly**. The plea might be for an extension of time on a loan, or some sort of legal proceedings may be involved. This proverb reports the ugliness of the world's behavior without approving of it.

22:7. The wealthy often have power that rivals that of government officials so that they can **rule over the poor**, who can seldom dispute the authority of those who dominate them. Poverty often leads to debt, which places even more control in the hand of the lender. The writer observes that a **borrower** becomes a **servant** or slave **to the lender**. This is true in an emotional sense, but in the ancient world it could be true in the most literal sense (2 Kgs. 4:1).

23:4–5. Hard work to provide the necessities of life is a virtue. Exhausting yourself to chase riches is foolishness. When you harness all your energies in the race for materialism, you sacrifice other, more important goals. You **wear yourself out** for something that can disappear almost instantly. Don't be a fool; **have the wisdom to show restraint** (literally, to desist from your purpose). Drop the plan!

The phrase **cast but a glance at riches** literally reads in Hebrew, "If you cause your eyes to fly after it." How ironic that you can fly after wealth, but it will fly away faster than you can flap your wings. Any amount of accumulated wealth can **sprout wings and fly off to the sky like an eagle**.

27:7. People often assume that the wealthy enjoy life more than other people. But luxury loses its thrill when you have too much of it. **Honey** was the sweetest food available in ancient Israel, yet a person could tire of it if he filled himself with delicacies. But the person who is **hungry** relishes even food that is **bitter**. Hunger improves our appreciation for anything that we receive.

28:8. One of the main means for extortion in the Old Testament was by abusive loans and excessive **interest**. An unscrupulous person could amass **wealth** by taking advantage of the poor when they were too weak to help themselves. But God has a special place in his heart for the helpless, and he promises to intervene at some point. All that wealth will eventually go to someone who treats **the poor** with compassion.

28:20–22. God says the path to blessing is to be **faithful** and trustworthy, to show devotion to duty. But many people prefer to pursue get-rich-quick schemes that usually involve devious, dishonest methods. Such unethical shortcuts to riches will not go **unpunished**, either directly by God or through the court system.

Proverbs mentions several things that are **not good**, and this is the final one in the series. God does not approve of showing **partiality**, either in personal matters or in a court setting. One would think that a judge could not be bribed, yet some people **will do wrong** for a price as small as **a piece of bread**.

A stingy man (literally, one with an evil eye, Prov. 23:6; Matt. 20:15) is eagerly grasping for riches and does not realize that his quest will be counterproductive. If you sell your integrity, you are likely to end in **poverty**, and your inner poverty will torment you even while the physical money lasts.

MAIN IDEA REVIEW: *It takes money to live! But that's much different than living for money. We readily appreciate the benefits of an ample income, and we are grateful for what we can earn, but we must also recognize the limitations and risks of wealth. Cash cannot meet our spiritual needs, and it can warp our character if we focus on it too much.*

III. CONCLUSION

Money Will Not Make You Content

Robinson Crusoe is a wonderfully entertaining adventure story that we are all familiar with. But what many people don't know is that it was originally written as an allegory, or a parable of the Christian life. It teaches, consciously and overtly, Daniel Defoe's understanding of how to live the Christian life. Crusoe was marooned on a desert island and before long came to accept the fact that he might not soon get off the island and might possibly never get off. There were no people on the island; there was no way off the island and little likelihood of anyone ever finding him.

After coming to grips with his desperate and hopeless circumstances, Crusoe said:

> I learned to look more upon the bright side of my condition, and less upon the dark side and to consider what I enjoyed, rather than what I wanted; and this gave me sometimes such secret comforts, that I cannot express them; and which I take notice here, to put those discontented people in mind of it, who cannot enjoy comfortably what God has given them, because they see and covet something that he has not given them. All our discontents about what we want appeared to me to spring from the want of thankfulness for what we have.

It is an eloquent and engaging way of saying what many others have said. Benjamin Franklin once wrote, "Discontentment makes a rich man poor while contentment makes a poor man rich." John Bunyan said, "If we have not 'quiet' in our minds, outward comfort will do no more for us than a golden slipper on a gouty foot."

Contentment is a virtue, and the insatiable lust for "more" is a vice. Solomon warns us to put our hopes not in money but in our Lord and the truth he reveals in his Word.

PRINCIPLES

- Money cannot buy the things that make life worthwhile.
- Money can serve you well if you keep it in perspective.
- If you live for money, it will harden your heart.

APPLICATIONS

- Choose to live within the standard of living God makes possible for you.

- Cultivate gratitude for what God has given you rather than ingratitude for what he has not given you.
- Be generous with your money, giving to the needs of the ministry and others. "Giving" is the only antidote for selfishness.

IV. LIFE APPLICATION

You Can't Take It with You

The old story is that you've never seen a hearse pulling a U-Haul. Why? Because you can't take it with you. But here's the Treasure Principle: you can't take it with you, but you can send it on ahead.

John D. Rockefeller was the Bill Gates of his day, one of the wealthiest men who ever lived. After he died, someone asked his accountant, "How much money did he leave?" The accountant said, "All of it." But Jesus' breathtaking revelation is, You can send it on ahead.

And why not? Once your basic needs are met, money does not make you happy. Benjamin Franklin once said, "Money never made a man happy yet, nor will it. There is nothing in its nature to produce happiness. The more a man has, the more he wants. Instead of its filling a vacuum, it makes one. If it satisfies one want, it doubles and triples that want another way."

Listen to these quotes from some of the wealthiest men in the twentieth century.

W. H. Vanderbilt said, "The care of $200 million [which would be equivalent to about $200 billion today] . . . is enough to kill a man. . . . There is no pleasure in it."

John Jacob Astor, another of the world's wealthiest men, said, "I am the most miserable man on earth."

John D. Rockefeller said, "I have made many millions, but they have brought me no happiness.

Andrew Carnegie said, "Millionaires seldom smile."

And Henry Ford said, "I was happier when doing a mechanic's job."

You've read the stories of lottery winners who are more miserable a few years after winning the lottery than before. The wealth they dreamed would bring them happiness didn't.

If we give instead of keep, if we invest in the eternal instead of the temporal, we store up treasures in heaven that we will never lose. Whatever treasures we store up on earth will be left behind. The money God entrusts to us here on earth is eternal investment capital. Every day is an opportunity to buy up more shares in his eternal kingdom.

Surely, this is the perspective on money that Solomon wants us to take away from the Book of Proverbs.

V. PRAYER

Father in heaven, help us to be content with our riches in heaven and not pine for the riches of this world. Free us from the love of money. Make us generous in spirit. May we be content with what you give us rather then dissatisfied for what you don't. Amen.

VI. DEEPER DISCOVERIES

A. Debt and Interest in the Old Testament

In Israel, it was the poor, not the rich, who owed money. Commercial debt was uncommon, and most loans were given to people who needed help because of a financial crisis. Lending to the poor was considered a good deed (Ps. 37:21), but the law forbade charging interest to a fellow Israelite (Lev. 25:35–38). Jews could, however, charge interest on loans to Gentiles (Deut. 23:19–20). The Mosaic law contained regulations designed to protect both the borrower and the lender, including the cancellation of all debts every seven years and at the year of jubilee every fifty years (Deut. 15:1–6; Lev. 25:28).

In the hands of unscrupulous people, lending often became the most common form of extortion. The borrower could lose his possessions, his children, or his freedom (Isa. 50:1). One of the Hebrew words for interest actually means the "bite" of a serpent.

B. Good, Better, and "Not Good"

Proverbs uses several common ways of phrasing the wise sayings that it contains, and the passages studied in this section provide examples of two of the most common structures.

Proverbs 28:21 is the last of six passages that proclaim, "It is not good" (17:26; 18:5; 19:2; 24:23; 25:27; 28:21). It is interesting to note that four of the six deal with the sin of partiality, particularly by a judge who is willing to render a false decision for his own purposes.

And Proverbs 28:6 provides the final example of an even more common form of proverb, which compares two things and declares which one is better. Many of the nineteen verses that take this form deal with money, showing that riches alone do not outweigh other factors such as a harmonious home or a clear conscience (15:16–17; 16:8,16; 17:1; 19:1,22; 21:9,19; 22:1; 25:24; 28:6). Other verses explain that the reality of wealth is better than the mere appearance of it (12:9).

Humility is better than arrogance (16:19), and self-control is better than military prowess (16:32). It is better to confront a bear robbed of its cubs than to meet a fool who is acting the part (17:12). Better to take a back seat and be invited forward than to take the best seat and be removed (25:7). Open rebuke is better than concealed love (27:5), and a neighbor nearby is a better help than a brother too far away to come to your aid (27:10).

VII. TEACHING OUTLINE

A. INTRODUCTION
1. Lead Story: Money Is a Terrible Master
2. Context: Solomon makes three things clear: money can meet life's needs, money cannot improve your standing with God or make you a better person, and money will harden your heart if you live for it.
3. Transition: If you think your life would be better with more money, stop and think about it. What would you use your money for? Would you spend it on yourself, or would you use it for good for God and others?

B. COMMENTARY
1. What Money Can Do
2. What Money Cannot Do
3. Attitudes About Money

C. CONCLUSION: MONEY WILL NOT MAKE YOU CONTENT

VIII. ISSUES FOR DISCUSSION

1. Do you honestly think more money will make you happier? Why or why not?
2. Do you think a Christian can be serious about making money without its ruining his life?
3. In what ways do you think a lot of money would corrupt you?

Chapter 24

The Challenge of Sharing

Proverbs 3:27–28; 11:24–26; 13:22–23; 14:21,31;
15:15; 16:8; 18:16; 19:17; 21:13; 22:9,16,22–23;
25:14; 28:27; 29:7,13

Quote

"We make a living by what we get;

we make a life by what we give."

Winston Churchill

Proverbs

11:24–28; 14:24–(?); 13:22–23;
14:21,31; 15:15, 16:8; 18:16;
19:17; 21:13; 22:9,16,22–23;
25:14; 28:27; 29:7,13

IN A NUTSHELL

God wants us to be generous in sharing with others. How much more would he oppose those who would take advantage of, or oppress, the poor.

The Challenge of Sharing

I. INTRODUCTION

Ten Times the Gift

*A*utomaker Henry Ford was vacationing in Ireland when he was asked to contribute toward a new orphanage. Ford wrote a check for two thousand pounds, which made headlines in the local newspaper. But the paper inadvertently reported the gift as *twenty* thousand pounds. The director of the orphanage apologized to Ford. "I'll phone the editor straight away and tell him to correct the mistake," he said.

"There's no need for that," Ford replied and promptly wrote a check for the additional eighteen thousand pounds.

A heart of generosity always responds to needs if it can. Of course, we cannot meet all the needs of the world, and we must all pray for guidance for which ones God wants us to meet. But if our heart is set toward generosity, the Lord can guide the wallet.

Solomon's great point in these passages is that God expects us to be generous in sharing with those less fortunate. He may ask us to give of our time, our talent, or our treasure. The resource and the amount are up to God. But having a heart of readiness to give, and thereby being open to his leading, is up to us.

II. COMMENTARY

The Challenge of Sharing

> **MAIN IDEA:** *God wants us to be concerned not only with how to acquire and use wealth for ourselves but also with how to share it with others. He makes clear that we have an obligation to help the poor; he loves to use his people as a channel of provision for those who cannot meet their own needs.*

Ⓐ Sharing with Generosity (3:27–28; 11:24–26; 13:22; 14:21; 18:16; 19:17; 21:13; 22:9; 25:14; 28:27)

> **SUPPORTING IDEA:** *Our natural instinct is to hoard our resources, just in case we might need a little extra some day. Like the rich man in Christ's parable who planned bigger barns to store a surplus, we always want just a little more. But when God provides us with resources beyond our needs, he wants us to show a generous spirit in looking for ways to pass them on to meet the needs of other people.*

3:27–28. This verse alerts us to a common sin of omission: failing to give people what they are entitled to. **Those who deserve it** is literally "its owners," so those who **withhold** this particular **good** or benefit are not merely inconsiderate (Deut. 24:14–15) but unjust (Lev. 19:13). This could refer to a legal obligation like a laborer's daily wage, a poor person's legitimate request for aid, or the sum awarded to a plaintiff in a court case. It applies especially to government officials and to the wealthy, who have the **power** to take action, but the principle could apply in any situation.

Proverbs 3:28 focuses particularly on the sin of procrastination. A laborer depended on daily payment of wages to provide his daily needs. Putting him off until **later** was a selfish, hurtful act.

11:24–26. These verses center on the concept of generosity versus selfishness. The first statement is a paradox, like some of Christ's teachings: He who **gives freely** will gain, not lose; and he who tries to keep everything for himself will lose in the end. The giving here primarily refers to voluntary donations to the poor but could also include fair pay for workers (cp. Jas. 5:1–4).

Like Proverbs 11:17, the second verse promises that **a generous man will prosper**. He will find that the effort he expends to refresh others will be repaid, both by those he has helped and by the Lord.

Verse 26 explores the issue of hoarding, a specific form of greed. In the Old Testament world, grain was a major form of exchange. Wealthy landowners could purposely choose to keep their grain off the market in an effort to drive up prices at the expense of the "little people." Naturally, those hurt by his schemes would **curse** him, while they would be grateful to the man who was willing to sell at a lower price.

13:22. How can a person amass enough prosperity to leave a sizable inheritance for the next generation? Be **good**, not wicked! Proverbs teaches consistently that God blesses the righteous, with the result that they have something to bequeath to their children. In fact, the effects of their godliness extend even to the grandchildren. There are exceptions to this principle, like Job, of course. But even when the godly do not have great material wealth, they can always pass down a spiritual **inheritance** that is even more important. In contrast, a sinner often gathers his hoard only to lose it through foolish handling of funds, the consequences of poor character, or the direct intervention of God.

14:21. Our attitude toward the poor is as important as our financial contributions. The Lord declares that it is a definite sin to despise, belittle, ridicule, or hold someone in contempt. Verse 20 observes that people tend to shun the poor, but this shows that it is morally wrong to do so. God's approval and blessing rest on the person **who is kind to the needy** (Prov. 14:31; 19:17; 28:27).

18:16. Several verses in Proverbs make the observation that justice can be twisted by bribes (17:8,23), but the word for **gift** here can refer either to a bribe or a legitimate present. Though there is the danger of misusing gifts, we may also use gifts as an innocent act of courtesy or appreciation (1 Sam. 17:18; Gen. 43:11). The verse simply states the fact that a gift can open doors but does not commend or forbid it.

19:17; 21:13. The word used for **poor** here can also mean "feeble," "weak," or "helpless." Since the poor are unable to help themselves, a compassionate person will be **kind** to them—not just feeling pity for them but taking some action to help them. The law of Moses approved such benevolence (Deut. 15:7–11). Giving to the poor in this way is like lending **to the** LORD because *he* will certainly **reward** such an act of love. You may not get your money back, but God will make it worth your while in some way.

The converse also holds true. If a person **shuts his ears** to the needy, he has a wicked heart, and he will be disregarded when he finds himself in need. The New Testament contains dramatic parallels in Matthew 25:31–46 and Luke 16:19–31.

22:9. Someone might object, "I can't afford to be that generous!" But Proverbs promises that the **generous man** will not have to do without. God rewards such liberality with blessing because willingness to share with the poor demonstrates the genuineness of the person's heart. **Generous** is literally "having a good eye," while a stingy man is described as having an "evil eye" (Prov. 28:22 NASB).

25:14. In an arid climate farmers waited eagerly for the **clouds and wind** that signaled a solid day of the rain they desperately needed. If the clouds passed without dropping any moisture, the disappointment would be bitter. In the same way, needy people will have their hopes dashed when an unethical person promises **gifts** but never gives anything. Better not to promise than to frustrate people by failing to carry through! The New Testament uses similar imagery to describe false prophets who try to win converts by making promises they have no intention of keeping (2 Pet. 2:19; Jude 12).

28:27. This verse summarizes several themes explored earlier. We can afford to be generous in sharing with the **poor** and hungry because God will ensure that our needs are met. But the person who ignores the needs of the poor will receive many **curses**, the resentment of the people around him, and the disapproval of God.

B The Sin of Oppressing the Poor (13:23; 14:31; 15:15; 16:8; 22:16,22–23; 29:7,13)

SUPPORTING IDEA: *Those who live in poverty are often vulnerable to mistreatment by those who wield greater wealth and power. And the Lord commits himself to protect those who cannot protect themselves. He opposes anyone who takes advantage of the weak.*

13:23. Hunger is sometimes the result of laziness or sinful attitudes (Prov. 13:25), but there are other cases where a poor person may work hard and still live in poverty because of **injustice**. In the Israelite economy, he might have a plot of land that produced **abundant food**, but if the political system offered no protection from injustice, all his work could be swept away.

14:31. This verse appears in a context containing many instructions for kings and other officials who are in a position to oppress **the poor**. It is easy to discuss such matters solely on the human level, as a social issue of oppressing the poor or being **kind to the needy**. But Proverbs pushes beyond to the spiritual issues involved. Contempt for the poor actually shows **contempt** for the God who created them. Kindness to the needy results from a heart that **honors God** and serves those whom he loves.

15:15. Oppression is not always inflicted on us by someone else; it may be an attitude that colors everything we experience. The **oppressed are** those who are bowed down, afflicted, and miserable. Hard circumstances may have contributed to their distress. The second half of the verse makes a contrast between oppression and cheerfulness, not oppression and prosperity. If you are emotionally bowed down, everything will seem bitter. But if your heart is **cheerful**, then life can be **a continual feast** that you can celebrate regardless of the circumstances.

16:8. Anyone would be pleased to have **much gain**, a high income. But if the cash flow depends on **injustice**, God is sure to send judgment eventually. It is better to be committed to **righteousness**, even if it means settling for a lower income.

22:16. The Hebrew in this verse is tightly compressed, and English translations vary widely in rendering it. But the overall thrust is a warning against two flagrant social sins: enriching yourself by exploiting **the poor** and seeking an advantage by ingratiating yourself with **the rich**. Both tactics may seem attractive, but both are doomed to eventual failure.

22:22–23. Even pagan writers of the ancient world were concerned for the poor, but only in Israel was God himself presented as the protector of the oppressed. The rich and powerful might strip the poor of their possessions through legal maneuverings, or they might take it by force. The word used for **poor** portrays them as weak and helpless, unable to defend themselves. But those who drag the needy into court will find themselves arraigned before a higher court, with God as the prosecutor. Those who **plunder** the poor will watch helplessly as God plunders them.

29:7. Righteous people want to see **justice for the poor** and helpless; they recognize and are personally concerned about their rights. **The wicked**, on the other hand, **have no such concern**. Literally, they "do not understand knowledge." They do not know right from wrong, particularly in regard to the issue of dealings with needy people.

29:13. Those who oppress the poor generally see themselves as superior to their victims, members of a different class of humanity. But God reminds us that both are equally dependent on God. The very fact that their **eyes** can see is not their own achievement; it is the gift of God.

> **MAIN IDEA REVIEW:** *God wants us to be concerned not only with how to acquire and use wealth for ourselves but also with how to share it with others. He makes clear that we have an obligation to help the poor; he loves to use his people as a channel of provision for those who cannot meet their own needs.*

III. CONCLUSION

Limited Good?

The Mazatec Indians of southwestern Mexico have a curious perspective on giving. They believe there is only "so much" of anything they have to give. For example, they seldom wish someone well. Not only that, they are hesitant to teach one another or to share the gospel with each other. If asked, "Who taught you to bake bread?" the village baker answers, "I just know," meaning he has acquired the knowledge without anyone's help. This odd behavior stems from the Indian's concept of "limited good." They believe there is only so much good, so much knowledge, so much love to go around. To teach another means you might drain yourself of knowledge. To love a second child means you have to love the first child less. To wish someone well—"Have a good day"—means you have just given away some of your own happiness, which cannot be reacquired.

This is absolutely the opposite of the truth. Scripture teaches us that God is able to make our resources abound for every good work *he* wants us to do, claiming that *he* owns the cattle on a thousand hills. It also teaches that the more you love, the more you can love. If you impart knowledge to someone, you double the amount of knowledge between you.

In God's economy, the more you give, the more you can have. Solomon teaches us that we need to think less like the Mazatec Indians and more like the Bible.

PRINCIPLES

- God gives us resources and expects us to trust him when we give them away.
- God expects those with surplus to help those in need. When you give to the poor, you are lending to the Lord.
- God is offended when we take advantage of those people who cannot help themselves.

APPLICATIONS

- Dedicate your resources to the Lord—your time, talent, and treasure.
- Trust the Lord to meet your needs as you tithe your income to him.
- Never take advantage of the poor or anyone else who cannot take care of himself. You are opposing God if you do.

IV. LIFE APPLICATION

Paderewski's Generosity

Generosity has a way of coming back to you.

There were once two young men working their way through Stanford University. Their funds got desperately low, and the idea came to one of them to engage Paderewski for a piano recital and devote the profits to their board and tuition. The great pianist's manager asked for a guarantee of two thousand dollars. The students, undaunted, proceeded to stage the concert.

They worked hard, only to find that the concert had raised only sixteen hundred dollars. After the concert, the students sought the great artist and told him of their efforts and results. They gave him the entire sixteen hundred dollars and accompanied it with a promissory note for four hundred dollars, explaining that they would earn the amount at the earliest possible moment and send the money to him.

"No," replied Paderewski, "that won't do." Then tearing the note to shreds, he returned the money and said to them: "Now, take out of this sixteen hundred dollars all of your expenses, keep for each of you 10 percent of the balance for your work, and let me have the rest."

The years rolled by—years of fortune and destiny. Paderewski had become premier of Poland. The devastating war came, and Paderewski was striving with might and main to feed the starving thousands of his beloved Poland. There was only one man in the world who could help Paderewski and his people. Thousands of tons of food began to come into Poland for distribution by the Polish premier. After the starving people were fed, Paderewski journeyed to Paris to thank Herbert Hoover for the relief sent him.

"That's all right, Mr. Paderewski," was Hoover's reply. "You don't remember, but you helped me once when I was a student at college and I was in a hole."

V. PRAYER

Father in heaven, help us to be generous in spirit. Then we will be ready to give away whatever we have, whether it be money or talent or knowledge or encouragement or love. Amen.

VI. DEEPER DISCOVERIES

A. The Case for Concern

Scripture consistently urges God's people to show concern for the poor and needy and to resist the temptation to mistreat those who cannot defend themselves. The Old Testament instructs us to recognize that rich and poor share equal standing in the eyes of God. Both rich and poor have a common origin: they are creatures of God (Job 31:13–15; Prov. 22:2). Both rich and poor share common blessings like life and sight (Prov. 29:13). And both groups will lose their distinctions in death (Job 3:19).

The New Testament adds to the list of reasons we should be concerned for the poor. In Matthew 25:35–40, Jesus explained that giving food or water to a needy person was equivalent to offering those ministries of love to him. James declares that God has chosen those who are poor in this world to be heirs of spiritual privilege in the future kingdom (Jas. 2:5). And John measures the sincerity of our love by the practical test of what we do to help fellow believers who are in need (1 John 3:17–18).

B. Treatment of the Poor

From the beginning, the Bible has promoted generous treatment of the poor. When Job was defending his upright character, he pointed to the way he delivered the poor and helped the orphans, encouraged the widows and delivered the defenseless (Job 29:12–17). The Mosaic law also commanded the Jews not to harden their hearts toward a brother in need but to open their hands freely to make available to him whatever he needed (Deut. 15:7–11).

VII. TEACHING OUTLINE

A. INTRODUCTION

1. Lead Story: Ten Times the Gift
2. Context: God expects us to be generous with those in need. How much more would he resent our oppressing the poor.
3. Transition: We need to set our heart in "generosity" mode. Then God can move us to give whatever he wants us to give, whether it be time, talent, or treasure.

B. COMMENTARY

1. Sharing with Generosity
2. The Sin of Oppressing the Poor

C. CONCLUSION: LIMITED GOOD?

VIII. ISSUES FOR DISCUSSION

1. Which are you most generous with: your time, your talent, or your treasure? Are you balanced in these areas? Are there significant changes you need to make in any or all three?
2. Are you sensitive to the needs of poor people? Have you ever sacrificed to meet the needs of someone in poverty? Have you allowed your heart to be touched by their need?
3. How much money is enough? Do you have enough, or do you need more? What would you do if you had more? How would it change your giving habits if you had more money?

Chapter 25

Common Sense Economics: Hard Work

Proverbs 6:9–11; 10:4,26; 12:24,27; 13:4; 14:23; 15:19; 16:26; 18:9; 19:15,24; 20:4,13; 21:17,25–26; 24:30–34; 26:14–15; 28:19

Quote

"*Work* as if you were going to live a hundred years;

pray as if you were going to die tomorrow."

B e n j a m i n   F r a n k l i n

Proverbs

6:9–11; 10:4,26; 12:24,27;
13:4; 14:23; 15:19; 16:26;
18:9; 19:15,24; 20:4,13;
21:17,25–26; 24:30–34;
26:14–15; 28:19

I N   A   N U T S H E L L

The wise person realizes that diligence is the price of financial security, as well as the source of many other blessings. A slothful person thinks hard work is beneath him, but his attitude brings hard consequences into his life. Sleep is good and necessary, but loving it is wrong and brings hardship on the lazy person.

Common Sense
Economics: Hard Work

I. INTRODUCTION

Working for the Lord

*C*olossians 3:22–24 tells us whom we should work for:

> Slaves, obey your earthly masters in everything; and do it, not only when their eye is on you and to win their favor, but with sincerity of heart and reverence for the Lord. Whatever you do, work at it with all your heart, as working for the Lord, not for men, since you know that you will receive an inheritance from the Lord as a reward. *It is the Lord Christ you are serving* (emphasis added).

That tells us who our boss is. That tells us who we are working for, no matter what we are doing.

If you are a child still living at home and you have chores to do or your room to keep clean or the bed to make, you do all these things not just for your parents but for the Lord. If you have gone out for volleyball or soccer, and you are supposed to do exercises to get better, you are doing it not just for yourself or for your coach or for the team but also for the Lord. You have been given gifts, such as athletic gifts, or musical gifts, or intellectual gifts, or gifts of being able to meet people well, or gifts of working well with your hands, or you can make things grow. We are to be diligent in exercising these gifts because they have been given to us by the Lord, and we are to improve them and give them back to the Lord.

If we are selling or working on an assembly line or teaching or crunching numbers, we should do our best, serving, first, the Lord.

Sometimes, it is for ministry, but sometimes, it is just so you and the Lord can enjoy it together. You might have a beautiful flower garden, and you don't minister with it, but you simply enjoy it, knowing that the Lord enjoys it too. We can use our gifts just for the joy of doing it. The Flying Scotsman, Eric Liddell, said, "When I run, I feel his pleasure."

We work for a new boss—Jesus. Do your work in a way that is pleasing to him.

II. COMMENTARY

Common Sense Economics: Hard Work

> **MAIN IDEA:** *No amount of clever scheming will make a lazy person into a prosperous one. According to Proverbs, the way to prosperity is hard work. And the person who tries to avoid honest labor, preferring the "couch potato" position relaxing in bed, dooms himself to poverty.*

A The Benefits of Diligence (10:4; 12:24; 13:4; 14:23; 15:19; 16:26; 18:9; 20:13; 21:17,25–26; 28:19)

> **SUPPORTING IDEA:** *Many people spend their energy trying to get out of work. But the wise person realizes that diligence is the price of financial security as well as the source of many other blessings.*

10:4. The equation is simple to understand: laziness results in poverty, but hard work results in wealth. Proverbs consistently holds up diligence as the surest way to gain prosperity and warns against laziness as the quickest path to poverty.

12:24. Solomon had drafted thousands of workers into forced labor to build the temple and then his palace, so he knew how the system worked. The man with **diligent hands** would ultimately be placed in charge, but **laziness** would result in **slave labor**, where the sluggard would be forced to work even harder than the rest.

13:4. The **sluggard** is driven by his cravings, those deep-seated physical appetites that dominate his thoughts. Those desires are never satisfied because he refuses to do the work necessary to fulfill them. The **diligent** person has more controlled **desires**, and because he is willing to labor, he is able to satisfy them. Literally, his soul grows fat, **fully satisfied**.

14:23. The lazy person would rather talk about work than actually do it, and this verse draws the contrast between the results of words versus action. **Hard work** is certain to produce at least some **profit**, but substituting **talk** for activity **leads** to nothing but **poverty**.

15:19. The slothful person continually complains that his path to success is blocked by various obstacles; failure is never his fault. And in fact, his pathway does seem to be **blocked** by thorn bushes. But the **upright** or straightforward person has a clear path; the **highway** stretches before him without the obstacles—partly because his diligence enables him to clear away anything that blocks his way and partly because God has promised to bless the upright.

16:26. Even a lazy person will work if he is hungry enough, so one might say that a little **hunger** is a good motivation to diligence. The New Testament uses the same principle in 2 Thessalonians 3:10–12. A realistic appraisal of human nature must acknowledge that we work most diligently when work is necessary to supply our needs.

18:9. Being **slack** in one's **work**, doing it poorly or carelessly, may not seem like a serious matter. But Proverbs declares that a person who does sloppy work is **brother** to (similar to) a person **who destroys** or demolishes the product. The result in either case is that the product is unusable.

20:13. **Love** of **sleep** is equated here to laziness, and staying **awake** is a hallmark of diligence. The sluggard who prefers to stay in bed will eventually end up going hungry because he lacks the discipline to produce any food. The farmer who works hard will have an abundance of **food**.

21:17. A quick way to become poor is to be one **who loves pleasure**, a lover of good times. Verse 15 pointed out that the man who aims to act justly will receive joy as a by-product, but verse 17 says that the person who pursues pleasure will find that, like a greased pig, it escapes his grasp. **Wine and oil** are some of the legitimate commodities that people connect with feasting and pleasure, but anyone who **loves** luxuries will soon be poor because he consumes all his income. Proverbs condemns neither pleasure nor food but warns of the danger of loving either.

21:25–26. The lazy man's life is a round of continual **craving**, and he substitutes wishing for working. As a result, he ruins himself and his story ends in **death**. He longs for things but refuses to work, so he eventually starves. **The righteous**, on the other hand, works hard and produces much. He is not a slave to his cravings, however, so he is free to **give** liberally to others.

28:19. Hard work is the only path to prosperity; there is no short cut. But the lazy person prefers to chase **fantasies** (literally, empty things). He wastes time on high-risk schemes and speculative ventures that promise instant wealth rather than doing the things that would actually make him prosper.

Ⓑ A Portrait of the Lazy Man (10:26; 12:27; 19:24; 26:14–15)

SUPPORTING IDEA: *A slothful person thinks of himself as too clever to do things the hard way and feels pity for the unimaginative people who simply work for a living. But those who observe him see a laughable figure, not a wise person.*

10:26. A **sluggard** is irritating to the employer who sends him on an errand because he inevitably fails to complete the task. **Vinegar** was made from wine that had gone sour, and no one enjoyed its taste. And **smoke** blowing into a person's **eyes** is just as unpleasant.

12:27. The Hebrew word translated **roast** here is of uncertain meaning, so some interpreters have thought the verse describes a man too lazy to go after food. But Jewish tradition and similar words in Arabic make it probable that it actually pictures a person too **lazy** to cook what he catches. The **diligent man**, on the other hand, values his **possessions** enough to care for them, so he takes full advantage of what he has gained.

19:24; 26:15. Here we find a tongue-in-cheek portrait of the lazy man. He refuses to be hurried, and though he **buries his hand** in a dish of food, he is too lazy to **bring it back** up to his mouth! If this description were literally true, the person would soon starve.

26:14. Now the **sluggard** is found in **bed**. In fact, that's the only place you can find him. He seems bolted to the bed, like **hinges** attached to a door jamb. Back and forth he rolls, but he never exerts the energy to get up and get moving.

ⓒ The Danger of Loving Sleep (6:9–11; 19:15; 20:4; 24:30–34)

> **SUPPORTING IDEA:** *The Bible presents sleep as a welcome respite from labor. But when a person sprawls in bed, wasting the morning rather than starting a good day of useful activity, sleep has become a danger. Sleep is good, but loving it is wrong.*

6:9–11. The writer attempts to motivate a slothful man to get up and start the day, asking twice **how long** he plans to lie in bed. Then he issues a warning—he who naps when he should be working will soon be victimized by poverty. It may seem like a **little** indulgence, but trouble will dog his steps. The word **bandit** literally means, "one who walks about" as a vagabond or vagrant. The NIV translation portrays his fate like that of a man who is attacked suddenly by scarcity, just as an unsuspecting victim would be assaulted by a bandit. It seems more likely, however, that it describes it not as an ambush but as the relentless badgering of the vagrants who hang around the door, always wanting more, siphoning off one's resources until everything is gone. Whether by robbery or vagrancy, the result is the same: **poverty**.

19:15. A lazy man may say, "I'll just rest for a minute," but he soon falls into a **deep sleep** or stupor (Job 4:13; 33:15). He is totally unaware how much time he is wasting. The word for *sleep* here is sometimes used for a heavy sleep induced by God (Gen. 2:21; 15:12; 1 Sam. 26:12). **The shiftless man** is literally a "man of laxness"—he relaxes when he should be working, so he **goes hungry**.

20:4. Laziness can be irrational, ignoring the laws of cause and effect. The slothful farmer would procrastinate, failing to **plow** at the right **season**. The phrase actually means the late autumn or the onset of winter. The weather would be getting cold, and the sluggard would be too soft to withstand the chill and do the hard work of plowing. But even though he has not plowed and planted at the right time, he still **looks** for a crop when it is **harvest time**. He forgets the fact that harvest happens only when the farmer is willing to do the planting at the right time.

24:30–34. This section tells a short story, followed by a lesson. The writer tells how he went past a **field** belonging to a **sluggard**. It contained a **vineyard**, and even the first glance made it plain that the owner suffered from a lack of judgment. The place was a mess—obviously neglected, with **weeds** and **thorns** choking out the crops. The **stone wall** around the field was not repaired, so animals could come in and eat the crops.

He stopped to think about it (v. 32) and drew this conclusion (vv. 33–34): laziness leads to poverty. In words very similar to Proverbs 6:10–11, he warns that such laziness would eventually ruin the place. Poverty would drain all a person's resources, leaving him as destitute as the victim of a robbery.

> **MAIN IDEA REVIEW:** *No amount of clever scheming will make a lazy person into a prosperous one. According to Proverbs, the way to prosperity is hard work. And the person who tries to avoid honest labor, preferring the "couch potato" position relaxing in bed, dooms himself to poverty.*

III. CONCLUSION

Widgets and Hard Work

General George C. Marshall once said, "Small deeds done are better than great deeds planned." And so it is. There is no profit in a half-baked cake, a partially painted house, or seeds planted but not harvested. Life depends on dependability. Life depends on people being willing to see their tasks through to completion. Whether it is a great task, such as sending a rocket ship to the moon, or a small task, such as mowing the lawn, it is only worth something when it is completed, and completing things requires diligence. The difference between success and failure is hard work.

It isn't a popular character trait today. Today we seem more interested in trying to get out of work rather than doing work. A college friend of mine went to work in a factory that was controlled by a union. It was a tool and die factory in which the laborers were paid by the number of pieces of work they completed. They had to complete a certain number of widgets an hour, and when they completed them, they got paid their hour's wage. However, it took only fifteen minutes to do that many widgets. So the workers worked for fifteen minutes, got their work done, then sat down and played cards for forty-five minutes, worked for fifteen minutes and played cards for forty-five minutes—the whole day

My friend didn't think it was right, plus he didn't know how to play cards and was bored, so he just kept making the widgets. He piled up an impressive number—four times the number of the other workers. They didn't like it. They told him to stop making so many widgets. Well, he wanted to be a good testimony, so he went to the boss and told him what he thought was wrong with the system, and that the factory could quadruple its production if it just required people to keep working. He thought he might get a Nobel Prize or something for rooting out this problem and exposing it.

Instead, his boss said in no uncertain terms, in a menacing voice, that he had negotiated with the union long and hard to get the number of widgets down to the number it was, and he didn't want anyone coming in and messing up the system, and that if he knew what was good for him he would make only the required number of widgets.

So much for hard work.

Hard work used to be an honored quality. Listen to some of the quotes from days gone by. Ralph Waldo Emerson said, "If a man has good corn, or wood, or boards, or pigs, to sell, or can make better chairs or knives, crucibles, or church organs than anybody else, you will find a broad, hard-beaten road to his house, though it be in the woods." Martin Luther King said, "If a man is called to be a street sweeper, he should sweep streets even as Michelangelo painted, or Beethoven composed music, or Shakespeare wrote poetry. He should sweep streets so well that all the hosts of heaven and earth will pause to say, 'Here lived a great street sweeper who did his job well.'"

Abraham Lincoln said, "The leading rule for a man is diligence." Oswald Chambers said, "If God is diligent, surely we ought to be diligent in doing our duty to him." Think how patient and diligent God has been with us. The character qualities to which we are to aspire are the character qualities of God. God is diligent. Therefore, we ought to be diligent.

PRINCIPLES

- Hard work is a requirement for a good living.
- Laziness brings financial hardship.
- Being careless, lazy, and irresponsible not only brings hardship into our lives; it also dishonors God.

APPLICATIONS

- Work hard, even at things that are beneath your ability. That is the doorway to advancement.

- Always remember: you are working for the Lord. Do your work well, and you will eventually get your reward from him.

- If you love others who depend on you, work hard for them, too. Laziness and carelessness hurt them, as well.

IV. LIFE APPLICATION

Taking Pleasure in Our Work

Proverbs 22:29 (NASB) says, "Do you see a man skilled in his work? He will stand before kings; he will not stand before obscure men." Proverbs 27:18 (NASB) says, "He who tends the fig tree will eat its fruit, and he who cares for his master will be honored."

If a person is diligent, he will gain recognition that will bring satisfaction. I remember as a college student working at a job in which one of my tasks was to keep the floor clear of sawdust, which was being continually created. The manager found odd jobs for me to do, and I did them, plus kept the floors swept. I only needed a job until the end of the semester in December, and he kept me on until then. I believe now that he kept me on simply because he saw that I was working hard and he liked to have a clean building. At Thanksgiving time, he went out of his way to look me up and give me a turkey, even though as a part-time, temporary employee, I wouldn't normally get one. I have always been grateful for the job and the turkey. But upon reflection, I think it was the principle of being rewarded for being diligent in my job.

It gave me great pleasure to be recognized and rewarded for doing a good job that was, frankly, beneath my abilities. We don't always get a reward for doing a good job. And we've probably all had jobs we didn't like. You may be in one you don't like right now. How do we take pleasure from our work when we don't get recognized and our work isn't pleasurable?

Recognize that you are contributing to God's plan of dominion over the earth. Genesis 1:26 says, "Then God said, 'Let us make man in our image, in our likeness; and let them rule over . . . the earth.'" We are to come together in social order. One is to make bread. Another is to make cheese. Another is to make plows. Another is to till the soil. And so on. Everything that we do— if it is not illegal or unethical or immoral—contributes to man's dominion over the earth.

Take the little example of driving your car to the grocery store. Someone had to make the roads, another the tires, another the gas, another the paint on the highway. Someone had to drill the oil well for the gas. Someone else had to supply the food. And on and on it goes. Ponder how interrelated we are and how, without each of us doing our part, we cannot all have our needs met.

- Consider your work environment part of the world God wants you to reach for Christ.
- Accept that you are working for God.
- Do your job as well as you can (not less well, and not better than you can; one approach underachieves, and the other gives ulcers).
- Be moral and have integrity.
- Treat other people with dignity and respect.
- Be prepared to give a verbal testimony of your faith in Christ.
- Leave all results to God.

V. PRAYER

Father in heaven, help me honor you by working hard and well at the tasks you have given me to do. May I find joy in whatever it is, knowing that I work for you, and that from you I will ultimately receive my reward. Amen.

VI. DEEPER DISCOVERIES

A. The Causes of Poverty

Proverbs recognizes the problem of poverty and warns against the oppression that often contributes to it. But it also emphasizes the fact that people often bring poverty on themselves by their foolish actions. The lazy person who talks instead of working is destined to be poor (14:23), as well as the person who is in a hurry to make money rather than diligently carrying out carefully made plans (21:5). The greedy person who tries to grasp everything for himself, withholding what is rightly due others, will lose it all eventually (11:24; 28:22). Another way to lose it all is to be a lover of pleasure, a person who consumes money as fast as it appears (21:17). And the person who oppresses the poor or fawns over the rich will find his tactics backfiring (22:16).

B. The Farmer's Year

The Israelite farmer generally raised several different crops on his acreage, which came ready for harvest at various times all the way through the dry summer months. Barley harvest took place in April or May, followed by the wheat harvest that could happen as late as July. Then figs, grapes, and other kinds of fruit became ripe in the later summer.

Once the last crops were harvested, the cycle would begin again. A farmer would plow his fields and prepare for planting during late September and early October, then sow the seed by mid-November, before winter made the ground hard. It would have been uncomfortably cold by the end of planting season, but the onset of winter made it vital to finish the task if there was to be a harvest the next year.

VII. TEACHING OUTLINE

A. INTRODUCTION
1. Lead Story: Working for the Lord
2. Context: Hard work carries its own blessings, while laziness carries its own curses.
3. Transition: We should see everything that we do as service to Christ. Whatever we do, in labor, profession, or hobby, we should do to the glory of God.

B. COMMENTARY
1. The Benefits of Diligence
2. A Portrait of the Lazy Man
3. The Danger of Loving Sleep

C. CONCLUSION: WIDGETS AND HARD WORK

VIII. ISSUES FOR DISCUSSION
1. Have you ever tasted the results of blessing for hard work or hardship for laziness or irresponsibility? How did it impact you? Did you learn from it?
2. What can you do to help instill a sense of responsibility and hard work into your children or those you are ministering to?
3. What area of your life is currently the greatest drawback to receiving the rewards of hard work?

Chapter 26

Common-Sense Economics: Working Smart

Proverbs 6:1–8; 10:5; 11:15; 12:11; 14:4; 17:18; 20:16; 21:20; 22:26–27,29; 24:27; 27:13,18,23–27

Quote

"*W*ork is not a curse, it is a blessing from God who calls man to rule the earth and transform it so that the divine work of creation may continue with man's intelligence and effort."

John Paul II

Proverbs
6:1–8; 10:5; 11:15; 12:11;
14:4; 17:18; 20:16; 21:20;
22:26–27,29; 24:27;
27:13,18,23–27

IN A NUTSHELL

*N*ot only must we work hard, but we must also make wise choices and avoid foolish risks. We must do the right thing at the right time and plan ahead. Do not let your concern for another person prompt you to take a foolish risk; you could both go down.

Common-Sense Economics: Working Smart

I. INTRODUCTION

Capitalizing on Opportunity

*M*uch of success lies in discernment: having the ability to make wise choices. In the passages in this chapter, Solomon is not exhorting us to work harder but smarter. Easier said than done! Peter Drucker, in his book *The Effective Executive* (New York: Harper & Row, 1967), wrote:

> A decision is a judgment. It is a choice between alternatives. It is rarely a choice between right and wrong. It is at best a choice between "almost right" and "probably wrong"—but much more often a choice between two courses of action, neither of which is probably more nearly right than the other.

That is why is takes discernment to work "smarter." But Solomon gives us valuable principles in these verses. It takes the ability to use biblical principles to guide us in the decision-making process. It takes the ability to see beyond the immediate moment and make decisions with long-term implications.

In his book *Quest for Character* (Grand Rapids: Zondervan, 1993), Chuck Swindoll tells the story of Tom Fatjo. He was a Rice University graduate, slated for a stable, predictable professional life. Things were progressing as planned when Tom found himself with a room of angry home owners in a southwestern suburb of Houston. The problem was that their city had refused to pick up their garbage at the back door of their homes, so they hired a garbage pickup service. But the new service was having serious problems, so the garbage was starting to back up on them. Flies were buzzing around trash cans at the backs of all the houses, and the situation was getting serious.

That night, Tom Fatjo couldn't sleep. A crazy idea was running through his head. He decided to buy a garbage truck and have the garbage picked up himself. That led to the purchase of another truck and then another. That evolved into the largest solid-waste disposal company in the world, Browning-Ferris Industries, Inc., with annual sales in excess of $500 million.

Of course, we cannot all do such a thing. But the point is, this man combined biblical principles with an opportunity and experienced success. On a lesser scale, we can probably all do the same.

II. COMMENTARY

Common-Sense Economics: Working Smart

> **MAIN IDEA:** *Mere activity never made a person prosperous. Though diligence is necessary, it is just as important to understand your job and spend your energy doing the things that make a difference. The right job done at the right time will produce the profit you want. And once you gain those profits, you will avoid foolish risks like cosigning that could cause you to lose it all needlessly.*

🅐 Do the Right Things (12:11; 14:4; 21:20; 22:29; 24:27; 27:18)

> **SUPPORTING IDEA:** *Working hard is not enough. We must invest our energy in the activities that will produce results. Tackle solid projects with good potential for growth; stay away from wild schemes.*

12:11. The farmer who simply **works his land** may seem like an unimaginative plodder, endlessly repeating the cycles of the seasons. But his steady labor produces results; he will produce ample supplies of **food**. In contrast, a different person may dream greater dreams. In fact, he may chase his visions frantically; the Hebrew for "chase" is an intensive word. But in the end, he has nothing but **fantasies** and empty, worthless schemes. He **lacks judgment** because he doesn't have sense enough to do his daily work.

14:4. Oxen were the tractors of the ancient world with the **strength** to pull a plow more effectively than any other animal. They were expensive, of course, and they required much labor to feed and to clean their stall. Life was simpler on the farm where there were no oxen. The **manger** or feed trough was **empty** (literally, "clean," a word which often describes moral purity), and the stall was orderly. You could escape the expense of feeding the oxen. But those are small advantages compared to the boost in productivity that the ox could bring. Sometimes we need to be ready to accept a certain amount of work and disruption as the price of growth.

21:20. Consumption versus investment is an issue that separates the wise from the foolish. A **wise** person has enough diligence to produce wealth and enough restraint to save what is needed for the future rather than using it all immediately. **Choice food** is literally "precious treasures" and applies to a broader range of possessions than just food stocks. The **foolish man** thinks only of the present, so he consumes everything immediately. As a result, he may run out of food before the next harvest replenishes his supply.

22:29. How can a worker gain a promotion? The best way to move ahead is to become **skilled** in your **work**. The word *skilled* can include the idea of quick or prompt. When a king or other leader discovers someone who does not stop with a job that is merely "good enough," he will want to employ him.

24:27. A young Israelite who was ready to start his own family would need to build a house for his bride and get his farm operating. Which is the first priority? Proverbs advises him to do the **outdoor work** first. He should get the **fields ready** because they were his source of income. The **house** was the place that provided personal comfort, but the crops were the means for supporting the farmhouse. In short, produce before you consume. And a young person contemplating marriage should set up a means to support his family before he starts one.

27:18. If you do a good job, you will get good results. This principle holds true for a farmer: when he nurtures and cultivates a **fig tree**, it will produce **fruit** that he can **eat**. In the same way, a person who faithfully attends to the business of his **master** will be **honored**.

🅱 Pick the Right Time (6:6–8; 10:5; 27:23–27)

> **SUPPORTING IDEA:** *A farmer must plant or harvest at the right time, or his opportunity will pass. And in any other field of endeavor, we must understand the cycles of the market and do what is needed at the appropriate time. Plan ahead, or deadlines will surprise you.*

6:6–8. The **ant** is a model of diligence, and Solomon recommends it as an object lesson for the lazy. Anyone who carefully considers its behavior will gain in wisdom.

Ants also display initiative, the willingness to take useful action even without direct supervision or orders from a superior. A colony of ants has no apparent **commander** of any kind, but it carries out coordinated work better than many people who have a leader!

In particular, ants have the apparent foresight to anticipate future needs. They gather and store **provisions** during the **summer**, at the time of **harvest**, when the **food** is readily available. Then they have plentiful supplies to carry them through the winter.

10:5. Just as the ant works at the proper time, farmers must reap the harvest at the moment the crops are ripe. A young man who is **wise**, having prudence and sound judgment, will have sense enough to move into action at the harvest time before the crops are ruined. A fool who **sleeps during harvest** has failed his family at the time when he is most needed; his uselessness will bring shame to his father.

27:23–27. These verses give a brief treatise on managing a farm, with principles that apply to any livelihood. First, Proverbs gives the basic command: pay **attention** to your **flocks** and **herds**! They need too much care, and too many things can go wrong, to assume that they can be neglected. Any occupation demands constant attention.

Riches do not endure forever; if you do not continue to monitor your investments, your wealth can disappear quickly. Even a king's **crown** is not automatically **secure**; maintaining a kingdom requires constant vigilance. And if these seemingly impregnable sources of wealth can be lost, then surely a farmer cannot afford to neglect his herds.

The person who recognizes the rhythm of nature and follows the cycle of his occupation will enjoy steady dividends. He will harvest **hay** at the proper time, so that he stockpiles food for his livestock. And then he can watch the **new growth** of grass beginning, even during the harvest, promising a fresh supply of food when it is needed. This person understands the cycles of his business, and he takes steps to keep up his resources.

Feed the flocks, and they will provide for your needs. The wool of the **lambs** gives **clothing**, and the **goats** can be sold to provide cash for a new **field**. In addition, **goats' milk** will provide nourishment for the entire household. And in any enterprise, the same principles can apply to provide for personal needs and fuel careful expansion.

Don't Take Another Person's Risk (6:1–5; 11:15; 17:18; 20:16; 22:26–27; 27:13)

SUPPORTING IDEA: *It may seem sensible or loving to cosign a loan for another person, but it puts you at great risk. You are responsible for the actions of someone you cannot control, and you could very well find yourself taking the loss when he acts irresponsibly or has bad luck.*

6:1–5. Solomon warns with surprising intensity of the foolishness of putting up security for a loan, making a commitment that could cause you to suffer great loss. He first describes the predicament in increasingly graphic terms. To **put up security for your neighbor** is to promise that you will pay back his loan if he is unable to do so. To strike **hands in pledge** is to formalize the agreement, as we would shake hands or sign on the dotted line. Anyone who makes such a deal is in a snare; he has been **trapped** by his own **words**. His financial fate is out of his control, resting solely on his neighbor's willingness to pay off the loan.

What is the appropriate response? Get out of the agreement! Gaining freedom from this dangerous position should be your top priority. You should take the initiative and go to the other party and plead to be released. Since you have signed the agreement, you cannot demand; you must **humble yourself** (literally, crush or tread yourself down, demean yourself, make yourself small). **Press your plea** aggressively; don't take *no* for an answer; push it even if you are almost obnoxious.

Finally, do not delay. Do not stop to take a nap; do it now! When a **gazelle** or a **bird** is caught in a trap, they do not nap for a while before they try to escape. They struggle immediately, knowing that it is only a matter of time before doom strikes. Debt works the same way; it is only a matter of time before the consequences arrive.

11:15. Simple rules of cause and effect come into play whenever we cosign for another person's loan. If you put up **security** for someone else, you will eventually **suffer** loss. But if you refuse to enter into such an agreement, you are **safe** (literally, free of care).

17:18. Proverbs 17:17 says, "A friend loves at all times." But he does not give rash loan guarantees that cause financial entanglements. A friend who needs such help is a bad risk, and you will almost certainly end by paying it all. It is better to give outright what you think is right, rather than giving a blind guarantee that enables the other person to sink deeper into trouble.

20:16; 27:13. Normally, a Jew was not allowed to keep a debtor's cloak or other **garment** as collateral for a loan (Exod. 22:26–27). But this proverb urges them to go ahead and take the garment if the person was foolish enough to sign as **security** for the loan of a **stranger** or a **wayward woman**. Loss of a garment is small penalty for a person who would risk his possessions for a questionable, perhaps sinful, relationship.

22:26–27. These verses remind us of the serious consequences of being entangled in someone else's debt. You will probably have to pay off the debt, and if you don't have the **means** or resources to do so, then you are the one who will lose everything—down to **your very bed**!

MAIN IDEA REVIEW: *Mere activity never made a person prosperous. Though diligence is necessary, it is just as important to understand your job and spend your energy doing the things that make a difference. The right job done at the right time will produce the profit you want. And once you gain those profits, you will avoid foolish risks like cosigning that could cause you to lose it all needlessly.*

III. CONCLUSION

The Wrong Business

Many years ago, there was a cartoon in the newspaper entitled *Pogo,* by Walt Kelly. It was the ongoing story of a possum, an alligator, a dog, and other assorted animals living in the Okeefenokee Swamp in South Georgia. One day's cartoon pictured Pogo fishing in the swamp. A duck came along and sat down beside Pogo, and said, "Has you seen my cousin?"

Pogo answered, "Your cousin?"

The duck said, "Yes, my cousin is migrating north by kiddy car."

"Kiddy car?" an astonished Pogo asked.

"Yep. He's afraid to fly. He's afraid he's gonna fall off."

"Then why don't he swim?" Pogo queried.

"Well, he don't like to swim 'cause he gets seasick."

Pogo concluded, "When your cousin decided to be a duck, he chose the wrong business" (Walt Kelley, *Pogo*, New York: Simon and Schuster, 1951, pp. 146–7).

A duck that won't fly or swim will have a hard life. He doesn't do the very things a duck needs to do. In the same way, each of us needs to decide what we're going to be and then do the things that are required of us. Each of us needs to decide that, whatever God wants us to do in life to make a living, we will go about it the way Solomon outlines in Proverbs. We must work hard. We must work smart. We must not borrow trouble by assuming responsibility for other people's debts. If we are scrupulous in following Solomon's teachings, life will go much better for us than if we ignore them.

PRINCIPLES

- Sometimes you have to spend money to make money, but it should always be done wisely, with full calculation and wise counsel.
- If you violate the principles of success, you will pay with failure.
- If you unduly risk yourself financially, you may be ruined financially.

APPLICATIONS

- Choose your work wisely. Work smarter as well as harder. Don't foolishly pursue avenues of work that will not pay off.
- Pay attention to the principles and forces that affect success. Just as a farmer has to be smart about the weather, so every worker needs to apply principles of success to his labor.
- Don't cosign for another person's loan. You will imperil your own financial well-being. You may be financially destroyed, along with the person you cosigned for.

IV. LIFE APPLICATION

Does God Care About Our Jobs?

The way we make our living can be a real challenge. Some jobs go smoothly and predictably, but many do not. Even adhering to the principles in Proverbs, the workplace can be a challenge. In a book written many years ago, *The Christian in Business* (Westwood, N.J.: Fleming H. Revel, 1962), John E. Mitchell wrote:

> Will Christianity and business mix? Is God interested in the way we do our work? Is he interested in a lathe operator and in the quantity and quality of his output? Is he interested in a watchman as he makes his rounds through the warehouse in the darkness and silence of the night? Is he interested in a stenographer, in the way she types her letters? Is he interested in a salesman and what he says to a prospect? Is God concerned about a businessman's business? Is God there when he makes out his income tax return or his expense account? Does he take an interest in the company's advertising campaign and the claims made for the product? Is he present at personal interviews, at conferences, director's meetings, labor union negotiations, trade conventions, business luncheons, and black-tie banquets? When a businessman succeeds or fails, is God interested?

To say *no* to these questions is to relegate God to a place of no importance in the very area of a person's life where he spends the most of his waking hours. On the other hand, he who answers *yes* to these questions, whether he be a Supreme Court justice or a garbage collector, transforms his career into a thing of dignity, high purpose, satisfaction, and excitement.

Yes, God cares about our vocations. That is why he inspired Solomon to write so prolifically and helpfully about workplace issues. He wants us to do well as we follow his principles. So, in addition to following Solomon's instructions carefully, we may also feel free to pray for God's blessing and guidance on all we do. If we are obedient to God, he will guide us into a rich life.

V. PRAYER

Father in heaven, tune our hearts to walk with you in all ways and at all times. Help us do the right things at the right times. Guide us as we refuse to entangle ourselves in the potentially ruinous traps of those in debt. May we honor you in all we do, and may you bless our faithful obedience. Amen.

VI. DEEPER DISCOVERIES

A. Lending and Cosigning

Though we do not have records of all the details of Israel's practices in borrowing and lending, the Old Testament law included basic regulations governing this practice. The primary purpose of Old Testament lending was to provide aid to a fellow Israelite who had fallen on hard times (Lev. 25:35–37). Therefore it was illegal to charge interest on loans to another Jew (Deut. 23:19–20); foreigners, however, could be charged interest. Every seven years, all debts were to be forgiven (Deut. 15:1–3) so that no one would be ruined by a crushing load of debt.

A lender could ask for various items as collateral to secure the loan but could not take anything like a millstone that was vital for the family's survival (Deut. 24:6–13). He could not enter the house to seize any property as collateral, and anything like a cloak that would be seriously missed was to be returned at night for use.

At various times in Israel's history, these laws were abused, even to the point where children were sold into slavery because of debt (2 Kgs. 4:1–7; Neh. 5:1–11).

In a fascinating passage, Job acknowledges that he was too bad a risk for anyone but God—so he asked the Lord to sign for him! And Psalm 119:122 (NASB) asks the Lord to "be surety" to his servant for good. It is comforting to realize that God's resources are never exhausted. He can take on our obligations, no matter what they are, and meet them according to his riches in glory.

VII. TEACHING OUTLINE

A. INTRODUCTION

1. Lead Story: Capitalizing on Opportunity
2. Context: Solomon has taught us to be on the lookout for doing the right thing at the right time. In addition he has warned us against potentially ruinous entanglements in the debt of others.
3. Transition: Each of us must choose to follow his wisdom, leaning on Scripture, prayer, and wise counsel to walk the road of success that Solomon lays out for us.

B. COMMENTARY

1. Do the Right Things
2. Pick the Right Time
3. Don't Take Another Person's Risk

C. CONCLUSION: THE WRONG BUSINESS

VIII. ISSUES FOR DISCUSSION

1. Are you well matched for the work you are doing? Do you understand how to be successful in what you are doing? This does not mean "rich" but that you understand how to do the job and what principles lead to success.
2. How could you learn how to do your job more effectively? Are there steps you should take to improve your success?
3. Do you have your debt under control? Are there changes you need to make in your life, not only not to take on someone else's debt but also to keep your own in check?

Chapter 27

❧ ❧

Abundant Family Relationships

Proverbs 1:8–9; 10:1; 11:22,29; 12:4; 14:1; 15:20; 16:31; 17:2,6,21,25; 18:22; 19:13–14,26; 20:20,29; 21:9,19; 23:22–25; 25:24; 27:15–16; 28:24

I. **INTRODUCTION**
The Building Block of All Society

II. **COMMENTARY**
A verse-by-verse explanation of these verses.

III. **CONCLUSION**
Pass the Salt or I'll Knock Your Block Off
An overview of the principles and applications from these verses.

IV. **LIFE APPLICATION**
The Power of a Godly Example
Melding these verses to life.

V. **PRAYER**
Tying these verses to life with God.

VI. **DEEPER DISCOVERIES**
Historical, geographical, and grammatical enrichment of the commentary.

VII. **TEACHING OUTLINE**
Suggested step-by-step group study of these verses.

VIII. **ISSUES FOR DISCUSSION**
Zeroing these verses in on daily life.

> ## Quote
>
> "*H*e is happiest, be he king or peasant,
>
> who finds peace in his home."
>
> G o e t h e

Proverbs
1:8–9; 10:1; 11:22,29; 12:4;
14:1; 15:20; 16:31; 17:2,6,21,25;
18:22; 19:13–14,26; 20:20,29;
21:9,19; 23:22–25; 25:24;
27:15–16; 28:24

IN A NUTSHELL

*C*hildren who honor their parents are a joy, while children who dishonor their parents are an annoyance. Marriage to a godly spouse is also one of life's greatest blessings, but life can be miserable if the relationship deteriorates. The Bible teaches that old age is an honor and encourages us to respect senior citizens.

Abundant Family Relationships

I. INTRODUCTION

The Building Block of All Society

*M*uch humor has been directed at the home. Humorist Robert Orbin once said, "Who can ever forget Winston Churchill's immortal words: 'We shall fight on the beaches, we shall fight on the landing grounds, we shall fight in the fields and in the streets, we shall fight in the hills.' It sounds exactly like our family vacation." Someone else once said, "To prove his love for her, he swam the deepest river, crossed the widest desert, and climbed the highest mountain. But she divorced him. He was never home."

We chuckle, and yet we instinctively believe what Samuel Johnson wrote, "To be happy at home is the ultimate result of all ambition, the end to which every enterprise and labour tends." The home is the building block of all society. As the home goes, so goes everything else.

Chuck Colson once said:

> No other structure can replace the family. Without it, our children have no moral foundation. Without it, they become moral illiterates whose only law is self. Ordained by God as the basic unit of human organization, the family is . . . the first school of human instruction. Parents take small, self-centered monsters, who spend much of their time screaming defiantly and hurling peas on the carpet, and teach them to share, to wait their turn, to respect others' property. These lessons translate into respect for others, self-restraint, obedience to law—in short, into the virtues of individual character that are vital to a society's survival (*Draper's Book of Quotations for the Christian World,* Edythe Draper, ed., Wheaton, Ill.: Tyndale House, 1992, p. 210).

Solomon knew and understood this. He loaded his proverbs with keen advice on what to do and what not to do for the family, dealing with children, husband and wife relationships, and the elderly.

II. COMMENTARY

Abundant Family Relationships

> **MAIN IDEA:** *Where can we find the deepest happiness? Not by being successful in business or becoming wealthy and well-known. Our most important source of satisfaction with life rests in committed relationships with others. God has designed the family to be the place where we naturally build such relationships.*

Parents and Children (1:8–9; 10:1; 11:29; 15:20; 17:2,6,21,25; 19:26; 20:20; 23:22–25; 28:24)

> **SUPPORTING IDEA:** *Nothing makes mom or dad happier than having their children turn out well. And grandchildren are better yet! But few sorrows burn more deeply than the pain of having a child who has strayed into destructive behavior.*

1:8–9. The first way a son can honor his parents is by listening attentively to them. Proverbs frequently issues the call to **listen** (4:1,10,20; 5:1,7; 7:24; 8:32; 19:20; 22:17; 23:19,22) because no parental wisdom will help a child who refuses to pay attention to it. Since the verse mentions both father and mother, it must be a reference to an actual family rather than a sage's advice to his disciples. Proverbs 1–9 is couched as the **instruction** of a father, and a mother is also involved in teaching (3:1; 6:20). The word **teaching** is *torah* in Hebrew, often translated "law." When God gives a *torah* directly, we call it "the law"; when a mother gives it, we call it "teaching." In either case, it guides a person's behavior at the same time that it teaches him how to live.

Attentiveness to parents reaps a reward. Just as **a garland** for the **head** or a gold **chain** for the **neck** enhances a person's attractiveness and symbolizes his prosperity and position, the counsel of wise parents produces a young person who commands respect and admiration.

10:1; 15:20. These two verses are very similar, both showing how much a parent's happiness is affected by a son's behavior. A **son** who heeds his father's instruction will become **wise**, and few things please a **father** more (Prov. 23:15; 27:11; 29:3; cp. 3 John 4). A headstrong fool, on the other hand, will bring **grief** to both **mother** and father (17:21,25; 19:13). He is so calloused that he **despises his mother**, with no qualms about inflicting pain on her.

11:29. When a son is a rebellious fool, he brings **trouble on his family**, much like Achan (Josh. 7:25–26) or King Ahab (1 Kgs. 18:17–18). He may assume that he can run wild and squander his father's estate, but the father will probably disinherit him, so that he will **inherit only wind** (i.e., nothing).

He may have expected to have wealth and servants, but he will be penniless, forced into servitude in order to survive.

17:2. In most cultures, a person's position was determined by his birth. Those born into wealthy families might expect to inherit a place of power. But Solomon points out that wisdom and sound character may trump lineage. A prudent **servant** who learns from instruction (as in Prov. 16:20) will sometimes be placed in a position of authority over a **son** who shames his parents. Such a reversal of fortune is illustrated by Solomon's own son Rehoboam, who lost most of his kingdom to Jeroboam, a former employee of his father.

17:6. When a family is properly related to God and to one another, it becomes a beautiful network of relationships, each generation proud of the others. Older people instinctively see their grandchildren as a **crown**, a cause for joy and a mark of honor. And it is healthy and normal for **children** to be proud of their **parents**. All of this is what God had in mind for the family, as a portrayal of the love that marks the Trinity.

17:21,25. Just as parents rejoice when their children display wisdom, they grieve when their sons turn out to be fools. In verse 21, the first use of **fool** is the Hebrew *kesiyl*, a dull, thick-headed person; **fool** in the second line is *nabal*, the boorish, obnoxious person. Verse 25 uses a particularly strong word for the father's **grief**, translated as sorrow (Eccl. 1:18; 7:3), provocation (Prov. 27:3); or annoyance (Prov. 12:16). In addition, such a son brings **bitterness** to his mother.

19:26. In the ancient world, few crimes were more serious than mistreating parents. It is a rejection of the most direct form of authority. The phrase **robs his father** means to assault or otherwise mistreat him; and the phrase **drives out his mother** implies actually seizing the family home and ejecting the parents. It is bad enough to disregard the instructions of a parent, but actually to abuse them is despicable. And receiving such treatment hurts even more when you receive it from your own son.

20:20. The Mosaic law provided for the death penalty when a son was an incorrigible rebel, and this proverb proposes a similar fate for a son who **curses** his parents. It actually calls down a curse on the man despicable enough to curse his own **father** and **mother**. Saying that **his lamp will be snuffed out** is a figurative expression referring to his physical death (Prov. 13:9; 24:20; Job 18:5–6; 21:17). The picture is strengthened by the closing phrase; **pitch darkness** is literally "the pupil [of the eye] of darkness," the darkest part of the middle of the night.

23:22–25. Here we find practical instruction in how to obey the fifth commandment. Verse 22 gives direct commands, while verses 23–25 present the same truth indirectly. The two focal points are **listen** and **do not despise**. Perhaps Proverbs repeats the command to listen so often because it is so easily forgotten. To despise is to hold in contempt, one of the sins that Proverbs hits hard.

To **buy the truth** is to spend whatever time or energy it takes to gain it—a call to discipline! The rest of this passage dramatizes once again the truth that the best way to honor your parents is to become wise and righteous. Nothing will make them happier.

28:24. For a son to rob his parents of their possessions has the same effect as destroying those items: they are lost to the parents. What could be a more obvious way to break the fifth commandment? To make matters worse, the ungrateful son claims he has done nothing **wrong.** Jesus condemned a sophisticated version of this sin in his day, the practice of *corban,* which allowed a person legally to escape his obligations to help his parents by declaring that those funds had been designated for the temple (Mark 7:11). The early church agreed in condemning a son who failed to help his parents (1 Tim. 5:4,8).

B Husbands and Wives (11:22; 12:4; 14:1; 18:22; 19:13–14; 21:9,19; 25:24; 27:15–16)

> **SUPPORTING IDEA:** *Men realize that marriage to a godly, capable woman is one of life's greatest blessings. But life together can be miserable if you let the relationship deteriorate!*

11:22. In a humorous saying, Proverbs notices the incongruity of physical beauty joined to moral ugliness. Israelite women often wore nose rings as part of their jewelry, but a **gold ring in a pig's snout** would be ludicrous and repulsive. It would not make the pig any more desirable. And if a woman **shows no discretion** (literally, turns away from discretion), mere physical attractiveness cannot compensate for her surrender to moral weakness.

12:4. A wife's character makes a great difference to her husband. A **wife** may be of **noble character,** exhibiting the strength and capability attributed to Ruth (Ruth 3:11) and to the woman portrayed in Proverbs 31:1–10. She is a **crown** to her husband, giving him dignity and honor. But a wife may be **disgraceful,** lacking in moral strength and solid character. The pain of the shame her husband bears because of her weakens him, just as a man can be incapacitated by physical **decay** of **his bones.**

14:1. This verse proclaims the power of a wife to build up her home or tear it down. Though it could theoretically refer to a physical **house,** it seems more likely that the writer is talking about her household. **The wise woman** cares for her family and causes it to flourish; **the foolish one** lives in a manner that causes it to deteriorate.

18:22. Even wise young men have difficulty discovering a good **wife;** they may choose a girl for the wrong reasons, then discover that their choice was hasty. It is only with guidance from God that a man can be assured of finding the right girl. So when a husband enjoys a wife who truly builds a happy home with him, he should recognize that he has received a **good** gift.

And as James 1:17 tells us, all good gifts come ultimately from God. He has received a token of God's **favor** or approval. The Lord is pleased to do him good.

19:13–14. Having a **foolish son** is a disaster. For the father, it is the **ruin** of his life; the word is related to "chasm," like falling over a cliff. And equally distressing is life with a **quarrelsome wife**. The word *quarrelsome* appears more often in Proverbs than any other book of the Bible, translated as "quarrelsome" (21:9,19; 25:24; 27:15); "dissension" (6:14,19; 10:12; 15:18; 28:25; 29:22); "disputes" (18:18–19); "quarrels" (17:14; 22:10; 26:20); and "strife" (23:27). The perpetual discord that she stirs up is as relentlessly irritating as a leaky roof. Just as a **constant dripping** can cause exasperation and permanent damage to a house, she can cause irreparable harm to the family relationships.

But nothing brightens a man's life more than the gift of a **prudent wife**, one who is capable and successful, who knows how to deal with people lovingly. She is his greatest asset. And even though a man would inherit property from his parents, including **houses and wealth**, God is the one who provides such a wife.

21:9,19; 25:24 How bad is life with a **quarrelsome**, ill-tempered **wife**? According to Proverbs, living cramped into the **corner** of their flat **roof** would be easier to handle than a house shared with such a person. In fact, it might be better to camp out in the **desert**! Some wives, of course, might legitimately ask for revised versions of these proverbs to describe life with quarrelsome men!

27:15–16. Verse 15 repeats the complaint of Proverbs 19:13, comparing the constant bickering of a **quarrelsome wife** to the way a roof leaks continually **on a rainy day**. Often the drips will continue long after the rain has stopped.

The Hebrew of verse 16 is tricky to translate. The word *restrain* is usually translated, "to keep in store, to treasure, to hide," as in Hosea 13:12. In this context, it may mean the husband is trying to ward off arguments by steering conversations away from touchy topics or by avoiding certain people. But such efforts are futile. You cannot keep **the wind** from blowing; you cannot pick up **oil** that has spilled; and you cannot prevent a wife from speaking her mind.

C The Older Generation (16:31; 20:29)

SUPPORTING IDEA: *In the Western world, people tend to look down on the elderly. But the Bible treats old age as an honor and encourages us to respect senior citizens.*

16:31. In the Old Testament world, elders were the respected members of society. **Gray hair** was not something to hide but a mark of honor, a thing of **splendor** or beauty. Proverbs teaches that long life is a reward for **righteous** living (9:6; 10:27), even though there are many exceptions to that rule. But a person who honors God over a long life can carry his gray hair like a **crown**; he has earned it!

20:29. Young people rely on **their strength**, which shows itself in vigorous actions. Older people rely on their wisdom and godly character, garnered over a long life. **Gray hair** is their mark of distinction. Both young and old have their own kind of excellence, and these are to be admired and respected.

> **MAIN IDEA REVIEW:** *Where can we find the deepest happiness? Not by being successful in business or becoming wealthy and well-known. Our most important source of satisfaction with life rests in committed relationships with others. God has designed the family to be the place where we naturally build such relationship.*

III. CONCLUSION

Pass the Salt or I'll Knock Your Block Off

Rearing our children doesn't always go as smoothly as we would like. Author Henry Brandt tells the story of when he and his wife invited to dinner the president of the college Brandt was attending as a young man. He and his wife had gone to great lengths to ready the house and to prepare their preschool children on how to act and what to say.

When the president came, they fell all over him. They got him to the table and sat him next to their little daughter who had barely learned to talk. That was a mistake. During the meal, the little tot said to the president in her birdlike voice, "Will you please pass the salt?"

Brandt writes:

> Nobody paid any attention. We were listening to the president. So she tried again.
>
> "Will you please pass the salt?" A small little voice that was easy to ignore as we strained at every word of the president.
>
> But the third time, this curly-haired tot single-handedly smashed all illusion about the offspring of the Brandt family we had so carefully constructed. She hammered our distinguished guest on the arm and yelled, "Pass the salt or I'll knock your block off!" (Brandt, *I Want to Enjoy My Children,* Grand Rapids: Zondervan, 1975, pp. 20–21).

And yet, though there are inevitable setbacks in the child-rearing process, character on the part of the parents, plus adherence to biblical principles, will win the day. As Solomon tells us, "Train a child in the way he should go, and when he is old he will not turn from it." While this is a not an ironclad guarantee, it is a statement of a principle that is generally true and a proverb that we can follow with confidence.

PRINCIPLES

- Older generations can have a strong, positive impact on younger generations if they will go about it in the right way.
- Young people can increase their pleasure in life and decrease its pain if they will choose wisdom over foolishness.
- Older people can take pride in their lives if they will continue to grow in wisdom all their days.

APPLICATIONS

- Listen to the warnings against fools! Put yourself in their place and see the pain you bring into your life by foolish behavior.
- Ponder the good that comes from a life of wisdom. Choose the good!
- Determine what you want your life to be like at its end, and then work toward that during the days you have left.

IV. LIFE APPLICATION

The Power of a Godly Example

In his book *A Spiritual Clinic* (Chicago: Moody Press, 1958), author J. Oswald Sanders recorded the classic observations about two Revolutionary War era families from New England, and the differing impacts each has had down through the generations. One family was the Max Jute family, and the other was the family of Jonathan Edwards, the well-known theologian and scholar who played such a prominent role in the early days of our nation.

Max Jute was a godless man who married a woman of like character. Among the known descendants, over 1,200 were studied:

> Three hundred and ten became vagrants; 440 lived a debauched lifestyle; 130 were sent to prison for an average of 13 years each, 7 of them for murder. There were over 100 alcoholics; 60 thieves; 190 prostitutes. Of the 20 who learned a trade, 10 of them learned the trade in prison. It cost the state about $1,500,000, and they made no contribution to society.

> In about the same era Jonathan Edwards, a man of God, married a woman of like character. From this marriage came 300 clergymen, missionaries, and theological professors; over 100 college professors; over 100 attorneys, 30 of them judges; 60 physicians; over 60 authors; and 14 university presidents. There were many giants in American industry. Three became United States congressmen, and one became the vice president of the United States.

The impact of a godly father and mother is enormous and can last for many generations. Those who follow the principle of Proverbs, backed up by godly character, will be blessed by God with a godly heritage that will bring great reward to them, great good to the world, and great glory to God.

V. PRAYER

Father in heaven, help us to take seriously the principles for a godly family found in Proverbs. May we live out our biblical responsibilities by the power and grace of the Holy Spirit, and may you bless our lives that others, especially our children and grandchildren, might be led to Jesus as a result. Amen.

VI. DEEPER DISCOVERIES

A. Leaky Roofs

A typical Israelite house featured a flat roof, which could be reached by stairs along the outside of the house. A builder would first lay down a series of wooden beams or palm tree trunks, then cover it with mats made from rushes or small branches. The whole roof would then be packed with clay, flattened by stone rollers.

Such a roof would provide good protection from the sun's heat or from storms. But if rain continued long enough, it could become saturated with water and would drip long after the storm ceased.

B. The Inheritance

The laws of inheritance in Old Testament Israel were simple and clearly defined. The land was the center of the inheritance, with boundaries fixed for each tribe and clan as far back as the Book of Joshua. When a father died, his land (including houses and vineyards) was divided among his sons. The eldest son received a double share, along with the responsibility to care for his mother and unmarried sisters. If no sons survived, the land could go to the daughters and then to other relatives, following a specified order.

A father could not take away the firstborn's birthright on a whim (Deut. 21:15–17), but he could disinherit a son who committed a trespass against the family (Gen. 49:4; 1 Chr. 5:1).

VII. TEACHING OUTLINE

A. INTRODUCTION
1.   Lead Story: The Building Block of All Society

2. Context: Immediate families are made up of parents, children, and grandparents. Proverbs is full of insightful and helpful instruction on how to fulfill each of these roles well, as well as what actions and attitudes each one should avoid.

3. Transition: Good families do not happen by accident. They are the result of dedicated parents following biblical principles. As the believer dedicates himself to fulfilling his role, God is able to use him to bring about great good.

B. COMMENTARY
1. Parents and Children
2. Husbands and Wives
3. The Older Generation

C. CONCLUSION: PASS THE SALT OR I'LL KNOCK YOUR BLOCK OFF

VIII. ISSUES FOR DISCUSSION

1. On a scale of 1 to 10, with 10 being the best, how well do you think you are fulfilling your biblical role of child, parent, or elder? What comes to your mind as the most important thing you could do to improve yourself in that role?

2. Young people are not young by choice. They simply have not lived long enough to get old, and they do not have the benefit of many years of living. The same is true of older people. They are not old by choice. It's the inevitable consequence of life's natural continuation. Depending on what generation you are in, are there any attitude adjustments you need to make toward others, to give them the respect Proverbs says we should?

3. When you die, what do you hope will be said of you? What changes do you need to make now so that this will happen?

Chapter 28

Toward Godly Leadership

Proverbs 13:17; 14:28,35; 16:10,12–15; 17:7,11;
19:12; 20:2,8,26,28; 21:1; 22:11; 23:1–3; 24:21–22;
25:1–7,13; 28:2–3,15–16; 29:4,12,14

I. **INTRODUCTION**
Leading by Public Opinion

II. **COMMENTARY**
A verse-by-verse explanation of these verses.

III. **CONCLUSION**
The Lessons of the Cranes

An overview of the principles and applications from these verses.

IV. **LIFE APPLICATION**
You Must Care

Melding these verses to life.

V. **PRAYER**
Tying these verses to life with God.

VI. **DEEPER DISCOVERIES**
Historical, geographical, and grammatical enrichment of the commentary.

VII. **TEACHING OUTLINE**
Suggested step-by-step group study of these verses.

VIII. **ISSUES FOR DISCUSSION**
Zeroing these verses in on daily life.

Q u o t e

"*In* order to be a leader a man must have followers. And to have followers, a man must have their confidence. Hence the supreme quality of a leader is unquestionably integrity."

D w i g h t   E i s e n h o w e r

Proverbs
13:17; 14:28,35; 16:10,12–15;
17:7,11; 19:12; 20:2,8,26,28;
21:1; 22:11; 23:1–3; 24:21–22;
25:1–7,13; 28:2–3,15–16;
29:4,12,14

I N   A   N U T S H E L L

A leader wields the power to make things happen, to reward or punish, so the prudent person will aim to please him. A leader must exemplify holiness in his conduct, as well as promote good and oppose evil. If a person can be trusted to carry out his responsibilities without campaigning for his own agenda, he will become a valued asset to the person whom he serves.

Toward Godly Leadership

I. INTRODUCTION

Leading by Public Opinion

*P*resident Harry Truman once commented with insight on the value of polls and public opinion on leadership.

> I wonder how far Moses would have gone if he'd taken a poll in Egypt? What would Jesus have preached if he'd taken a poll in Israel? Where would the Reformation have gone if Martin Luther had taken a poll? It isn't the polls or public opinion of the moment that counts. It is right and wrong and leadership—men with fortitude, honesty, and a belief in the right—that makes epochs in the history of the world.

How true this is. And how fully Solomon agrees. In Proverbs, Solomon speaks eloquently on the subject of leadership, telling us that leaders must lead with character and integrity, and that their primary responsibility is to further the causes of justice and righteousness in the world. In dangerous and crucial times, such a leader must be willing to stand alone because it is right and be willing to pay the price to let right be done.

II. COMMENTARY

Toward Godly Leadership

MAIN IDEA: *When Proverbs was written, Solomon ruled as king, so he could speak as an expert on the privileges and pitfalls of leadership. He understood how to wield power, but he also realized that God gives people authority so they can bring justice to a nation. In addition, he knew exactly what a leader looks for in his subordinates. The principles Proverbs presents apply to employers and to elected officials as well as to kings.*

A The Leader's Clout (14:28; 16:15; 19:12; 20:2; 21:1; 25:1–3)

SUPPORTING IDEA: *Life at the top does have its perks. The leader lives in the limelight, and he enjoys the recognition that comes with his position. He wields the power to make things happen, to reward or punish, so the prudent person will aim to please him.*

14:28. What good is a lofty leadership position if you have no one to lead? A king's greatest resource is his people, and his title is meaningless unless he has a **large population** of citizens. A **prince** who rules so foolishly that he loses his following is bound to be **ruined**.

16:15. The king has great influence over the welfare of his subjects, and he can provide great benefits for those who please him. When his **face brightens** with approval, no one needs to fear death; he will see that you enjoy **life**. And to those who enjoy his **favor**, the king is a giver of good gifts, as welcome as a **rain cloud in spring** that enables farmers to enjoy an ample crop.

19:12; 20:2. These parallel verses warn that it is important to stay in the king's good graces. To run afoul of his **wrath** (Prov. 14:35; 16:14; 20:2) is as dangerous as hearing the **roar of a** ferocious **lion** (Prov. 28:15), ready to pounce on its prey. Enjoying the king's **favor** is as refreshing as the **dew on the grass**, but if he becomes enraged, you can easily forfeit your **life**. In our daily lives, the anger of a superior rarely results in death, but it can lead to unpleasant consequences!

21:1. Although a king may seem to make his decisions unhindered by anyone, God still sits on his throne. He retains control of history, and he uses rulers to carry out his plans for justice. Just as a farmer channels water into irrigation ditches, directing it into the fields of his choice, so God **directs** the **heart** of a king. He turns it **wherever he pleases**, just as he determines the steps of less prominent people (Prov. 16:1,9).

25:1–3. King **Solomon** was the prime example of leadership in his day, so it is natural that he included numerous **proverbs** on leadership and the running of government. Well over a century after Solomon's death, **Hezekiah king of Judah** valued his predecessor's advice enough to commission scholars to add an appendix to the Book of Proverbs.

A **king** needs to know what is going on in his realm, so it is his **glory**, a sign of his administrative skill, to probe all the aspects of his kingdom. **God**, on the other hand, already knows everything, so he never needs to carry out an investigation. Part of his **glory** rests in the fact that his knowledge extends far beyond our ability to comprehend. We know as much as he chooses to reveal, and there is deep truth that remains a mystery to us (Deut. 29:29). Recognizing the depth of God's wisdom leads us to approach him with awe and reverence.

Proverbs 25:3 carries on the parallel between God's ultimate kingship and the limited authority of human kings. Just as the **heavens** and the **earth** stretch far beyond the limited comprehension of an individual, the affairs of a ruler are often **unsearchable**, hidden from the common citizen. It is impossible to read a king's heart, and a ruler must be able to hide certain plans until the time is right to reveal them.

ⒷThe Leader's Standard (16:10,12; 17:7; 20:8,26,28; 25:4–5; 28:2–3,15–16; 29:4,12,14)

> **SUPPORTING IDEA:** *Great power can be used for good or evil, so it is crucial that a leader maintain high standards of justice and righteousness. He must not only exemplify holiness in his own conduct but also carry out the mandate of promoting good and opposing evil.*

16:10. Proverbs 16:10–15 deals with various aspects of a king's leadership. Like many of the other verses in Proverbs, it describes what a king should be like, not necessarily what every king actually does. In the ancient world, **an oracle** was a priest or prophet who supposedly passed on messages from a god. Their word carried authority because of the divine source. And in the same way, **a king** can **speak** with finality because God has placed him in power. Because he speaks for God, he must be just, or he will misrepresent the Lord (Deut. 17:18–20).

16:12. A king who recognizes his responsibility—and his own best interests—will **detest** any form of **wrongdoing** and will value righteousness and truth. Only through **righteousness** will his place on the **throne** be **established**, made firm or secure.

17:7. **Arrogant lips** are literally "lips of excess," a description of a person who talks too much. The **fool** (Heb. *nabal*) in this verse is the sort of crude, insensitive rascal who does not realize how much he reveals himself by his speech. But if it is inappropriate for a fool to show his arrogance, it is even worse for a **ruler** or official to lie. A leader must be trustworthy, and the person who breaks his trust is worse than an arrogant fool.

20:8,26. A king serves as the source of justice; Solomon, for instance, served as the highest court of appeal (1 Kgs. 3:16–28). So it was vital to discern the good from the **evil**. As a farmer **winnows** the grain, sifting out the chaff from the wheat, so the king must scrutinize the actions and motives of those before him, so he can come to a righteous verdict.

And once the guilty have been detected, he must inflict the punishment that justice requires. Farmers would thresh wheat by spreading the stalks on a solid surface, then rolling a heavy **wheel** across them to separate the grain from the stalks and loosen the kernels from the chaff. The same severe treatment is sometimes necessary to deal with the criminal.

20:28. Severity (v. 26) is balanced by kindness here. **Love** (Heb. *chesedh*) is the loyalty and **faithfulness** that belong to those who are in a covenant relationship with one another. When a king displays the kindness and reliability that go with his office, his subjects will respond with loyalty. He will be **safe**, and his kingdom will be **secure**. This proverb points to the truth that political power cannot rest long on brute force.

25:4–5. Rulers must not tolerate corruption, even if it seems harmless. A **silversmith** takes great pains to skim off the impurities in the molten ore so that he can produce a work of art formed of pure silver. In the same way, a ruler must remove any **wicked** associates from his **presence**. When he exposes and expels such people from his staff, he establishes or gives stability to **his throne**.

28:2–3. Stability is one of the key symptoms of good government; regimes that come and go are a sign of deep flaws in leadership. When a leader has deep **understanding and knowledge**, he will be able to maintain order. When a ruler lacks character, his nation will erupt in rebellion. The history of Israel furnishes ample illustration of this principle.

The Hebrew in verse 3 literally speaks of a "poor man" who **oppresses** his fellows in poverty; the NIV has made a slight change in spelling to read "ruler" or "chief man." In either case, mistreating those who are poor and helpless is an unnatural cruelty. It is **like a driving rain that** destroys the crops it should nourish, turning a life-giving shower into a cloudburst that unleashes its power without restraint.

28:15–16. Any **wicked man** can cause plenty of trouble, but a tyrant can devastate an entire country! Here such a rogue ruler is compared to a **lion** or a **bear** because his viciousness is more like a wild animal than a human being. Daniel 7 portrays world empires using the same beasts.

In Proverbs 28:16, **a tyrannical ruler lacks** the basic **judgment** or understanding that all people should have; once again he is presented as subhuman. On the other hand, a leader who refuses to abuse his power for personal **gain will** receive God's favor, and he can look forward to an extended **life**.

29:4. According to Proverbs, a ruler can achieve national stability by ruling with understanding (28:2), righteousness (16:12), love and faithfulness (20:28), and **justice** (29:4). On the other hand, a person who is **greedy for bribes** (literally, a man of offerings) squanders the nation's wealth and empties its coffers.

29:12,14. The **ruler** must set high standards of integrity and justice if he wants to build a kingdom that lasts. When he takes the advice of liars, he creates a climate where deceit can flourish. But when people realize that he consistently rewards honesty, honesty will increase. And when the king treats **with fairness** those who are helpless and unable to bring any pressure to bear on his decisions, both the Lord and the people will be pleased with him.

C The Follower's Role (13:17; 14:35; 16:13–14; 17:11; 22:11; 23:1–3; 24:21–22; 25:6–7,13)

SUPPORTING IDEA: *Leaders cannot succeed without good followers. So Proverbs gives wise counsel on how to make your authority successful. If you can be trusted to carry out your responsibilities without campaigning for your own agenda, you will become a valued asset to the person you serve.*

13:17. Though there is some variation in the precise translation, the overall thought of this verse is simple: a **wicked messenger** is unreliable, for a variety of reasons, and will not only cause trouble for others, but will get in **trouble** himself. A **trustworthy envoy**, on the other hand, will enjoy health himself and will bring **healing** to others.

14:35. Here we see the contrast between a **wise** or prudent **servant** and one who causes shame for himself and his master (cp. 10:5; 19:26; 29:15). The first one pleases the king, but the second will have to endure a blast of anger. If you are constantly in trouble with the boss, the problem could be your performance, not his favoritism.

16:13–14. How does a person please a king? First, be completely **honest** when you speak to the king. He will take pleasure in finding someone he can trust. Second, do whatever it takes to **appease** the king if he becomes angry at you. **A king's wrath** comes with the power to order the **death** penalty, and rulers can be unpredictable. So a prudent person learns how to stay in the king's good graces. In principle, of course, this applies to our relationship with anyone in authority over us.

17:11. When a person's heart is **evil**, he lives for himself and finds it almost impossible to submit to authority. He becomes a confirmed troublemaker, **bent only on rebellion**. A verbal rebuke does nothing to change him, so the government will eventually send a **merciless official** to bring him into line. The treatment he receives will be severe, but it will be precisely what he deserves.

22:11. It is rare to find a person who combines rugged integrity with charm. When a leader finds someone who has a **pure heart** and whose **speech is gracious**, he welcomes him as a personal **friend**.

23:1–3. This passage gives wise advice to the social climber who has been invited to **dine with a ruler**. He might find it easy to be awed by the king's splendor and spend his time congratulating himself on his good fortune and gorging on the banquet before him. But Proverbs warns, "Be careful." He must be cautious and aware of his surroundings. If he is **given to gluttony**, he should put the **knife** to his **throat**, not in the meat! The powerful seldom give away favors for nothing; they often want something in return. So a person cannot afford to be blinded by the lavish meal; it is **deceptive** (literally, bread of lies). You may end up the loser in the exchange.

24:21–22. This passage is echoed in 1 Peter 2:17 and Romans 13:4, clinching the point that believers should submit to governmental authority. Both **the LORD and the king** he has placed on the throne wield authority, and the two of them will punish the **rebellious** (literally, those given to change). **Sudden destruction** and **calamities** will strike those who assume they are immune from retribution.

25:6–7. Jesus built a parable on this saying (Luke 14:7–10), showing that those who compete for the best spots at the royal court will end up being humiliated. It is far wiser to take a back seat and have the king invite you to **come** forward, than to make a spectacle of yourself by choosing a **place among great men** and then being ushered to the rear.

25:13. An actual snowstorm covering the crops **at harvest time** would be a disaster. But to workers sweating in the heat of harvest, nothing could be more refreshing than snow carried down from the mountains. In the same way, a **trustworthy messenger** is refreshing to those who use his services. Perhaps this verse hints at the scarcity of reliable couriers.

> **MAIN IDEA REVIEW:** *When Proverbs was written, Solomon ruled as king, so he could speak as an expert on the privileges and pitfalls of leadership. He understood how to wield power, but he also realized that God gives people authority so they can bring justice to a nation. In addition, he knew exactly what a leader looks for in his subordinates. The principles Proverbs presents apply to employers and to elected officials as well as to monarchs.*

III. CONCLUSION

The Lessons of the Cranes

Bruce Larson, in his book *Wind and Fire* (Dallas, Tex.: Word Books, 1984), points out some interesting facts about sandhill cranes:

> These large birds, who fly great distances across continents, have three remarkable qualities. First, they rotate leadership. No one bird stays out in front all the time. Second, they choose leaders who can handle turbulence. And then, all during the time one bird is leading, the rest are honking their affirmation. That's not a bad model for the church. Certainly we need leaders who can handle turbulence and who are aware that leadership ought to be shared. But most of all, we need a church where we are all honking encouragement.

This is a good example of Solomon's teachings in Proverbs. He teaches us that we need leaders of ability and integrity but that we need followers, too.

Let us determine to lead when God asks us to lead, and to follow when God asks us to follow, and to trust him that he will get us where we need to go.

PRINCIPLES

- Leaders must have integrity in order for people to trust them enough to follow.
- Leaders must do unto others as they want others to do to them.
- The goal of a follower is to make the person you are following successful.

APPLICATIONS

- If God calls you to leadership—as he does everyone in one capacity or another—be sure to build all your leadership on the foundation of character and integrity.
- If God calls you to follow—as he does everyone in one capacity or another—be sure you follow with character and integrity.
- Whether leading or following, bathe everything in prayer, since it is God's blessing that will bring good out of anything.

IV. LIFE APPLICATION

You Must Care

In his book, *A Passion for Excellence* (New York: Random House, 1985), Tom Peters quotes from a speech by the late Lieutenant General Melvin Zais:

> The one piece of advice which I believe will contribute more to making you a better leader and commander, will provide you with greater happiness and self-esteem and at the same time advance your career more than any other advice I can provide you . . . and it doesn't call for any specific personality and it doesn't call for any certain chemistry . . . any one of you can do it . . . and that advice is that you must care.
>
> How do you know if you care? Well, for one thing, if you care, you *listen* to your junior officers and your soldiers. Now, when I say listen, I don't mean that stilted baloney that so many officers engage in and stand up to an enlisted man and say, "How old are you son? Where are you from? How long have you been here? Thank you very much. Next man!" That's baloney.
>
> To care you must listen. Really listen. You care if you really wonder what the soldiers are doing when you are out playing golf. What

are the airmen doing? What are the sailors doing? Where do they go when I play golf?

You care if you go to the mess hall, and I don't mean go in with your white gloves and rub dishes and pots and pans and find dust. You care if you go to a mess hall and you notice that the scrambled eggs are in a puddle of water and twenty pounds of toast has been done in advance and it's all lying there hard and cold, and the bacon is lying there dripping in the grease and the cooks got all their work done way ahead of time, and the cold pots of coffee are sitting on the tables getting even colder. If that really bothers you, if it really gripes you, if you want to tear up those cooks, you care.

And I can't make you do this. But you really, you really need to like soldiers. You need to be amused at their humor, you need to be tolerant of their bawdiness, and you have to understand that they're as lousy as you let them be and as good as you make them be. You just have to really like them and feel good about being with them.

That is what it means to care. And that is what makes a good leader in the military. But it is also what makes a good leader anywhere. To care about the same things God cares about, and to show that concern by taking a personal interest in helping the right thing be done. If leaders in the church show the same level of care about all the others in the church, great things can be done with a sense of unity and harmony.

V. PRAYER

Father in heaven, help us to care about the same things you care about. We find ourselves caring deeply about things you don't care about. By the power of your Word through the presence of the Holy Spirit, may our hearts be formed to care as you would care if you were in our shoes. And then, dear Father, may we lead, or follow as you see fit, with integrity. Amen.

VI. DEEPER DISCOVERIES

A. Irrigation Canals and Kings

Proverbs 21:1 compares the way God directs the heart of a king to the way farmers directed watercourses or irrigation canals. The Israelites were familiar with the Egyptian practice of using water from the Nile River to flood their fields, but agriculture in most parts of the land of Canaan depended on rainfall rather than man-made canals. Irrigation was common in areas like Jericho and the edges of the Jordan valley.

B. The Soul of Gluttony

The word *gluttony* in Proverbs 23:2 is a translation of the Hebrew *nephesh,* a word that occurs over seven hundred times in the Bible and is usually translated "soul." In Genesis 2:7, God breathed into Adam's nostrils the breath of life and he became "a living being" or soul (*nephesh*). Deuteronomy 6:5 commands Israel to love God with all the heart, soul (*nephesh*), and strength. In the Old Testament, this word often refers to the many strong desires and appetites of the human heart, so it is sometimes translated "appetite" as in this verse. When we let our soul do what comes naturally, we generally end up satisfying our cravings.

VII. TEACHING OUTLINE

A. INTRODUCTION
1. Lead Story: Leading by Public Opinion
2. Context: In the mix of life, God calls some people to be leaders and some to be followers.
3. Transition: Whether we lead or whether we follow, we must do so with integrity.

B. COMMENTARY
1. The Leader's Clout
2. The Leader's Standard
3. The Follower's Role

C. CONCLUSION: THE LESSONS OF THE CRANES

VIII. ISSUES FOR DISCUSSION

1. Are you a natural leader? Has God asked you to lead in some area, whether or not you are a natural leader? Do you think you measure up to the standard of leadership? Is there some way in which you should improve?
2. When you follow, do you follow with integrity? Is your goal to make the leader you are following successful? Or is your goal to get your way? Is there something you need to change about how you follow leadership?
3. Do you trust God to lead in imperfect situations through imperfect people?

Chapter 29

The Rewards of Following God

Proverbs 3:25–26; 13:12,19; 14:10,13,32;
15:13,30; 16:17; 17:22; 18:14; 22:1,3,5,13;
23:17–18; 24:10; 25:9–10,20,25; 26:13;
27:11–12,20; 28:1; 29:6

---

*"H*ope: a continual looking forward

to the eternal world."

C . S . L e w i s

Proverbs

3:25–26; 13:12,19; 14:10,13,32;
15:13,30; 16:17; 17:22; 18:14;
22:1,3,5,13; 23:17–18;
24:10; 25:9–10,20,25; 26:13;
27:11–12,20; 28:1; 29:6

IN A NUTSHELL

*T*he wise man avoids blundering into dangerous situations but, at the same time, has courage to go wherever God leads. A good name, based on character and integrity, is one of the most valuable things in life, and God's child should value it as such. True joy comes from following God, not from pursuing the enticements of the world, and in placing our hope in heaven.

The Rewards of Following God

I. INTRODUCTION

In the End, All Will Be Well

*I*n this chapter we see proverbs that Solomon wrote about courage balanced by caution, reputation based on reality, and joy built on hope. These are the rewards of following God. Of all three of these subjects, hope is the power that keeps us moving in God's direction. Hope gives us the courage to follow God and to be tenacious about tending our reputation. Hope is a critical ingredient to the life God wants us to live.

In his book *Man's Search for Meaning* (Boston: Beacon Press, 1962), Viktor Frankl tells of his dreadful years in the German concentration camps of Auschwitz and Dachau. Treated worse than an animal, he was condemned to a living death filled with cold, starvation, pain, lice, exhaustion, and dehumanization. Frankl wrote that he was able to survive because of hope. He never stopped believing that he would survive. Those prisoners who lost hope were doomed. When a prisoner lost hope, Frankl said, he gave up and died from the inside out.

This usually happened quite suddenly. One morning a prisoner would just refuse to get out of bed. He wouldn't get dressed or wash or go outside or eat. No amount of pleading by his fellow prisoners would help, nor would any threatening by his captors. He would lie there in his own excrement until he died. Yet those who continued to hope often found the strength to continue, and of those who survived, all survived on hope.

This is, of course, because God created us this way . . . to be creatures of hope. Then, because he created us creatures of hope, he gave us the greatest of all hope—heaven. So we live on hope in this world, but we also cling to the hope that no matter what this world brings, in the end, all will be well.

II. COMMENTARY

The Rewards of Following God

MAIN IDEA: *All through Proverbs God has promised to bless the person who fears God, chooses wisdom, and walks in righteousness. Such people enjoy a truly abundant life, just as Jesus promised in John 10:10. They will handle today's challenges with courage; they will look to the future with joy. And others will recognize the work of God in their lives.*

🅰 Courage Balanced by Caution (3:25–26; 14:32; 16:17; 22:3,5,13; 24:10; 26:13; 27:12; 28:1)

SUPPORTING IDEA: *Blundering into danger is not bravery; it's heedlessness. The wise person knows where the traps are, and he avoids them. But when the occasion arises, the person who fears God never needs to surrender to any other fear.*

3:25–26. In this passage, Solomon lists the benefits that come to those who pay attention to his exhortation to hold tightly to wisdom (3:21). When you commit yourself to using discernment and exercising sound judgment, you will be able to look to the future with **confidence**, knowing that the **LORD** will keep you from falling into the traps set by the **wicked**. It is important to note that a person is not preserved from **disaster** by his own common sense or competence. Those resources soon run out. Only the protection of God is a solid basis for our confidence.

14:32. Some interpreters have worried that this proverb could be used to justify suicide because the Hebrew literally reads, "The righteous seeks refuge in his death." But such an idea runs contrary to the rest of Scripture and ignores the theme in Proverbs that death is a terrible consequence of ignoring God's precepts. The point of the passage is that **calamity** is sheer disaster for the **wicked** because they have no hope. But God is a **refuge** for the **righteous**, even if they must face **death**.

16:17. Like many other proverbs, this passage pictures the godly person walking down a road, choosing the route that **avoids evil** and guarding his pathway carefully. The word *evil* can mean either a misfortune or moral evil, and the latter is more likely here (cp. 3:7; 8:13; 16:6). He who **guards his way** by maintaining upright conduct **guards his life**, literally "his soul." This too could describe protection from physical harm, but it probably refers to preservation from temptation and moral collapse.

22:3; 27:12. Courage does not require you to walk blindly into danger. Boldness must be balanced with prudence or shrewdness, so that you look ahead, observe the threat, and take **refuge** from it. It is the **simple** person (not merely ignorant but headstrong) who keeps on going even when danger is visible; he will **suffer** the consequences of his rashness.

22:5. Here the writer shows that it is more than just naivete that makes a person walk carelessly into trouble. It is the **wicked**, or twisted, person who chooses the **paths** choked with **thorns and snares**. Thorns impede their progress, and snares stop them completely. Unfortunately, their predicament is avoidable; the person who heeds God's warnings will keep his **soul** safe by staying as far away from trouble as possible.

22:13; 26:13. Sometimes cowardice is actually a cover-up for laziness. These verses spotlight the far-fetched excuses that a sluggard will use to escape his work. Although lions seldom entered towns, this fellow claims that a fierce **lion** is lurking right outside! Or he worries that he might be **murdered** if he goes out into the **streets**. It is amazing how readily we can think of reasons to postpone or cancel a job that we don't want to do.

24:10. Trouble reveals either our courage or our weakness. Problems are inevitable, and our responsibility in life is to meet each challenge with God's help. He has designed us to rise to the occasion and has promised to provide his strength. So when we **falter in times of trouble**, we simply demonstrate how inadequate we are. Our **strength** is **small**, so we need to lean on the Lord.

28:1. When we have a clear conscience, we will not flee from lions or anything else. The **wicked** carry a guilty conscience around with them, and they realize that they have broken the law. Like criminals, they flee even when **no one pursues** them, imagining that the law is after them. The **righteous**, on the other hand, can be as **bold as a lion**. They do not need to keep looking over their shoulders because they know they have done nothing wrong.

🅱 Reputation Based on Reality (22:1; 25:9–10)

SUPPORTING IDEA: *Anyone can build a reputation by launching a slick public relations campaign. But the only way to establish a good name that outlasts the hoopla is to develop rock-solid character. What counts is what remains when people discover the reality behind the appearances.*

22:1. Riches can be a blessing from God, but they are useless (Prov. 1:19; 10:2; 13:11) if they are gained at the cost of a good reputation. A **good name** involves an honorable reputation gained by displaying good character. And such a name is far more important than the size of your bank account.

25:9–10. One of the quickest ways to ruin a person's reputation is to reveal a **confidence** as you settle a dispute in court. You may win the case, but you will lose the trust of your friend and any others who learn about this cheap shot. God, of course, marks such heartless sins. But the person you have targeted may retaliate, exposing your duplicity and shattering your reputation.

ⓒ Joy Built on Hope (13:12,19; 14:10,13; 15:13,30; 17:22; 18:14; 23:17–18; 25:20,25; 27:11,20; 29:6)

SUPPORTING IDEA: *So many people chase dreams and stock-pile possessions in a vain attempt to capture happiness. But Proverbs makes clear that genuine joy comes to the person who loves God and walks according to his wisdom. God promises to bless such a person, and we can rest our hope on his word. We can be joyful when we know that the story of our life has a happy ending.*

13:12,19. A person cannot live without hope, but we suffer greatly even when our hopes are delayed. **Hope** is **deferred** when a promise is put off, standing unfulfilled for a long time. God often works more slowly than we wish, and our **heart** can be **sick** with disappointment if we fail to remember that fact. When our **longing** is finally **fulfilled**, our **soul** is revived. Like a life-giving tree, the answer refreshes us. It is sweet to our soul. The second half of verse 19 may seem disconnected from the rest of the verse, but it may imply that the fool who detests **turning from evil** or his sin should not expect God to fulfill his hopes.

14:10,13. We know what is in our **heart**, but none of us can fully share someone else's emotions of **bitterness** or **joy**. In that sense we are solitary. But God knows our deepest secrets, and he can understand us more deeply than any human. People can only see the exterior, and **laughter** may just mask deep emotional pain. A person may be experiencing **joy** for the moment, but both our circumstances and our emotions shift quickly, and the joy could turn to **grief** in a moment.

15:13,30; 17:22. Taken together, these verses show how a cheerful face and a cheerful heart go together. When your **heart** is **happy**, it will produce a smile. And when you have a **cheerful look** (literally, bright eyes), it will encourage not only your own spirit but the hearts of those around you. On the other hand, the depression of a **heartache** can eventually crush **the spirit**. These verses make clear that the most important factor in happiness is not our situation but our thoughts.

Proverbs 17:22 declares that a happy or **cheerful heart** is a **good medicine** or cure for the physical body as well as the emotions. A depressed or **crushed spirit**, however, **dries up the bones**. Proverbs often emphasizes the effect of the inner life on our health; in 15:30, it declares that **good news gives health to the bones**.

18:14. Like 17:22, this verse proclaims that our attitude is the single most important factor in confronting adversity. A person with a strong, encouraged spirit can keep going in **sickness**, but when your **spirit** is **crushed**, your inner strength is gone, and there is little that medicine can do to overcome such a collapse.

23:17–18. These verses show us where to fix our gaze: not on **sinners**, envying them and wishing we could do what they do (3:31; 24:1,19; Ps. 37:1), but turning to **the LORD**, being **zealous** to **fear** them. It is also profitable to keep looking to the **future** because God's people can live with a **hope** that is more than wishful thinking, resting on the promises of God.

25:20. Cheerfulness is a good thing, but it is important to blend it with sensitivity. When a person is depressed, burdened with a **heavy heart**, it is tactless to sing mindless ditties to him, ignoring the depth of his distress. Such a thoughtless approach just makes him more miserable; it is as bad as stealing his coat and letting him shiver, unprotected **on a cold day**. Or it may lead to an explosive reaction, just as **vinegar poured on soda** fizzes quickly.

25:25. One thing that gives us joy is **good news from a distant land**. In the ancient world news traveled slowly. Whether you were waiting for word about the sale of goods that you had shipped to a foreign port or hoping to hear from a friend or relative, the delay could be long. So when the message finally arrived, the joy was intense. Receiving what you had waited for was as refreshing as a cup of **cold water** to a weary person.

27:11. Proverbs mentions repeatedly that a **wise** son brings **joy** to a father's **heart** (10:1; 15:20; 23:15,24; 29:3). Godly children are your best credentials, and they will give you an **answer** for the critic who holds you in **contempt**.

27:20. The writer first portrays **Death and Destruction** (literally Sheol and Abaddon; see 15:11) as persons whose hunger is **never satisfied**. The grave always yawns wide, ready to receive another body. In the same way, **the eyes of man** are never satisfied. This might mean the curiosity that always wants to see new things, but it is more likely the covetousness that always wants to own new things. Such greed shows that a person has not learned contentment, and he will therefore never be satisfied.

29:6. An **evil** person is caught in a trap of his own making, but the **righteous** man can be joyful and carefree, knowing that he need not worry about his actions coming back to haunt him. He can **sing and be glad** with a clear conscience and joyful heart.

MAIN IDEA REVIEW: *All through Proverbs, God has promised to bless the person who fears God, chooses wisdom, and walks in righteousness. Such people enjoy a truly abundant life, just as Jesus promised in John 10:10. They will handle today's challenges with courage; they will look to the future with joy. And others will recognize the work of God in their lives.*

III. CONCLUSION

Hope Is a Theological Virtue

C. S. Lewis wrote clearly and insightfully on the subject of hope.

> Hope is one of the theological virtues. This means that a continual looking forward to the eternal world is not, as some modern people think, a form of escapism or wishful thinking, but one of the things a Christian is meant to do. It does not mean that we are to leave the present world as it is. If you read history you will find that the Christians who did most for the present world were just those who thought most of the next. The Apostles themselves, who set on foot the conversion of the Roman Empire, the great men who built up the Middle Ages, the English Evangelicals who abolished the Slave Trade, all left their mark on Earth, precisely because their minds were occupied with Heaven. It is since Christians have largely ceased to think of the other world that they have become so ineffective in this. Aim at heaven, and you will get earth thrown in. Aim at earth, and you will get neither (*Mere Christianity*, New York: Macmillan, 1952, p. 118).

So Christian, student of Proverbs, hope in the next world as your basis for joy and meaning in this world.

PRINCIPLES

- Hope is an essential part of the human mind. Without it we cannot survive.
- Hope is a powerful factor in earthly matters, but for the Christian there is always the hope of heaven after life on earth.
- Hope is the basis for all joy.

APPLICATIONS

- When you are in the midst of life's trials, find reasons to hope, as a biblical way of coping.
- In addition to earthly hope, be sure to place your hope in heaven, knowing that no matter how difficult life gets on earth, in the end, all will be well.
- Help other people find hope, too. You will have a powerful influence in the lives of others if you do.

IV. LIFE APPLICATION

Hope Springs Eternal

For the Christian, no matter how hard life is, there is still hope—hope that one day, in heaven, all will be well. In Revelation 21, the heavenly city, the New Jerusalem, comes down out of heaven. Then, the Scriptures say, "He will wipe every tear from their eyes. There will be no more death or mourning or crying or pain, for the old order of things has passed away" (Rev. 21:4). This is our hope—that in the presence of Jesus, there will be untarnished joy forever.

Many stories of hope come from war times. In World War II, twenty-five thousand soldiers were held in POW camps in inhumane conditions, and many of them died. Yet others survived and eventually returned home. There was no reason to believe that the ones who survived where physically any stronger or healthier than the ones who died. The survivors, however, were different in one major respect: they expected to be released some day.

They talked about the kinds of homes they would have, the jobs they would choose, and even described the kind of person they would marry. They drew pictures on the walls to illustrate their dreams. Some even found ways to study subjects related to the kind of career they wanted to pursue when they got back home.

Researchers have even learned that a hopeful attitude can lead to physiological changes that improve the immune system, making the body more effective at fighting physical problems. That is the power of hope.

As we face the hardships of life on earth, there are times when things look grim. Even when things look bad on earth, there is reason to hope. In an old 1930s film about the attack of the Spanish Armada on England, a fearful court attendant asked the queen of England if there were reason for hope. The queen replied, "I have seen darker fears turned to hope. Hope until you know there is none!" That is the perspective of hope for this earth. Hope until you know there is none.

But Christians have the ability to look beyond earth. Even if we come to the end of hope in this world, we can look to heaven, where there is ultimate hope. For the believer hope never dies. Peter wrote in his first epistle:

> Blessed be the God and Father of our Lord Jesus Christ, who according to His great mercy has caused us to be born again to a living hope through the resurrection of Jesus Christ from the dead, to obtain an inheritance which is imperishable and undefiled and will not fade away, reserved in heaven for you, who are protected by the power of

God through faith for a salvation ready to be revealed in the last time" (1 Pet. 1:3–5 NASB).

Then he went on to say, "Therefore, prepare your minds for action, keep sober in spirit, fix your hope completely on the grace to be brought to you at the revelation of Jesus Christ" (1 Pet. 1:13 NASB).

That is the power and purpose of hope—to give us strength to face the trials of today and to give us joy in anticipating the future. Hebrews 12:2 says that for the joy that was set before him in heaven, Jesus endured the cross. So fix your hope in heaven. Let the unshakable truth of our home in heaven steady and strengthen you through the ups and downs of this life. Just as surely as the jonquils and daffodils and dogwoods will come out again every spring as they have done since the creation of the world, so when we die, we will come to a new and beautiful life in heaven. Because Jesus rose, we will rise. There is no better news. There is no greater hope.

V. PRAYER

Father in heaven, thank you that we have the ultimate hope of heaven, deliverance from the penalty, power, and presence of sin. Help us be hopeful in this world as we draw on your grace for the hard times. But also, help us place our final hope in heaven, and give us joy and power as a result. Amen.

VI. DEEPER DISCOVERIES

A. Old Testament Medicine

When Proverbs 17:22 declares that a cheerful heart is good medicine, it chooses a word for "medicine" that appears nowhere else in the Old Testament. Rather than a specific medication or treatment, the word simply means "a cure, that which relieves the distress."

The ancient world practiced numerous therapies for their ailments. Ointments and bandages were applied to wounds (Isa. 1:6), and Hezekiah's boil was treated with a paste made of figs (Isa. 38:21). Ezekiel spoke of bandaging the broken arm of the Pharaoh (Ezek. 30:21), and Jeremiah mentioned the "balm of Gilead" (Jer. 8:22; 46:11; 51:8) as a medicinal ointment.

The sanitary and dietary laws of the Israelites served as protection against many diseases that plagued the neighboring nations. Their medical practice emphasized prevention more than cure.

B. The Insatiable Eye

Proverbs 27:20 declares that human eyes are never satisfied, any more than death is. Some interpreters have taken this as a reference to healthy human curiosity, as Ecclesiastes 1:8 observes. But other passages suggest that it refers to greed. Proverbs 30:15–16 lists four insatiable things: the grave, a barren womb, dry ground, and fire; two are destructive, and two are constructive. Isaiah 5:14 speaks of the grave enlarging itself to make room for more of the dead resulting from God's judgment. And Habakkuk 2:5 uses the same imagery to describe the arrogant person who yearns to control everything around him.

VII. TEACHING OUTLINE

A. INTRODUCTION

1. Lead Story: In the End, All Will Be Well
2. Context: There are wonderful rewards for following the Lord. There is the reward of courage in the face of danger, though tempered by caution; there is the legitimate pride in a good name, built on character and integrity; and there is joy built on hope. These are the context of this chapter.
3. Transition: As we study these passages, stretch your mind to embrace the wisdom and importance of the truth they contain. Power and joy are yours if you do.

B. COMMENTARY

1. Courage Balanced by Caution
2. Reputation Based on Reality
3. Joy Built on Hope

C. CONCLUSION: HOPE IS A THEOLOGICAL VIRTUE

VIII. ISSUES FOR DISCUSSION

1. There is sometimes a fine line between courage and foolhardiness. Do you evaluate dangers before taking action so that you can have courage that you are doing something reasonable?
2. How good is your reputation? Do you care deeply about it? Is there anything you need to do to repair it or to keep it in good repair?
3. Do you think your joy is as great as it could be? What would you need to do, according to Proverbs, to experience more joy in life?

Chapter 30

A Comforting Life Perspective

Proverbs 30:1–33

| Q u o t e |

"*A* sharp tongue is the only edge tool that grows

keener with constant use."

W a s h i n g t o n   I r v i n g

Proverbs
30:1-33

I N   A   N U T S H E L L

*B*y looking upward in humility, we see the matchless power and wisdom of God. His words are the supreme source of truth. Then, by taking a thoughtful look around, we can draw practical lessons from the world of human behavior and the animal kingdom.

A Comforting Life
Perspective

I. INTRODUCTION

Hey, Buddy, Can You Spare a Dime?

J. Wilbur Chapman, a minister from a previous generation, told the story of a gentleman he had met who had grown up in a wealthy family but who had become estranged, something like the prodigal son. He became destitute, was broken in spirit, and had taken to a life of begging. As the man told the story, he said:

"I got off at the Pennsylvania depot as a tramp, and for a year I begged on the streets for a living. One day, I touched a man on the shoulder and said, 'Hey mister, can you give me a dime?' As soon as I saw his face I as shocked to see that it was my own father. I said, 'Father, do you know me?'

"Throwing his arms around me and with tears in his eyes, he said, 'Oh, son, at last I've found you. I've found you. You want a dime? Everything I have is yours.'

"Think of it. I was a tramp. I stood begging my own father for ten cents when for eighteen years, he had been looking for me to give me everything he had."

What a compelling story! And how like us it is. We go around tapping the world on the shoulder, asking for a dime, when our heavenly Father is seeking us to give us everything he has.

When we have turned, or returned, to our heavenly Father, then we can receive what he is pleased to give us. And wisdom is one of those good gifts. It was the spirit of awe and submission in Agur's life that enabled him to make the keen, original observations of truth that are so helpful to us today. May we have a spirit of awe about our heavenly Father, and may it produce in our hearts wisdom to guide us and those whom we love.

II. COMMENTARY

A Comforting Life Perspective

> **MAIN IDEA:** *An unknown writer ponders the world of nature, seeking lessons for life. But with all of his investigations, he concludes that God alone truly understands the universe and its meaning. It is humbling but comforting to recognize that he holds the secrets of life.*

Ⓐ A Humble Look Upward (30:1–9)

> **SUPPORTING IDEA:** *Though we can delve deeply into the workings of the physical universe, our understanding is no more than a child's play compared to the matchless power and wisdom of God. His words are the supreme source of truth.*

30:1. Proverbs 30 adds a separate discourse to the main body of Proverbs, much like an appendix, and the first verse provides the introduction. The writer is **Agur**, and his readers are **Ithiel** and **Ucal**. Scholars have produced many interesting theories about the names, but nothing is known about them with any certainty.

30:2–4. Agur begins by declaring his ignorance. It is a sincere expression of humility but so extreme that it appears to contain a little irony. He claims to be **the most ignorant of men**, a word that implies an intellect as dull as an animal, below normal human level—hardly a literal description of a person who could compile a chapter like this! With all his searching, he has not attained the **knowledge** possessed by God **the Holy One**.

Verse 4 is a series of rhetorical questions, like the later chapters of Job, and in each case the obvious reply is "God." **Who**, he asks, **has gone up to heaven and come down** with knowledge of truth? **Who has** sufficient power to hold the **wind in** his **hands**? **Who** has **wrapped up the waters** of the clouds **in his cloak**? And, **Who has established all the ends of the earth** in its place? God, of course.

The final question asks for the identity of any person who can fit the description. No human can measure up, so God is the obvious choice. When Agur asks for **the name of his son**, an Old Testament reader might see only an extension of the argument, showing that no human could achieve such power. But the New Testament reader cannot help but wonder if this is a subtle reference to Jesus, the Son of God.

30:5–6. If no person can find truth by his own intellect or power, then God is the only infallible source of truth. His **word** is **flawless**; it has stood the test. And those who trust him and his word will find that he protects them like **a shield**.

Because God's Word is already flawless, we must not attempt to **add** to or improve on it or take away from it (Deut. 12:32; Rev. 22:18).

30:7–9. Many of the sections in this chapter are numerical sayings like this one. The writer asks God for **two things** that will be important as long as he lives. First, he begs the Lord to preserve him from **falsehood and lies**. He longs to maintain his integrity, no matter what. Second, he requests that God provide his **daily** necessities, not too much or too little. He recognizes the distinctive temptations that go with either extreme. Too much money, and we are tempted to forget God and trust in our own resources (Deut. 8:12–17). Too little, and desperation may tempt us to steal. Either way, we **dishonor the name of** our **God**.

B A Thoughtful Look Around (30:10–33)

> **SUPPORTING IDEA:** *A wide-ranging collection of observations draws practical lessons from the world of human behavior and the animal kingdom. The writer ponders the parallels between nature and society.*

30:10. Do not meddle in the affairs of another household by slandering a **servant**. The **master** may curse you for making a false accusation, and such a **curse** will hit home (unlike Prov. 26:2) because it is deserved. The Hebrew phrase **pay for it** actually means "to be guilty."

30:11–14. This paragraph describes four kinds of particularly obnoxious sinners. The first group dishonor their parents, even to the point of cursing them (cp. Prov. 20:20). The second group consists of hypocrites who think they are morally clean but are too dense to realize how badly they smell of filth. The word for **filth** here is used of vomit (Isa. 28:8) and human excrement (Isa. 36:12). The third group of sinners are the arrogant, who look down on others, certain of their own superiority (unlike Agur's humble words in Prov. 30:1–4). The final group are like ferocious beasts who brutally plunder the helpless. The **poor** here are those who are afflicted and humbled, and the **needy** are those who cannot survive without aid. Of course, a person could be so wicked that all four descriptions would fit him.

30:15–17. This paragraph gives a series of graphic pictures of the greedy person. First, he is compared to a **leech** sucking the blood from a body and producing two offspring just as voracious. The words **they cry** are not in the Hebrew, so the **two daughters** are actually named **Give** and **Give**.

The next section presents a list of four things that are never satisfied, just like a greedy person. The phrase **three . . . four** is a Hebrew idiom showing that the list is specific but not intended to be all-inclusive. Two items are destructive and two are life-giving, but they all provide clear images of the person who is insatiable. The **grave**, or death, never stops taking in more people who have died. A woman with a **barren womb** never stops wanting a child. Especially in the arid climate of Canaan, the **land** immediately sucks up all the rain that falls. And once a **fire** begins burning, it continues as long as there is fuel to consume.

Verse 17 looks back to verse 11 and shows the end of those who are arrogant and disrespectful to parents. To scorn **obedience** is to ridicule it or hold it in contempt. Such disdain for human authority goes with rebellion against divine authority. And God warns that such a person will die a violent death and his corpse will lie unburied, so that the **ravens** and **vultures** will mutilate it.

30:18–20. The writer declares that there are **four** things that amaze him and go beyond his understanding, but scholars have disagreed on precisely what common denominator ties them together. In each case, it appears that progress would be impossible, yet somehow each one moves toward the goal, leaving no track behind. An **eagle** soars high above without even moving its wings; a **snake** slithers across a rock even though it has no legs; a **ship** slides through the sea with nothing to push it but a breeze; and a **man** makes his way into the heart of a woman in similarly mysterious ways.

Verse 20 adds one other surprising, yet revolting, picture: an **adulteress** so promiscuous that her conscience has been deadened. Illicit sex means no more to her than eating a meal. She simply **wipes her mouth** and denies that she has **done** anything **wrong**.

30:21–23. Here are four people we could do without; they cause so much trouble that the **earth trembles**! A **servant** who moves directly into the role of **king** has neither the training nor the experience to rule well. The **fool** (Heb. *nabal*, a boorish, insufferable person) who is **full of food** will be even more insensitive to the needs of those around him. A **woman** desperate for love will bring her deep hurts into marriage and find it hard to relate properly to her husband. And a **maidservant** who steps into the place of her **mistress** will surely flounder, perhaps because she does not know how to direct others.

30:24–28. This section portrays **four** animals that compensate for their **small** size and lack of strength, and manage to thrive despite their limitations. **Ants** do not have much strength, at least in comparison with a man, but God has given them the foresight to store food in the summer, even though it will not be needed until much later. **Coneys**, which are like small marmots, cannot defend themselves, but they have learned to make their home among rugged rocks where they can quickly dive to safety. **Locusts** appear to have no leader, but they can instinctively gather in such orderly formations that they can devastate crops. A **lizard** may be so helpless that a person can capture it with a quick grab of the hand, but it finds free access to the palaces of kings. God has provided for the needs of these little animals, so he can certainly do the same for his people.

30:29–31. Agur uses **three** impressive animals as comparisons to the noble appearance and regal bearing of a king. The **lion**, of course, has the reputation of being king of the beasts, dominant over the others. **Roosters**, too, have a natural strut that reminds one of the pomp of a king's court. The **he-goat** at the head of a flock of goats puts on an aggressive front intended to show any rivals that he is in charge. A **king** surrounded by **his army** instinctively takes on a similar appearance, acting the part of the proud and noble monarch.

30:32–33. Acting the part of a king is appropriate for a king, but it can be a disaster for a **fool** (Heb. *nabal,* inconsiderate, obstinate fool). Anyone insensitive enough to exalt himself or plan evil against an innocent person is likely to get punched in the nose! The writer warns him to **clap** his **hand** over his **mouth** before he gets in more trouble because he is stepping in the way of an inevitable sequence of cause and effect. The same Hebrew word is used for **churning, twisting,** and **stirring up**, and it means to squeeze or wring out.

Everyone in Israel knew that twisting a skin bottle full of milk would produce butter, and it is clear that twisting a person's nose will cause a nosebleed. In the same way, the person foolish enough to aggravate a person who is already angry should not be surprised to find that he has sparked a hot conflict.

MAIN IDEA REVIEW: *An unknown writer ponders the world of nature, seeking lessons for life. But with all of his investigations, he concludes that God alone truly understands the universe and its meaning. It is humbling but comforting to recognize that he holds the secrets of life.*

III. CONCLUSION

Mysteries of the Universe

Though Agur, author of this chapter of Proverbs, was a keen observer of the mysteries of God and nature, such keen insights are easier read than made. We may try to plumb the depths of mysteries but fail.

Oliver Wendell Holmes Sr. was a doctor and therefore was interested in the use of ether. In order to know how his patients felt under its influence, he once had a dose administered to himself. As he was going under, in a dreamy state, a profound thought came to him. He believed that he had suddenly grasped the key to all the mysteries of the universe. When he regained consciousness, however, he was unable to remember what the insight was.

Because of the great importance this thought would be to mankind, Holmes arranged to have himself given ether again. This time he had a stenographer present to take down the great thought. The ether was administered, and sure enough, just before passing out, the insight reappeared. He mumbled the words, the stenographer took them down, and he went to sleep confident in the knowledge that he had succeeded.

Upon awakening, he turned eagerly to the stenographer and asked her to read what he had uttered. This is what she read: "The entire universe is permeated with a strong odor of turpentine."

Not exactly the key to all the mysteries of the universe!

Even less insightful was a student of William Phelps, who taught English literature at Yale for forty-one years until his retirement in 1933. Grading an examination paper shortly before Christmas one year, Phelps came across this note: "The Lord only knows the answer to this question. Merry Christmas." Phelps returned the paper with this note: "The Lord gets an A. You get an F. Happy New Year."

These examples are given to make the point that original, keen observations worth passing down from one generation to another are not easy to make. The Holy Spirit inspired Agur to make some observations in this chapter that are worthy of being passed down to succeeding generations until the Lord returns. First, he expresseed his own humility and the exaltedness of God. Such is an ageless observation. Second, he gleaned insights from life and nature, warned us of foolishness, and called us to wisdom.

PRINCIPLES

- Seeing the exaltedness of God depends on a sense of personal humility.

- There is danger in both poverty and riches.

- Exalting yourself will backfire.

APPLICATIONS

- Do not set your heart on wealth. The Bible repeatedly warns against it. It is a trap. Be content with how much money the will of God brings you.

- Honor your father and mother. Throughout Scripture we see blessings for doing so and negative consequences for failing to do so.

- Correct yourself quickly if you have exalted yourself. It will inevitably bring negative consequences.

IV. LIFE APPLICATION

The Mysteries of Life

In his book *The Tale of the Tardy Oxcart* (Dallas, Tex.: Word Publishing, 1984), Chuck Swindoll wrote:

> A lot of things about life are mysteries. Death is like that. No one has ever come back and told us what it's about, so it remains a distinct enigma, a riddle, mystery. So is the sea. It's strange marriage to the moon that controls its tide continues to be in the poet's mind a great, constant, moving mystery.
>
> So are the spaces above us. Who can fathom the mysterious movement of that masterful piece of time that stays on track, continually, twenty-four hours a day, 365 days a year. If we look long enough through a telescope, our eyes bug out against the lens and our mouths drop open as we try to fathom the mystery of the spaces above us.
>
> Consider also the invisible world around us that can be seen only through the lens of a microscope. Whether it's telescopic or microscopic, life seems to be shrouded in mystery. Did you realize that if an electron could be increased in size until it became as large as an apple, and if a human being could be increased by the same proportion, that person could hold the entire solar system in the palm of his hand and would have to use a magnifying glass in order to see it? (Swindoll, 407).

Then there are the mysteries of time and space. When you look back in time, you cannot come to a beginning point. If you could, you would have to ask the question, What happened just before that beginning point? The same thing is true with space. Go straight up from the North Pole at a million times the speed of light for a hundred billion years, and you would still not come to the end of space. Or if you did, what would be just on the other side of the end of space?

The mysteries of life are profound and unimaginable when we get even a small glimpse of them. Things that cannot be must be, and things that must be cannot be. While we cannot grasp the mysteries of life, we can make sense of some of them. Agur made sense of some of them. He looked at mysteries of life and nature and drew principles and truths from them. But sometimes he stopped and marveled. We can do the same. Sometimes we can draw spiritual truths from the mysteries of life, such as the eternality of time and infinity of space give us a picture of the eternality and infinity of God. But other times, we must stop and marvel at a God who is so great, so magnificent, so wonderful, so awesome that with our earthbound brains, we cannot take him in.

But just because we cannot understand everything about God does not mean we cannot understand some things. And the things we do understand cause us to bow our knees in gratitude and worship. This much we may grasp: Jesus loves me, this I know, for the Bible tells me so.

V. PRAYER

Father in heaven, give us an eternal perspective that leads us to value the things in life that really matter. May we live each day in the knowledge that you hold the key to the mysteries of life.

VI. DEEPER DISCOVERIES

A. Agur

Agur, the mysterious writer of Proverbs 30, is mentioned nowhere else in the Bible. The name means "hireling" or "gatherer" in Hebrew, and many rabbis and church fathers have suggested that this is an alternate name for Solomon. But there is no apparent reason King Solomon should use such a pen name. Some have suggested that the word *oracle* in verse 1 may actually be Massah, the name of a place. One of Ishmael's descendants was named Massa (Gen. 25:14), but evidence for this view is scanty. Agur was most likely a non-Israelite wise man like the sages mentioned in 1 Kings 4:30–31.

B. Lizards, Coneys, and Roosters

There is a surprising amount of variation in the translation of certain names of animals in this chapter, reflecting the fact that the ancient world did not use precise names for different types of wildlife.

The coney (30:26), for instance, is actually a small mammal about the size of a rabbit, somewhat like a marmot or badger. It is more accurately called the Syrian hyrax. It appears to chew its cud and stays close to its hiding places on rocky slopes.

The lizard (30:28) appears as "spider" in a few translations. Either is possible because the Hebrew word actually means "one who creeps or crawls." But the majority of modern versions prefer "lizard."

The rooster (30:31) renders a Hebrew word that has been translated as "greyhound, war horse, or starling"—a strange combination of options. The word appears to mean "thin at the waist," and the evidence for ancient usage is uncertain. "Rooster" seems to be the most likely choice.

VII. TEACHING OUTLINE

A. INTRODUCTION

1. Lead Story: Hey, Buddy, Can You Spare a Dime?

2. Context: God dwells in mystery, and the truth he reveals to us often dissolves into mystery. Yet there are some things we can understand, even if we cannot understand everything.

3. Transition: In order to grasp as much of God and his truth as possible, we must begin with a humble look upward . . . to him, submitting ourselves to him. Then we must take a thoughtful look around, seeing what he has created, and looking to him for insight on how his truth can be used in our lives.

B. COMMENTARY

1. A Humble Look Upward (30:1–9)

2. A Thoughtful Look Around (30:10–33)

C. CONCLUSION: MYSTERIES OF THE UNIVERSE

VIII. ISSUES FOR DISCUSSION

1. It has been said that you must believe in order to see (just backwards from the idea that you must see in order to believe). This makes Agur's humble look upward at the beginning of chapter 30 very important. He looks first to God and then sees all things, as much as possible, through God's eyes. How well do you follow the Augur principle? Do you tend to see things through God's eyes, or do you tend to see things simply through your own eyes? Is there a change you need to make in this area?

2. What do you think of Agur's prayer to "give me neither poverty nor riches" (Prov. 30:8)? Most people clearly do not want poverty, but many would say, if they had a choice, "Give me riches." Do you want poverty? Do you want riches? Do you want something in between? Explain your answer.

3. Agur prayed, "Two things I ask of you, O LORD; do not refuse me before I die" (Prov. 30:7). If you were praying that, what two things would you ask of the Lord?

Chapter 31

Wisdom from Two Women

Proverbs 31:1–31

I. **INTRODUCTION**
The Total Woman

II. **COMMENTARY:**
A verse-by-verse explanation of these verses.

III. **CONCLUSION**
Men Versus Women?

An overview of the principles and applications from these verses.

IV. **LIFE APPLICATION**
Circles of Authority

Melding these verses to life.

V. **PRAYER**
Tying these verses to life with God.

VI. **DEEPER DISCOVERIES**
Historical, geographical, and grammatical enrichment of the commentary.

VII. **TEACHING OUTLINE**
Suggested step-by-step group study of these verses.

VIII. **ISSUES FOR DISCUSSION**
Zeroing these verses in on daily life.

Quote

"The woman was formed out of man—not out of his

head to rule over him; not out of his feet to be trampled

upon by him; but out of his side to be his equal, from

beneath his arm to be protected, and from near his heart to

be loved."

Matthew Henry

Proverbs
31:1–31

 IN A NUTSHELL

A king should avoid wine and women and concentrate on ruling with justice and righteousness. In addition, a godly woman can make full use of the resources available to her. She is a key factor in her husband's success and is worthy of the highest respect.

Wisdom from Two Women

I. INTRODUCTION

The Total Woman

We are living in a day of shifting values about women. On the one extreme, there are some who hold to an antiquated, backwoods stereotype that women should be kept ignorant, barefoot, and in the kitchen. On the other extreme, there are those who think that women should be men . . . that they are the same as men with incidental anatomical variations, and that therefore, their jobs should be the same as men, their responsibilities should be the same as men, and even their restrooms should be the same as men.

This opinion was championed in the 1960s, with the feminist movement, which began and attempted through political means to improve the plight of women. During that time, Charlotte Whitton said, "Whatever women do they must do twice as well as men to be thought half as good. Luckily, this is not difficult." Yet many believe they went too far in their push for equality. Even Gloria Steinem, a leader in the feminist movement, said, "Some of us are becoming the men we wanted to marry."

Then, a backlash began. A book hit *The New York Times* best-sellers list like a storm. It was called *The Total Woman*. It offered advice for extreme femininity that some felt was inspired, while others bitterly ridiculed it.

The culture wars have continued for ensuing decades between those who embrace a traditional role for women in society and those who embrace a progressive role. Most views are somewhere in between, but in an age of shifting cultural values, we can look to the Scripture for what a women should be.

While the New Testament passages are often criticized by feminists for suggesting that wives should be submissive to husbands, Proverbs 31 presents a picture of a wife who is anything but passive, underproductive, and unappreciated. Here we see a woman of extraordinary skill, great drive, and expansive involvement who is valued by her husband and known in the community for her achievements and stature. When all the passages of Scripture are taken together, a picture becomes clear of a woman who is free to become all that God intended her to be. Proverbs 31 is a central passage in creating this picture.

II. COMMENTARY

Wisdom from Two Women

MAIN IDEA: *The closing chapter of Proverbs centers on remarkable women. Just as the book opened by advising a young man to pursue the figurative Lady Wisdom, it concludes with sound counsel from a mother and a portrait of the literal woman worth pursuing for a wife.*

🅐 A Mother's Advice on Leadership (31:1–9)

SUPPORTING IDEA: *Even a king can benefit from the instructions of his mother, especially one who can so succinctly summarize the core of good leadership: avoid wine and women and concentrate on ruling with justice.*

31:1. Like chapter 30, this section is attributed to an unknown source, **King Lemuel.** The name means "belonging to God," but there is no known link to any Jewish king. A slightly different punctuation would change **an oracle** to "King Lemuel of Massa," a location in northern Arabia, and he was possibly head of a tribe in that region. These verses report the weighty message he received from his **mother**—a shift from the typical pattern in Proverbs of instruction centered in the father but not totally unknown (1:8; 6:20).

31:2–3. She begins by addressing her son in terms of endearment. **O my son** is literally "What, my son?" And all three addresses begin with the same implied question, "What shall I tell you?" or "What will you do?" She refers to him as the **son of my vows,** suggesting that she may have devoted him to the Lord, as Hannah did Samuel (1 Sam. 1:11).

The first fundamental of good leadership is moral purity. He must not dissipate his energy **on women,** catering to his own lusts rather than the needs of his people. Immorality carries a hefty price tag, both physically and spiritually (Prov. 2:16–19; 5:1–14; 7:1–27; 22:14; 23:27–28).

31:4–7. This wise mother gives a second warning: beware of alcohol. **Beer** clouds a man's memory and distorts his judgment, and a king cannot afford to **forget** the law's demands. Too much **wine** turns a leader into a tyrant who deprives **the oppressed of their rights.**

Perhaps drink may be appropriate for those people who need an anesthetic for their physical or mental pain, especially if they are **perishing.** But it has no place in the life of a leader.

31:8–9. The third word of instruction is a positive one: stand for justice! A king's role is to **speak up for those who cannot** plead their own cause, those who are in no position to threaten or reward him. He must **judge fairly,**

giving equal treatment to the **destitute** (those who are insecure), the **poor** (afflicted, humble) and the **needy** (easily oppressed).

Ⓑ A Pattern for the Ideal Wife (31:10–31)

SUPPORTING IDEA: *Here is a poetic description of the ideal wife—the woman of godliness and ability who can make full use of the resources available. She is a key factor in her husband's success and is worthy of the highest respect.*

31:10. The opening verse states the theme of the poem: the value of a good **wife**, a wife of noble character. The Hebrew word for **noble character** implies strength and ability and is repeated in verse 29. Ruth was called a noble woman (Ruth 3:11). When used of men, it is often translated in the phrase, mighty man of "valor." It is not impossible to find a woman like the one described here, but such a woman is valuable because she is rare, like a precious stone. The word **rubies** is uncertain and has sometimes been rendered "coral" or "pearls." But it definitely implies something of rare beauty and value.

31:11–12. The husband appears in verses 11–12 and in verses 23,28. He can have **full confidence** in such a wife; literally, "His heart trusts in her." She is completely faithful in every area, and one result is that her husband **lacks nothing of value**. The word means "booty," the rich plunder of a victorious army, a vivid metaphor for the good things she brings into the home.

She is a continual asset to her husband, bringing him **good, not harm**. And this faithfulness is consistent. It continues **all the days of her life**.

31:13–19. These verses describe her diligence—one of her outstanding traits. In the culture of ancient Israel, women had to stay busy in their spare moments spinning wool and making clothes. Doing this faithfully was a feminine virtue, and this woman was faithful. Weaving cloth and sewing clothes were a major part of her work (vv. 13,19,22,24). She selected the materials, either **wool** or **flax** (from which linen was made), and **works with eager hands**, literally "with the delight of her hands." She evidently took pleasure in creating something of beauty and usefulness.

Not only does she provide clothing for her family, but she also produces a surplus that she sells. She functions like the **merchant ships**, bringing home items that the family cannot produce for itself.

Unlike the sluggard mentioned often in Proverbs, she gets up early, before dawn, to ensure that **food** is ready **for her family**, as well as **portions for her servant girls**. "Portion" is literally "that which is appointed," and some interpreters have suggested that it actually refers to her instructions for the servants. But it more naturally describes her carefulness in making sure that even the servants are properly nourished.

She has a keen business sense and has managed to save enough money **out of her earnings** (literally, from the fruit of her hands) to purchase **a field**. Some have questioned whether women in ancient Israel could buy property, but this one certainly was able to. And her husband would have been available to help with any legal issues.

The wife described here is a woman of strength. The NIV rendering **sets about her work vigorously** is literally "girds her loins with strength," a Hebrew idiom for having great stamina.

Previous business ventures have been successful, so she is encouraged to move forward with more. In some passages, a **lamp** going out is used as a picture of calamity (Job 18:6; Prov. 13:9; 20:20; 24:20), but here it seems to be a reference to the fact that she not only gets up early (31:15) but stays up late to finish her work.

The section on diligence concludes with another description of her hard work. She even uses a **distaff**, or stick, and **spindle** to twist wool or flax into thread. The whole process goes through her hands!

31:20. This woman's **hands** may be busy with her work, but she is willing to stretch them out to help the **needy** as well. All through Proverbs, generosity to the poor is presented as one of the marks of wisdom. And, as verse 26 explains, the wife in this household is a model of wisdom.

31:21. Because she has been faithful in providing clothing for her family, they are prepared for the cold of winter and need not **fear** snow. Some ancient versions have substituted "double thickness" for **scarlet**, referring to the protection provided by thicker garments. But the Hebrew text definitely says scarlet; scarlet clothing was expensive, of the highest quality, and would be adequate for chilly weather.

31:22. Not only does she make clothes; she also takes on larger projects such as bed **coverings**. And her own clothes are of the finest quality. **Linen** was made from flax and was usually imported from Egypt. **Purple** cloth was produced by dye extracted from shellfish and was available from Phoenicia. A woman who dressed well and decorated her home, she brought beauty and luxury to her family.

31:23. With a wife like this, it is no surprise that her husband is **respected** by the leaders of the city. Those who gather **at the city gate** are the ones who transact the legal and judicial affairs of the town. And though the wife's merit is well-known (v. 31) among them, she enhances her husband's prestige rather than overshadowing him.

31:24. Proverbs 31:14,18 hint that she had developed a business making and selling garments. She was skillful and industrious enough to supply **merchants** with luxury items like **linen garments** and **sashes**.

31:25. The wife in this household had no fear of cold in verse 21; here she has no fear of the future. The **days to come** may be uncertain (Prov.

27:1), but she has the character to face them with confidence. Although her literal wardrobe is impressive, the figure of speech here shows her **clothed** even more regally with **strength and dignity**.

31:26. In verse 20, she is a giver of help; here she is a giver of **wisdom**, like Lady Wisdom in chapter 1. She shares her wisdom with her husband and instructs her children and servants.

31:27. This verse provides a one-sentence glimpse of her diligence, presented in more detail in verses 13–19. She gives herself both in management of others (watching over the household affairs) and in her own labor. To **eat the bread of idleness** is a Hebrew expression for laziness, and nothing could be further from this woman than idleness!

31:28–29. The wife and mother in this home receives the appreciation she deserves, as her family acknowledges how she has blessed their lives. The **children** call her **blessed**, implying that she sees her lot in life as a gift from God, not as an intolerable burden. Her positive approach and zest for life inspire **her husband** to echo the children's praise. He tells her that **many women** are **noble** (same word as in v. 10), but she surpasses **them all**—she is the best!

31:30–31. The NIV punctuates this as a closing summary, rather than a continuation of the husband's praise, but this is uncertain. The woman who has been described so well is charming and beautiful, but she is far more. **Charm** can be **deceptive**, and **beauty** eventually fades. But godly character counts most. Proverbs began with a call to fear the Lord (1:7), and it is fitting that it closes with a portrait of a woman who **fears the LORD**.

She deserves the praise of her family, and she has **earned** the right to be rewarded with gratitude and respect. In fact, she is recognized and honored by the leaders at the **city gate**, an unusual honor for a woman, but then she is an unusual woman!

MAIN IDEA REVIEW: *The closing chapter of Proverbs centers on remarkable women. Just as the book opened by advising a young man to pursue the figurative Lady Wisdom, it concludes with sound counsel from a mother and a portrait of a literal woman worth pursuing for a wife.*

III. CONCLUSION

Men Versus Women?

Theologian Donald Bloesch has said:

> The model of women in tribal patriarchalism is the brood mare; in hedonistic naturalism, she is the bunny or plaything; in feminist

ideology, she is the self-sufficient career women; in romanticism, she is the fairy princess or maiden in distress waiting to be rescued; in biblical faith, she is the partner in ministry.

This perspective is biblical and helpful. God created Adam and Eve, making the point that it took both a man and a woman to reflect the image of God (Gen. 1:27). Eve is described as a helper suitable for Adam (Gen. 2:18). Each gender has a specific role to play, just as God the Father, God the Son, and God the Holy Spirit have different roles to play within the Trinity. The genders are equal in the sight of God, and as they are seen as equal in the sight of mankind, everyone will benefit.

This helpful chapter lifts women to their rightful stature and challenges men to live up to their end of the bargain as well. Properly understood, the chapter can create a vision for a Christian woman to pursue, as well as to establish standards that a godly man can use in seeking a wife.

PRINCIPLES

- All biblical leadership is based on moral authority and is to strive to advance justice and righteousness.
- Women should aspire to the character of the Proverbs 31 women.
- Men should fully appreciate their wives, and all women, as they exercise their God-given gifts and roles.

APPLICATIONS

- Make sure your own leadership is based, first on the moral authority of an authentic pursuit of God's will, as well as a clear conscience.
- If you are a woman, study Proverbs 31 as a model for your life. If you are a man, create your own scriptural picture of a model Christian man and follow it.
- If you are a woman, take pride in the gifts and roles God has given you. If you are a man, affirm and appreciate the gifts and roles of the women in your life.

IV. LIFE APPLICATION

Circles of Authority

Everyone is in a circle of authority. A husband may be in authority at home and under authority at work. A wife may be under authority at home and in authority at work. The children are under authority to their parents but in authority over the cat. We are all in authority and under authority. God has deemed it so.

There are five sets of relationships in Scripture that depict these authority relationships: husband/wife (Eph. 5:22–33), parent/child (Eph. 6:1–4), master/slave (Eph. 6:5–9), government/citizen (1 Pet. 2:13–14), and church/member (1 Pet. 5:1–5). We cannot get out of authority relationships. They are God ordained.

Scripture makes clear, however, that authority is never given so that a person can abuse or neglect someone else. In Scripture, authority is given only so the person in authority can exercise his authority for the benefit of the people under him. All authority is to be benevolent authority, and it is to be submissive to the needs of those under him. At the same time, the person in authority is not free to disregard the authority of the people over him. The first creates tyranny while the second creates anarchy. Only the biblical balance works. The person under authority must, of course, disobey if the authority asks him to do something wrong (Acts 5:29).

If you are so fortunate as to be under another who exercises his authority for your benefit, that is the best situation and one in which you can thrive. That is the case with the Proverbs 31 woman. She is under authority. But she is under benevolent, appreciative, supportive authority. And, as a result, she thrives and becomes all that she was meant by the Lord to be.

This has several lessons for us. First, we can try to be sure we end up under benevolent, appreciative, and supportive authority. This is especially important when a woman decides whether to marry a man. If he is a biblical man, she will thrive. If not, she will suffer. The same thing is true of employees (slaves). If we can get a job under someone who helps us, it will be to our advantage. But there are some things we have no control over, such as our parents or the country in which we were born. In those cases, principles for submission may be found in other places in Scripture.

The point here, however, is that the Proverbs 31 woman is under authority yet thrives. It should be used for women as an example for their own behavior and attitudes and for men in choosing a wife who will have a biblical attitude toward life.

V. PRAYER

Father in heaven, help us all, whether a man or a woman, to pursue your ideal for our lives. We know that you want us to be like Christ. May we accept all the guidance available in the Scriptures to do so, and may your Holy Spirit do his work of transformation in our lives. Amen.

VI. DEEPER DISCOVERIES

A. Acrostics and Chiasms

The poetic description of an exemplary wife in 31:10–31 follows a complicated structural pattern. First, it is an acrostic; each verse begins with the successive letters of the Hebrew alphabet. Second, it follows a pattern known as "chiasm," in which the writer moves through a series of thoughts until he reaches a climax, then retraces his steps, approaching the subjects in reverse order. Here is the structure as presented by Duane A. Garrett in *The New American Commentary, Vol. 14: Proverbs, Ecclesiastes, Song of Solomon* (Nashville: Broadman Press, 1993), 248:

A High value of a good wife (31:10)
  B Husband benefitted by wife (31:11–12)
    C Wife works hard (31:13–19)
      D Wife gives to poor (31:20)
        E No fear of snow (31:21a)
          F Children clothed in scarlet (31:21b)
            G Coverings for bed, wife wears linen (31:22)
              H Public respect for husband (31:23)
            G′ Sells garments and sashes (31:24)
          F′ Wife clothed in dignity (31:25a)
        E′ No fear of future (31:25b)
      D′ Wife speaks wisdom (31:26)
    C′ Wife works hard (31:27)
  B′ Husband and children praise wife (31:28–29)
A′ High value of a good wife (31:30–31)

Note that the central point is the high level of respect that comes to the husband of such an amazing woman. This may suggest that the description is addressed to the young man choosing a bride as much as to the young woman who aspires to such excellence.

B. Producing Clothes

Jewish women generally produced their own clothes, a time-consuming process that required several steps. First, they would attach wool or flax to a rod called the distaff and use a spindle to spin the fibers into threads. Next they would use the thread to weave cloth, running thread vertically on a wooden frame or loom, and using a shuttle to run the thread crosswise over and under the vertical threads. The cloth could then be cut and sewn into various items of clothing. The Jews were known for their skill in embroidery.

VII. TEACHING OUTLINE

A. INTRODUCTION

1. Lead Story: The Total Woman

2. Context: Solomon creates a picture of the model godly woman, based on character and hard work.

3. Transition: As women look at this chapter, they should see it as a picture of the character and lifestyle they should strive for. As men look at this chapter, they should have two responses. First, they should affirm and appreciate the gifts and roles of the women in their lives. Second, they should pursue their own vision of the godly man that can be found in other passages in Scripture.

B. COMMENTARY

1. A Mother's Advice on Leadership (31:1–9)

2. A Pattern for the Ideal Wife (31:10–31)

C. CONCLUSION: MEN VERSUS WOMEN?

VIII. ISSUES FOR DISCUSSION

1. In the first part of this chapter, King Lemuel is instructed by his mother not to give in to the temptations of women or alcohol. Assuming those two areas have been mastered, the broader principle is that a king must lead wisely, with a clear head and with moral authority. In the areas of life in which you give leadership (work, home, church), are you clearheaded, and do you lead with moral authority? Is there anything in your life about these options that needs to be addressed?

2. If you are a woman, how well do you think you match the standards of a godly woman in this chapter? What is the most important thing you could work on to improve in this area? If you are a man, how well do you think you match the standards of being a godly man found throughout Scripture? What is the more important thing you could do to improve in this area?

3. If you were going to write an equivalent chapter of Proverbs for the godly man, what would you put into it?

Glossary

Agur—author of Proverbs 30; most likely a non-Israelite wise man like the sages mentioned in 1 Kings 4:30–31

coney—rodent-like rock-dwelling mammal

fear—to have an attitude of honor and trust that causes a person to esteem and obey God

fool—a person who is stubborn and bullheaded, with a closed mind, or who lacks spiritual perception, or a person who is arrogant, coarse, and hardened in his ways

glutton—an extreme and habitual overeater

harlot—a woman who engages men for personal income. Harlots were common in the time of Proverbs and were a snare to foolish young men.

heart—has many different potential meanings, including intellect, emotion and will, or the inner man, the real "you"

leech—a parasitic worm that sucks blood from its host

Lemuel—unknown author of Proverbs 31. Some speculate it was Solomon. A slightly different punctuation would change "an oracle" to "King Lemuel of Massa," a location in northern Arabia, and he could possibly be head of a tribe in that region.

pride—the attitude that one is better than another person, or too good for certain things

righteous—the person who embraces the values of God and strives to live in a way that pleases him

rod—an instrument of punishment, in the same way as a whip or paddle

rooftop—the flat upper roof of a house suitable for use as an outdoor room

scales—an instrument for weighing things, with a beam that is supported freely in the center and has two pans of equal weight suspended from its ends. It was used to determine how much of a commodity could be bought for a certain price.

Sheol—the grave, or the place of the departed dead

sluggard—an extremely and habitually lazy person who suffers harm for himself and those dependent on him, rather than doing hard work

understanding—good common sense; the ability to think through a complex set of factors and reach a wise conclusion

weights—small metal objects used on one tray of scales to determine how much something on the other tray of scales weighs, to determine the price of something being purchased

wicked—the person who is willing to do what is wrong, no matter what the consequences to his reputation or well-being

wisdom—skill in living life. A wise person is one who has expertise in living in a way that makes life go as well as possible for him.

Bibliography

Buzzell, Sid S. *Proverbs* in The Bible Knowledge Commentary. John Walvoord and Roy Zuck, editors. Wheaton, Ill.: Victor Books, 1985.

Garrett, Duane A. *Proverbs, Ecclesiastes, Song of Songs,* in The New American Commentary. Nashville, Tenn.: Broadman Press, 1993.

Kidner, D. *Proverbs.* Downers Grove, Ill: InterVarsity, 1964.

Kidner, D. *The Wisdom of Proverbs, Job, and Ecclesiastes.* Downers Grove: InterVarsity, 1985.

Ross, Allen P. *Proverbs* in The Expositor's Bible Commentary. Frank E. Gabelein, editor. Grand Rapids: Zondervan, 1983.

Waltke, Bruce K. *The Book of Proverbs: Chapter 1–15* in the New International Commentary on the Old Testament. Grand Rapids: Eerdmans, 2003.

Waltke, Bruce K. *The Book of Proverbs: Chapter 16–31* in the New International Commentary on the Old Testament. Grand Rapids: Eerdmans (this volume is forthcoming as of this printing).

HOLMAN REFERENCE

ALSO AVAILABLE:

THE HOLMAN COMMENTARIES SERIES – *Retail $19.99 ea.*

Old Testament

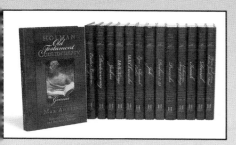

9-780-805-494-617	Genesis (Vol. 1)
9-780-805-494-624	Exodus, Leviticus, Numbers (Vol. 2)
9-780-805-494-631	Deuteronomy (Vol. 3)
9-780-805-494-648	Joshua (Vol. 4)
9-780-805-494-655	Judges, Ruth (Vol. 5)
9-780-805-494-662	1 & 2 Samuel (Vol. 6) *forthcoming*
9-780-805-494-679	1 & 2 Kings (Vol. 7)
9-780-805-494-686	1 & 2 Chronicles (Vol. 8)
9-780-805-494-693	Ezra, Nehemiah, Esther (Vol. 9)
9-780-805-494-709	Job (Vol. 10)
9-780-805-494-716	Psalms 1-75 (Vol. 11)
9-780-805-494-815	Psalms 76-150 (Vol. 12)
9-780-805-494-723	Proverbs (Vol. 13)
9-780-805-494-822	Ecclesiastes, Song of Songs (Vol. 14)
9-780-805-494-730	Isaiah (Vol. 15)
9-780-805-494-747	Jeremiah, Lamentations (Vol. 16)
9-780-805-494-754	Ezekiel (Vol. 17)
9-780-805-494-761	Daniel (Vol. 18)
9-780-805-494-778	Hosea, Joel, Amos, Obadiah, Jonah, Micah (Vol. 19)
9-780-805-494-785	Nahum-Malachi (Vol. 20)

New Testament

9-780-805-402-018	Matthew
9-780-805-402-025	Mark
9-780-805-402-032	Luke
9-780-805-402-049	John
9-780-805-402-056	Acts
9-780-805-402-063	Romans
9-780-805-402-070	1 & 2 Corinthians
9-780-805-402-087	Galatians-Colossians
9-780-805-402-094	1 Thessalonians-Philemon
9-780-805-402-117	Hebrews, James
9-780-805-402-100	1 & 2 Peter-Jude
9-780-805-402-124	Revelation

9-780-805-428-285 **NT Boxed Set Sale Price $179.97** (Reg. $239.88)
(All Volumes Hardcover)

1.800.233.1123 www.BHPublishingGroup.com